Love Me, Love Me Not

1

IO SAKISAKA

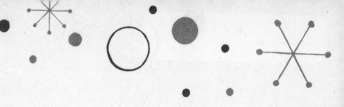

Contents

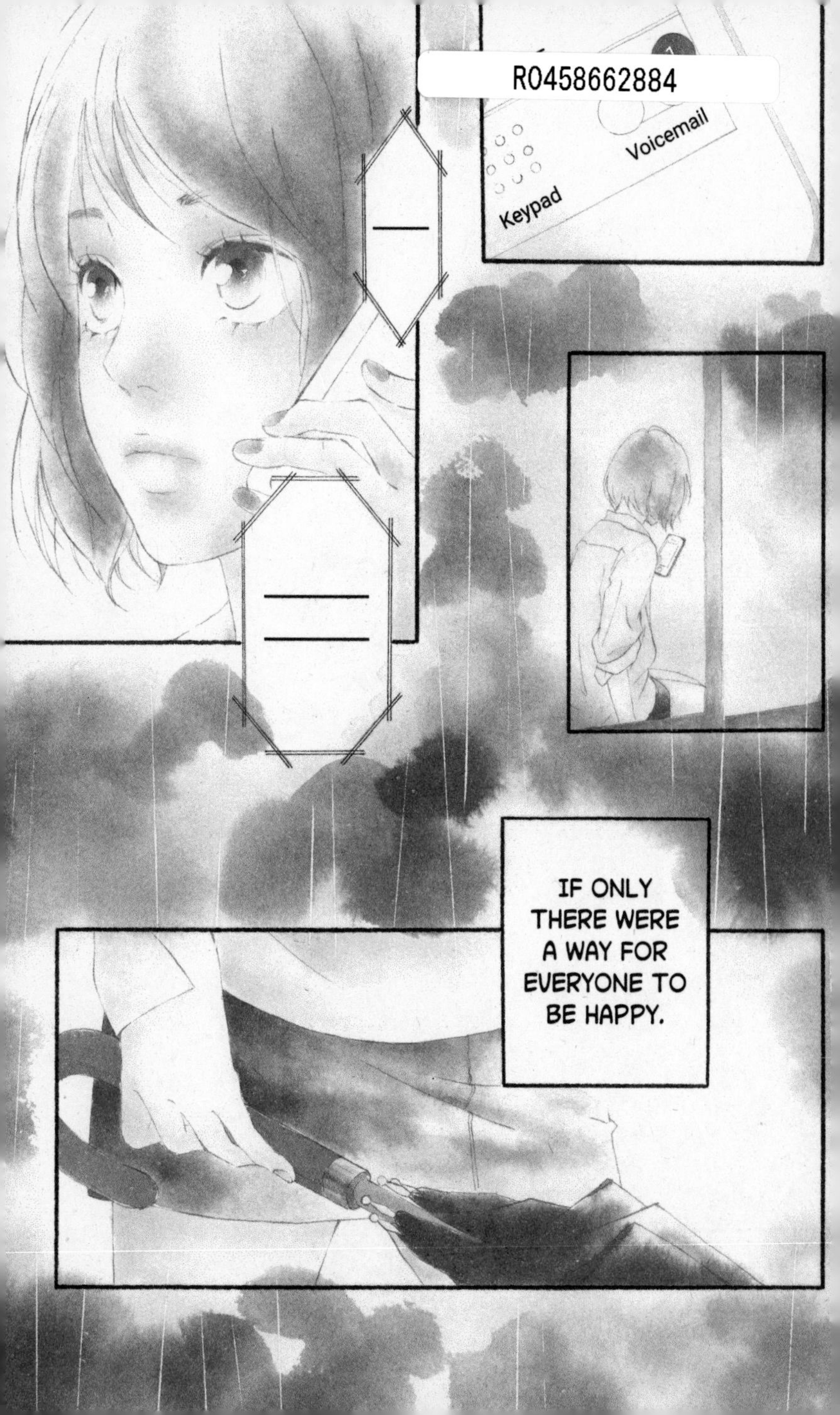
Voicemail
Keypad
—
— —
IF ONLY THERE WERE A WAY FOR EVERYONE TO BE HAPPY.

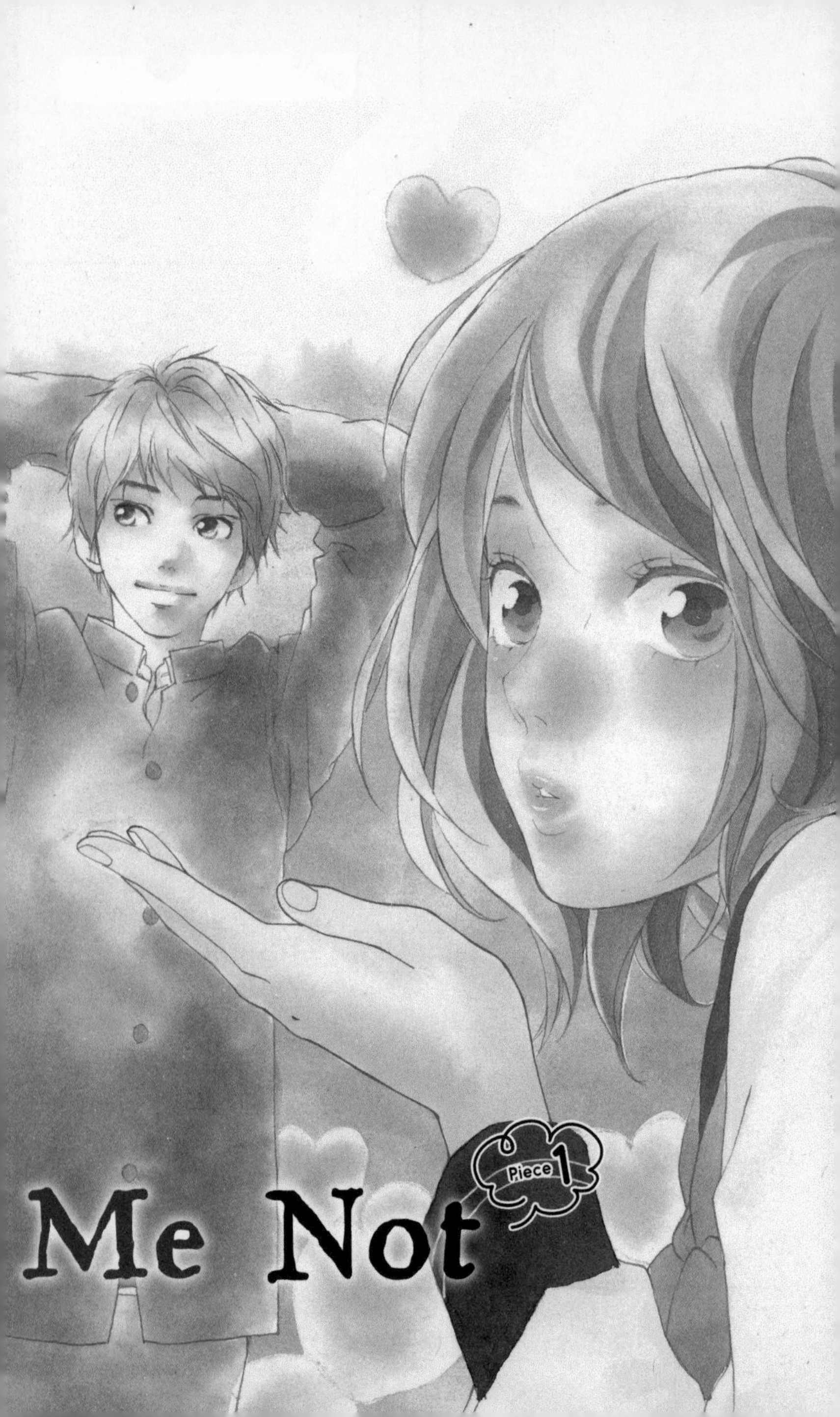
Piece 1
Me Not

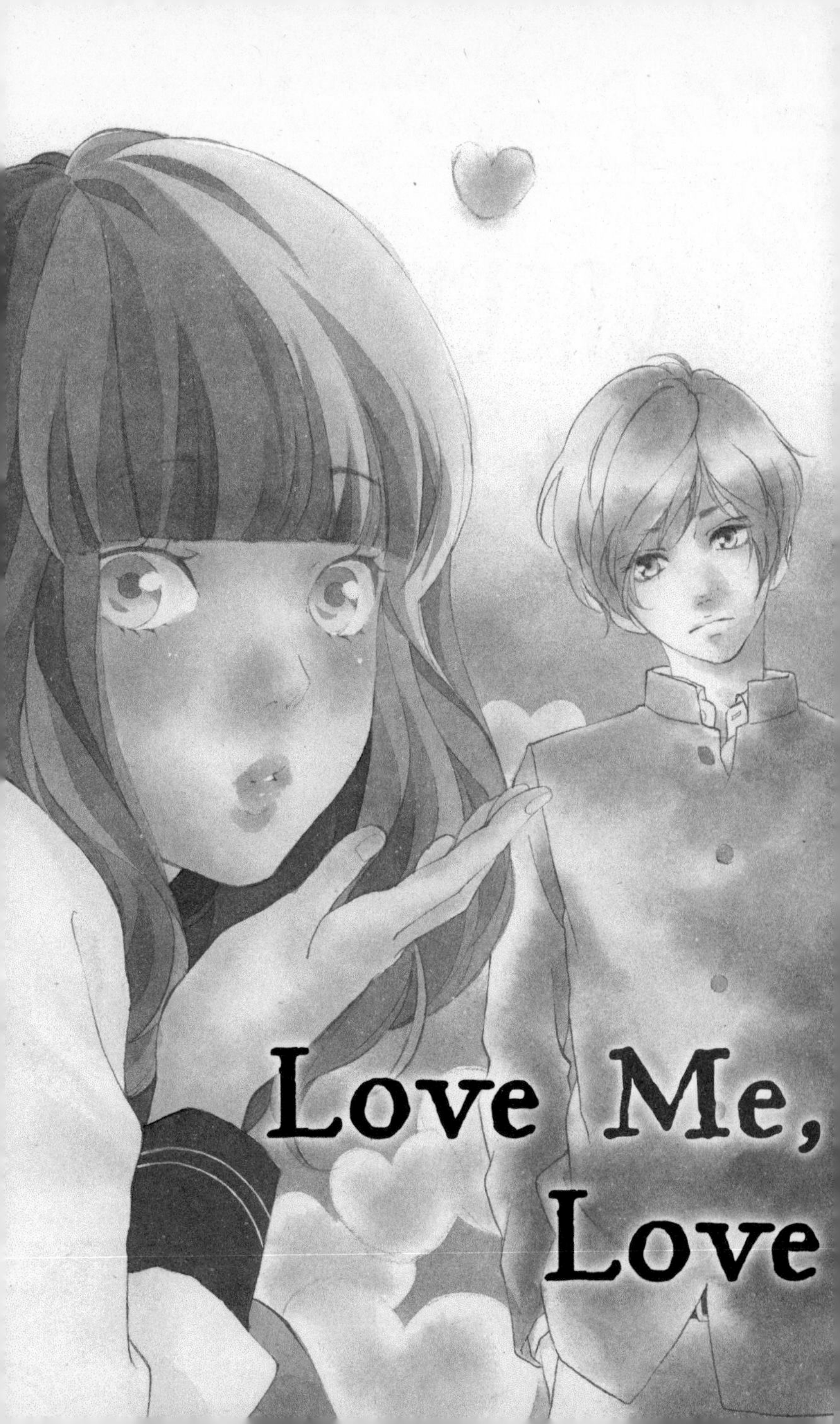
Love Me,
Love

GREETINGS

Hello. I'm Io Sakisaka.
Thank you very much for picking up
volume 1 of Love Me, Love Me Not.

In this story there are two heroines.
These two girls have completely different
views on love. Their views are simply
differences of opinion—neither is right
or wrong. If I had made just one girl the
heroine, it might influence my readers to
think the heroine's view is right and the
other view is wrong. But that is not my
intent, so I've made them both heroines.
I want to enjoy portraying the love story
of each girl, and I hope you all enjoy the
journey with me.

Io Sakisaka

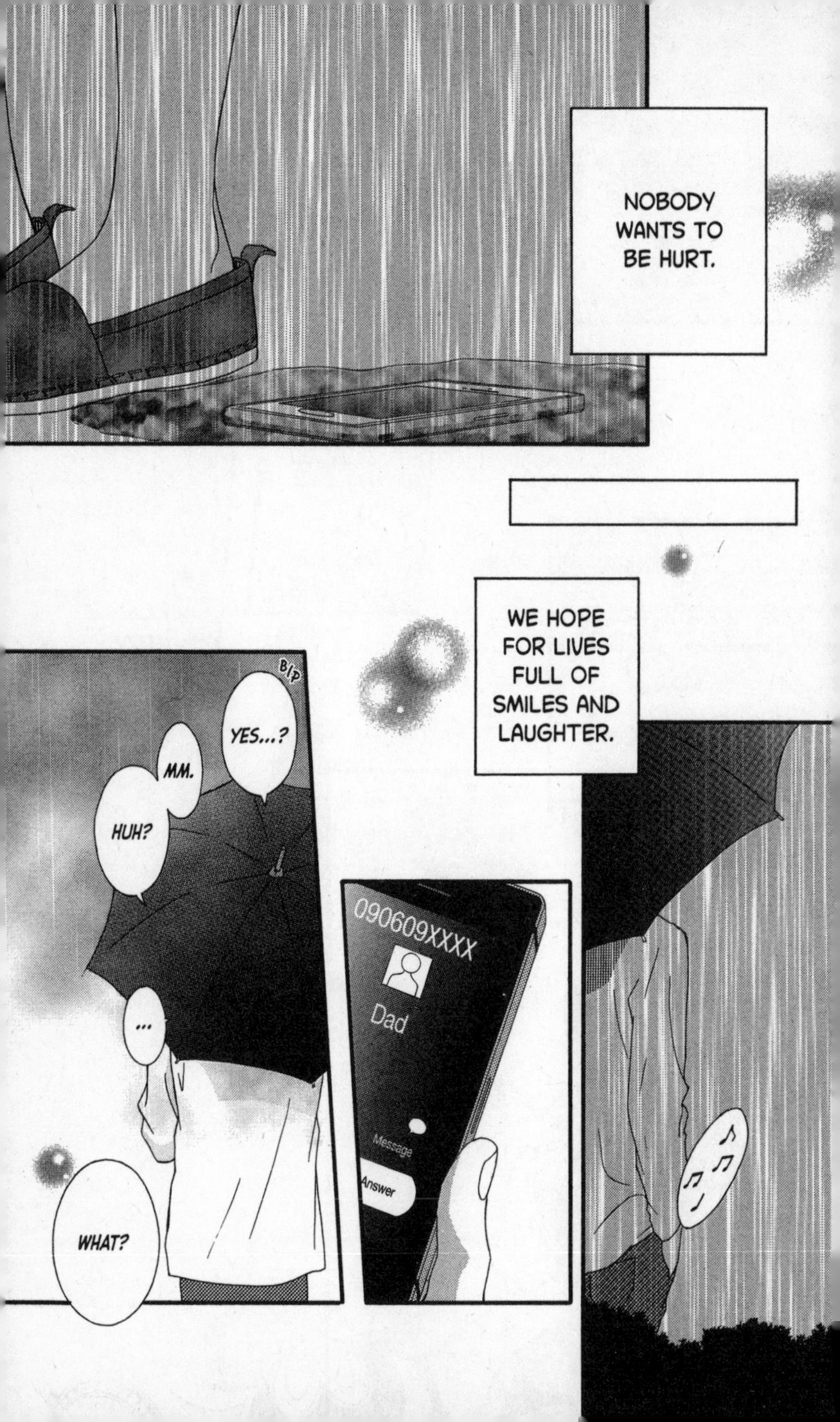
NOBODY WANTS TO BE HURT.
WE HOPE FOR LIVES FULL OF SMILES AND LAUGHTER.
090609XXXX
Dad
Message
Answer
BIP
YES...?
MM.
HUH?
...
WHAT?

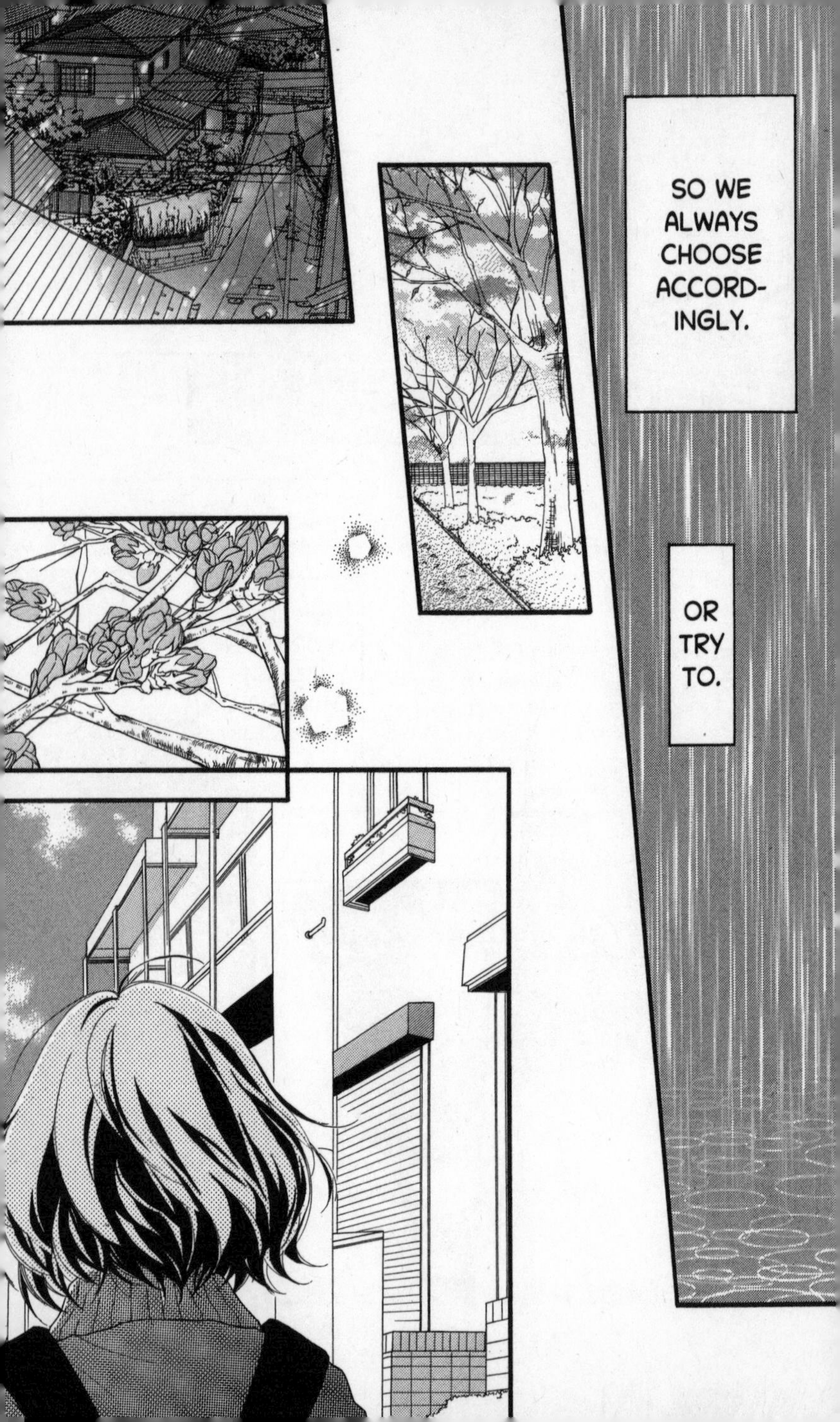
SO WE ALWAYS CHOOSE ACCORD-INGLY.
OR TRY TO.

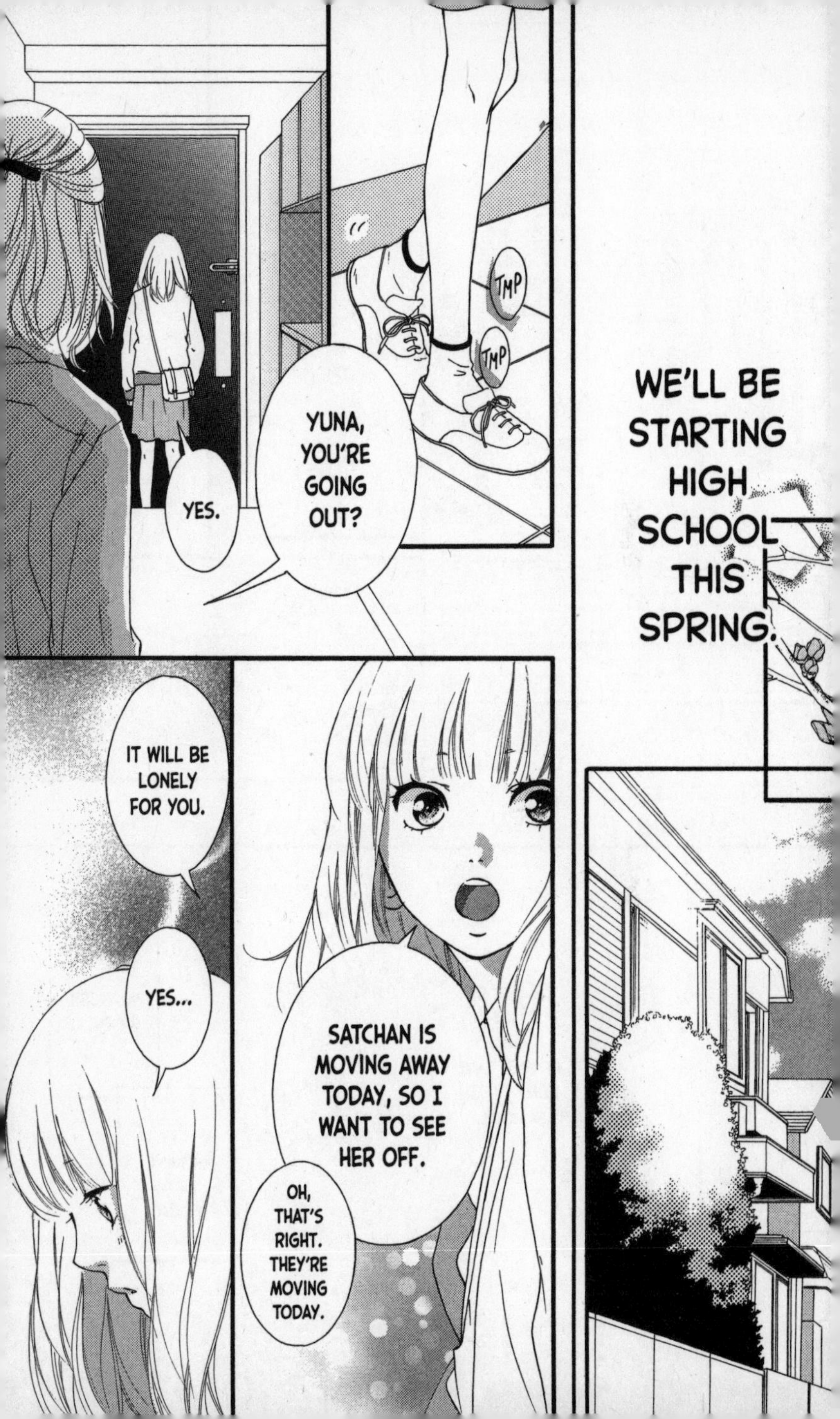
WE'LL BE STARTING HIGH SCHOOL THIS SPRING.
TMP
TMP
YUNA, YOU'RE GOING OUT?
YES.
SATCHAN IS MOVING AWAY TODAY, SO I WANT TO SEE HER OFF.
OH, THAT'S RIGHT. THEY'RE MOVING TODAY.
IT WILL BE LONELY FOR YOU.
YES...

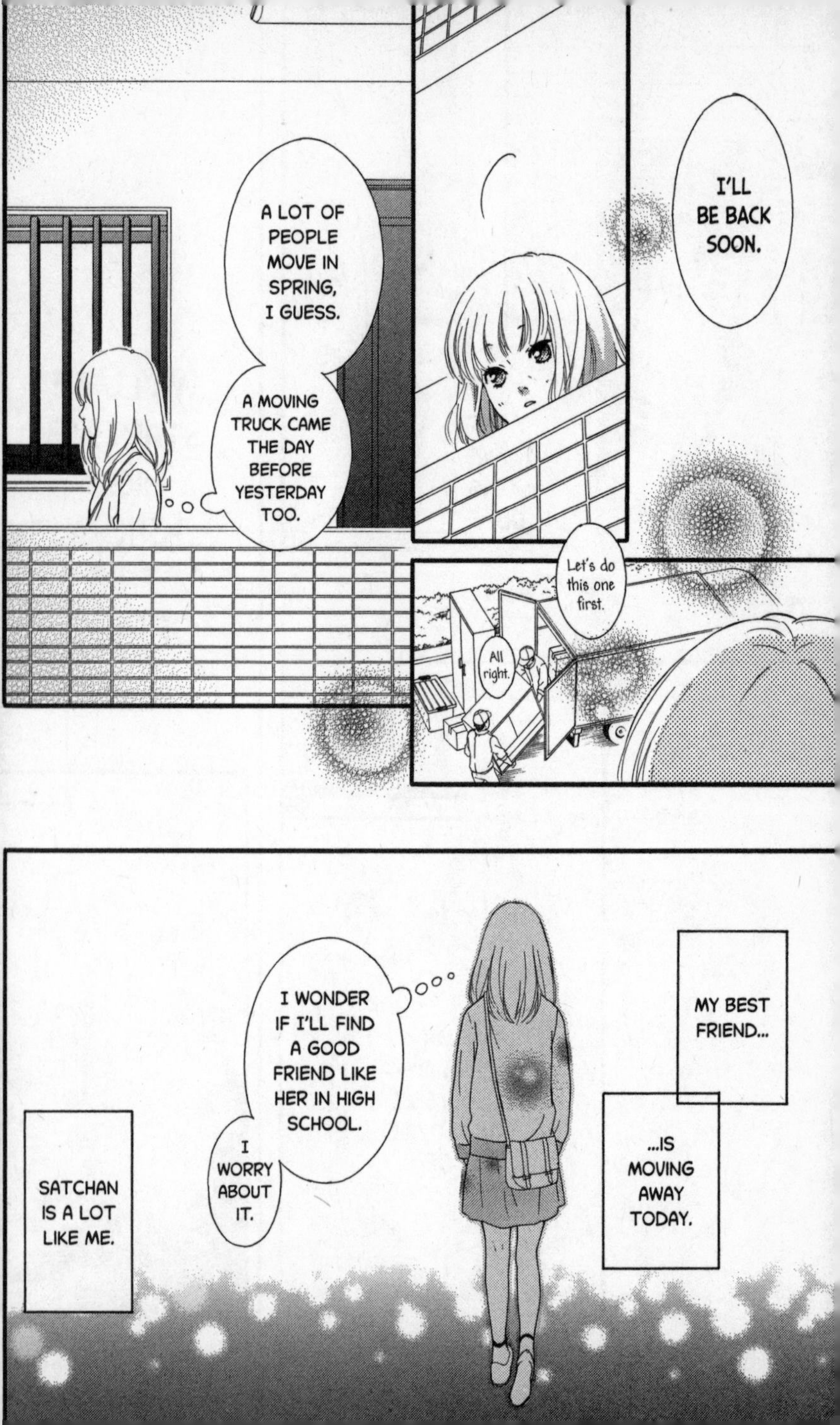
I'LL BE BACK SOON.
Let's do this one first.
All right.
A LOT OF PEOPLE MOVE IN SPRING, I GUESS.
A MOVING TRUCK CAME THE DAY BEFORE YESTERDAY TOO.
MY BEST FRIEND...
...IS MOVING AWAY TODAY.
I WONDER IF I'LL FIND A GOOD FRIEND LIKE HER IN HIGH SCHOOL.
I WORRY ABOUT IT.
SATCHAN IS A LOT LIKE ME.

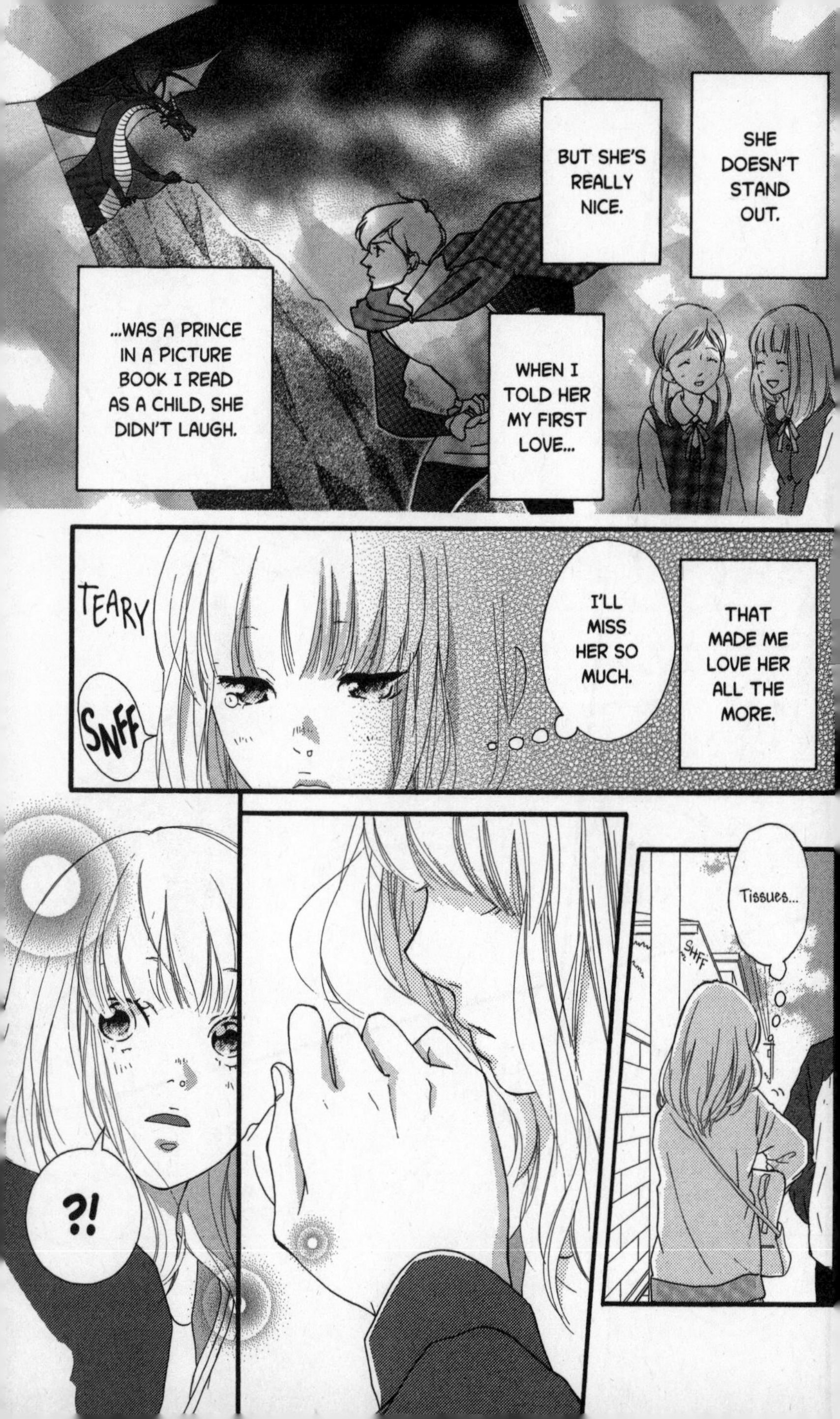
SHE DOESN'T STAND OUT.
BUT SHE'S REALLY NICE.
WHEN I TOLD HER MY FIRST LOVE...
...WAS A PRINCE IN A PICTURE BOOK I READ AS A CHILD, SHE DIDN'T LAUGH.
THAT MADE ME LOVE HER ALL THE MORE.
I'LL MISS HER SO MUCH.
TEARY
SNFF
Tissues...
SHFF
?!

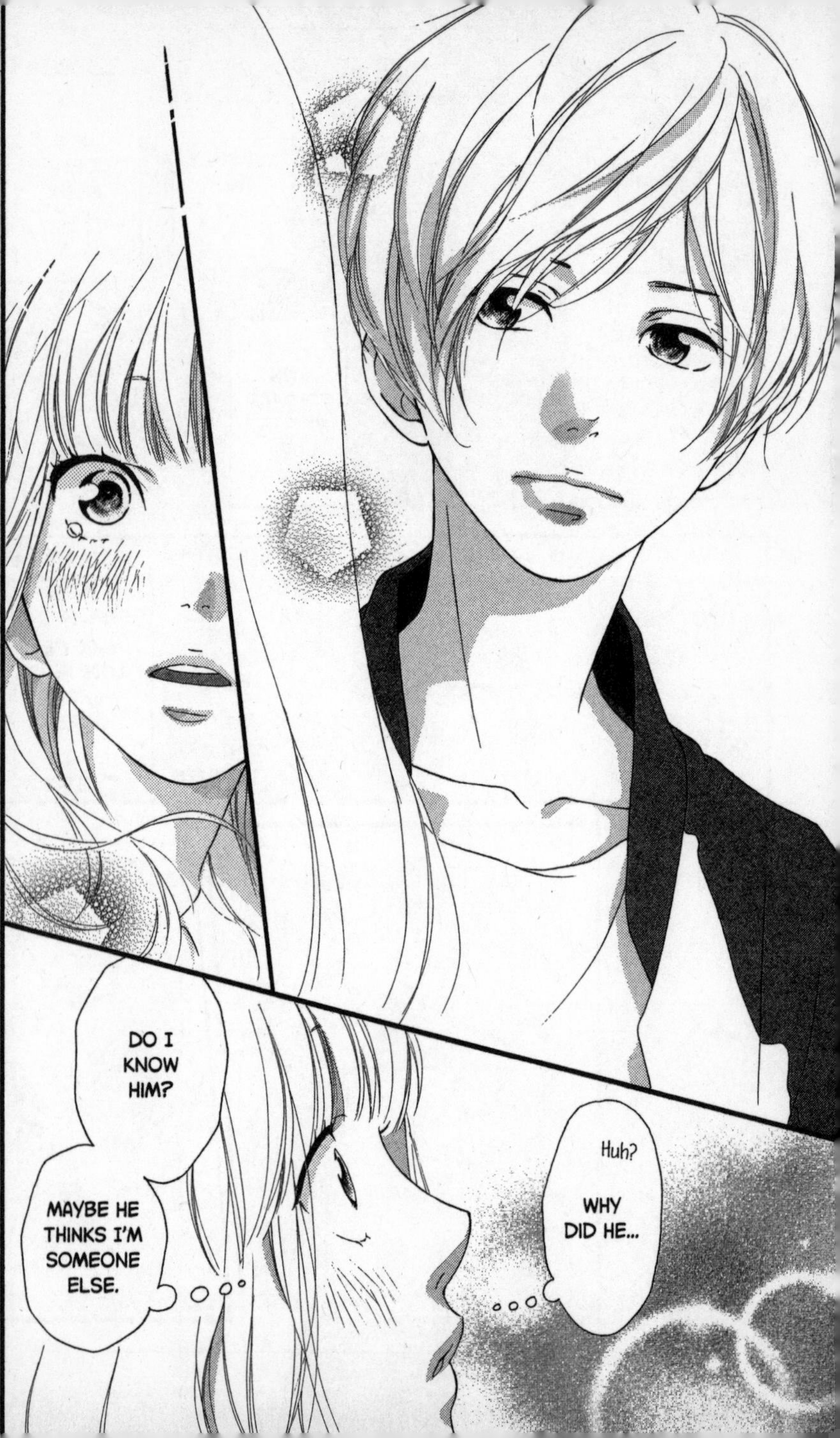
Huh?
WHY DID HE...
DO I KNOW HIM?
MAYBE HE THINKS I'M SOMEONE ELSE.

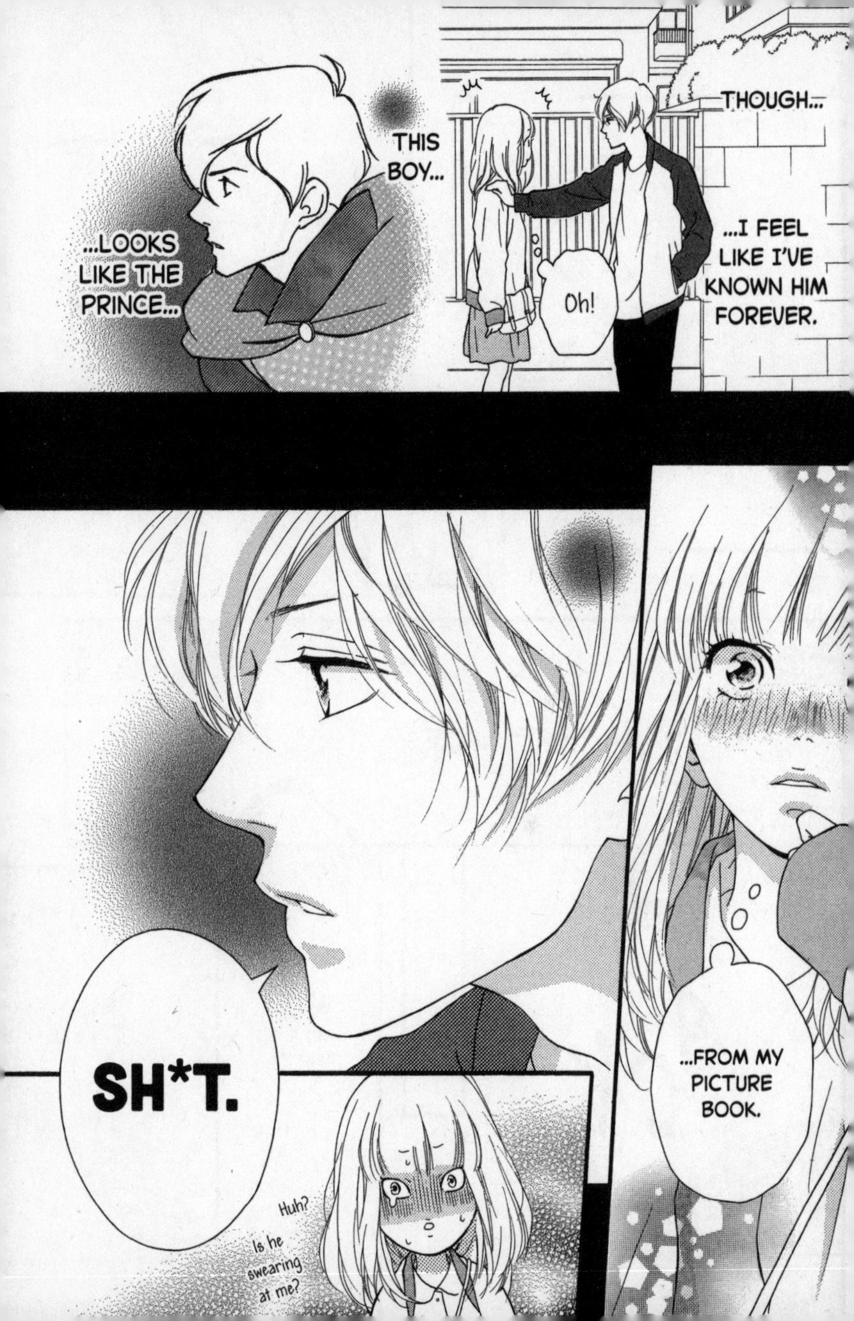
THOUGH...
...I FEEL LIKE I'VE KNOWN HIM FOREVER.
Oh!
THIS BOY...
...LOOKS LIKE THE PRINCE...
...FROM MY PICTURE BOOK.
SH*T.
Huh?
Is he swearing at me?

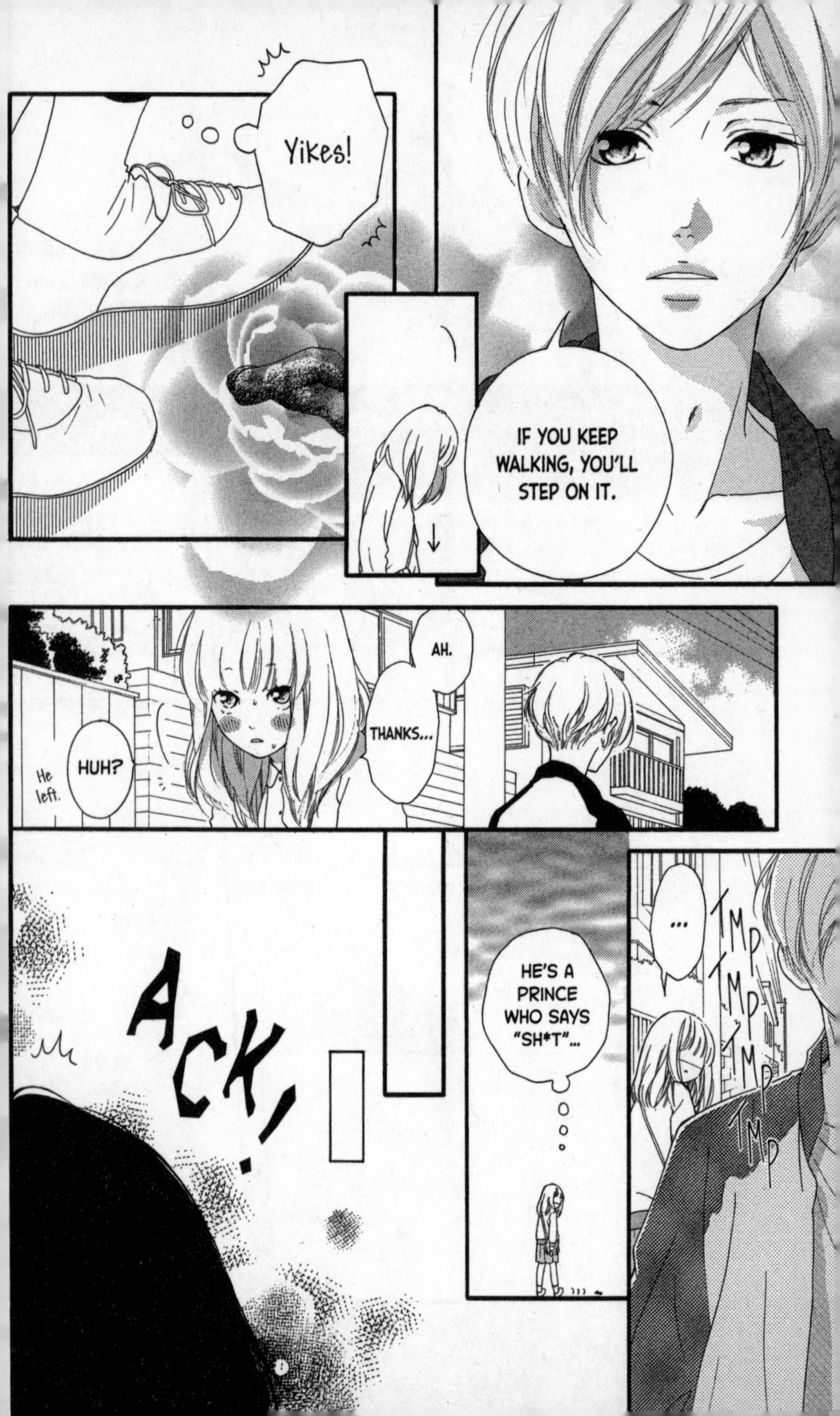
IF YOU KEEP WALKING, YOU'LL STEP ON IT.
Yikes!
AH.
THANKS...
HUH?
He left.
...
TMP TMP TMP TMP
HE'S A PRINCE WHO SAYS "SH*T"...
ACK!

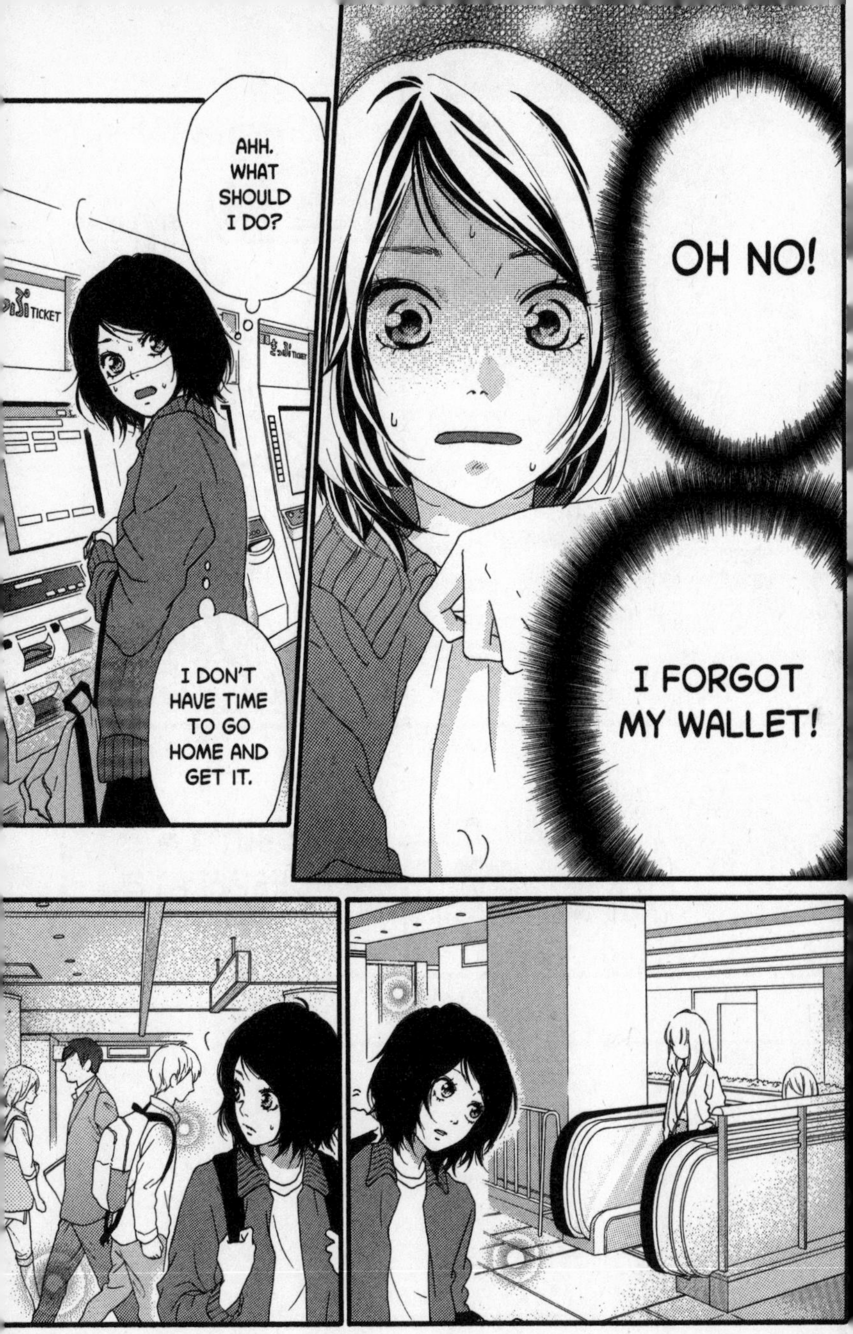
OH NO!
I FORGOT MY WALLET!
AHH. WHAT SHOULD I DO?
I DON'T HAVE TIME TO GO HOME AND GET IT.

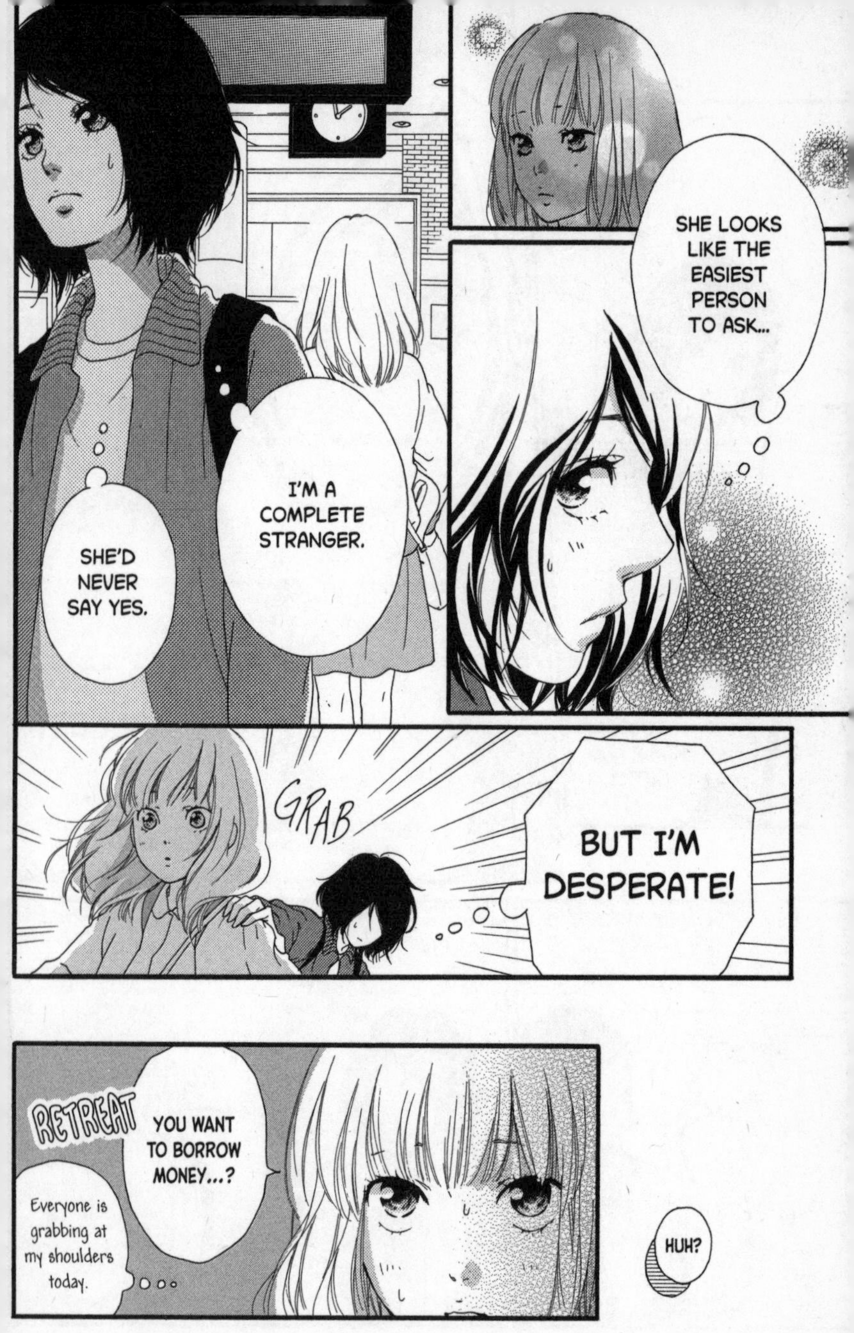
SHE LOOKS LIKE THE EASIEST PERSON TO ASK...
I'M A COMPLETE STRANGER.
SHE'D NEVER SAY YES.
BUT I'M DESPERATE!
GRAB
HUH?
YOU WANT TO BORROW MONEY...?
RETREAT
Everyone is grabbing at my shoulders today.

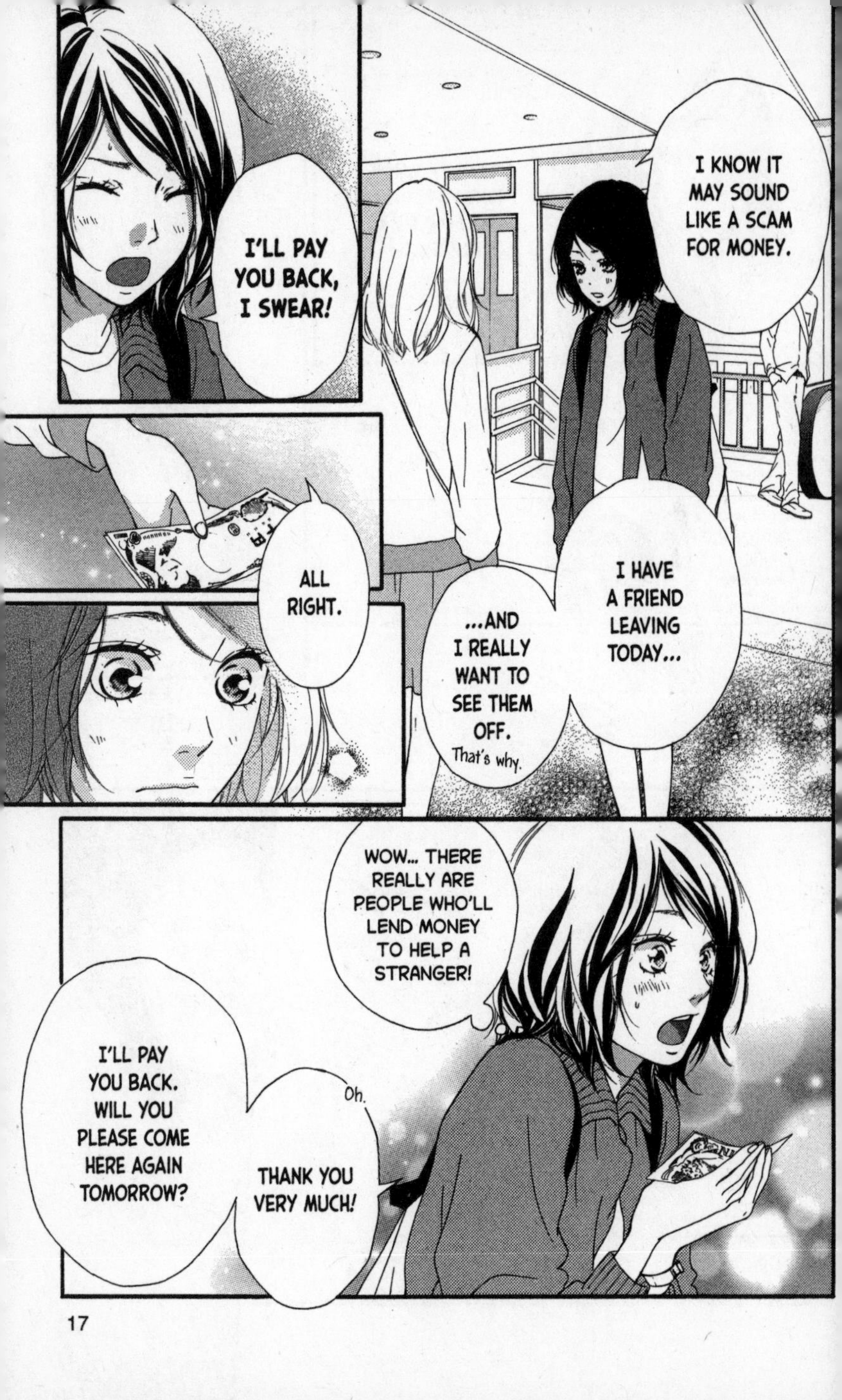
I KNOW IT MAY SOUND LIKE A SCAM FOR MONEY.
I HAVE A FRIEND LEAVING TODAY...
...AND I REALLY WANT TO SEE THEM OFF.
That's why.
I'LL PAY YOU BACK, I SWEAR!
ALL RIGHT.
WOW... THERE REALLY ARE PEOPLE WHO'LL LEND MONEY TO HELP A STRANGER!
Oh.
THANK YOU VERY MUCH!
I'LL PAY YOU BACK. WILL YOU PLEASE COME HERE AGAIN TOMORROW?

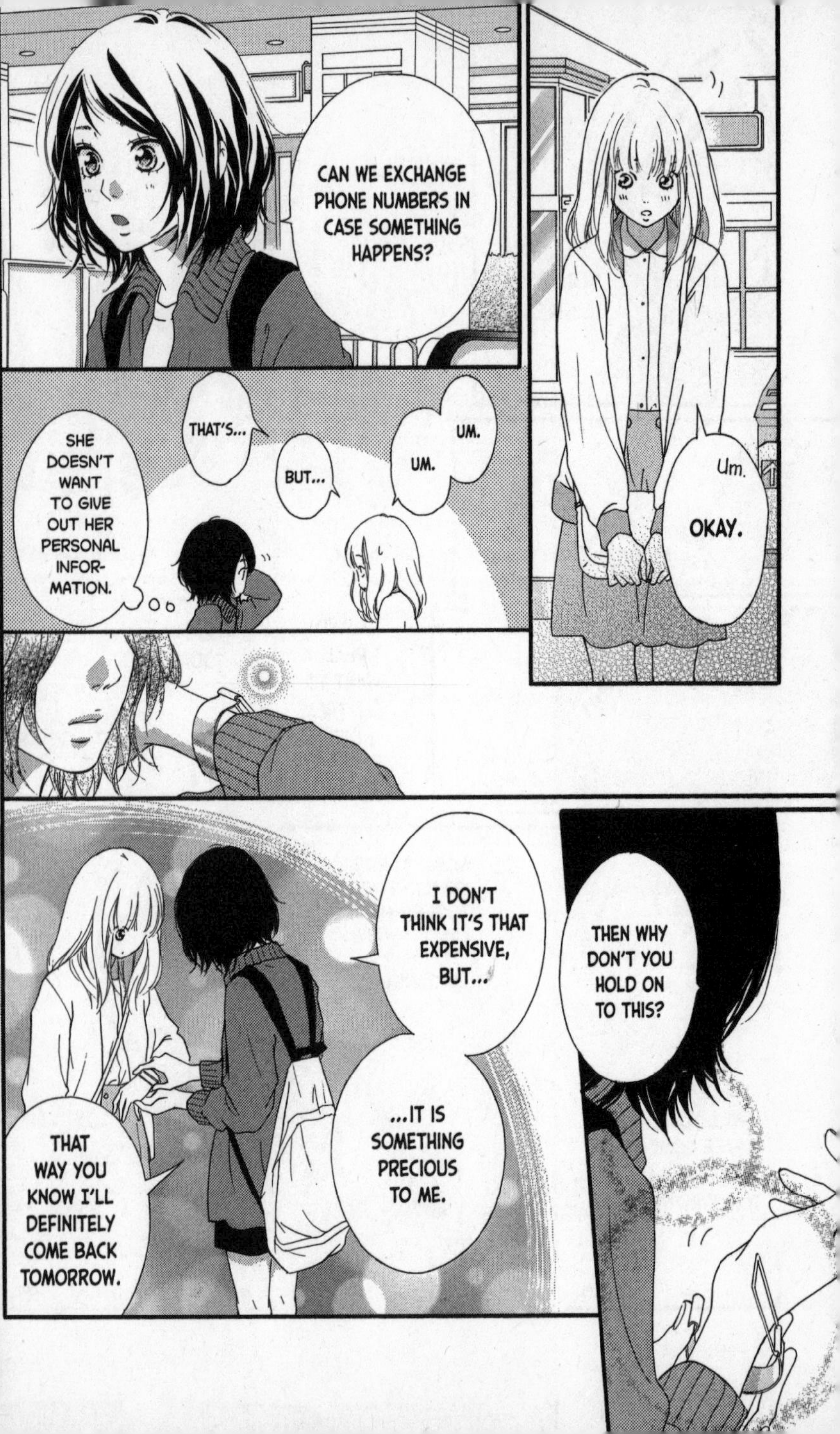
Um.
OKAY.
CAN WE EXCHANGE PHONE NUMBERS IN CASE SOMETHING HAPPENS?
UM.
UM.
BUT...
THAT'S...
SHE DOESN'T WANT TO GIVE OUT HER PERSONAL INFOR-MATION.
THEN WHY DON'T YOU HOLD ON TO THIS?
I DON'T THINK IT'S THAT EXPENSIVE, BUT...
...IT IS SOMETHING PRECIOUS TO ME.
THAT WAY YOU KNOW I'LL DEFINITELY COME BACK TOMORROW.

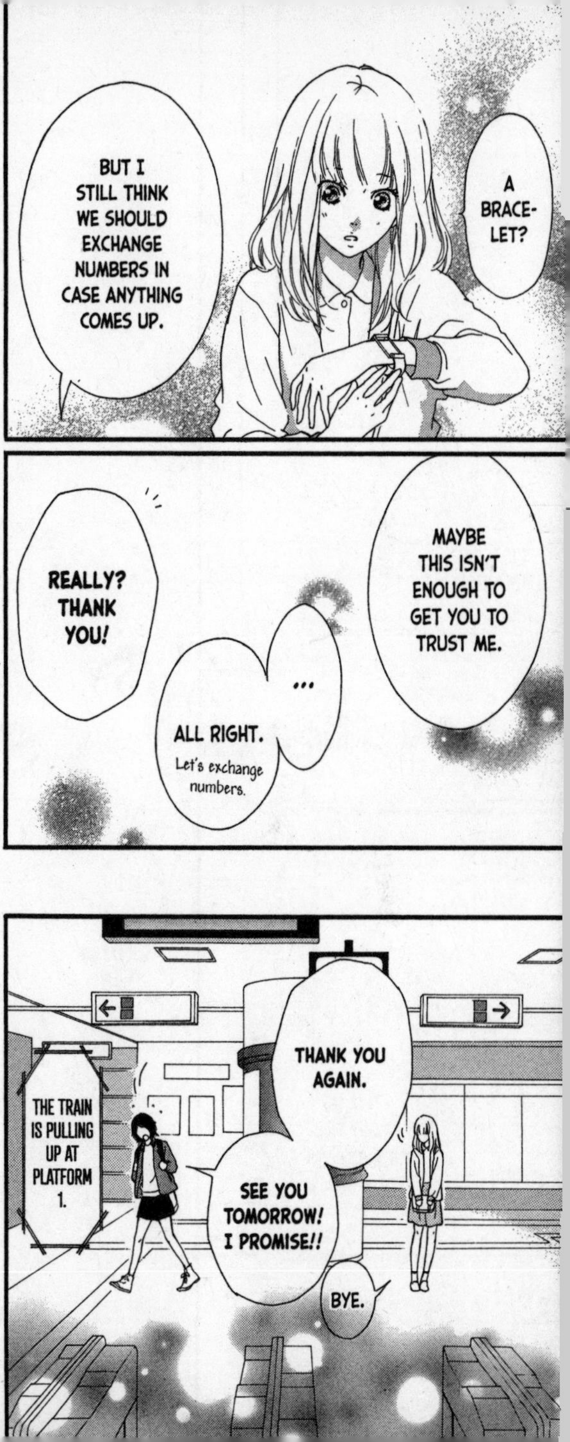
A BRACELET?
BUT I STILL THINK WE SHOULD EXCHANGE NUMBERS IN CASE ANYTHING COMES UP.
MAYBE THIS ISN'T ENOUGH TO GET YOU TO TRUST ME.
...
ALL RIGHT.
Let's exchange numbers.
REALLY? THANK YOU!
THANK YOU AGAIN.
SEE YOU TOMORROW! I PROMISE!!
BYE.
THE TRAIN IS PULLING UP AT PLATFORM 1.

Love Me, Love Me Not

I debated over what title to give this series until the very last minute. I wanted to use a phrase that was familiar and that would fit the sweet scenes as well as the sad ones. The other title I'd thought of seemed a tad too poetic, and it's a little too embarrassing for me to mention. When the phrase *omoi omoware, furi furare* came to me, I was sincerely relieved. It's a saying in a love-divination game according to where a pimple appears on your face. I thought it might be a good title because it connects with young people. I think it's cute, and I hope you think so too!

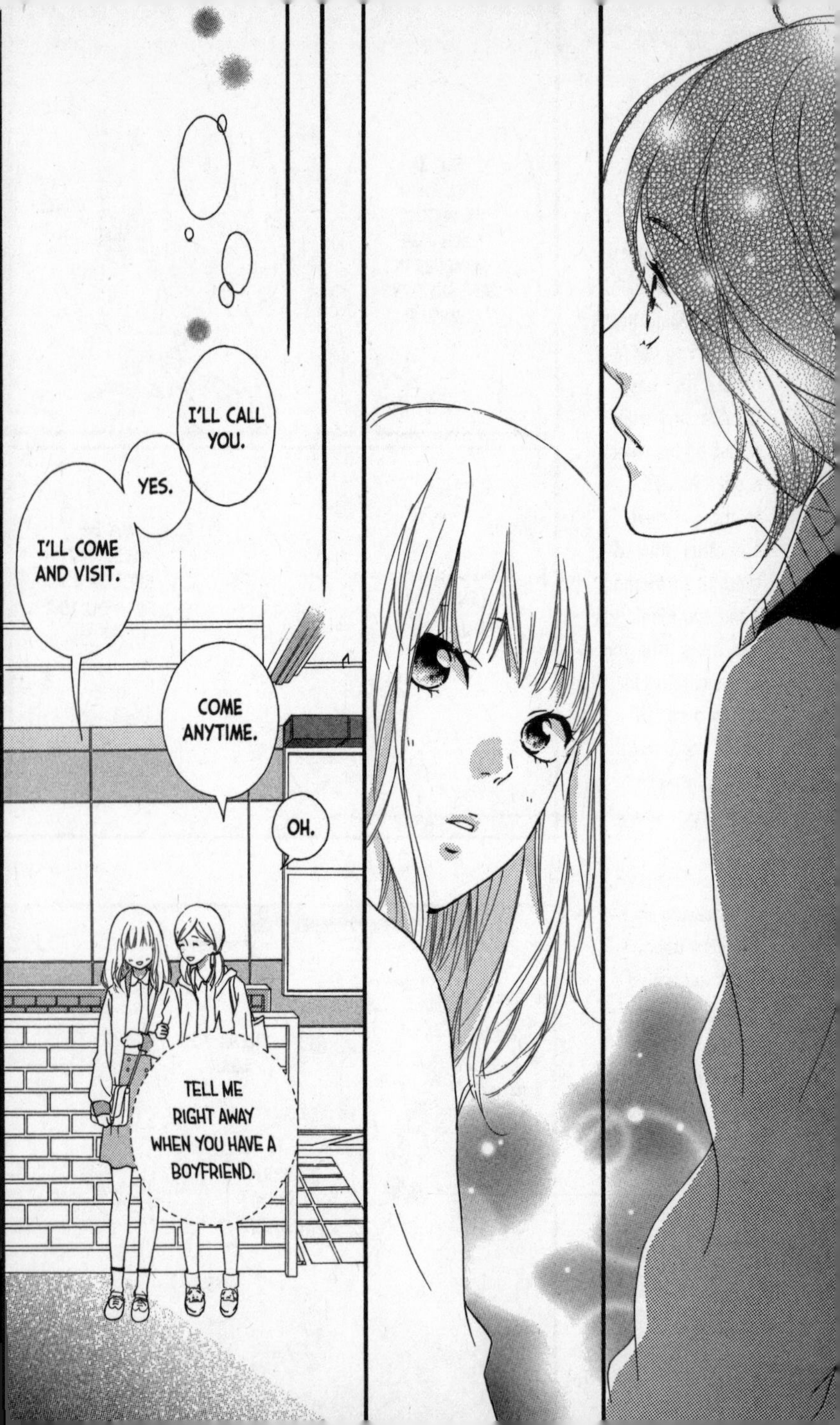
I'LL CALL YOU.
YES.
I'LL COME AND VISIT.
COME ANYTIME.
OH.
TELL ME RIGHT AWAY WHEN YOU HAVE A BOYFRIEND.

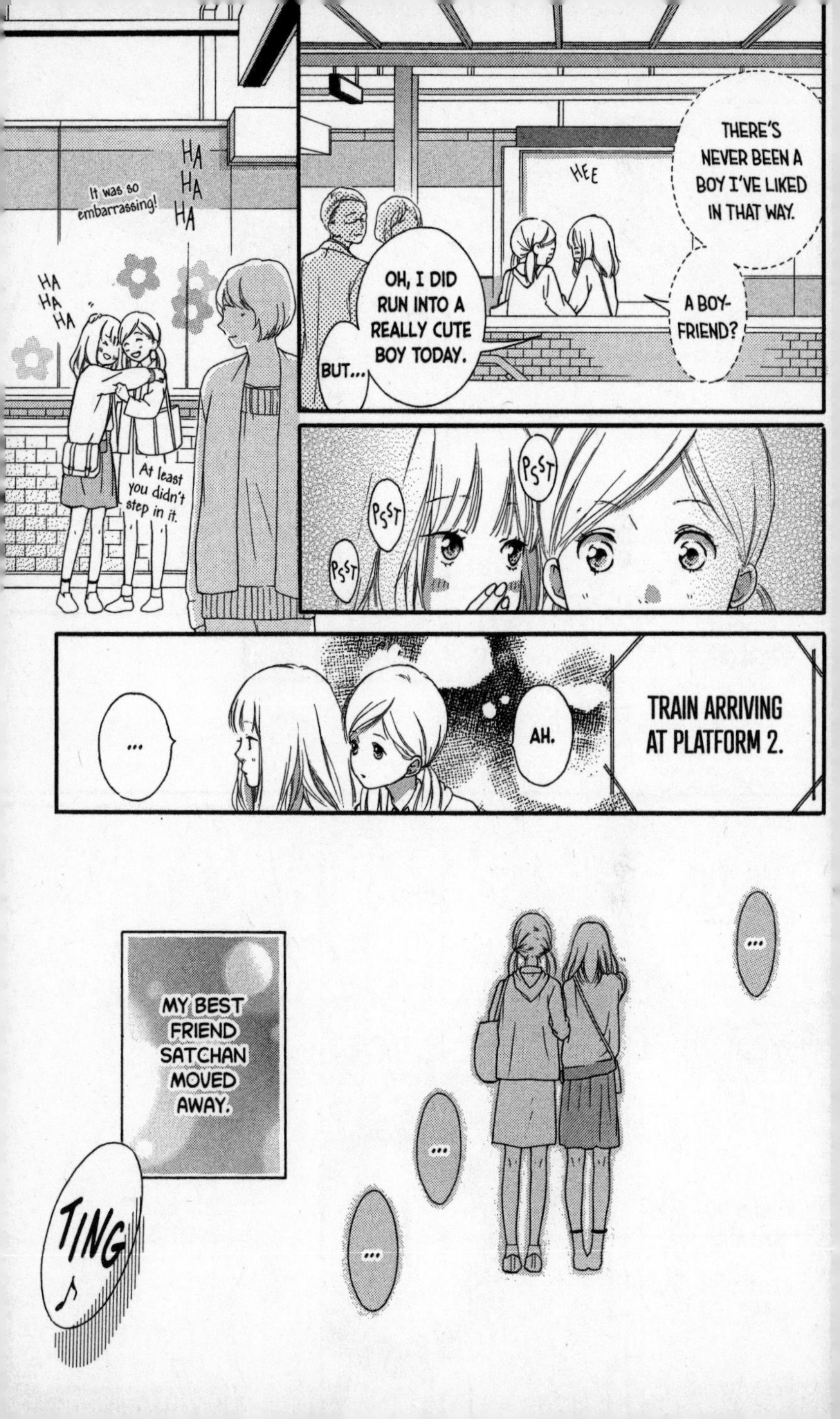
THERE'S NEVER BEEN A BOY I'VE LIKED IN THAT WAY.
A BOY-FRIEND?
HEE
OH, I DID RUN INTO A REALLY CUTE BOY TODAY.
BUT...
PSST
PSST
PSST
HA HA HA
It was so embarrassing!
HA HA HA
At least you didn't step in it.
TRAIN ARRIVING AT PLATFORM 2.
AH.
...
...
MY BEST FRIEND SATCHAN MOVED AWAY.
...
...
TING ♪

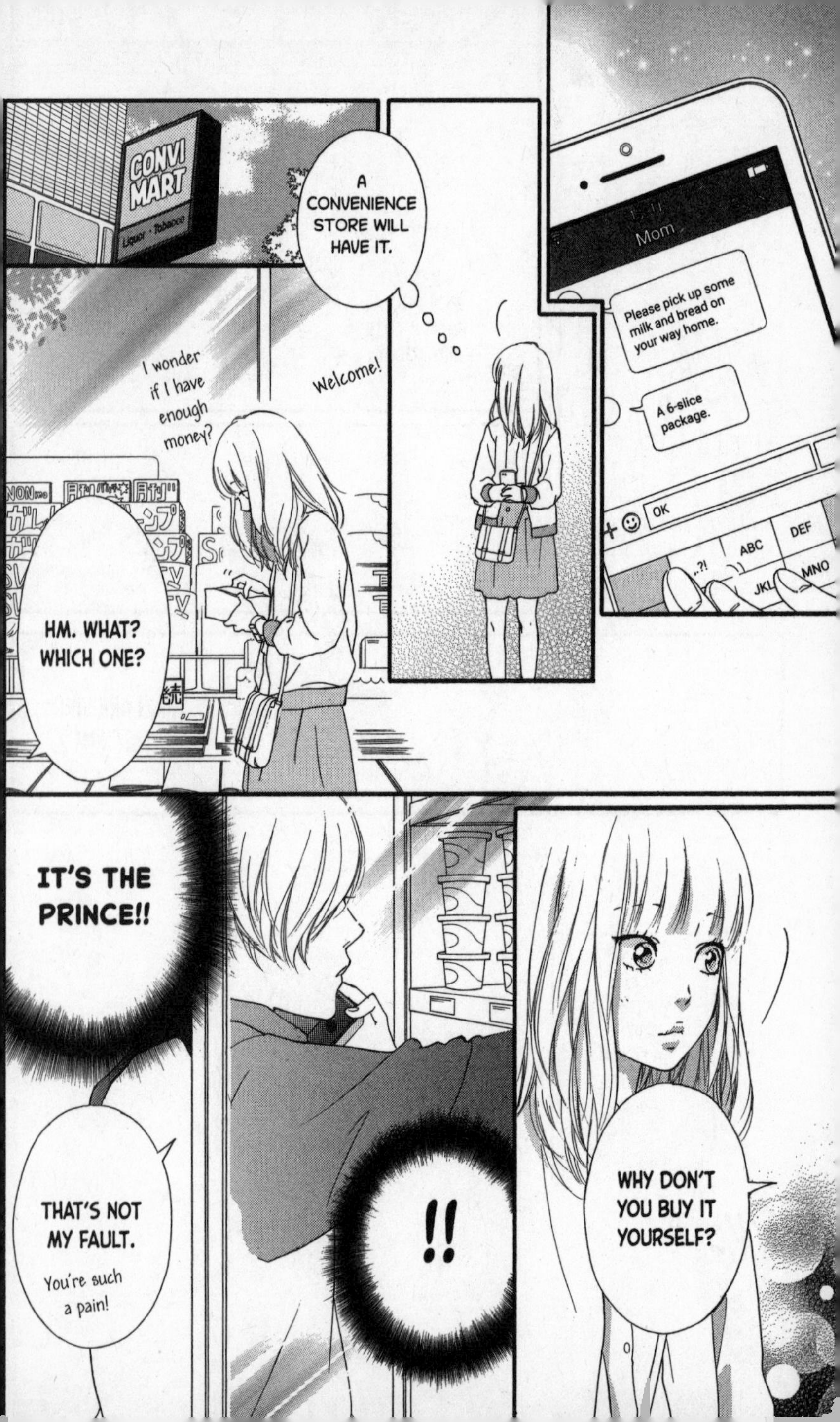
Mom
Please pick up some milk and bread on your way home.
A 6-slice package.
OK
A CONVENIENCE STORE WILL HAVE IT.
CONVI MART
Liquor · Tobacco
Welcome!
I wonder if I have enough money?
HM. WHAT? WHICH ONE?
WHY DON'T YOU BUY IT YOURSELF?
!!
IT'S THE PRINCE!!
THAT'S NOT MY FAULT.
You're such a pain!

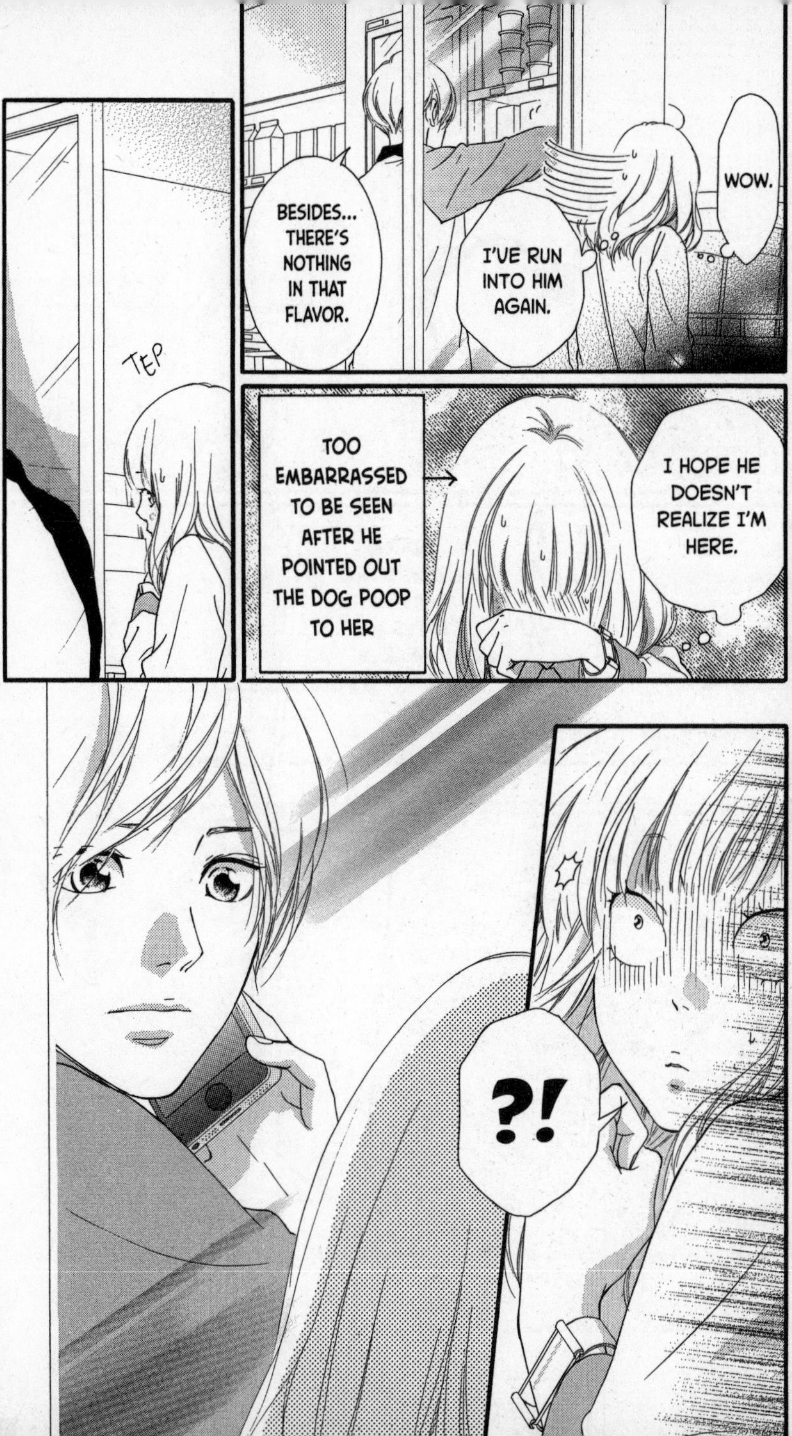
WOW.
I'VE RUN INTO HIM AGAIN.
BESIDES... THERE'S NOTHING IN THAT FLAVOR.
I HOPE HE DOESN'T REALIZE I'M HERE.
TOO EMBARRASSED TO BE SEEN AFTER HE POINTED OUT THE DOG POOP TO HER
TEP
?!

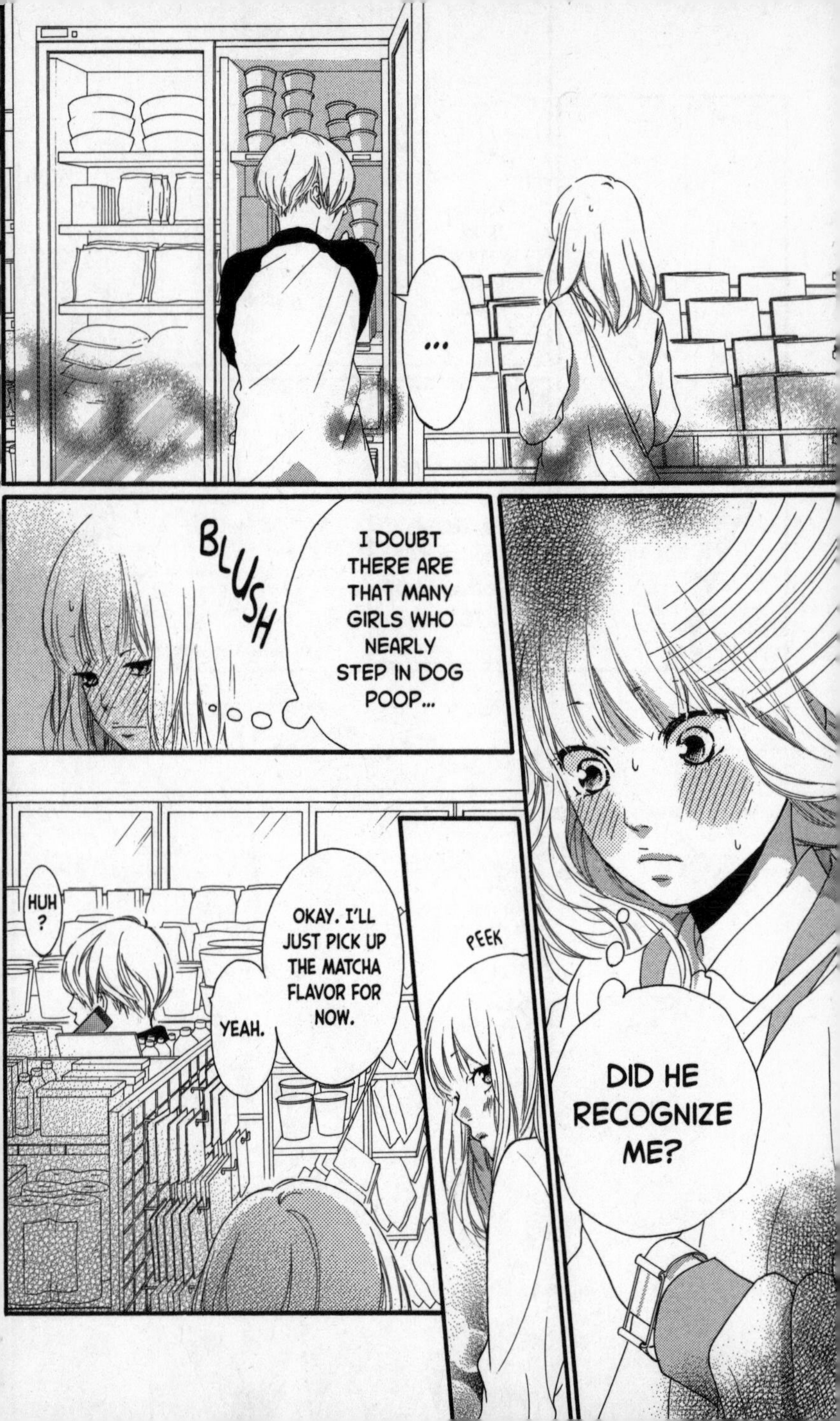
...
DID HE RECOGNIZE ME?
I DOUBT THERE ARE THAT MANY GIRLS WHO NEARLY STEP IN DOG POOP...
BLUSH
PEEK
OKAY. I'LL JUST PICK UP THE MATCHA FLAVOR FOR NOW.
YEAH.
HUH?

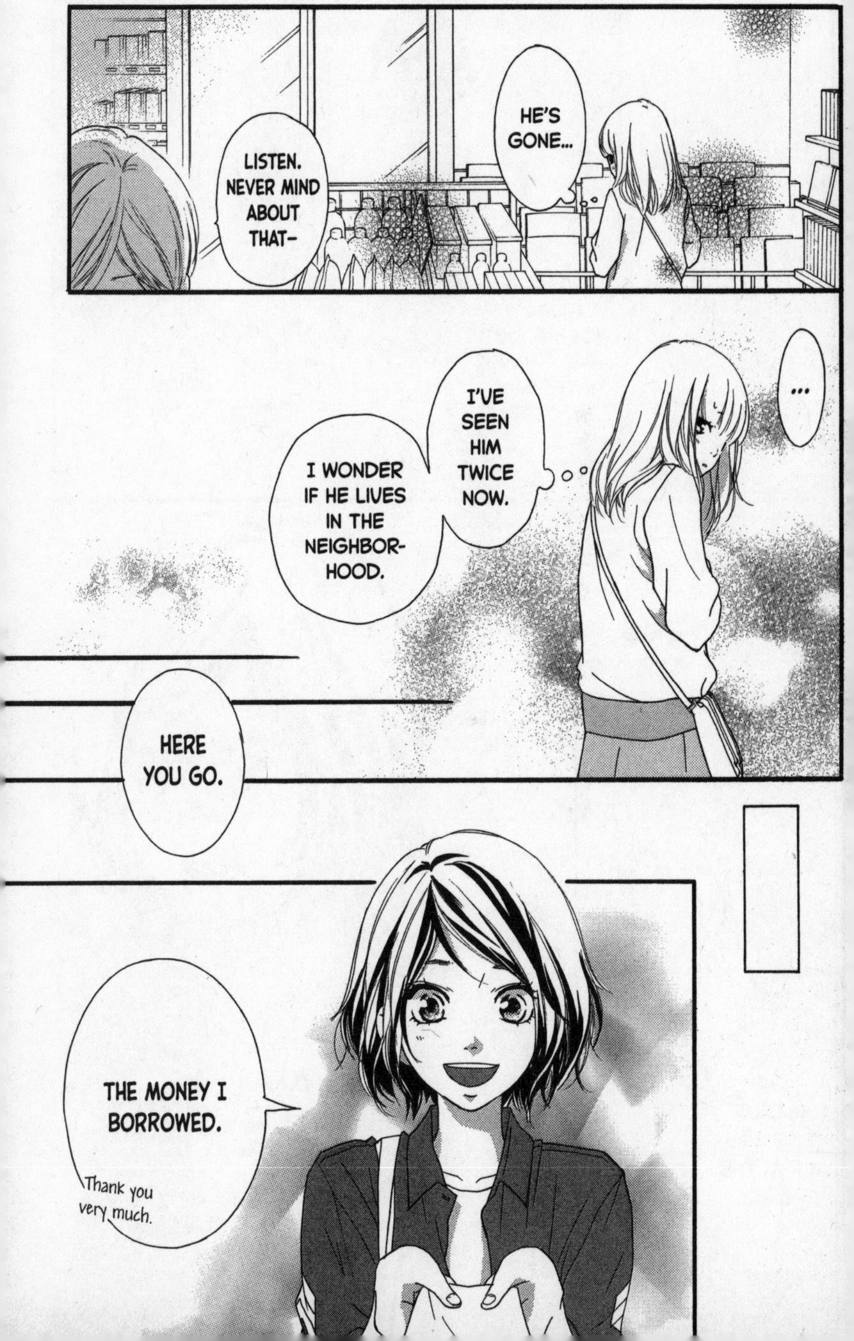
HE'S GONE...
LISTEN. NEVER MIND ABOUT THAT–
...
I'VE SEEN HIM TWICE NOW.
I WONDER IF HE LIVES IN THE NEIGHBOR-HOOD.
HERE YOU GO.
THE MONEY I BORROWED.
Thank you very much.

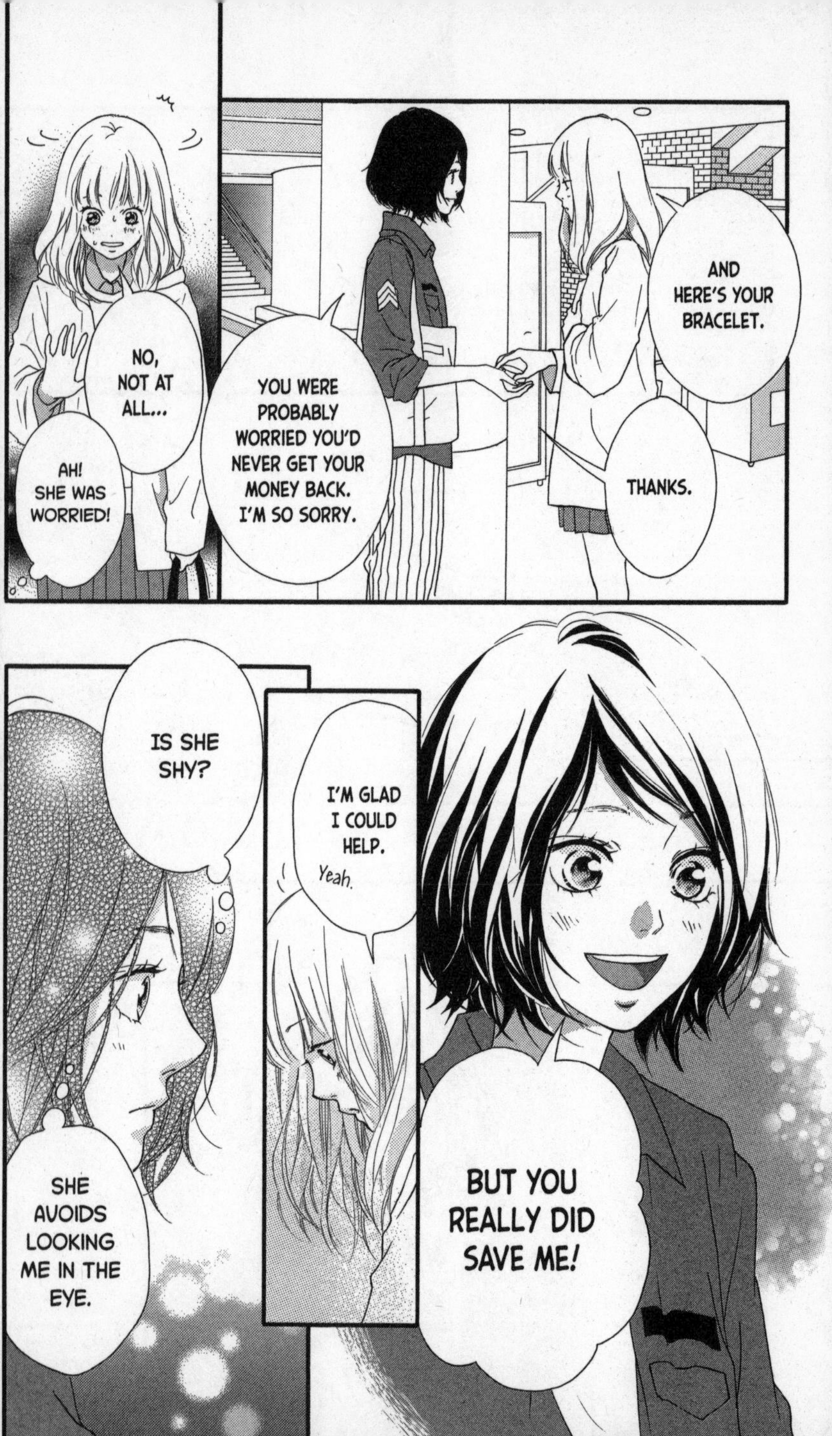
AND HERE'S YOUR BRACELET.
THANKS.
YOU WERE PROBABLY WORRIED YOU'D NEVER GET YOUR MONEY BACK. I'M SO SORRY.
NO, NOT AT ALL...
AH! SHE WAS WORRIED!
BUT YOU REALLY DID SAVE ME!
I'M GLAD I COULD HELP.
Yeah.
IS SHE SHY?
SHE AVOIDS LOOKING ME IN THE EYE.

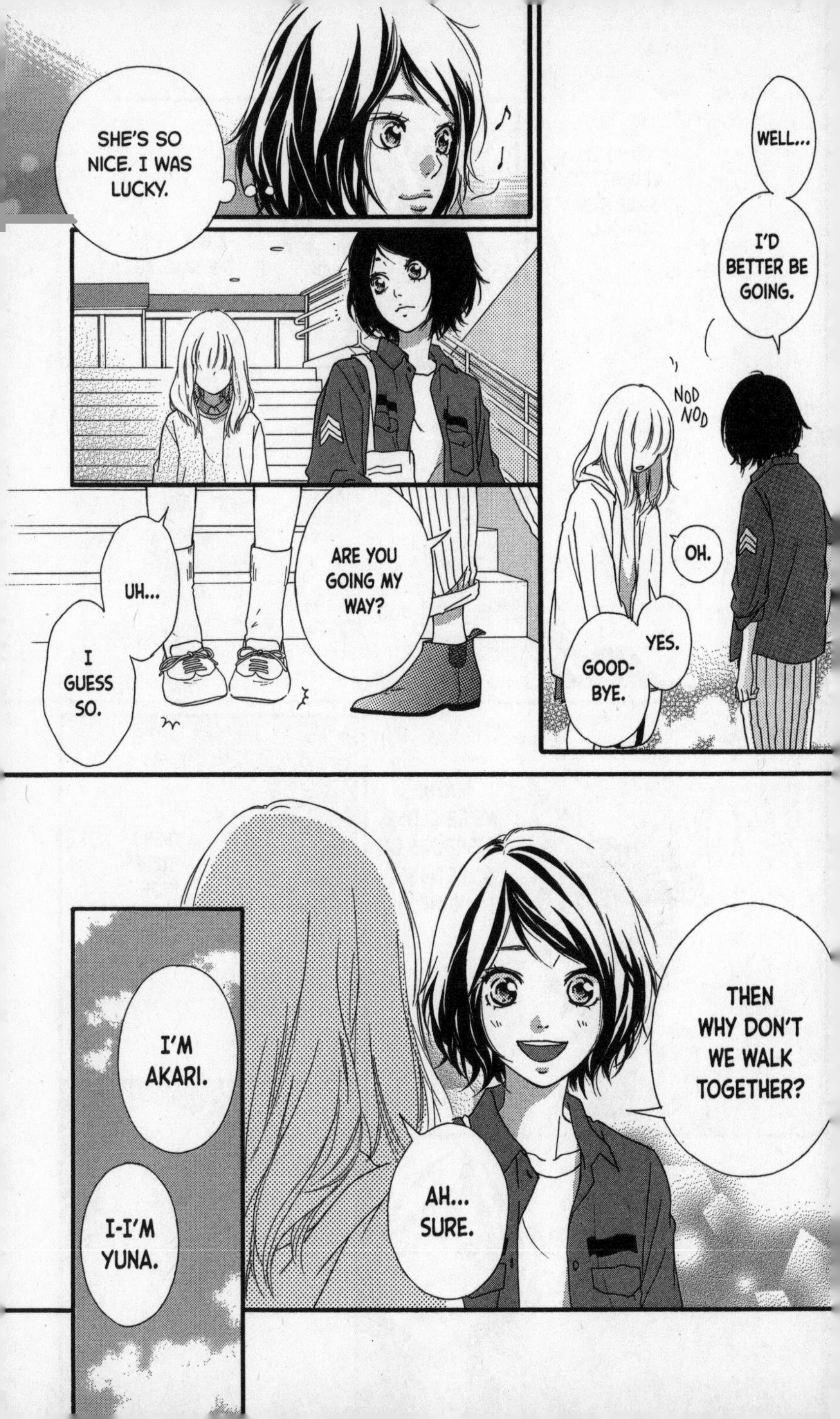
WELL...
I'D BETTER BE GOING.
NOD NOD
OH.
YES.
GOOD-BYE.
SHE'S SO NICE. I WAS LUCKY.
ARE YOU GOING MY WAY?
UH...
I GUESS SO.
THEN WHY DON'T WE WALK TOGETHER?
AH... SURE.
I'M AKARI.
I-I'M YUNA.

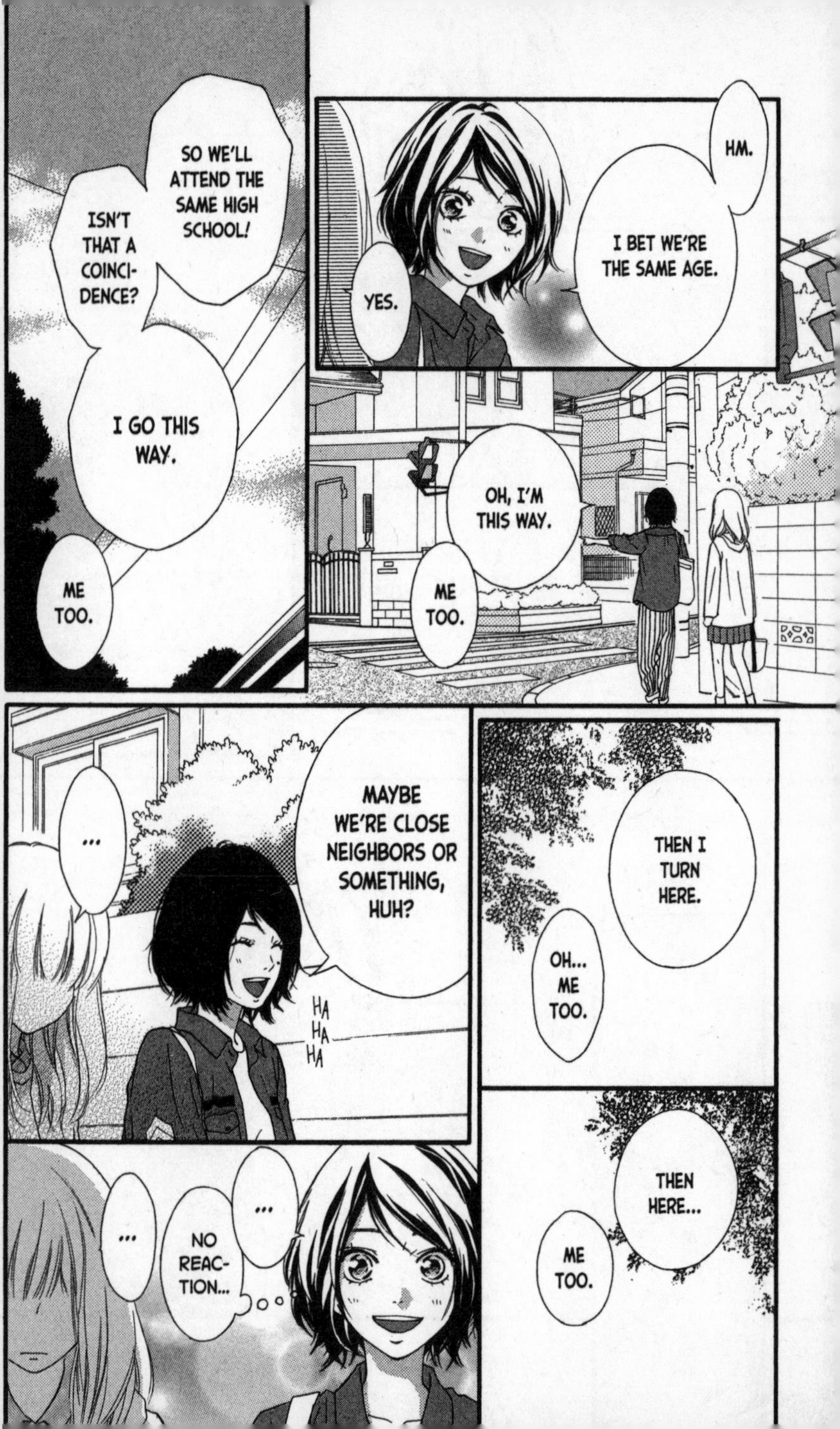
HM.
I BET WE'RE THE SAME AGE.
YES.
OH, I'M THIS WAY.
ME TOO.
SO WE'LL ATTEND THE SAME HIGH SCHOOL!
ISN'T THAT A COINCI-DENCE?
I GO THIS WAY.
ME TOO.
THEN I TURN HERE.
OH... ME TOO.
THEN HERE...
ME TOO.
MAYBE WE'RE CLOSE NEIGHBORS OR SOMETHING, HUH?
...
HA HA HA
...
NO REAC-TION...
...

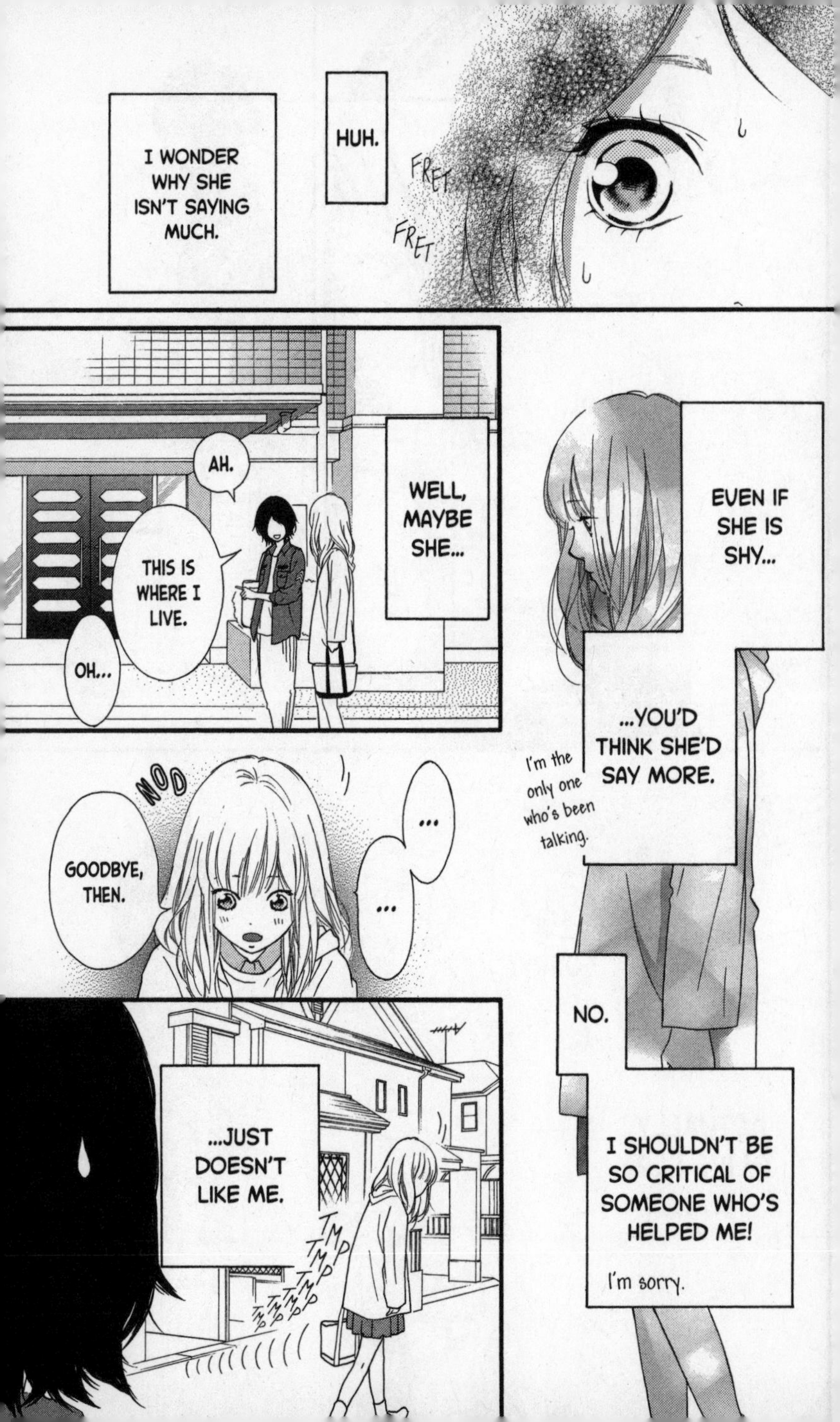
HUH.
FRET
FRET
I WONDER WHY SHE ISN'T SAYING MUCH.
EVEN IF SHE IS SHY...
...YOU'D THINK SHE'D SAY MORE.
I'm the only one who's been talking.
NO.
I SHOULDN'T BE SO CRITICAL OF SOMEONE WHO'S HELPED ME!
I'm sorry.
WELL, MAYBE SHE...
AH.
THIS IS WHERE I LIVE.
OH...
...
...
NOD
GOODBYE, THEN.
...JUST DOESN'T LIKE ME.
TMP TMP TMP TMP TMP TMP

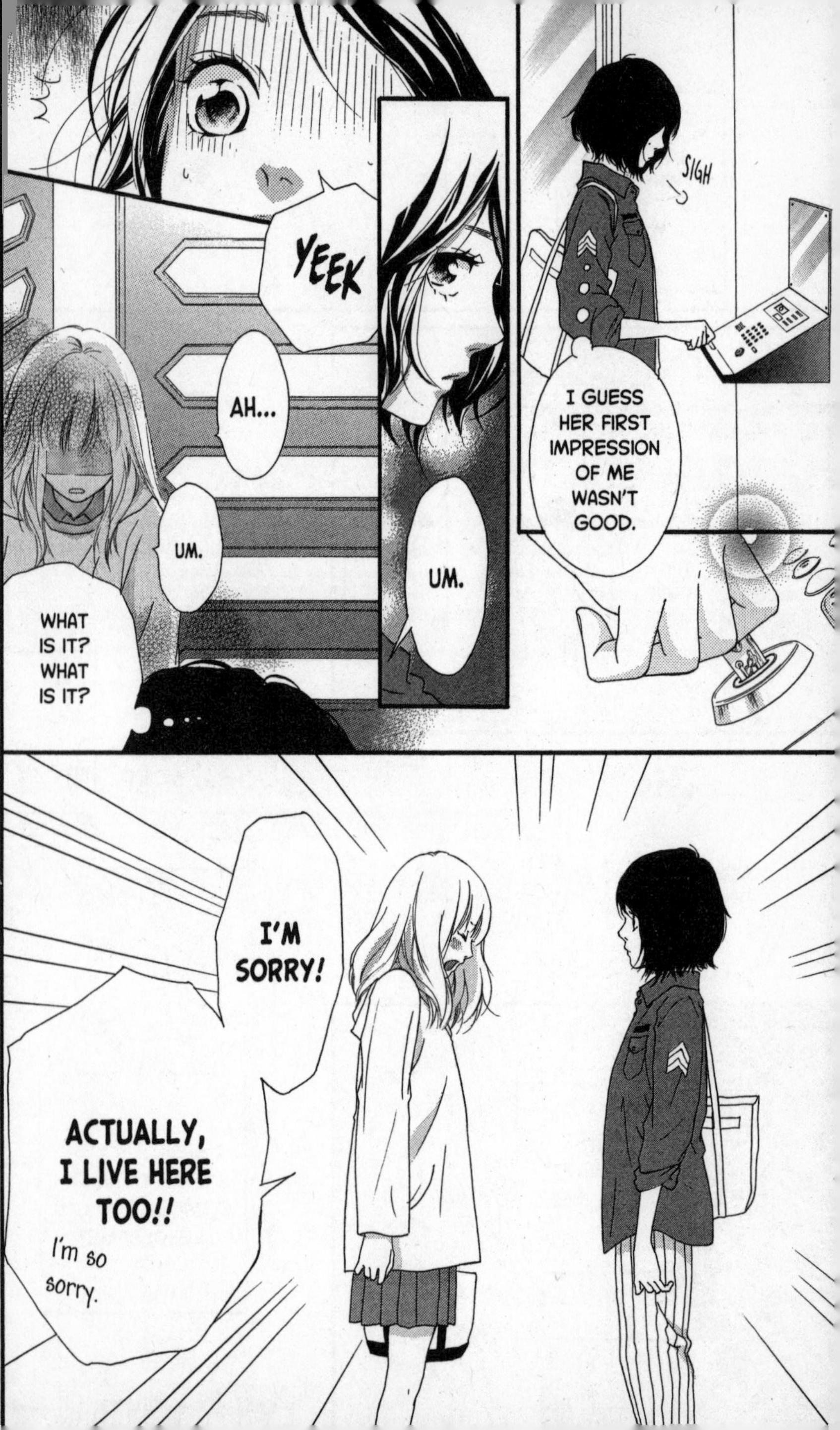
SIGH
I GUESS HER FIRST IMPRESSION OF ME WASN'T GOOD.
UM.
YEEK
AH...
UM.
WHAT IS IT? WHAT IS IT?
I'M SORRY!
ACTUALLY, I LIVE HERE TOO!!
I'm so sorry.

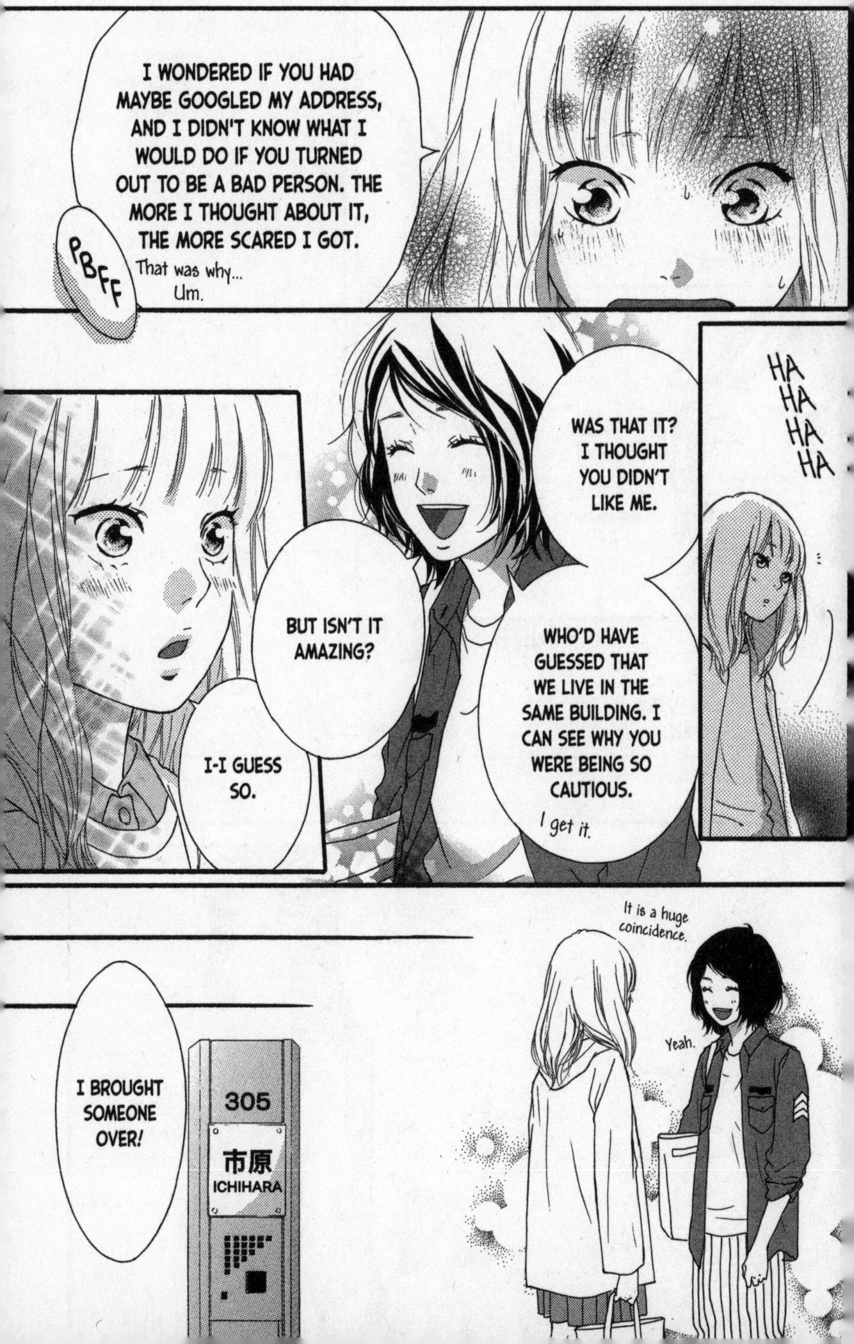
I WONDERED IF YOU HAD MAYBE GOOGLED MY ADDRESS, AND I DIDN'T KNOW WHAT I WOULD DO IF YOU TURNED OUT TO BE A BAD PERSON. THE MORE I THOUGHT ABOUT IT, THE MORE SCARED I GOT.
That was why... Um.
PBFF
HA HA HA HA
WAS THAT IT? I THOUGHT YOU DIDN'T LIKE ME.
WHO'D HAVE GUESSED THAT WE LIVE IN THE SAME BUILDING. I CAN SEE WHY YOU WERE BEING SO CAUTIOUS.
I get it.
BUT ISN'T IT AMAZING?
I-I GUESS SO.
It is a huge coincidence.
Yeah.
305
市原
ICHIHARA
I BROUGHT SOMEONE OVER!

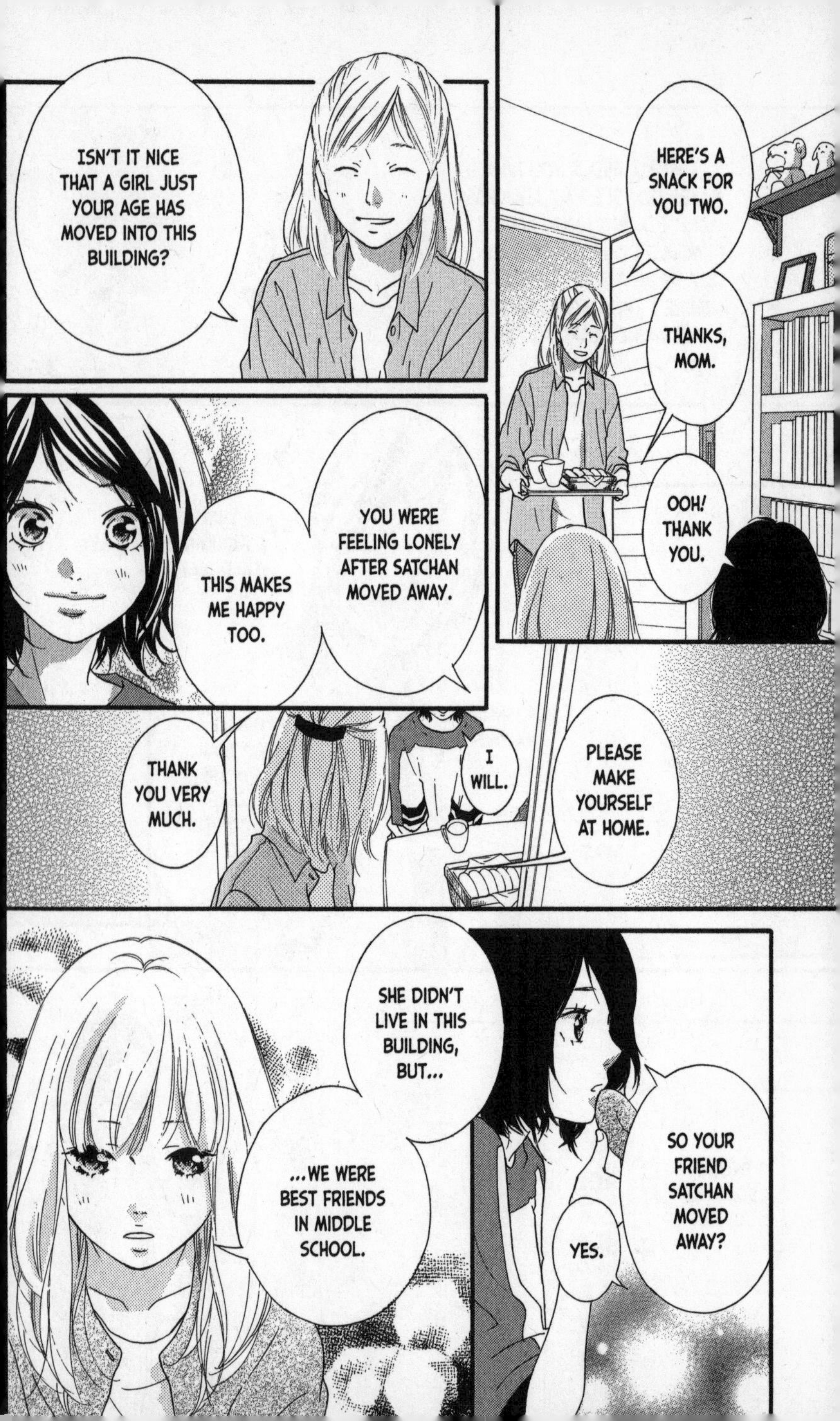
HERE'S A SNACK FOR YOU TWO.
THANKS, MOM.
OOH! THANK YOU.
ISN'T IT NICE THAT A GIRL JUST YOUR AGE HAS MOVED INTO THIS BUILDING?
YOU WERE FEELING LONELY AFTER SATCHAN MOVED AWAY.
THIS MAKES ME HAPPY TOO.
PLEASE MAKE YOURSELF AT HOME.
I WILL.
THANK YOU VERY MUCH.
SO YOUR FRIEND SATCHAN MOVED AWAY?
YES.
SHE DIDN'T LIVE IN THIS BUILDING, BUT...
...WE WERE BEST FRIENDS IN MIDDLE SCHOOL.

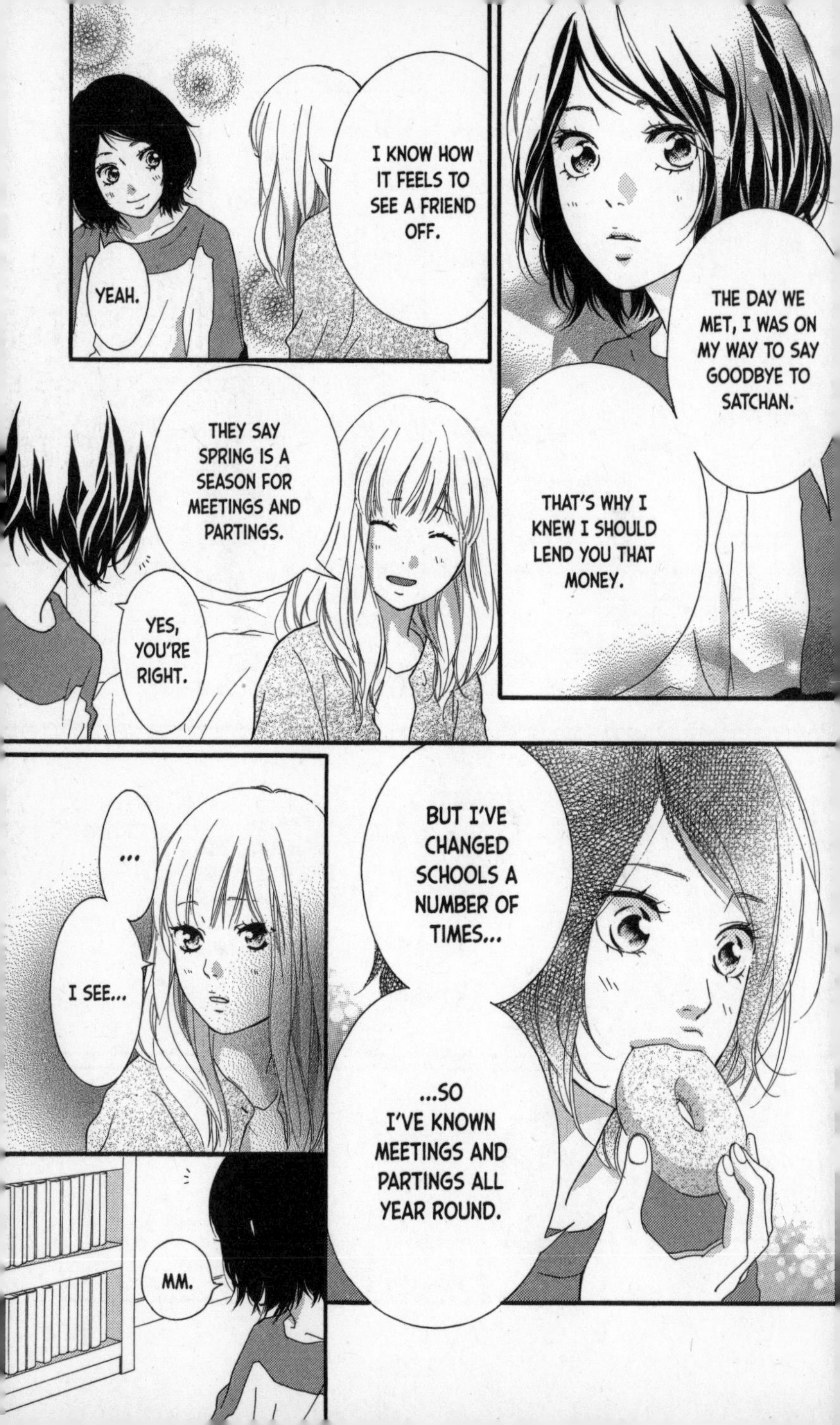
THE DAY WE MET, I WAS ON MY WAY TO SAY GOODBYE TO SATCHAN.
THAT'S WHY I KNEW I SHOULD LEND YOU THAT MONEY.
I KNOW HOW IT FEELS TO SEE A FRIEND OFF.
YEAH.
THEY SAY SPRING IS A SEASON FOR MEETINGS AND PARTINGS.
YES, YOU'RE RIGHT.
BUT I'VE CHANGED SCHOOLS A NUMBER OF TIMES...
...SO I'VE KNOWN MEETINGS AND PARTINGS ALL YEAR ROUND.
...
I SEE...
MM.

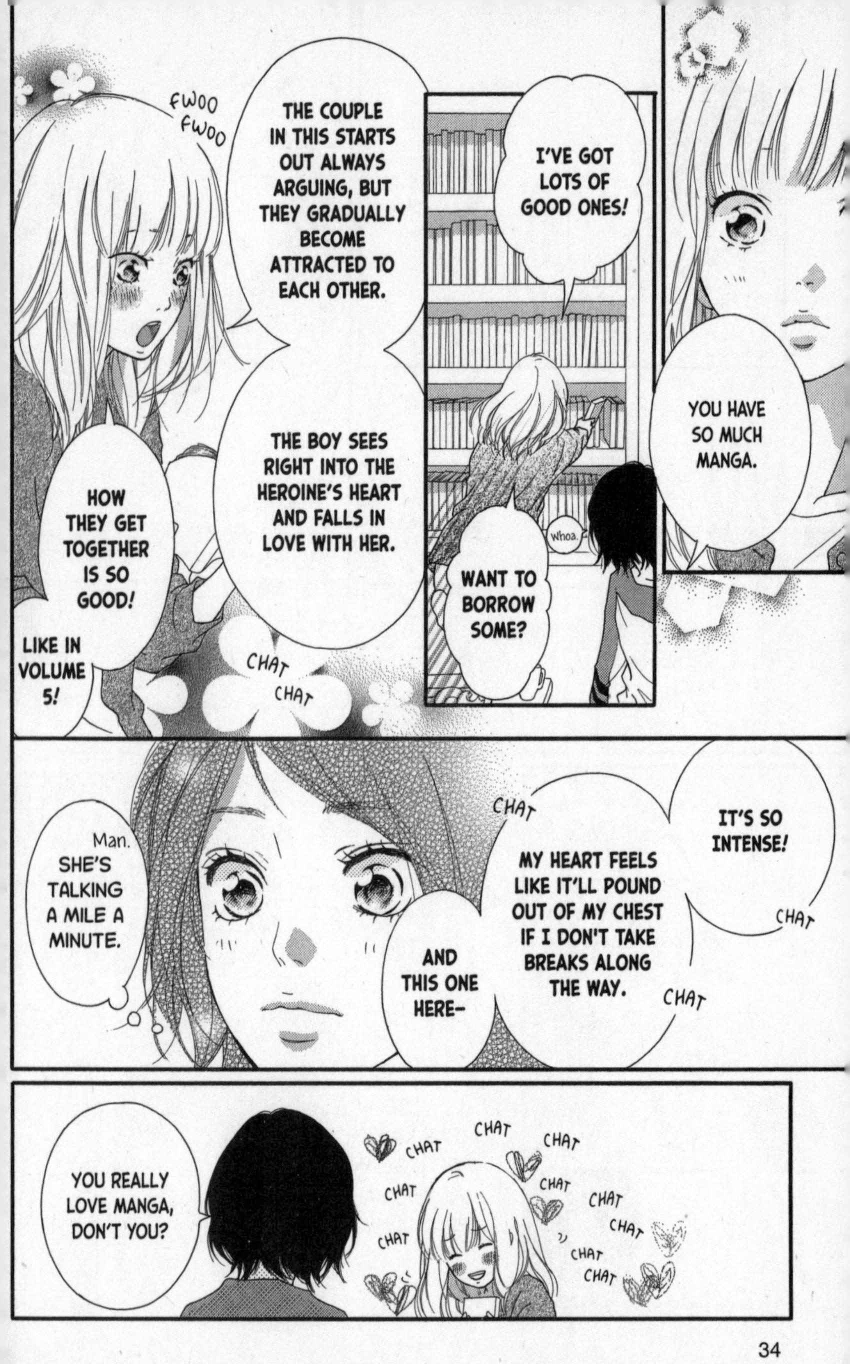
YOU HAVE SO MUCH MANGA.
I'VE GOT LOTS OF GOOD ONES!
Whoa.
WANT TO BORROW SOME?
FWOO FWOO
THE COUPLE IN THIS STARTS OUT ALWAYS ARGUING, BUT THEY GRADUALLY BECOME ATTRACTED TO EACH OTHER.
THE BOY SEES RIGHT INTO THE HEROINE'S HEART AND FALLS IN LOVE WITH HER.
HOW THEY GET TOGETHER IS SO GOOD!
LIKE IN VOLUME 5!
CHAT CHAT
IT'S SO INTENSE!
CHAT
CHAT
MY HEART FEELS LIKE IT'LL POUND OUT OF MY CHEST IF I DON'T TAKE BREAKS ALONG THE WAY.
CHAT
AND THIS ONE HERE–
Man. SHE'S TALKING A MILE A MINUTE.
CHAT CHAT CHAT CHAT CHAT CHAT CHAT CHAT CHAT CHAT
YOU REALLY LOVE MANGA, DON'T YOU?

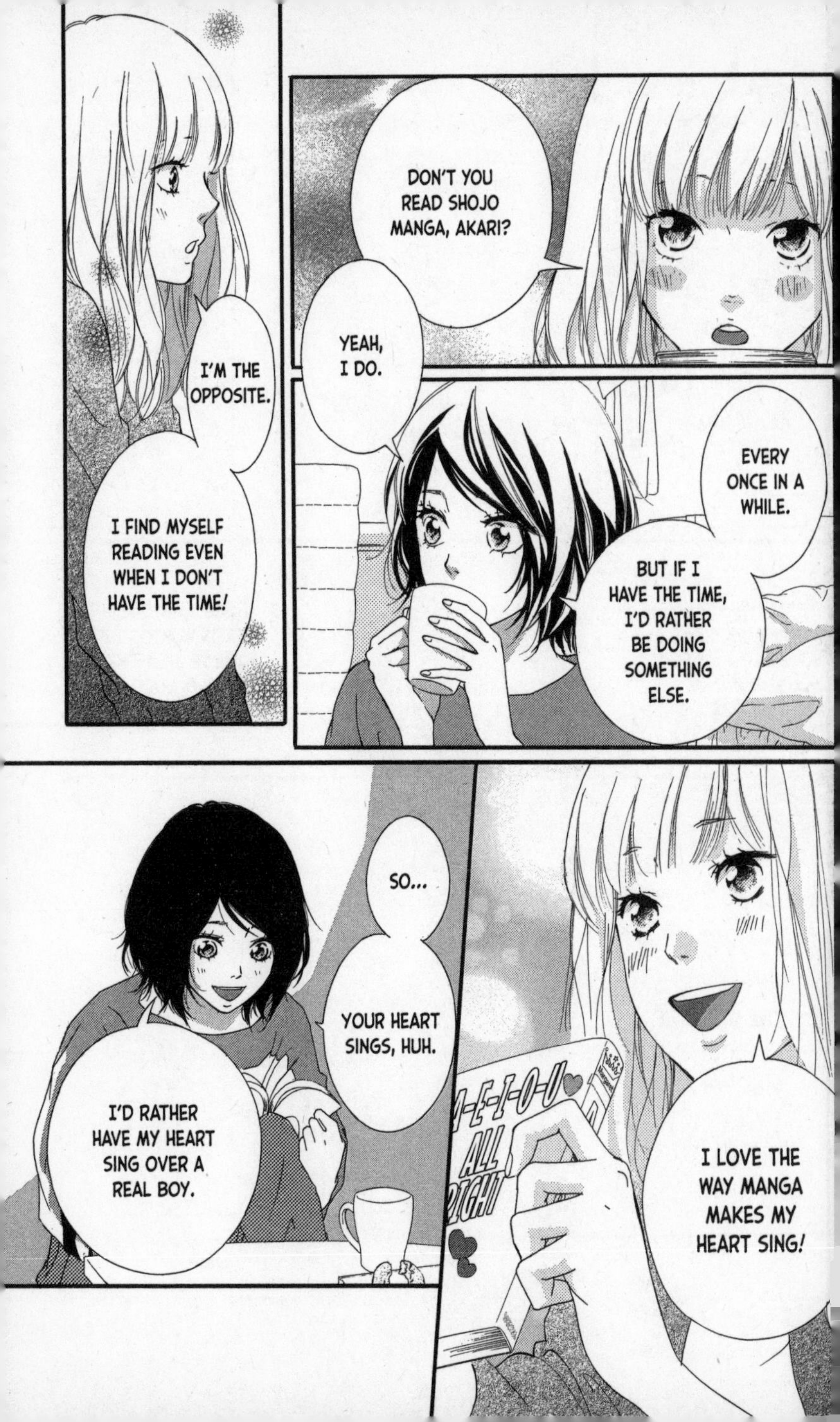
DON'T YOU READ SHOJO MANGA, AKARI?
YEAH, I DO.
EVERY ONCE IN A WHILE.
BUT IF I HAVE THE TIME, I'D RATHER BE DOING SOMETHING ELSE.
I'M THE OPPOSITE.
I FIND MYSELF READING EVEN WHEN I DON'T HAVE THE TIME!
I LOVE THE WAY MANGA MAKES MY HEART SING!
SO...
YOUR HEART SINGS, HUH.
I'D RATHER HAVE MY HEART SING OVER A REAL BOY.

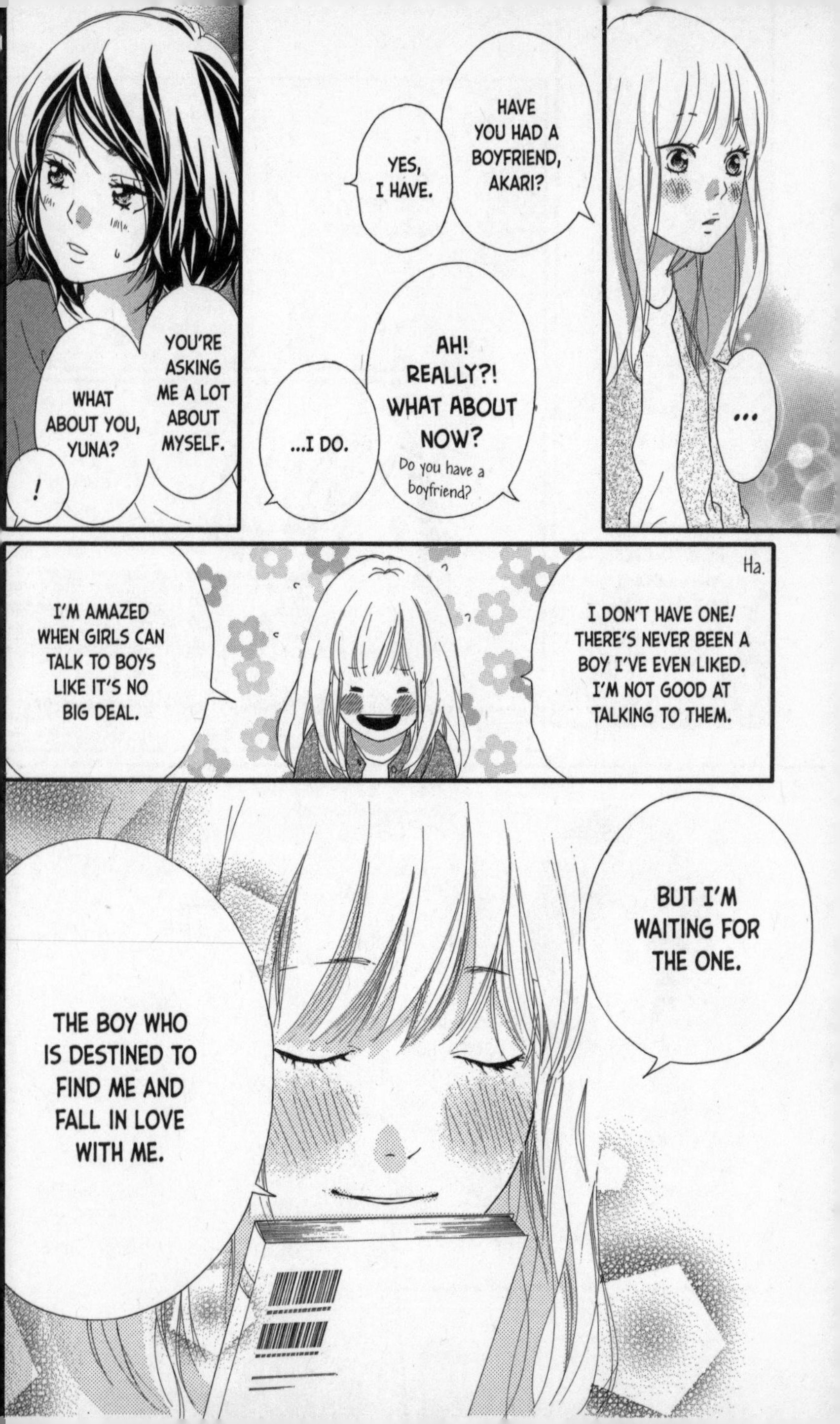

HAVE YOU HAD A BOYFRIEND, AKARI?
YES, I HAVE.
AH! REALLY?! WHAT ABOUT NOW? Do you have a boyfriend?
...I DO.
...
YOU'RE ASKING ME A LOT ABOUT MYSELF.
WHAT ABOUT YOU, YUNA?
!
Ha.
I DON'T HAVE ONE! THERE'S NEVER BEEN A BOY I'VE EVEN LIKED. I'M NOT GOOD AT TALKING TO THEM.
I'M AMAZED WHEN GIRLS CAN TALK TO BOYS LIKE IT'S NO BIG DEAL.
BUT I'M WAITING FOR THE ONE.
THE BOY WHO IS DESTINED TO FIND ME AND FALL IN LOVE WITH ME.

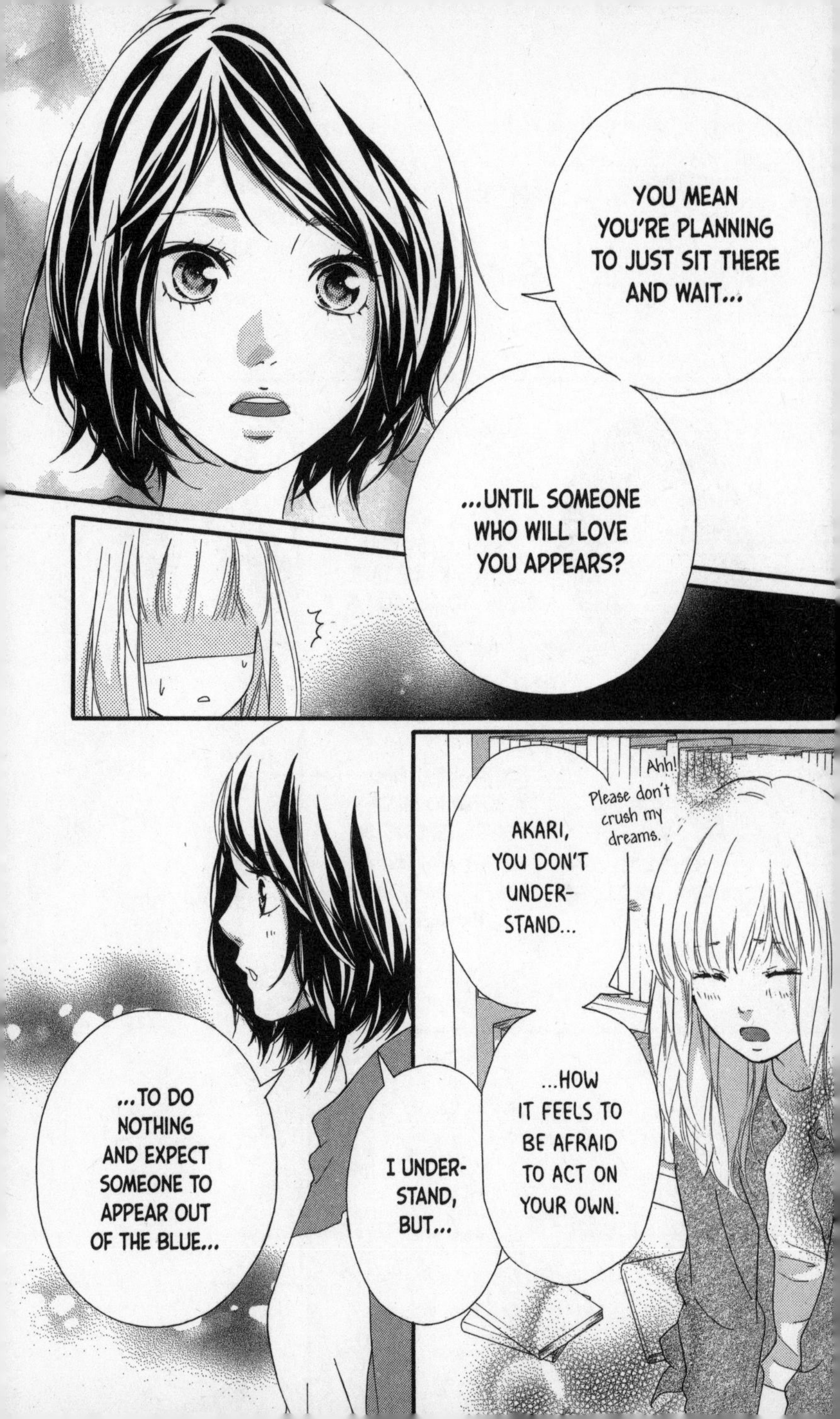
YOU MEAN YOU'RE PLANNING TO JUST SIT THERE AND WAIT...
...UNTIL SOMEONE WHO WILL LOVE YOU APPEARS?
Ahh! Please don't crush my dreams.
AKARI, YOU DON'T UNDER-STAND...
...HOW IT FEELS TO BE AFRAID TO ACT ON YOUR OWN.
I UNDER-STAND, BUT...
...TO DO NOTHING AND EXPECT SOMEONE TO APPEAR OUT OF THE BLUE...

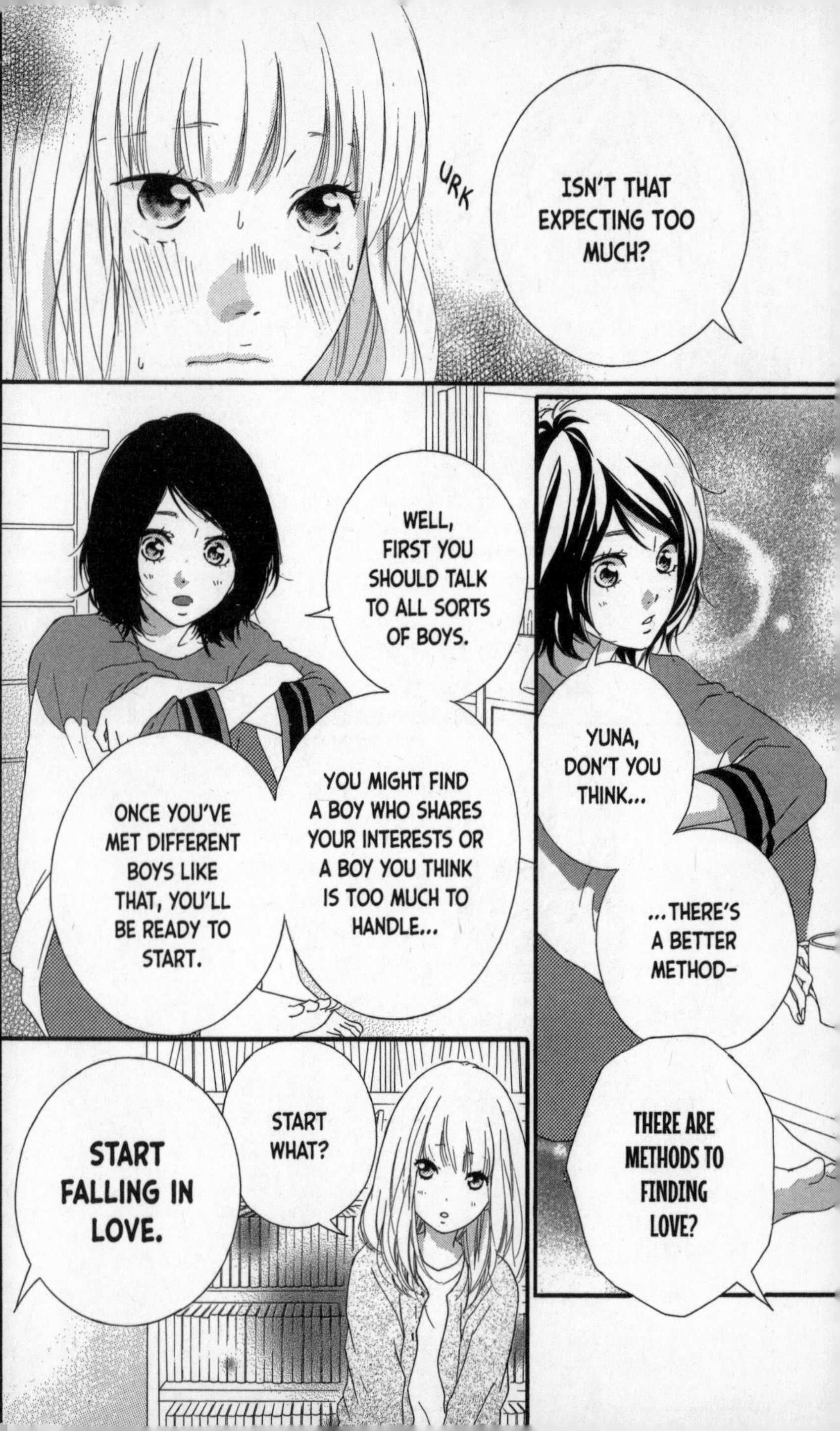
ISN'T THAT EXPECTING TOO MUCH?
URK
YUNA, DON'T YOU THINK...
...THERE'S A BETTER METHOD-
THERE ARE METHODS TO FINDING LOVE?
WELL, FIRST YOU SHOULD TALK TO ALL SORTS OF BOYS.
YOU MIGHT FIND A BOY WHO SHARES YOUR INTERESTS OR A BOY YOU THINK IS TOO MUCH TO HANDLE...
ONCE YOU'VE MET DIFFERENT BOYS LIKE THAT, YOU'LL BE READY TO START.
START WHAT?
START FALLING IN LOVE.

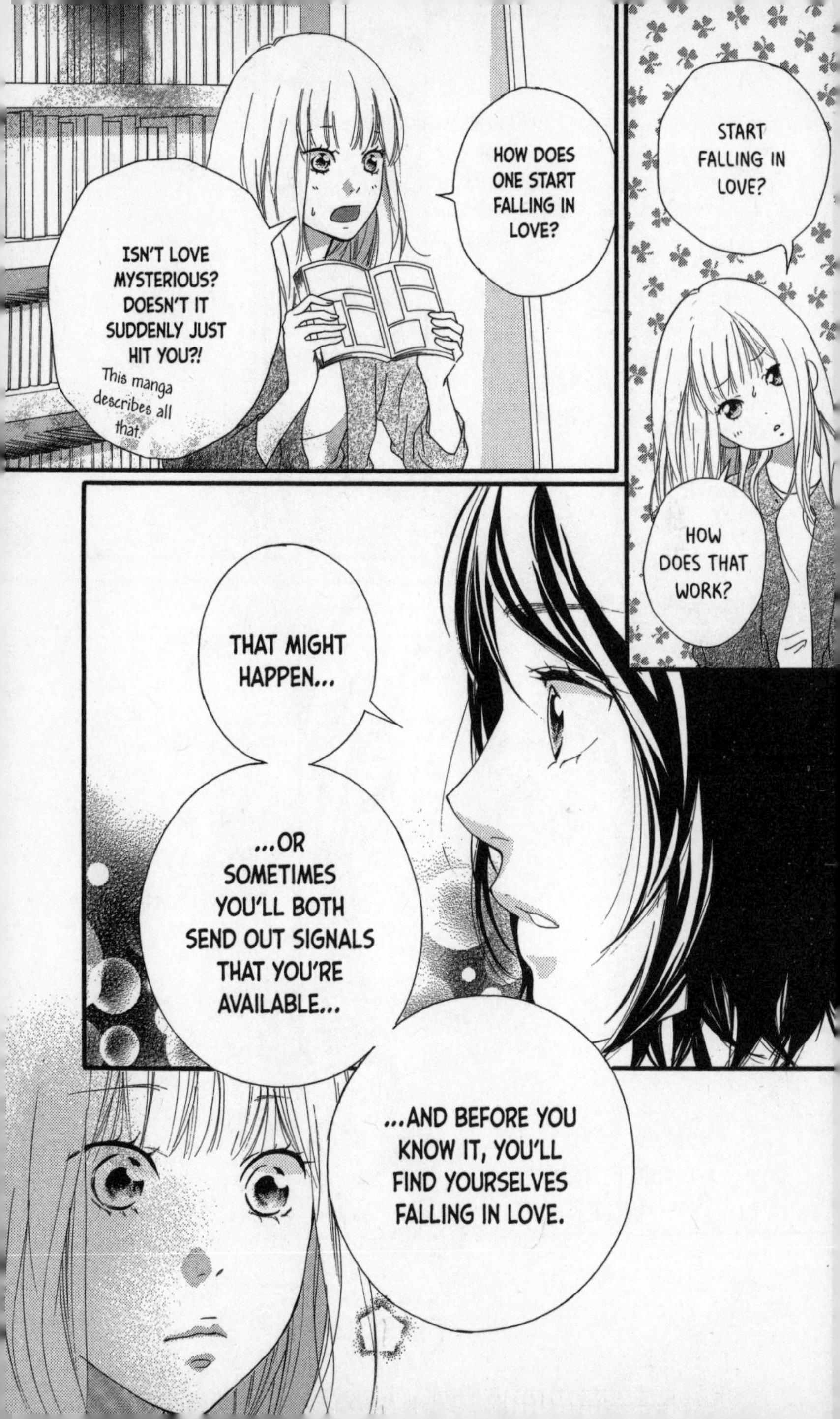
ISN'T LOVE MYSTERIOUS? DOESN'T IT SUDDENLY JUST HIT YOU?!
This manga describes all that.
HOW DOES ONE START FALLING IN LOVE?
START FALLING IN LOVE?
HOW DOES THAT WORK?
THAT MIGHT HAPPEN...
...OR SOMETIMES YOU'LL BOTH SEND OUT SIGNALS THAT YOU'RE AVAILABLE...
...AND BEFORE YOU KNOW IT, YOU'LL FIND YOURSELVES FALLING IN LOVE.

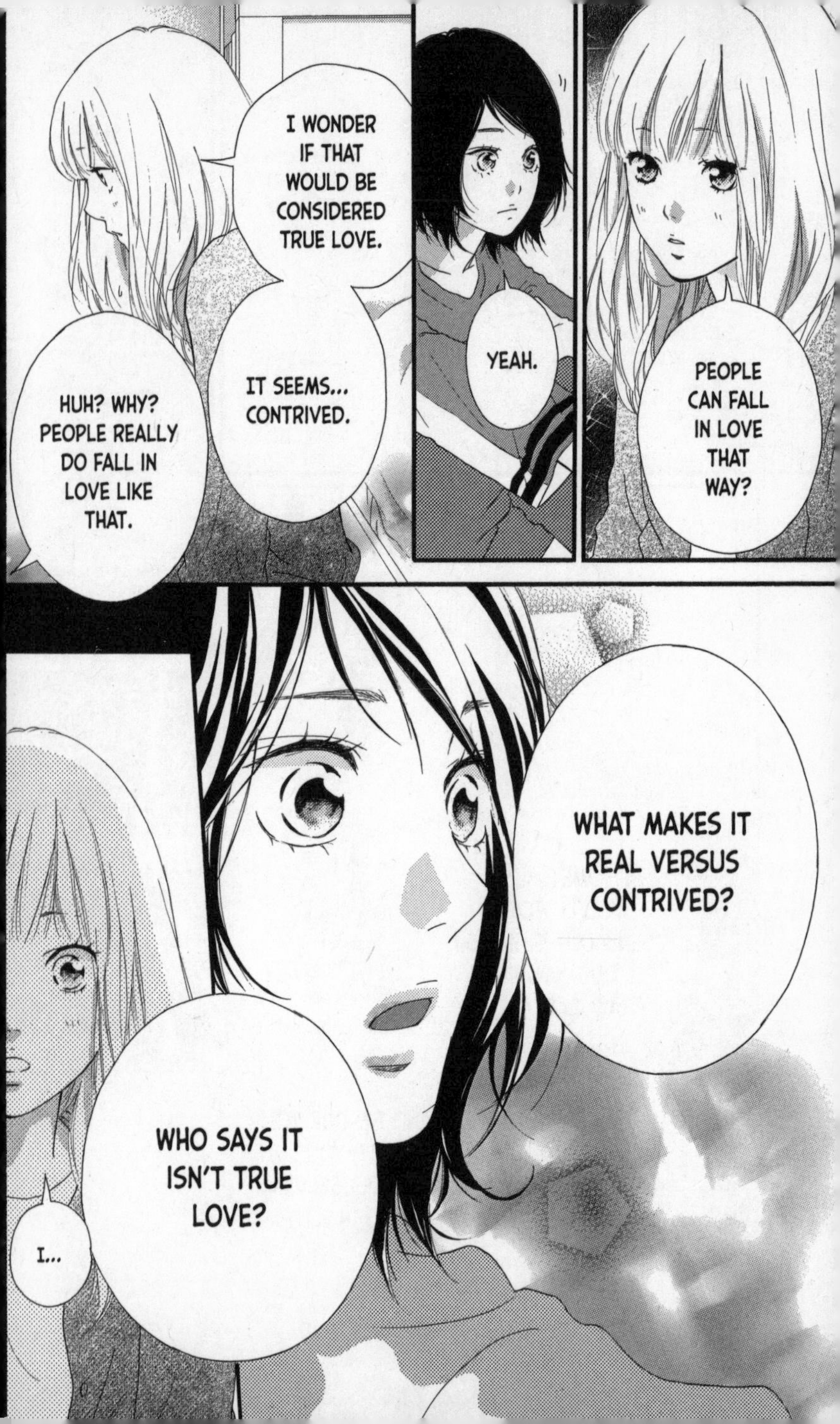
PEOPLE CAN FALL IN LOVE THAT WAY?
YEAH.
I WONDER IF THAT WOULD BE CONSIDERED TRUE LOVE.
IT SEEMS... CONTRIVED.
HUH? WHY? PEOPLE REALLY DO FALL IN LOVE LIKE THAT.
WHAT MAKES IT REAL VERSUS CONTRIVED?
WHO SAYS IT ISN'T TRUE LOVE?
I...

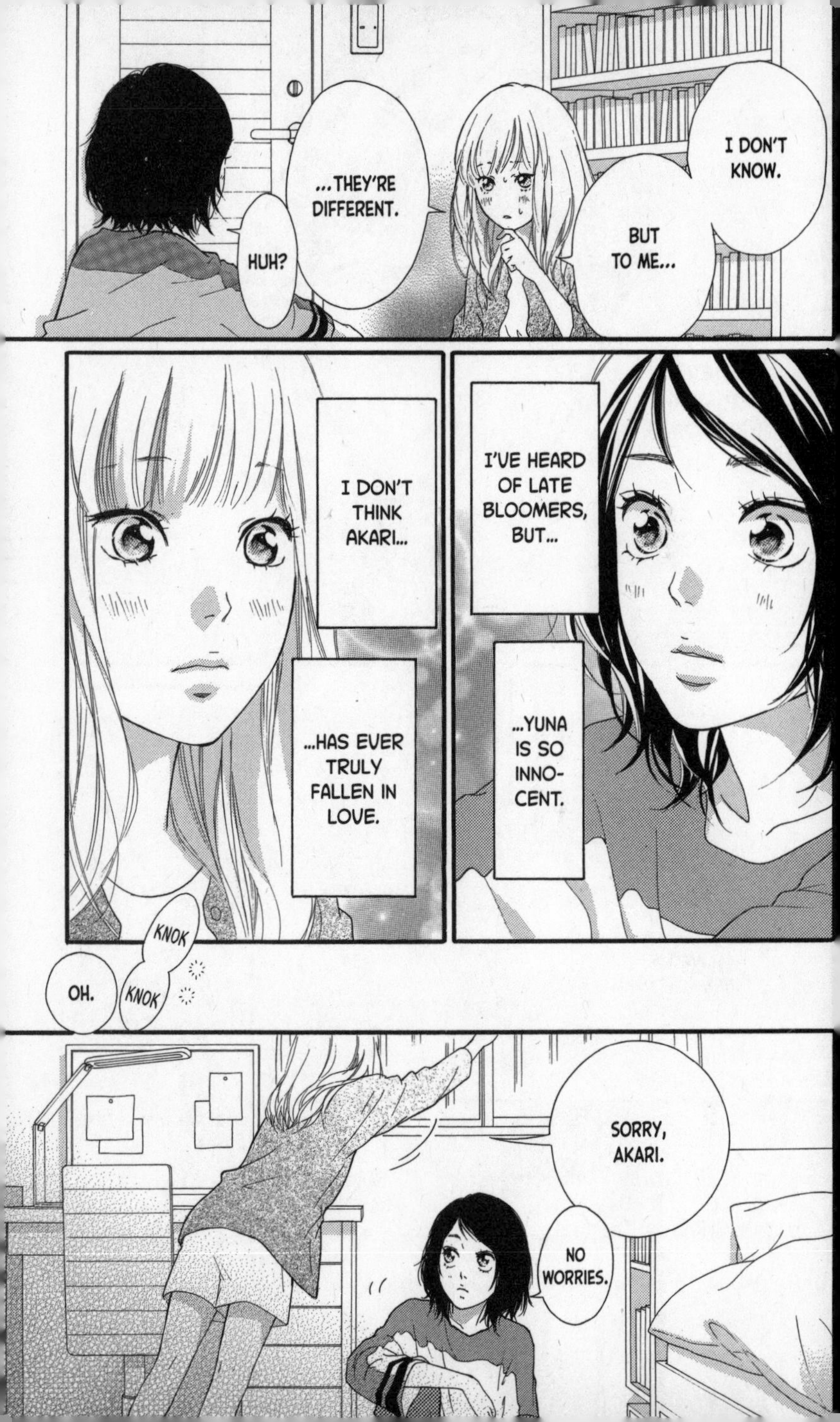
I DON'T KNOW.
BUT TO ME...
...THEY'RE DIFFERENT.
HUH?
I'VE HEARD OF LATE BLOOMERS, BUT...
...YUNA IS SO INNO-CENT.
I DON'T THINK AKARI...
...HAS EVER TRULY FALLEN IN LOVE.
KNOK
KNOK
OH.
SORRY, AKARI.
NO WORRIES.

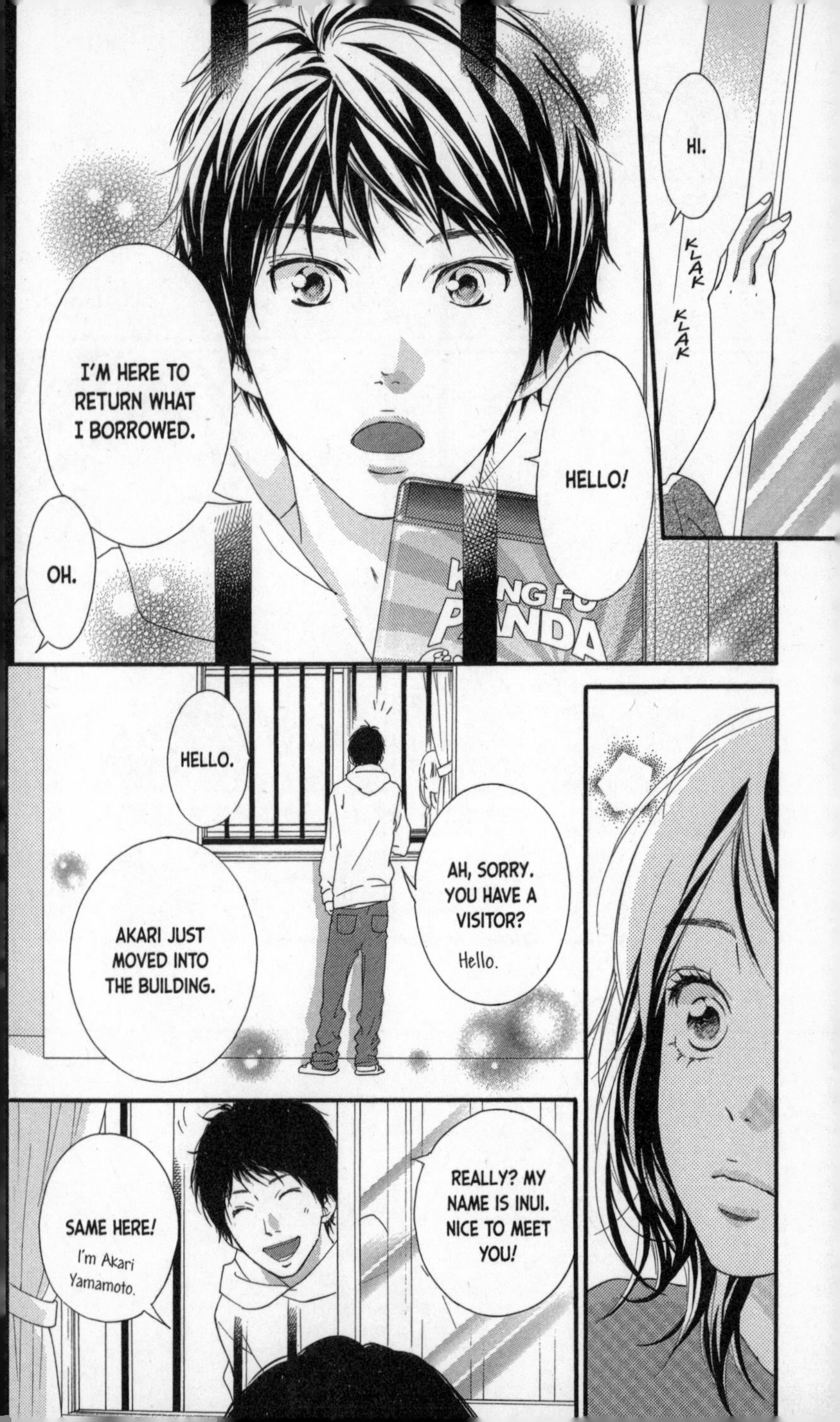
HI.
KLAK KLAK
HELLO!
I'M HERE TO RETURN WHAT I BORROWED.
OH.
AH, SORRY. YOU HAVE A VISITOR?
Hello.
HELLO.
AKARI JUST MOVED INTO THE BUILDING.
REALLY? MY NAME IS INUI. NICE TO MEET YOU!
SAME HERE!
I'm Akari Yamamoto.

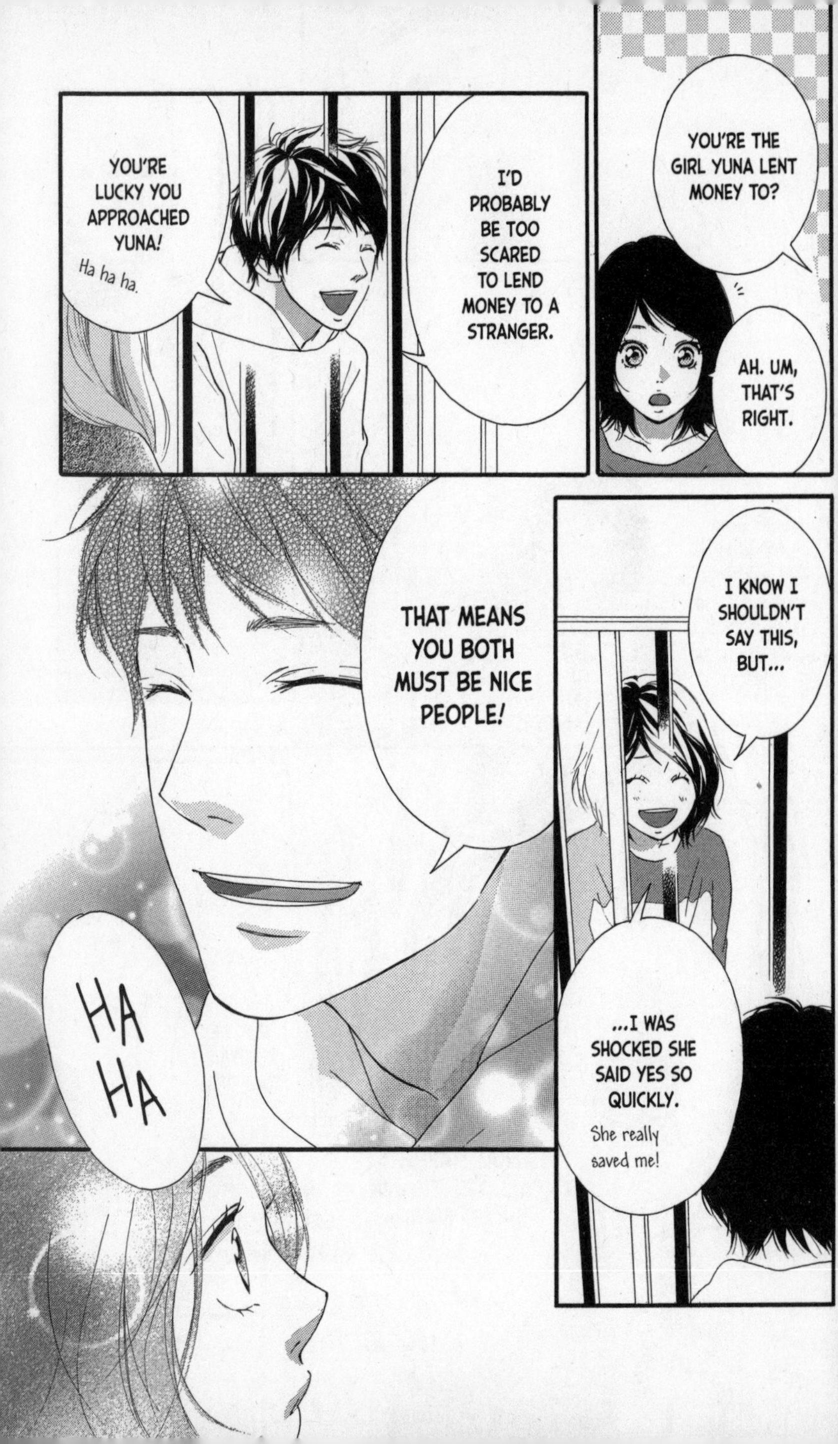
YOU'RE THE GIRL YUNA LENT MONEY TO?
AH. UM, THAT'S RIGHT.
I'D PROBABLY BE TOO SCARED TO LEND MONEY TO A STRANGER.
YOU'RE LUCKY YOU APPROACHED YUNA!
Ha ha ha.
I KNOW I SHOULDN'T SAY THIS, BUT...
...I WAS SHOCKED SHE SAID YES SO QUICKLY.
She really saved me!
THAT MEANS YOU BOTH MUST BE NICE PEOPLE!
HA HA

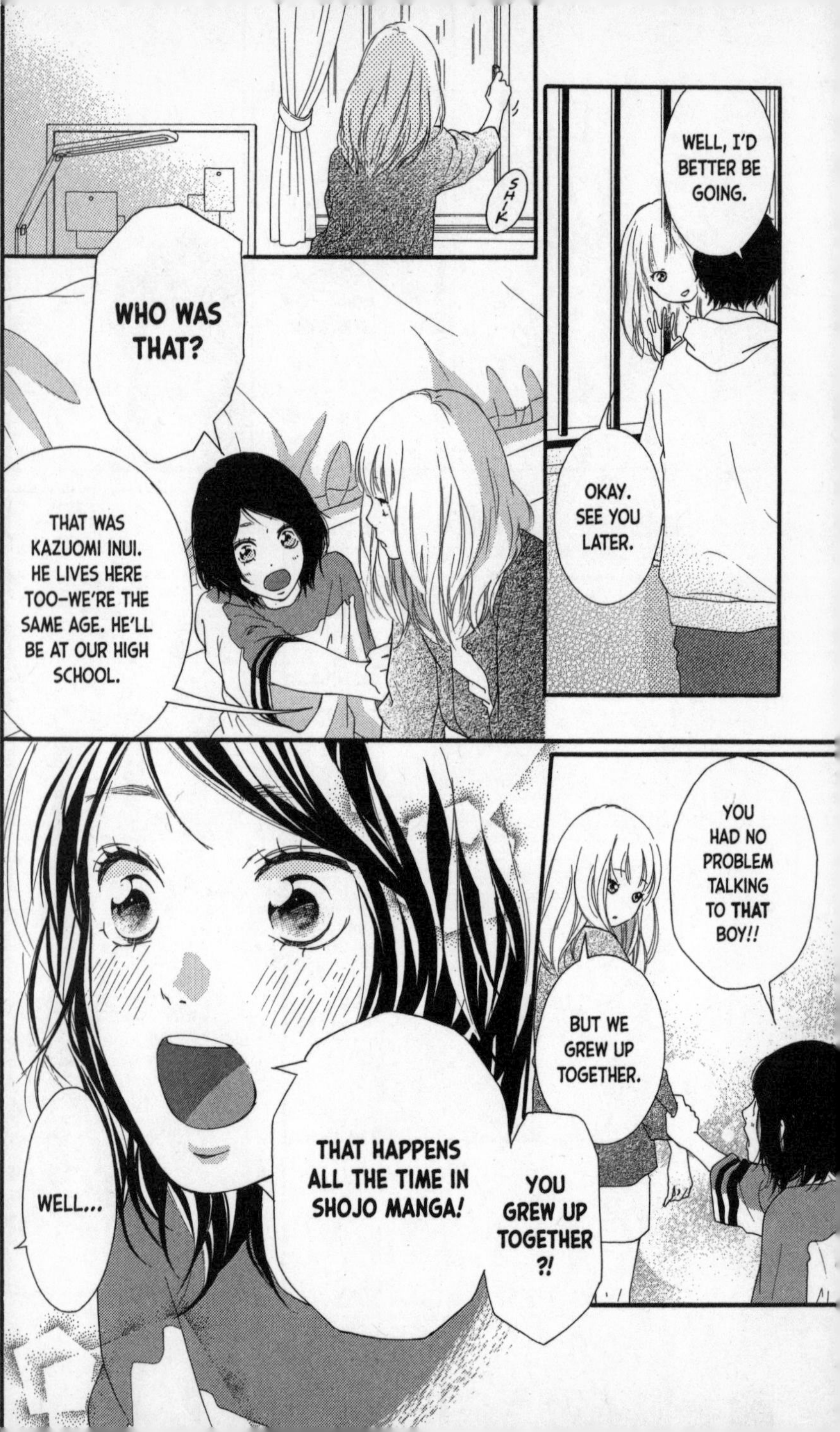
WELL, I'D BETTER BE GOING.
OKAY. SEE YOU LATER.
SHIK
WHO WAS THAT?
THAT WAS KAZUOMI INUI. HE LIVES HERE TOO—WE'RE THE SAME AGE. HE'LL BE AT OUR HIGH SCHOOL.
YOU HAD NO PROBLEM TALKING TO THAT BOY!!
BUT WE GREW UP TOGETHER.
YOU GREW UP TOGETHER ?!
THAT HAPPENS ALL THE TIME IN SHOJO MANGA!
WELL...

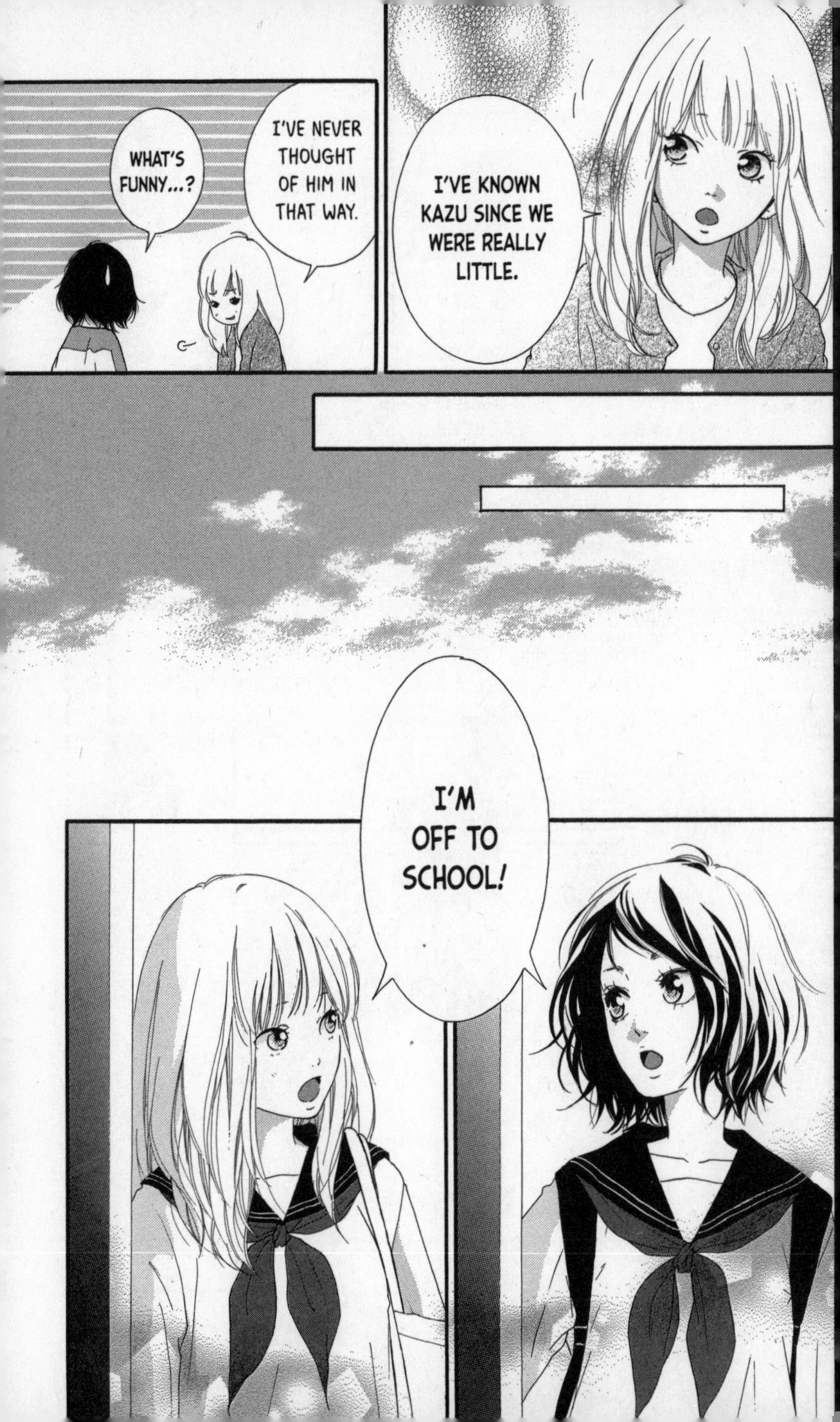
I'VE KNOWN KAZU SINCE WE WERE REALLY LITTLE.
I'VE NEVER THOUGHT OF HIM IN THAT WAY.
WHAT'S FUNNY...?
I'M OFF TO SCHOOL!

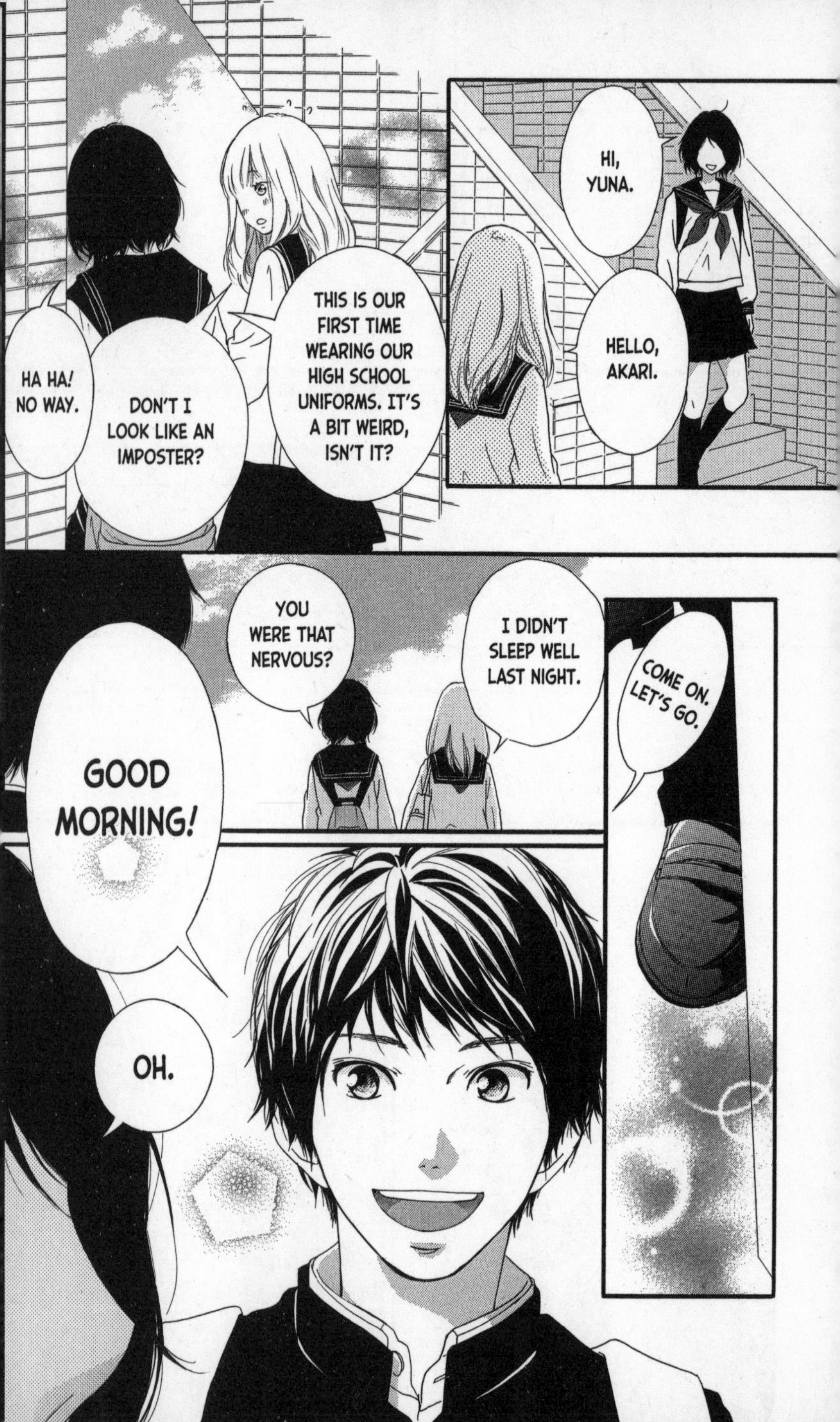
HI, YUNA.
HELLO, AKARI.
THIS IS OUR FIRST TIME WEARING OUR HIGH SCHOOL UNIFORMS. IT'S A BIT WEIRD, ISN'T IT?
DON'T I LOOK LIKE AN IMPOSTER?
HA HA! NO WAY.
COME ON. LET'S GO.
I DIDN'T SLEEP WELL LAST NIGHT.
YOU WERE THAT NERVOUS?
GOOD MORNING!
OH.

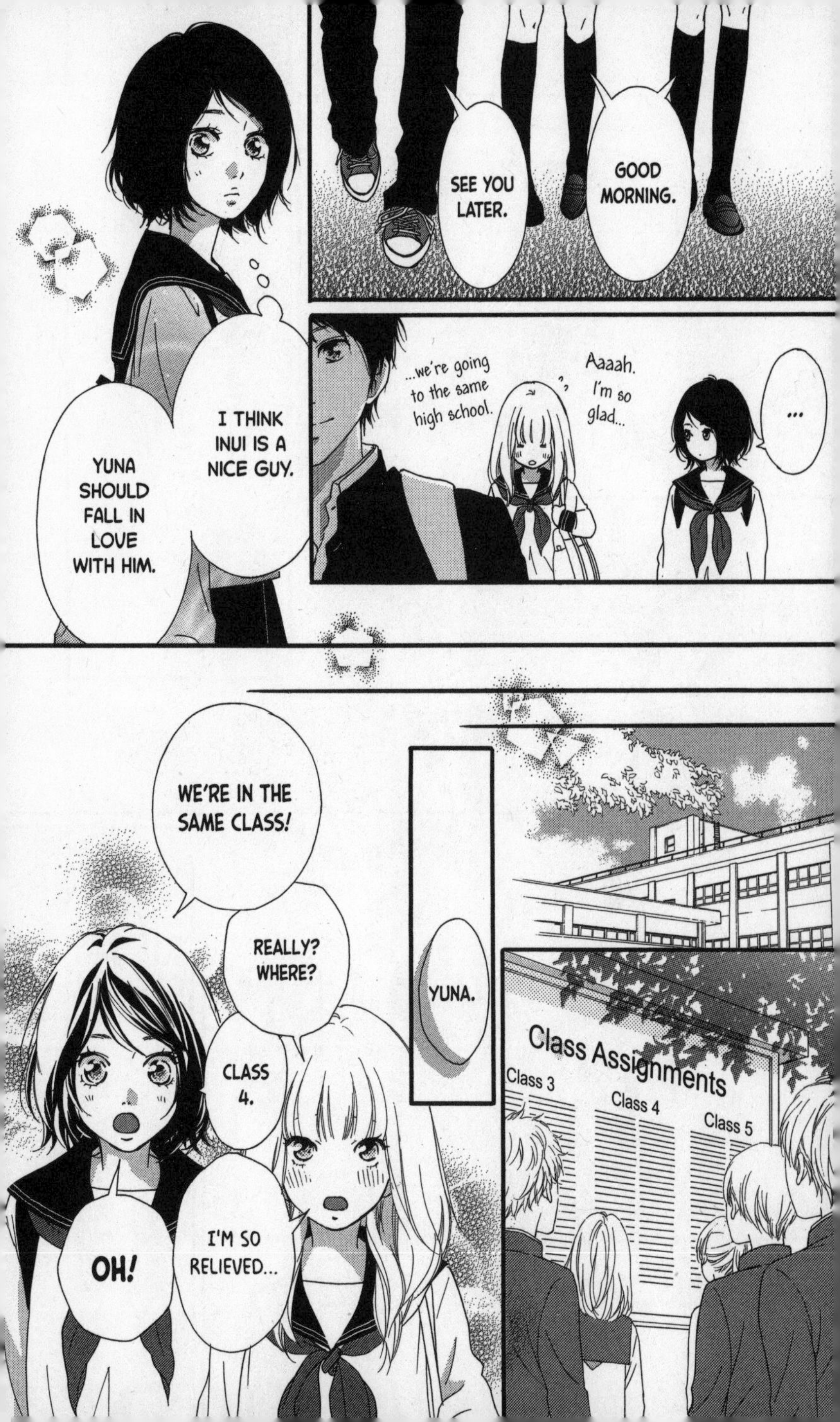
GOOD MORNING.
SEE YOU LATER.
...
Aaaah. I'm so glad...
...we're going to the same high school.
I THINK INUI IS A NICE GUY.
YUNA SHOULD FALL IN LOVE WITH HIM.
Class Assignments
Class 3
Class 4
Class 5
YUNA.
WE'RE IN THE SAME CLASS!
REALLY? WHERE?
CLASS 4.
I'M SO RELIEVED...
OH!

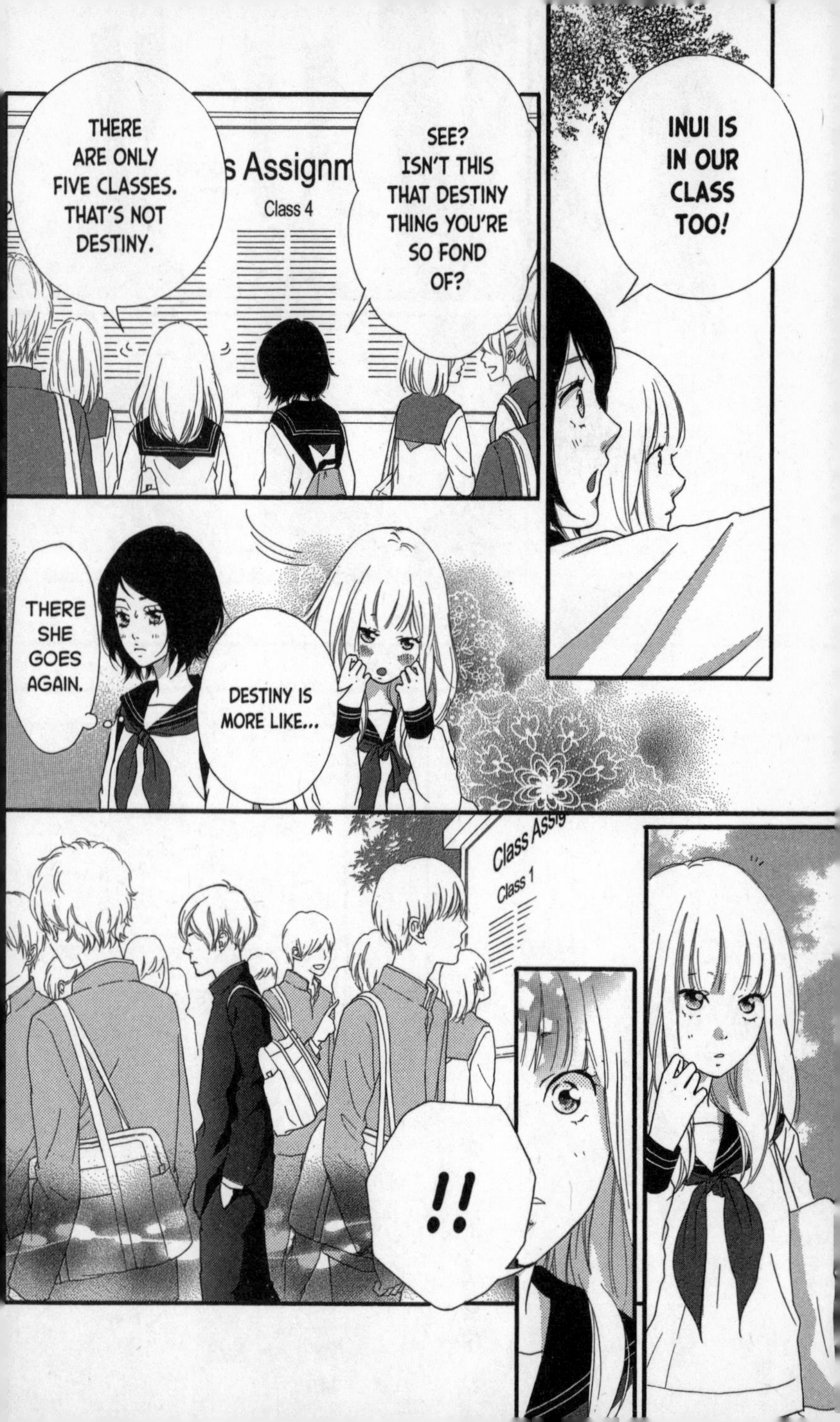
INUI IS IN OUR CLASS TOO!
SEE? ISN'T THIS THAT DESTINY THING YOU'RE SO FOND OF?
THERE ARE ONLY FIVE CLASSES. THAT'S NOT DESTINY.
Class 4
DESTINY IS MORE LIKE...
THERE SHE GOES AGAIN.
!!
Class 1

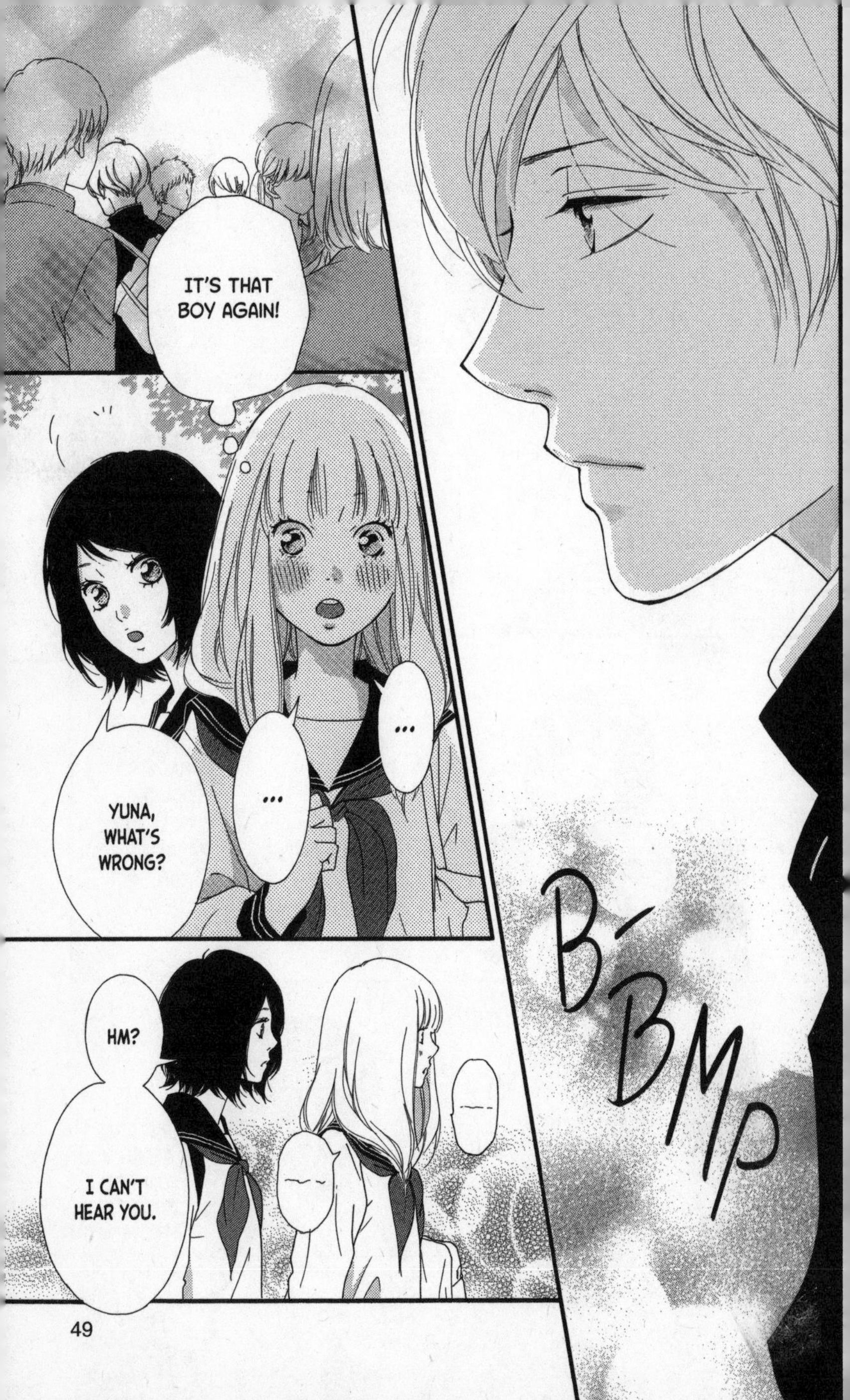
B-BMP
IT'S THAT BOY AGAIN!
...
...
YUNA, WHAT'S WRONG?
——
——
HM?
I CAN'T HEAR YOU.

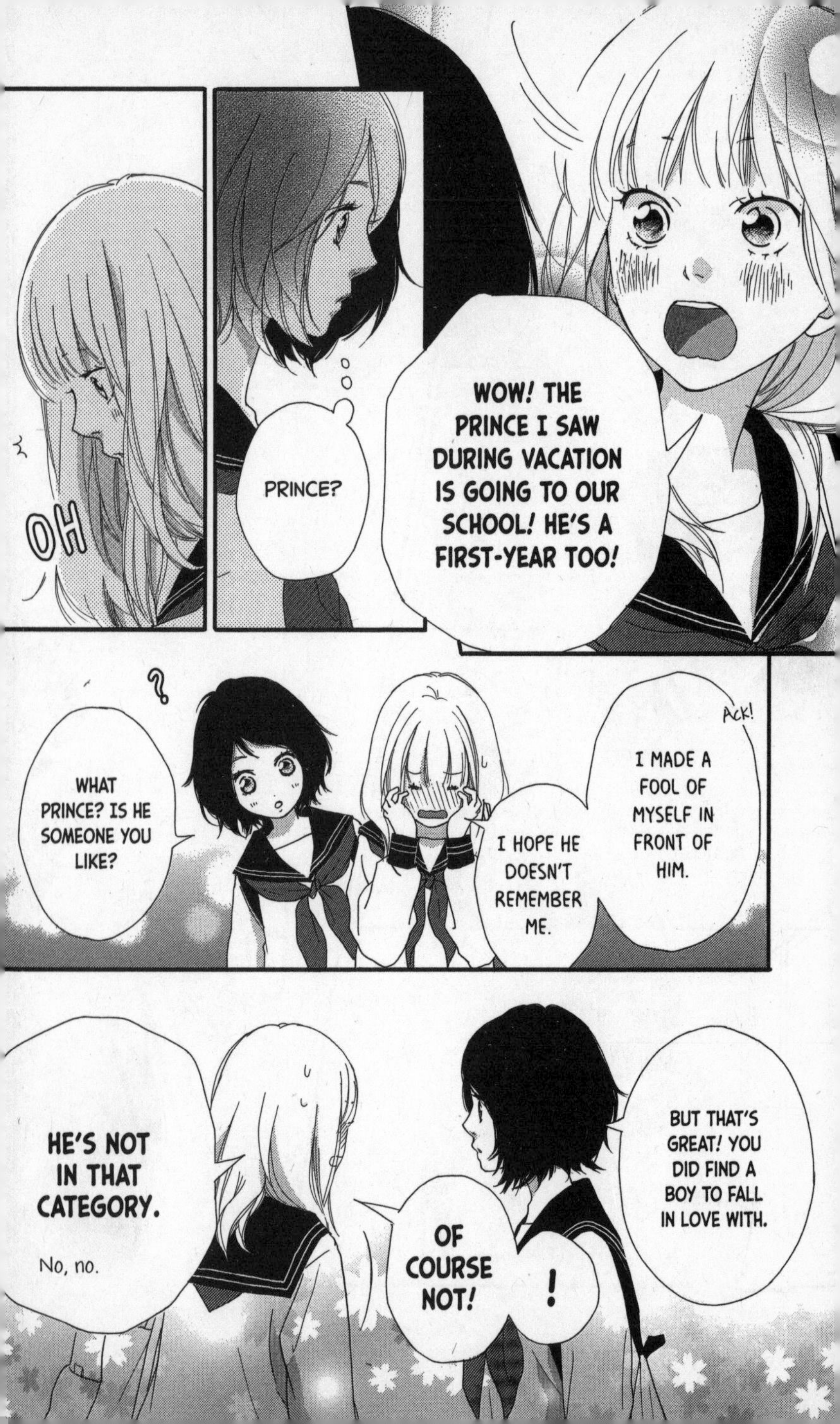
WOW! THE PRINCE I SAW DURING VACATION IS GOING TO OUR SCHOOL! HE'S A FIRST-YEAR TOO!
PRINCE?
OH
ACK!
I MADE A FOOL OF MYSELF IN FRONT OF HIM.
I HOPE HE DOESN'T REMEMBER ME.
?
WHAT PRINCE? IS HE SOMEONE YOU LIKE?
BUT THAT'S GREAT! YOU DID FIND A BOY TO FALL IN LOVE WITH.
!
OF COURSE NOT!
HE'S NOT IN THAT CATEGORY.
No, no.

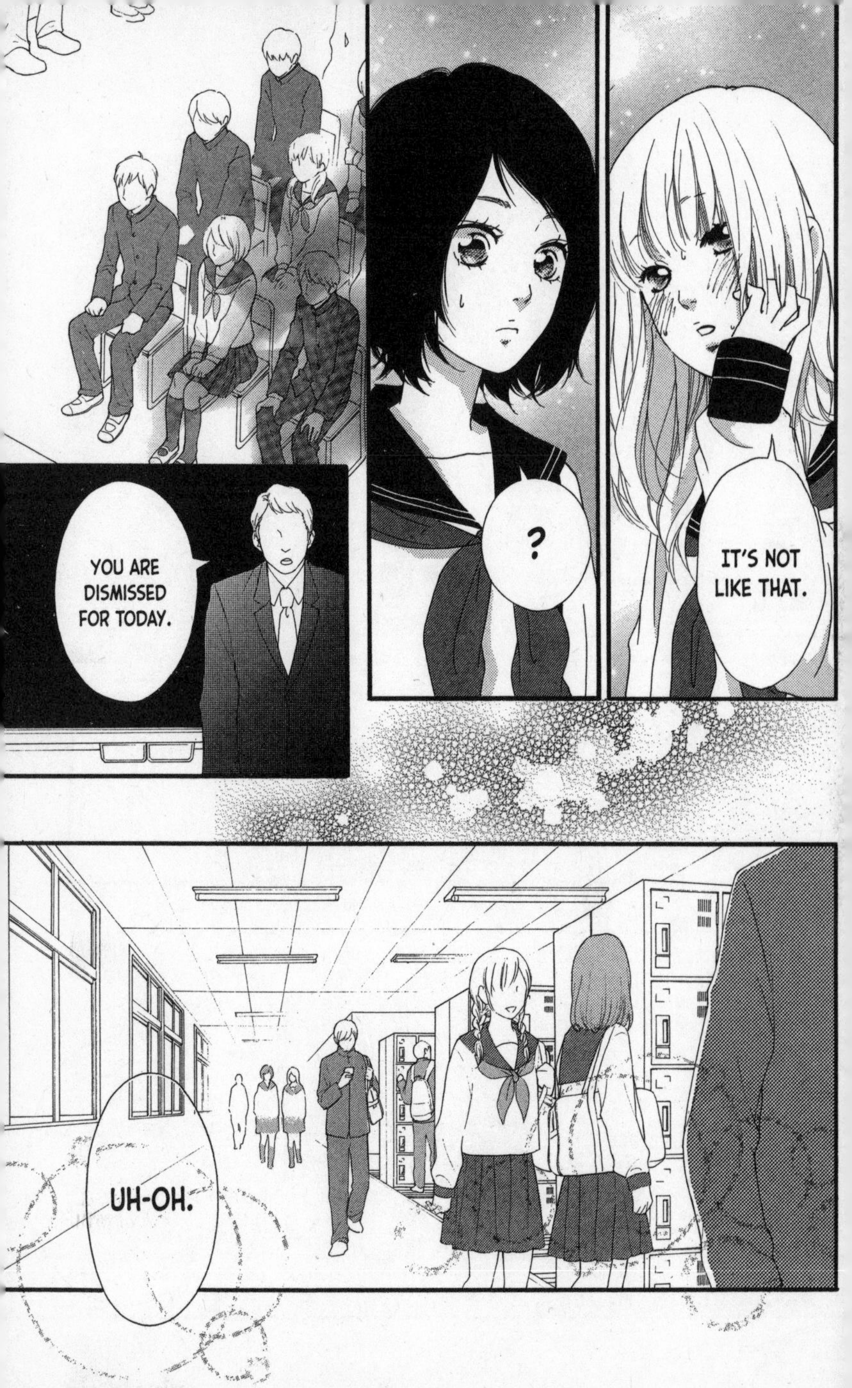
IT'S NOT LIKE THAT.
?
YOU ARE DISMISSED FOR TODAY.
UH-OH.

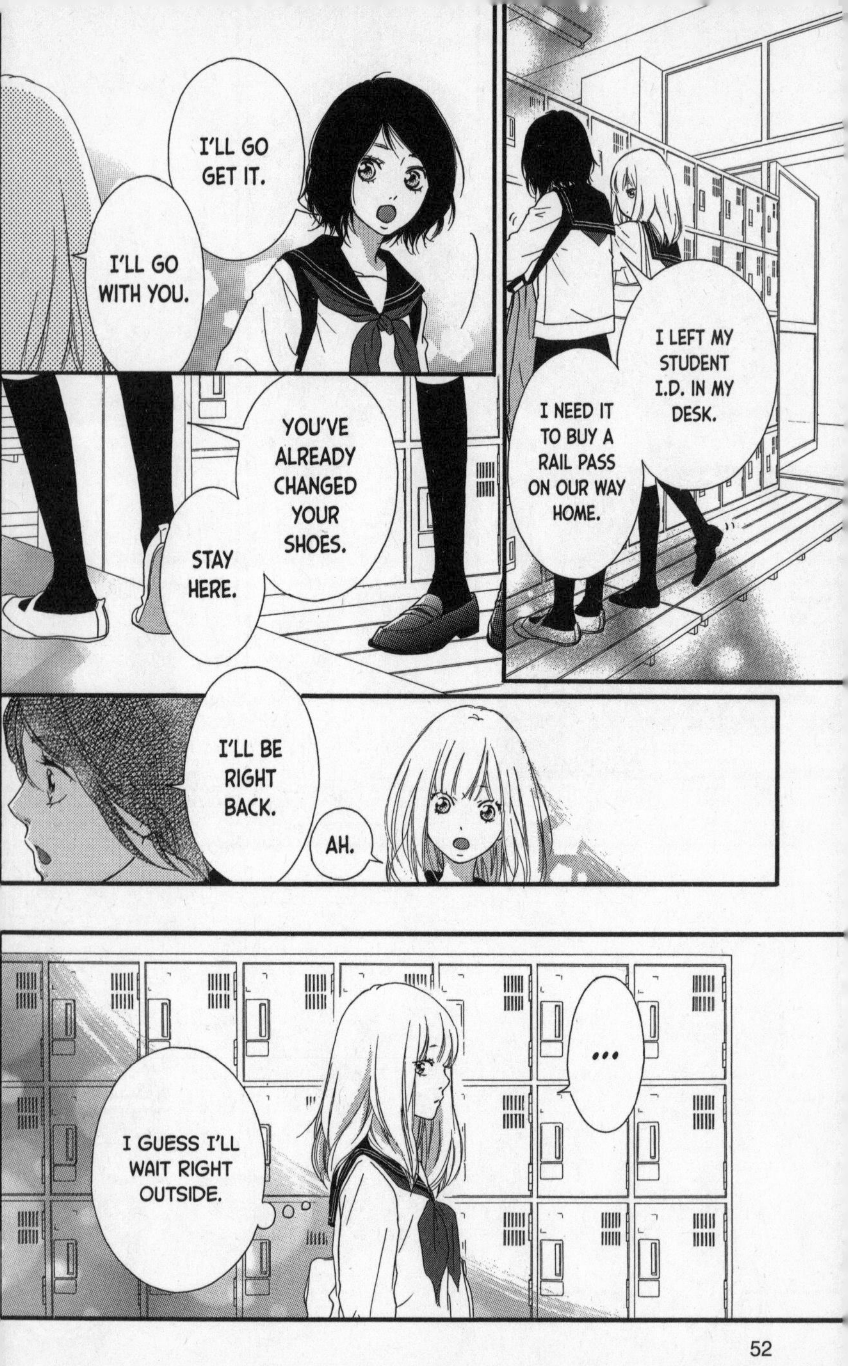
I LEFT MY STUDENT I.D. IN MY DESK.
I NEED IT TO BUY A RAIL PASS ON OUR WAY HOME.
I'LL GO GET IT.
I'LL GO WITH YOU.
YOU'VE ALREADY CHANGED YOUR SHOES.
STAY HERE.
I'LL BE RIGHT BACK.
AH.
...
I GUESS I'LL WAIT RIGHT OUTSIDE.

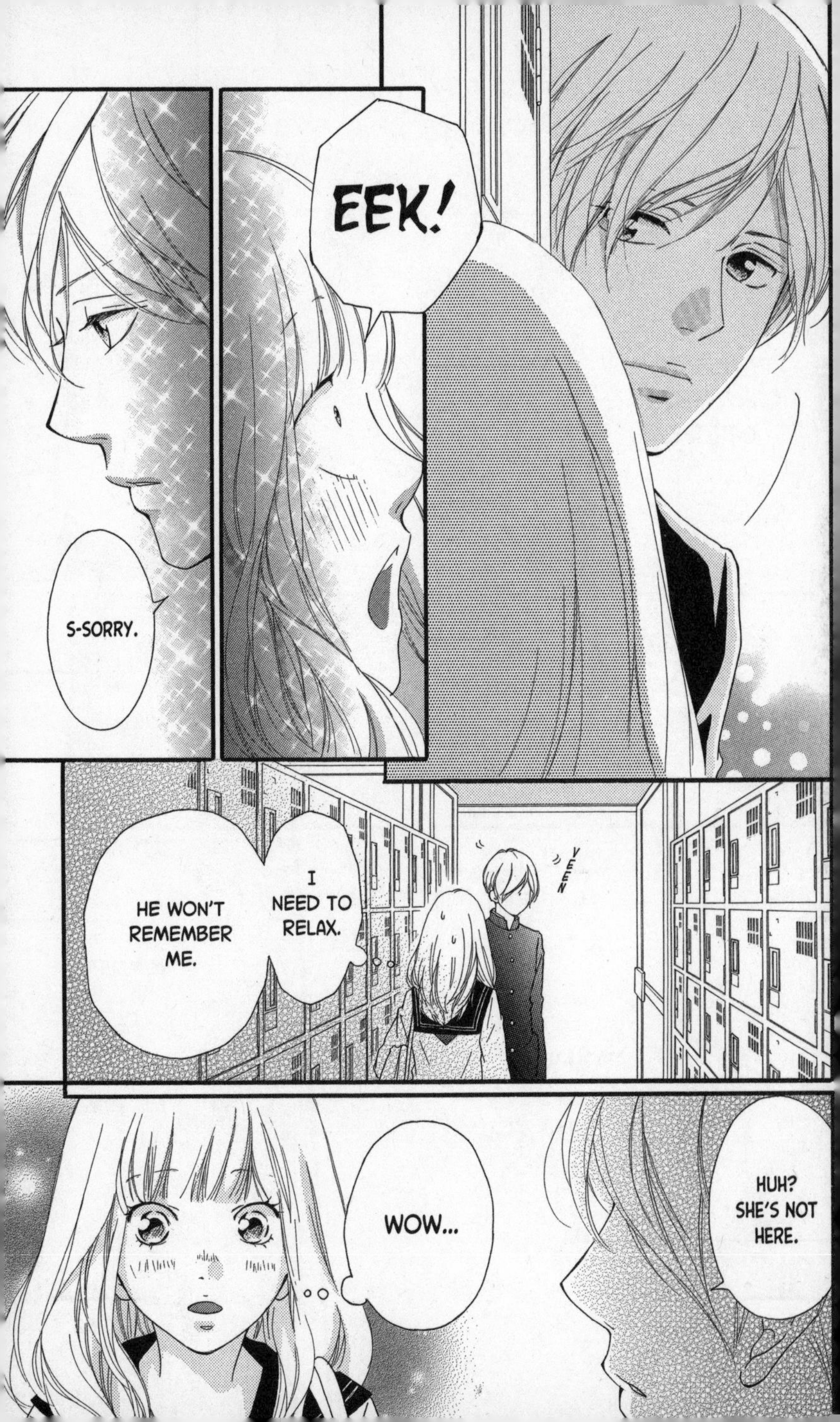
EEK!
S-SORRY.
VEEN
I NEED TO RELAX.
HE WON'T REMEMBER ME.
HUH? SHE'S NOT HERE.
WOW...

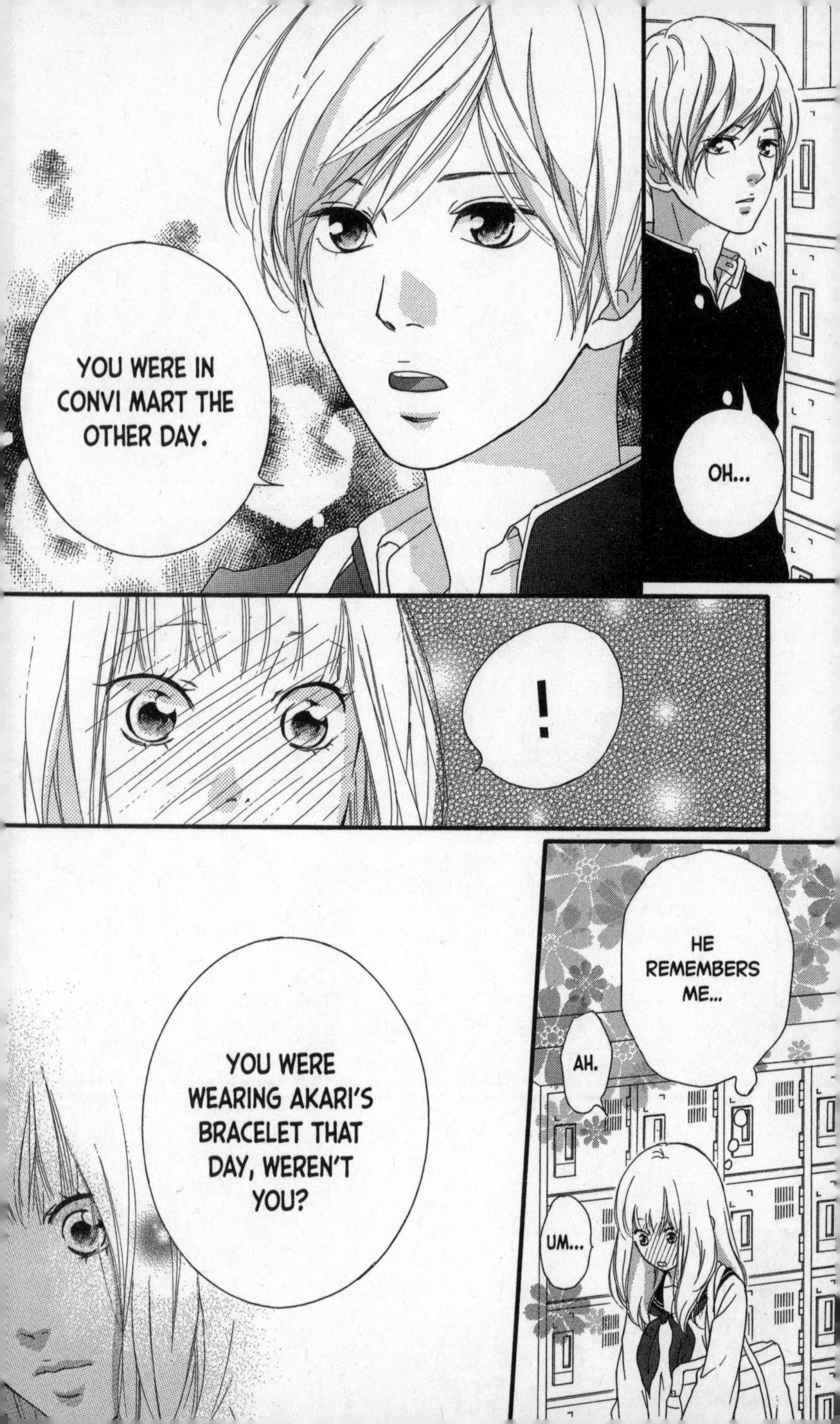
OH...
YOU WERE IN CONVI MART THE OTHER DAY.
!
HE REMEMBERS ME...
AH.
UM...
YOU WERE WEARING AKARI'S BRACELET THAT DAY, WEREN'T YOU?

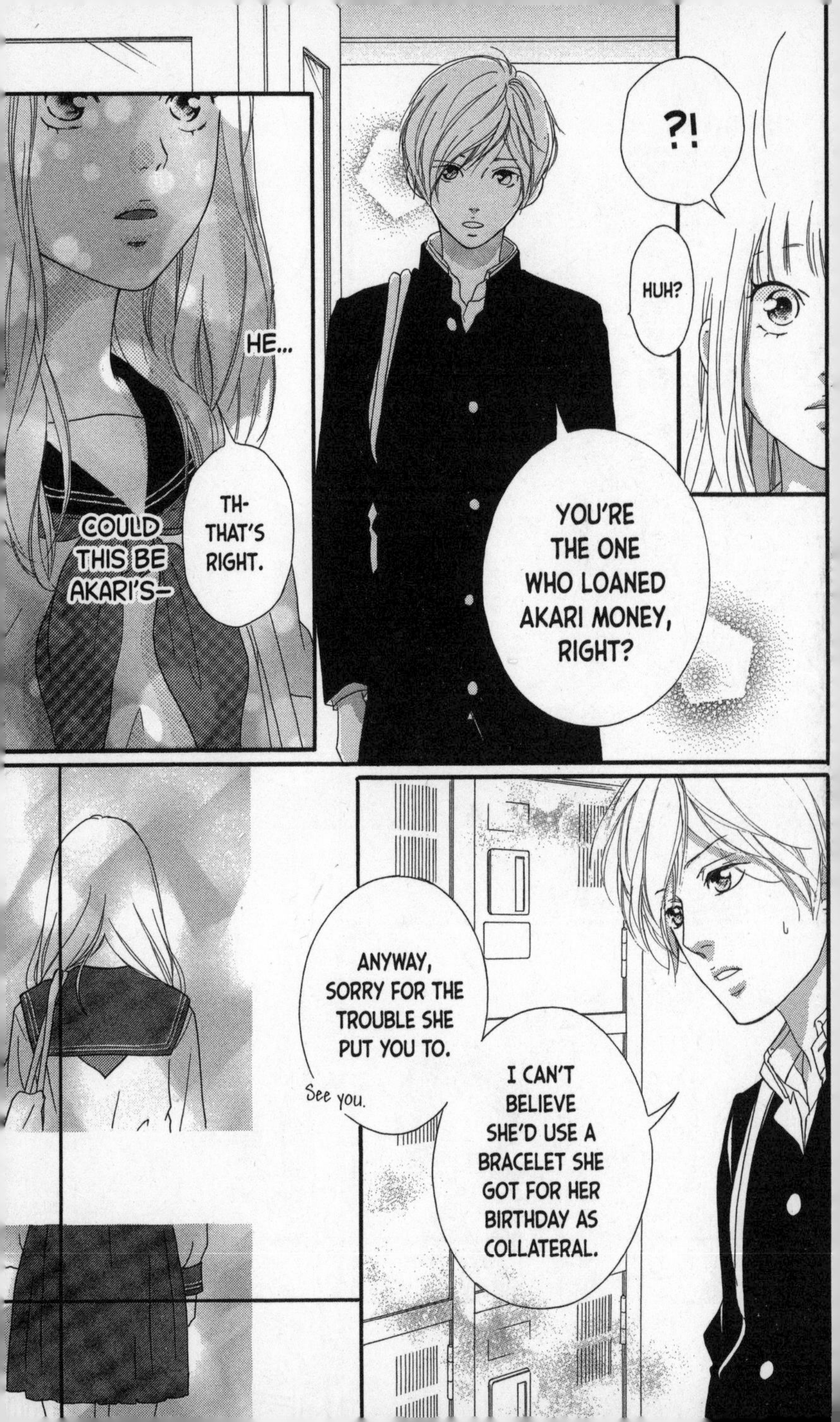
?!
HUH?
YOU'RE THE ONE WHO LOANED AKARI MONEY, RIGHT?
HE...
TH- THAT'S RIGHT.
COULD THIS BE AKARI'S—
I CAN'T BELIEVE SHE'D USE A BRACELET SHE GOT FOR HER BIRTHDAY AS COLLATERAL.
ANYWAY, SORRY FOR THE TROUBLE SHE PUT YOU TO.
See you.

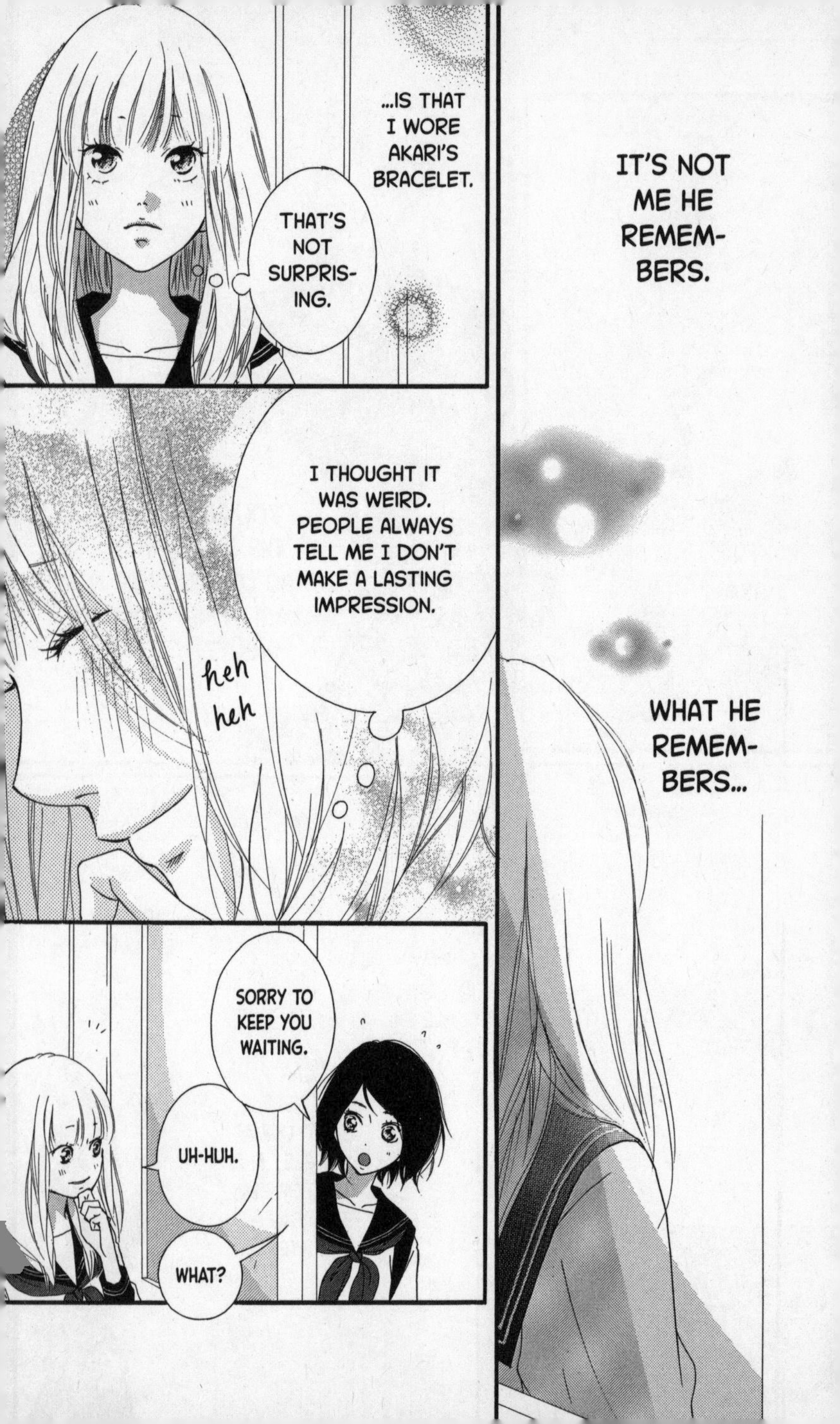
IT'S NOT ME HE REMEMBERS.
WHAT HE REMEMBERS...
...IS THAT I WORE AKARI'S BRACELET.
THAT'S NOT SURPRISING.
I THOUGHT IT WAS WEIRD. PEOPLE ALWAYS TELL ME I DON'T MAKE A LASTING IMPRESSION.
heh heh
SORRY TO KEEP YOU WAITING.
UH-HUH.
WHAT?

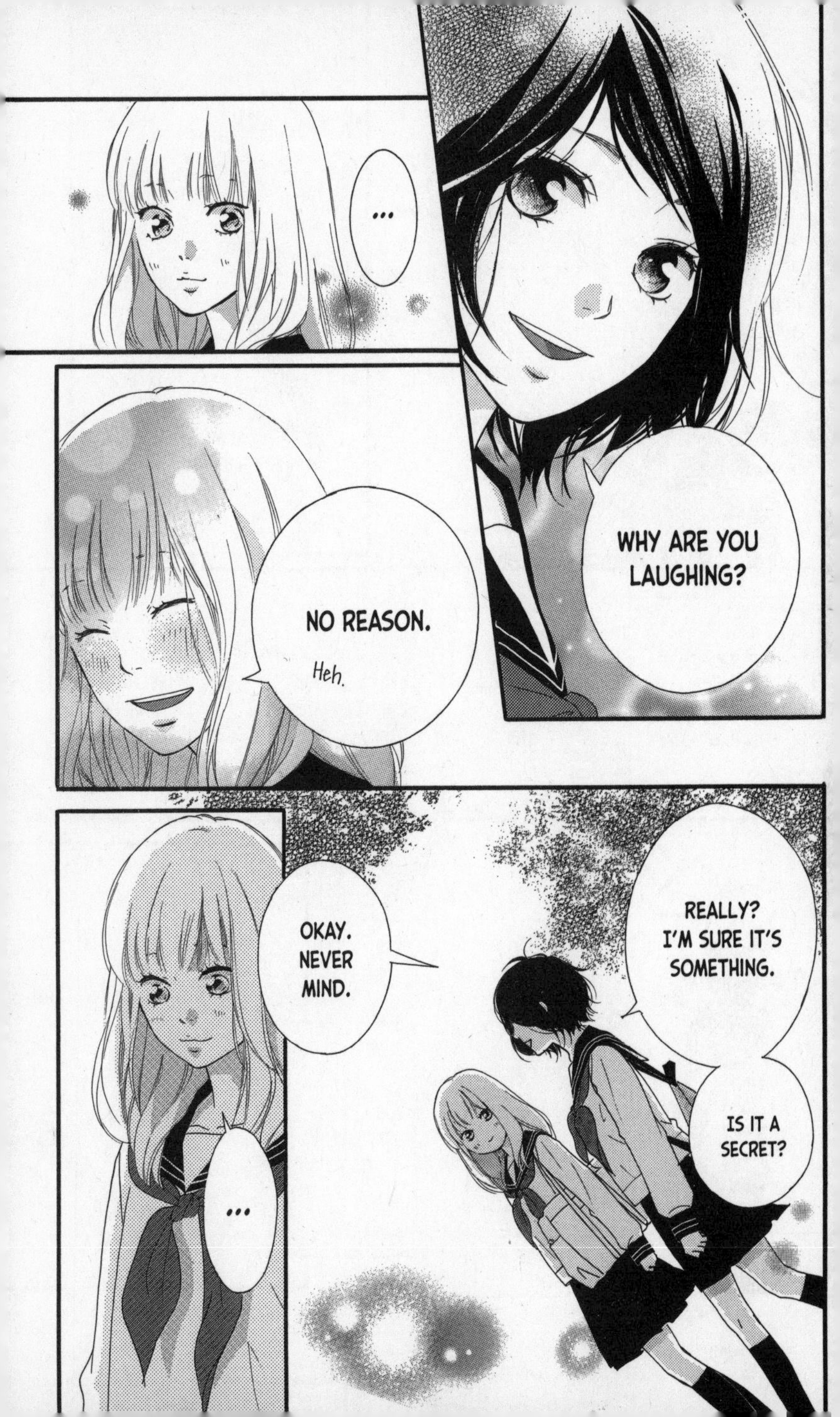
WHY ARE YOU LAUGHING?
...
NO REASON.
Heh.
REALLY? I'M SURE IT'S SOMETHING.
IS IT A SECRET?
OKAY. NEVER MIND.
...

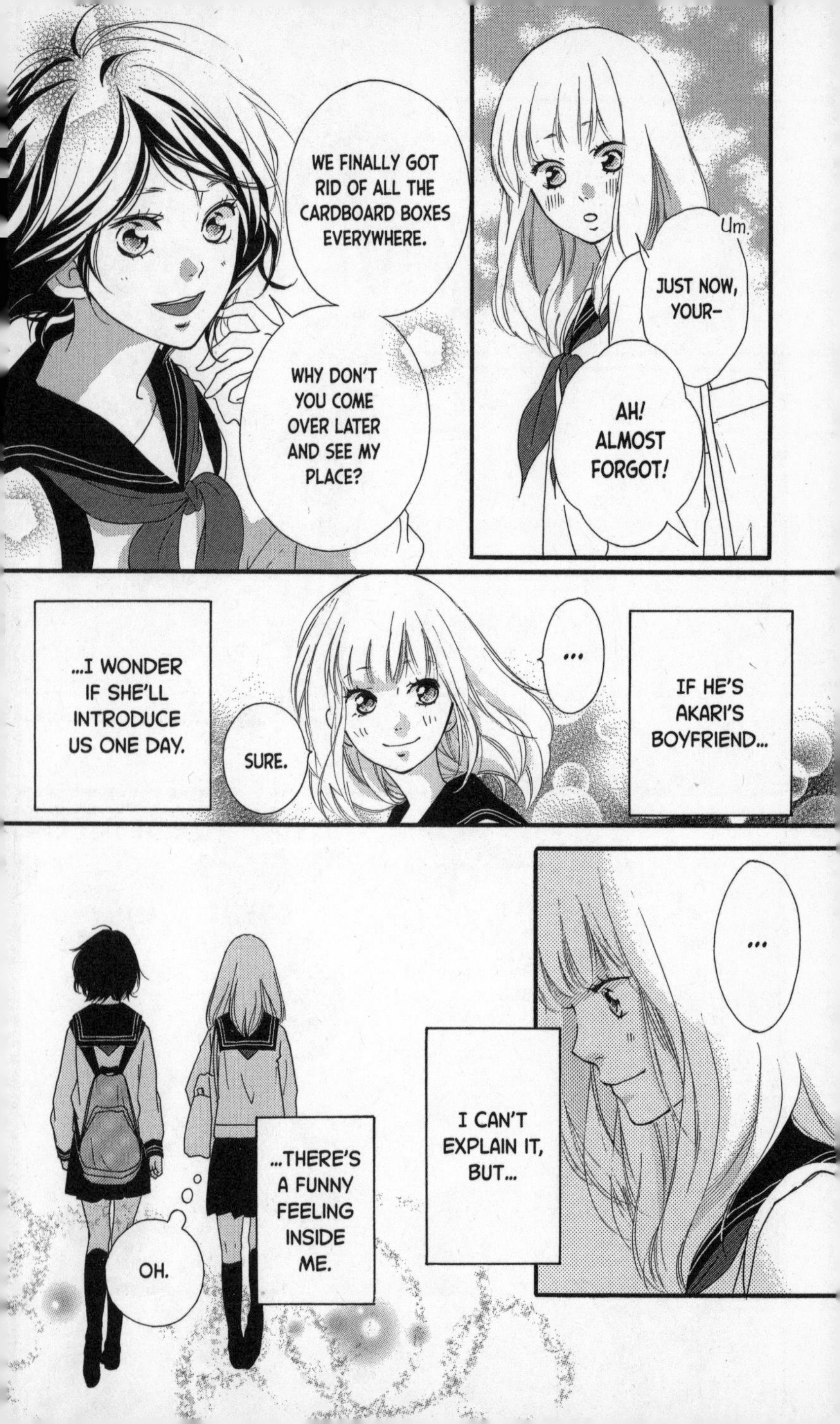
Um.
JUST NOW, YOUR–
AH! ALMOST FORGOT!
WE FINALLY GOT RID OF ALL THE CARDBOARD BOXES EVERYWHERE.
WHY DON'T YOU COME OVER LATER AND SEE MY PLACE?
IF HE'S AKARI'S BOYFRIEND...
...
SURE.
...I WONDER IF SHE'LL INTRODUCE US ONE DAY.
...
I CAN'T EXPLAIN IT, BUT...
...THERE'S A FUNNY FEELING INSIDE ME.
OH.

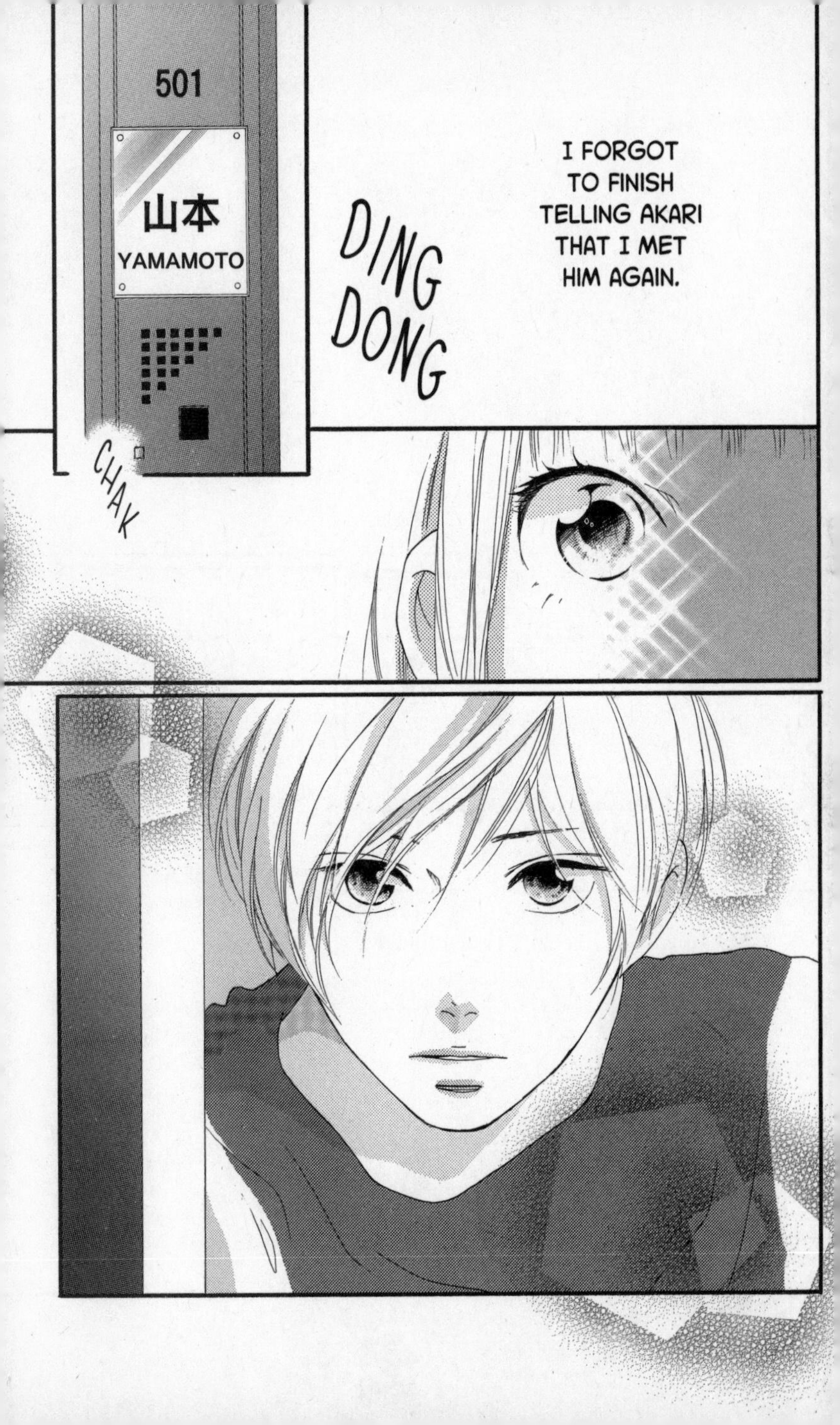
I FORGOT TO FINISH TELLING AKARI THAT I MET HIM AGAIN.
DING DONG
501
山本
YAMAMOTO
CHAK

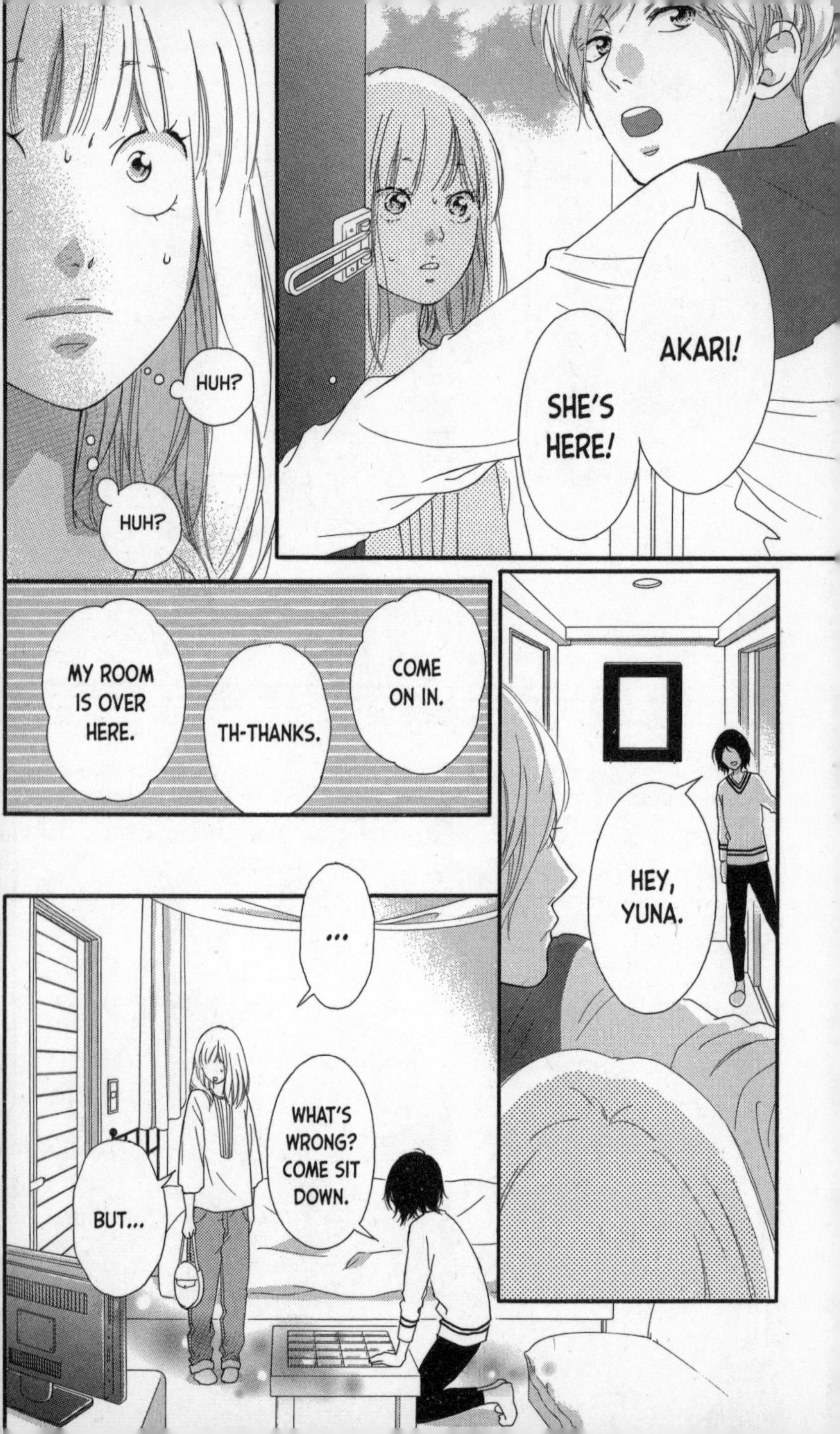
AKARI!
SHE'S HERE!
HUH?
HUH?
HEY, YUNA.
COME ON IN.
TH-THANKS.
MY ROOM IS OVER HERE.
...
WHAT'S WRONG? COME SIT DOWN.
BUT...

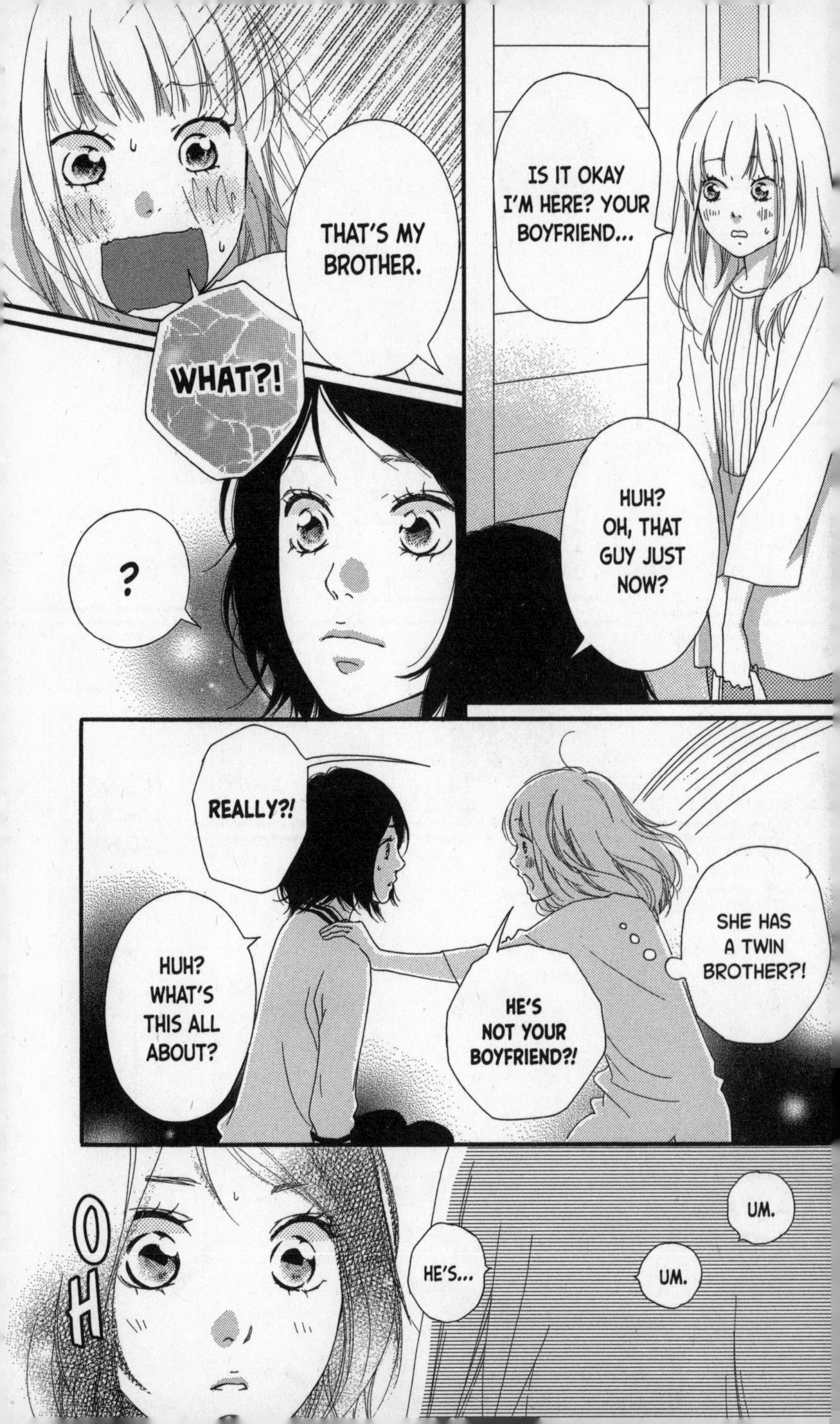
IS IT OKAY I'M HERE? YOUR BOYFRIEND...
HUH? OH, THAT GUY JUST NOW?
THAT'S MY BROTHER.
WHAT?!
?
SHE HAS A TWIN BROTHER?!
HE'S NOT YOUR BOYFRIEND?!
REALLY?!
HUH? WHAT'S THIS ALL ABOUT?
UM.
UM.
HE'S...
OH

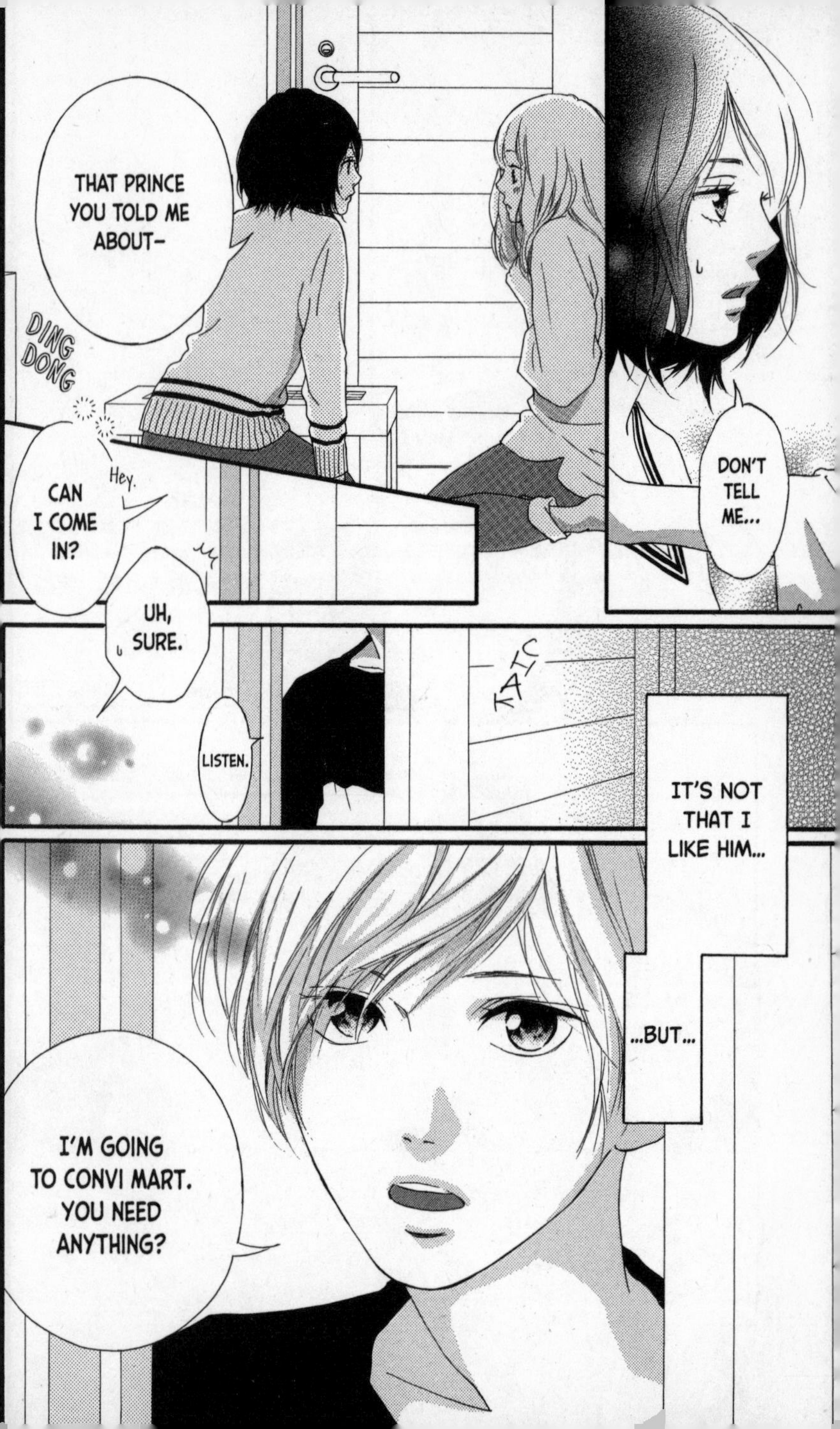
DON'T TELL ME...
THAT PRINCE YOU TOLD ME ABOUT–
DING DONG
Hey.
CAN I COME IN?
UH, SURE.
IT'S NOT THAT I LIKE HIM...
LISTEN.
...BUT...
I'M GOING TO CONVI MART. YOU NEED ANYTHING?

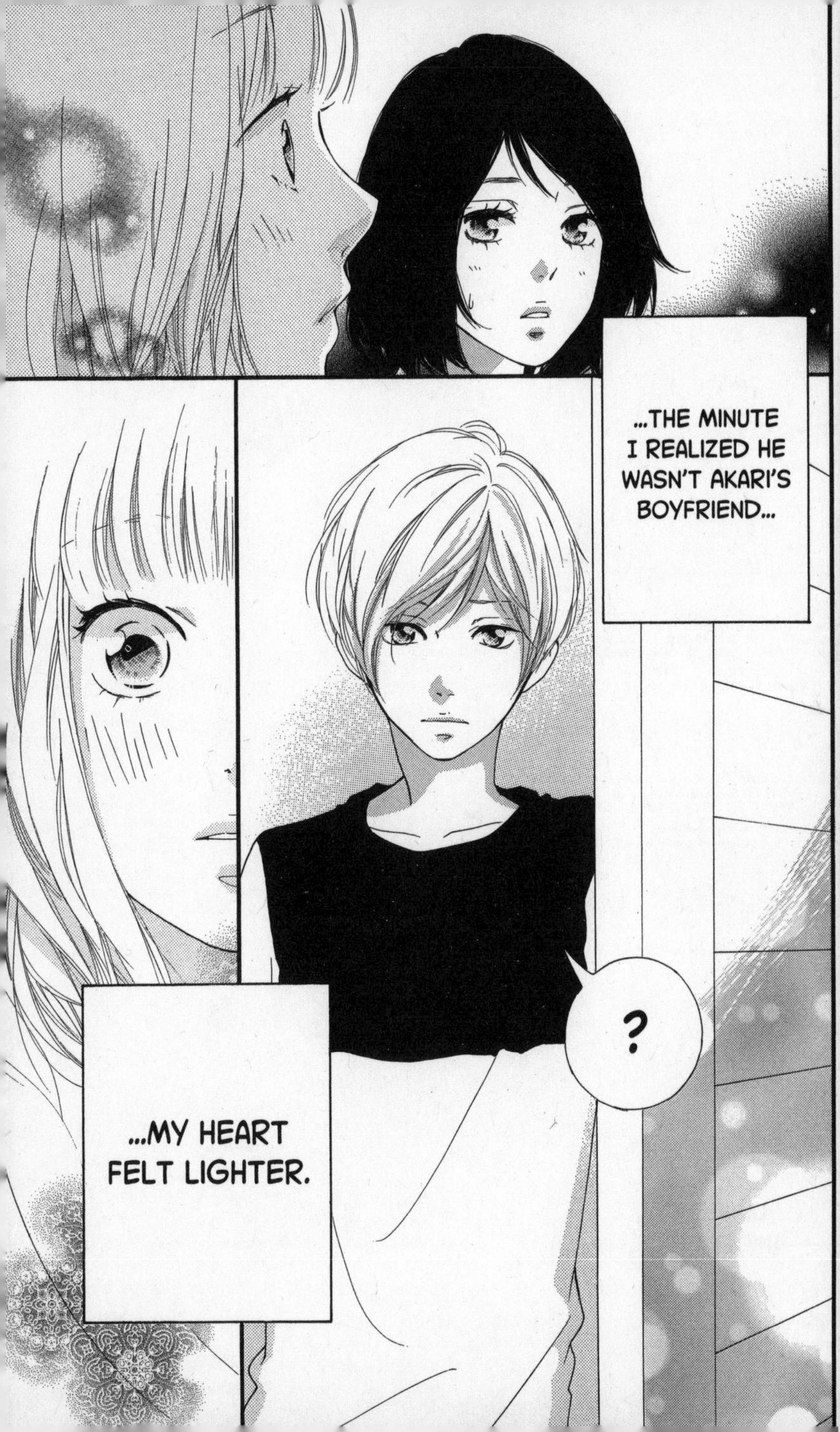
...THE MINUTE I REALIZED HE WASN'T AKARI'S BOYFRIEND...
?
...MY HEART FELT LIGHTER.

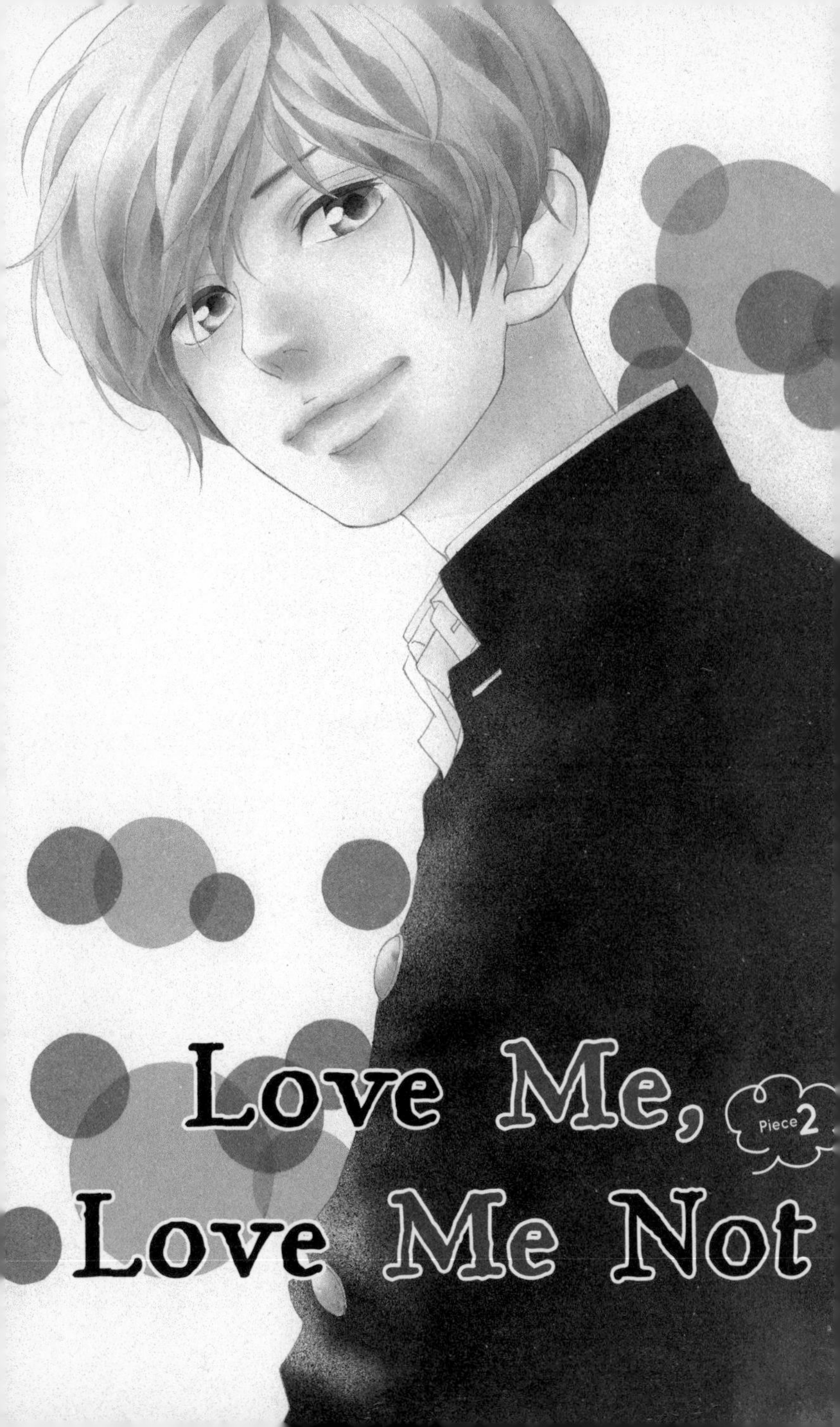
Love Me, Love Me Not
Piece 2

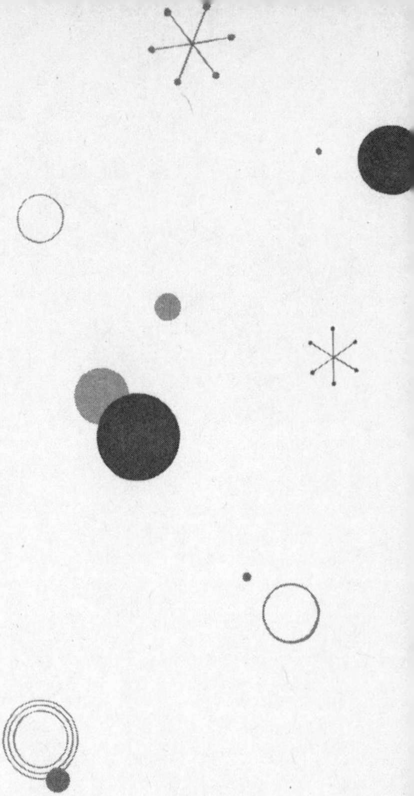

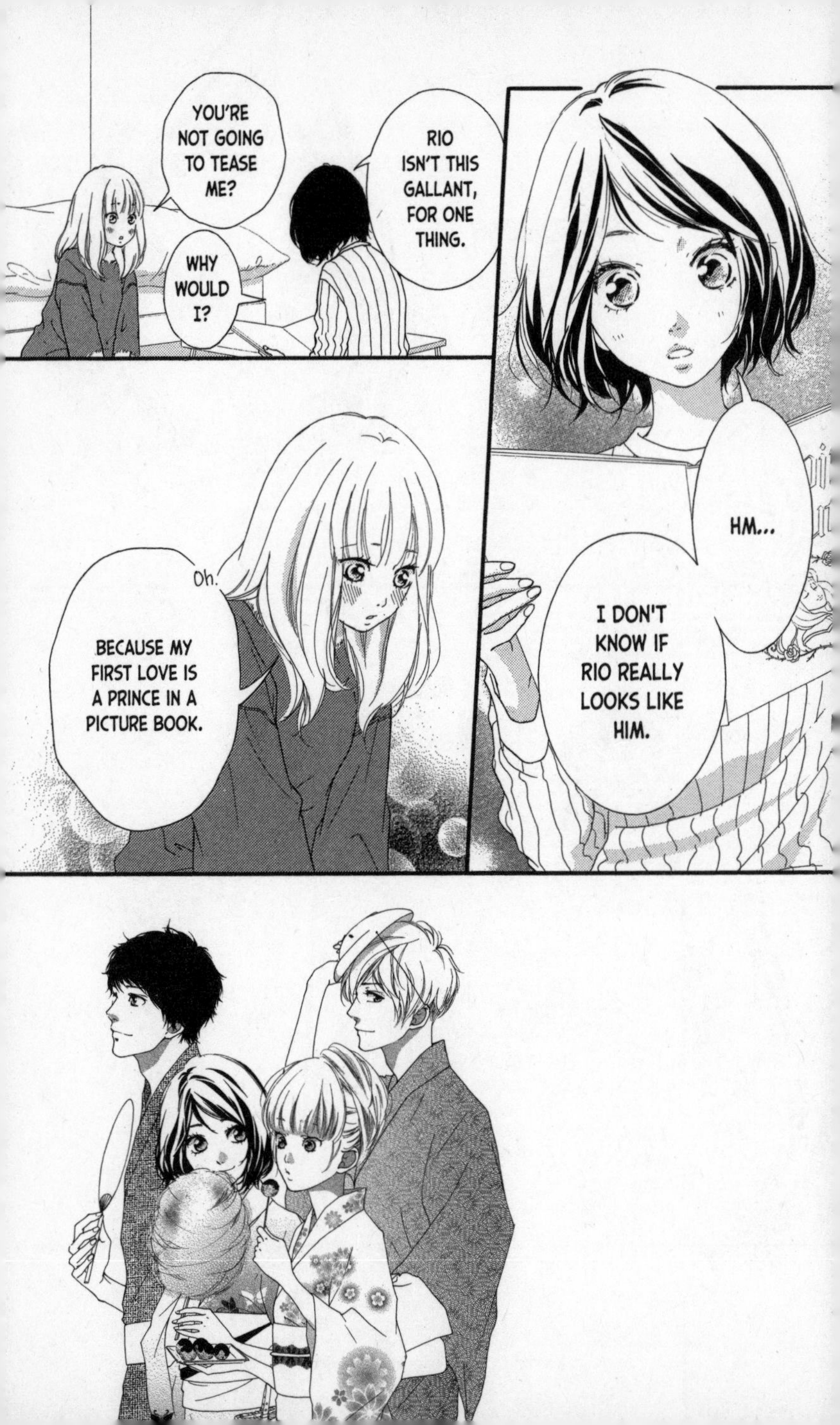
HM...
I DON'T KNOW IF RIO REALLY LOOKS LIKE HIM.
YOU'RE NOT GOING TO TEASE ME?
WHY WOULD I?
RIO ISN'T THIS GALLANT, FOR ONE THING.
Oh.
BECAUSE MY FIRST LOVE IS A PRINCE IN A PICTURE BOOK.

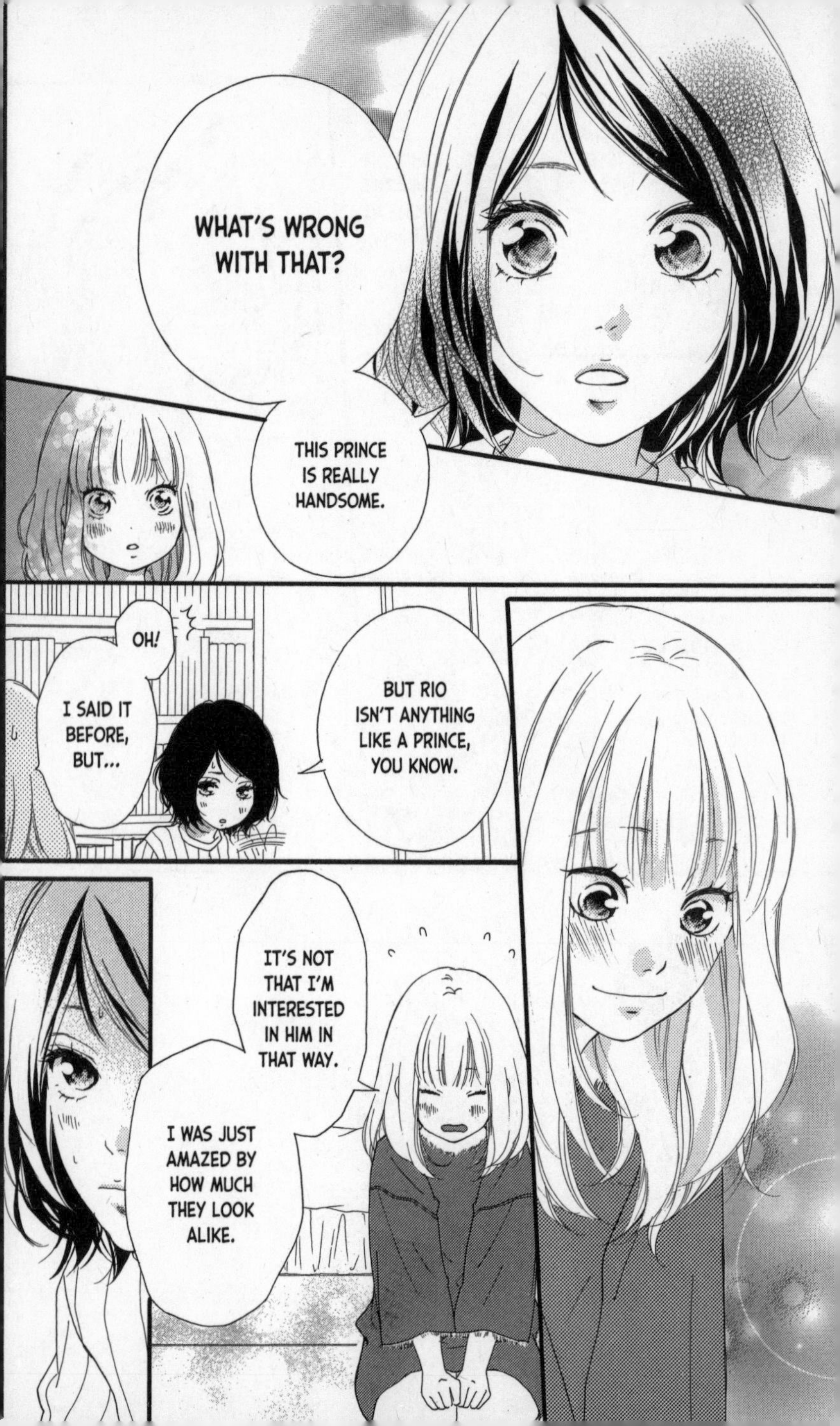
WHAT'S WRONG WITH THAT?
THIS PRINCE IS REALLY HANDSOME.
BUT RIO ISN'T ANYTHING LIKE A PRINCE, YOU KNOW.
OH!
I SAID IT BEFORE, BUT...
IT'S NOT THAT I'M INTERESTED IN HIM IN THAT WAY.
I WAS JUST AMAZED BY HOW MUCH THEY LOOK ALIKE.

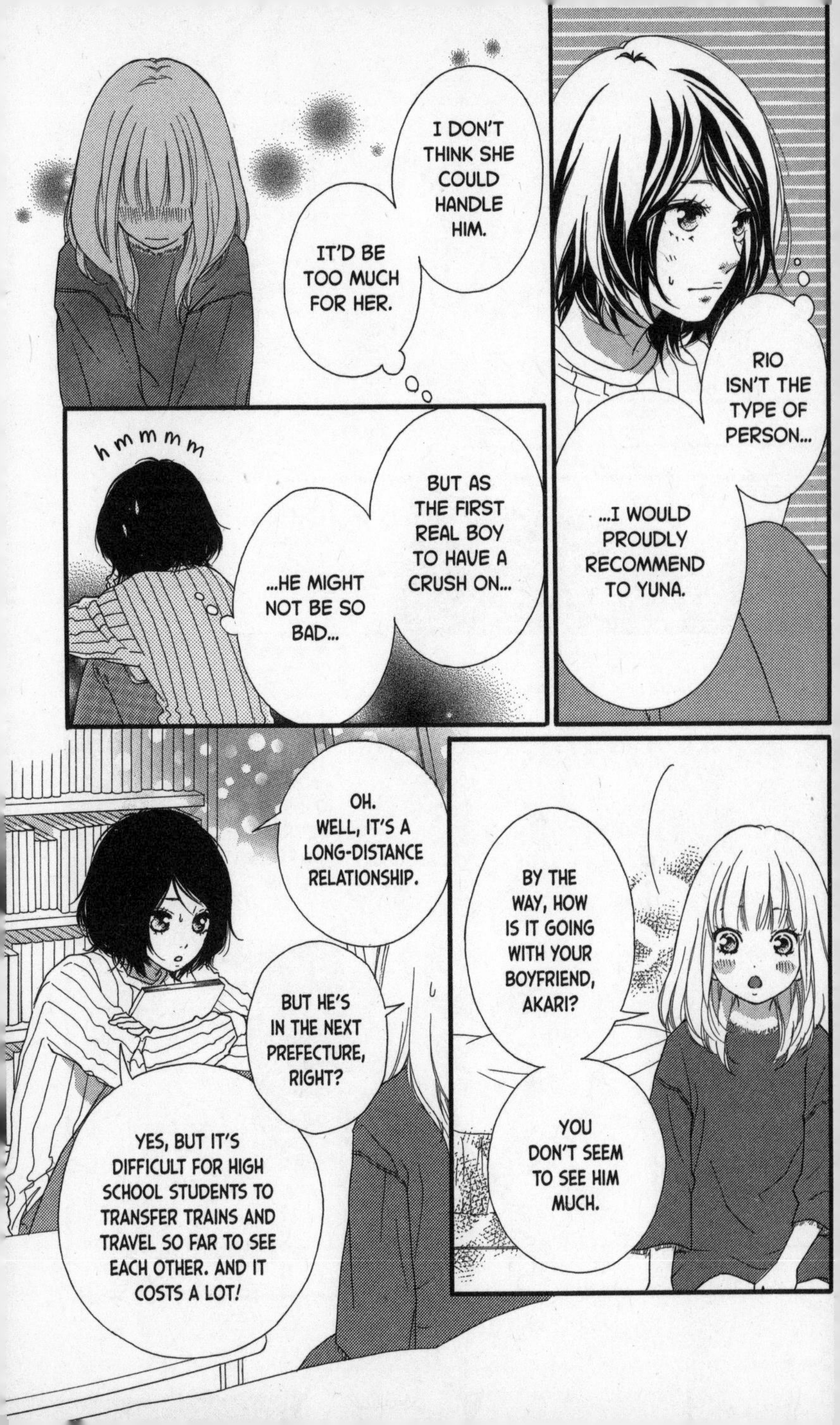
RIO ISN'T THE TYPE OF PERSON...
...I WOULD PROUDLY RECOMMEND TO YUNA.
I DON'T THINK SHE COULD HANDLE HIM.
IT'D BE TOO MUCH FOR HER.
hmmmmm
BUT AS THE FIRST REAL BOY TO HAVE A CRUSH ON...
...HE MIGHT NOT BE SO BAD...
BY THE WAY, HOW IS IT GOING WITH YOUR BOYFRIEND, AKARI?
YOU DON'T SEEM TO SEE HIM MUCH.
OH. WELL, IT'S A LONG-DISTANCE RELATIONSHIP.
BUT HE'S IN THE NEXT PREFECTURE, RIGHT?
YES, BUT IT'S DIFFICULT FOR HIGH SCHOOL STUDENTS TO TRANSFER TRAINS AND TRAVEL SO FAR TO SEE EACH OTHER. AND IT COSTS A LOT!

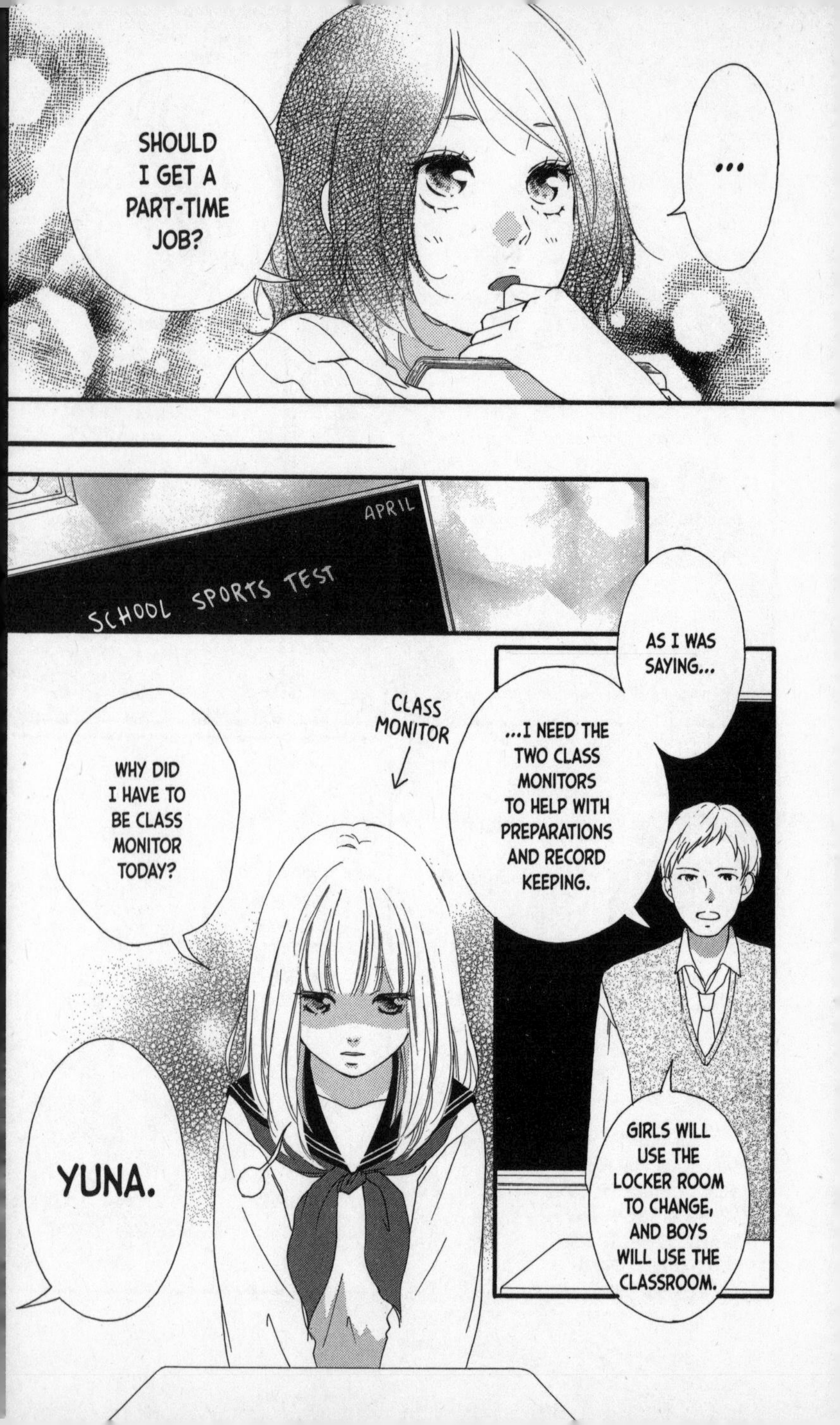
...
SHOULD I GET A PART-TIME JOB?
APRIL
SCHOOL SPORTS TEST
AS I WAS SAYING...
...I NEED THE TWO CLASS MONITORS TO HELP WITH PREPARATIONS AND RECORD KEEPING.
GIRLS WILL USE THE LOCKER ROOM TO CHANGE, AND BOYS WILL USE THE CLASSROOM.
CLASS MONITOR
WHY DID I HAVE TO BE CLASS MONITOR TODAY?
YUNA.

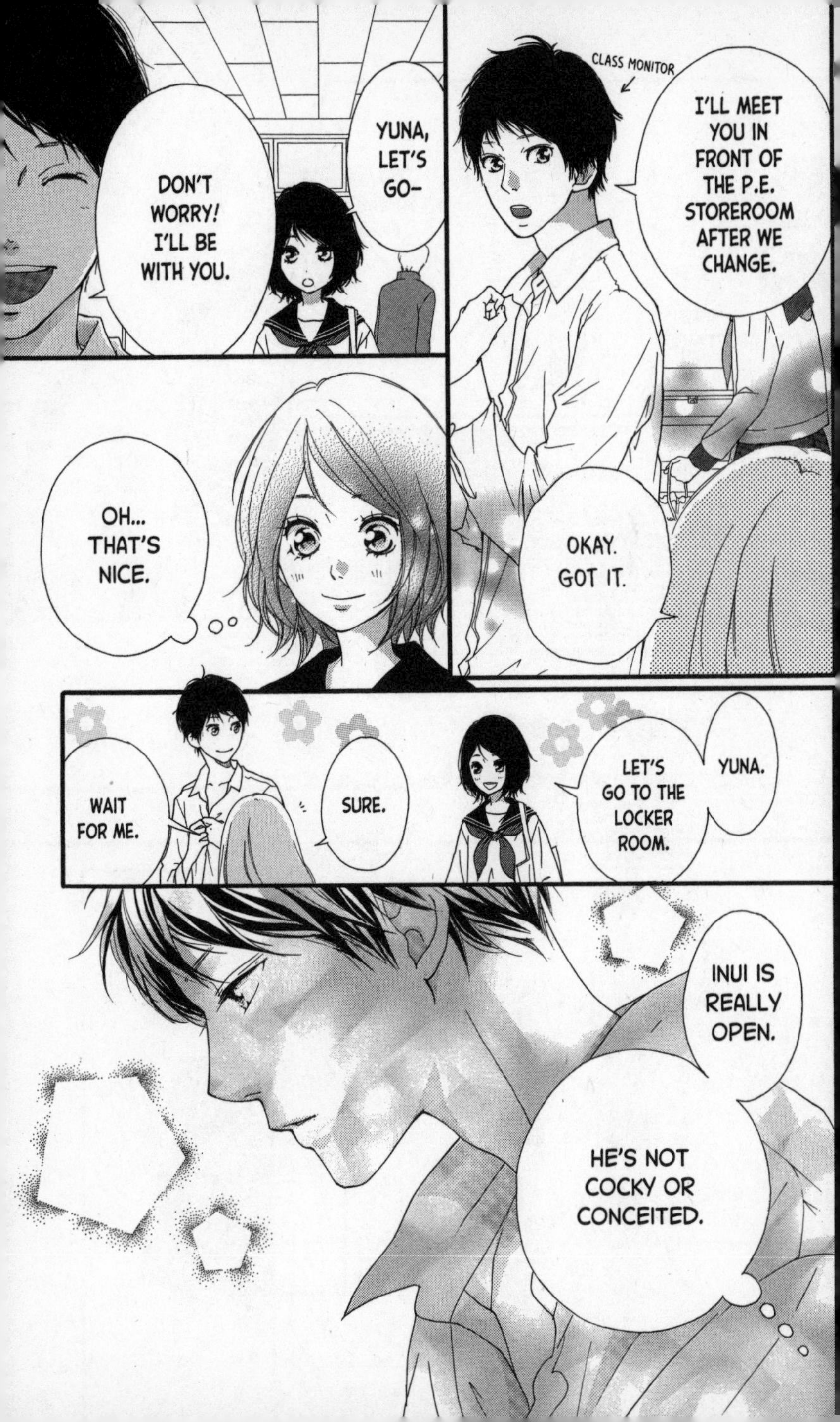
CLASS MONITOR
I'LL MEET YOU IN FRONT OF THE P.E. STOREROOM AFTER WE CHANGE.
OKAY. GOT IT.
YUNA, LET'S GO–
DON'T WORRY! I'LL BE WITH YOU.
OH... THAT'S NICE.
YUNA.
LET'S GO TO THE LOCKER ROOM.
SURE.
WAIT FOR ME.
INUI IS REALLY OPEN.
HE'S NOT COCKY OR CONCEITED.

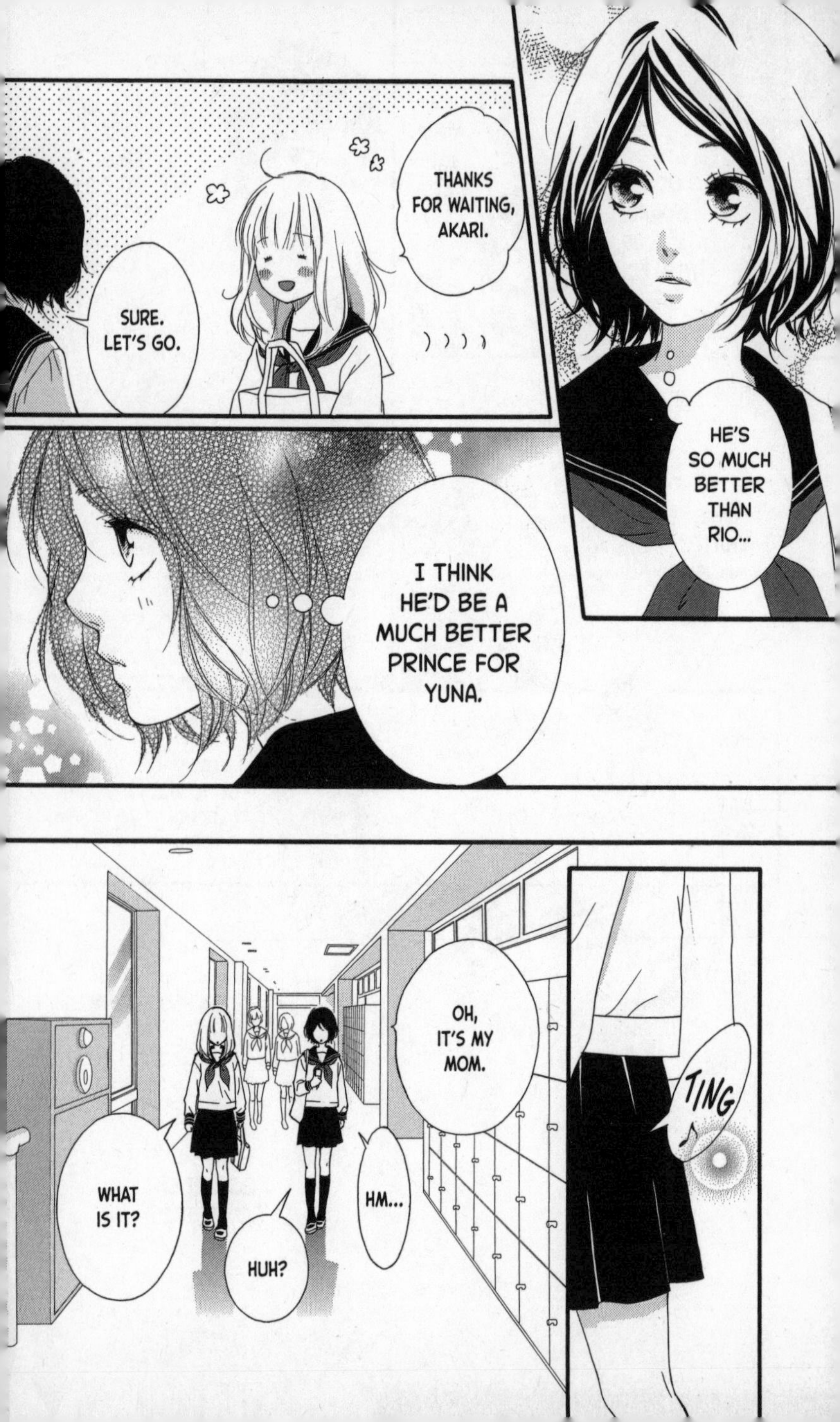
HE'S SO MUCH BETTER THAN RIO...
THANKS FOR WAITING, AKARI.
SURE. LET'S GO.
I THINK HE'D BE A MUCH BETTER PRINCE FOR YUNA.
TING
OH, IT'S MY MOM.
HM...
HUH?
WHAT IS IT?

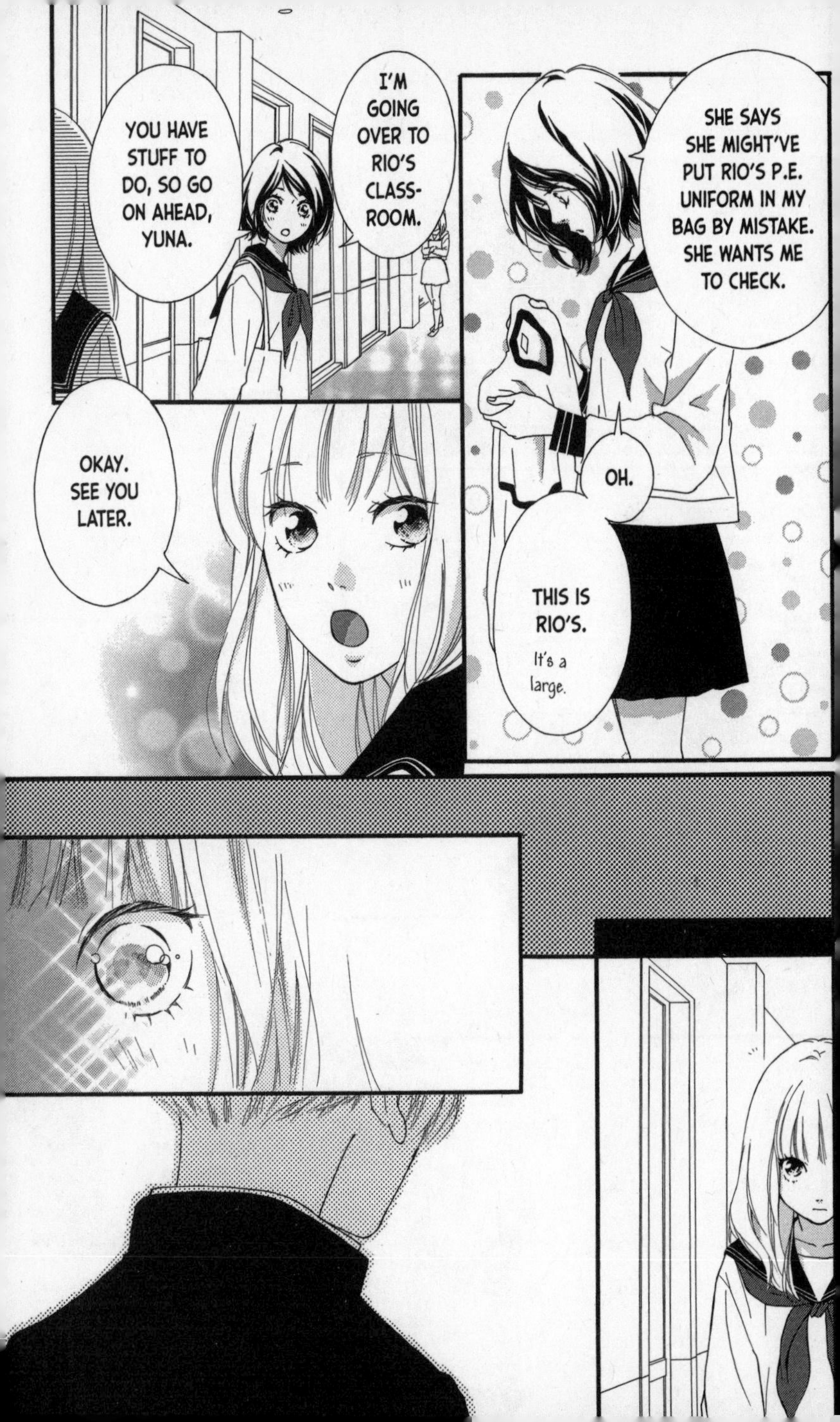
SHE SAYS SHE MIGHT'VE PUT RIO'S P.E. UNIFORM IN MY BAG BY MISTAKE. SHE WANTS ME TO CHECK.
OH.
THIS IS RIO'S.
It's a large.
I'M GOING OVER TO RIO'S CLASS-ROOM.
YOU HAVE STUFF TO DO, SO GO ON AHEAD, YUNA.
OKAY. SEE YOU LATER.

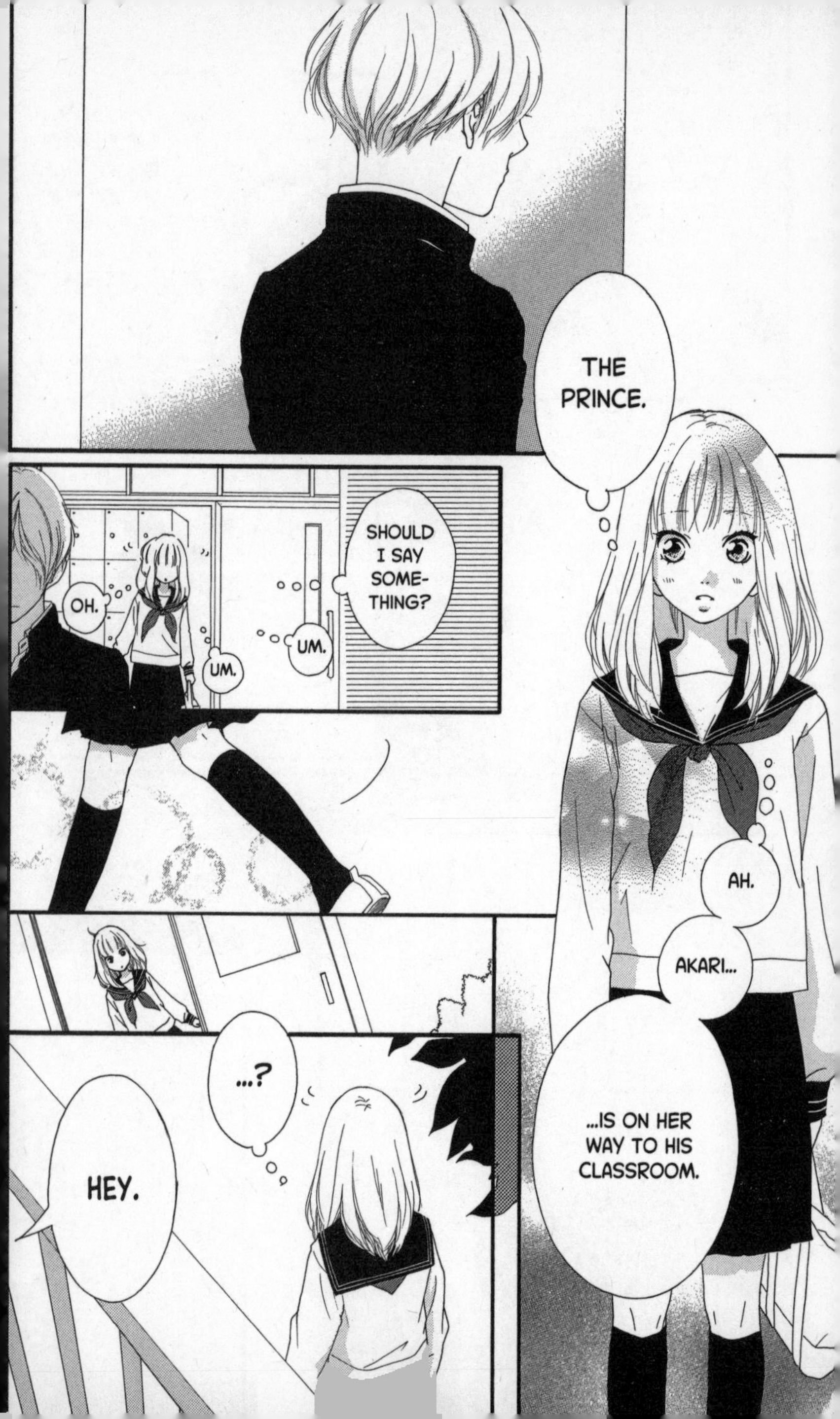

THE PRINCE.
AH.
AKARI...
...IS ON HER WAY TO HIS CLASSROOM.
SHOULD I SAY SOME-THING?
UM.
UM.
OH.
...?
HEY.

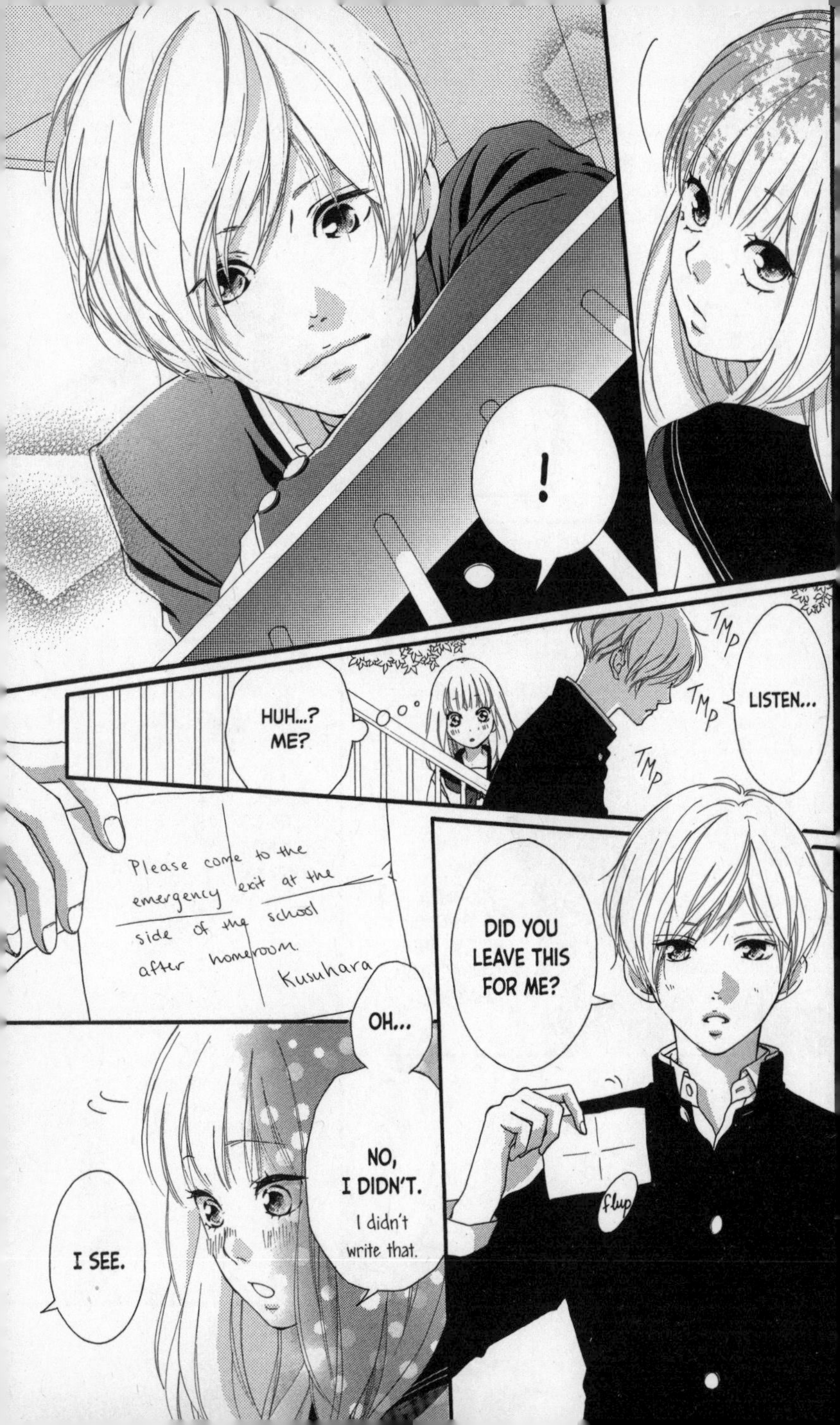
!
TMP
TMP
TMP
LISTEN...
HUH...? ME?
DID YOU LEAVE THIS FOR ME?
Please come to the emergency exit at the side of the school after homeroom.
Kusuhara
flup
OH...
NO, I DIDN'T.
I didn't write that.
I SEE.

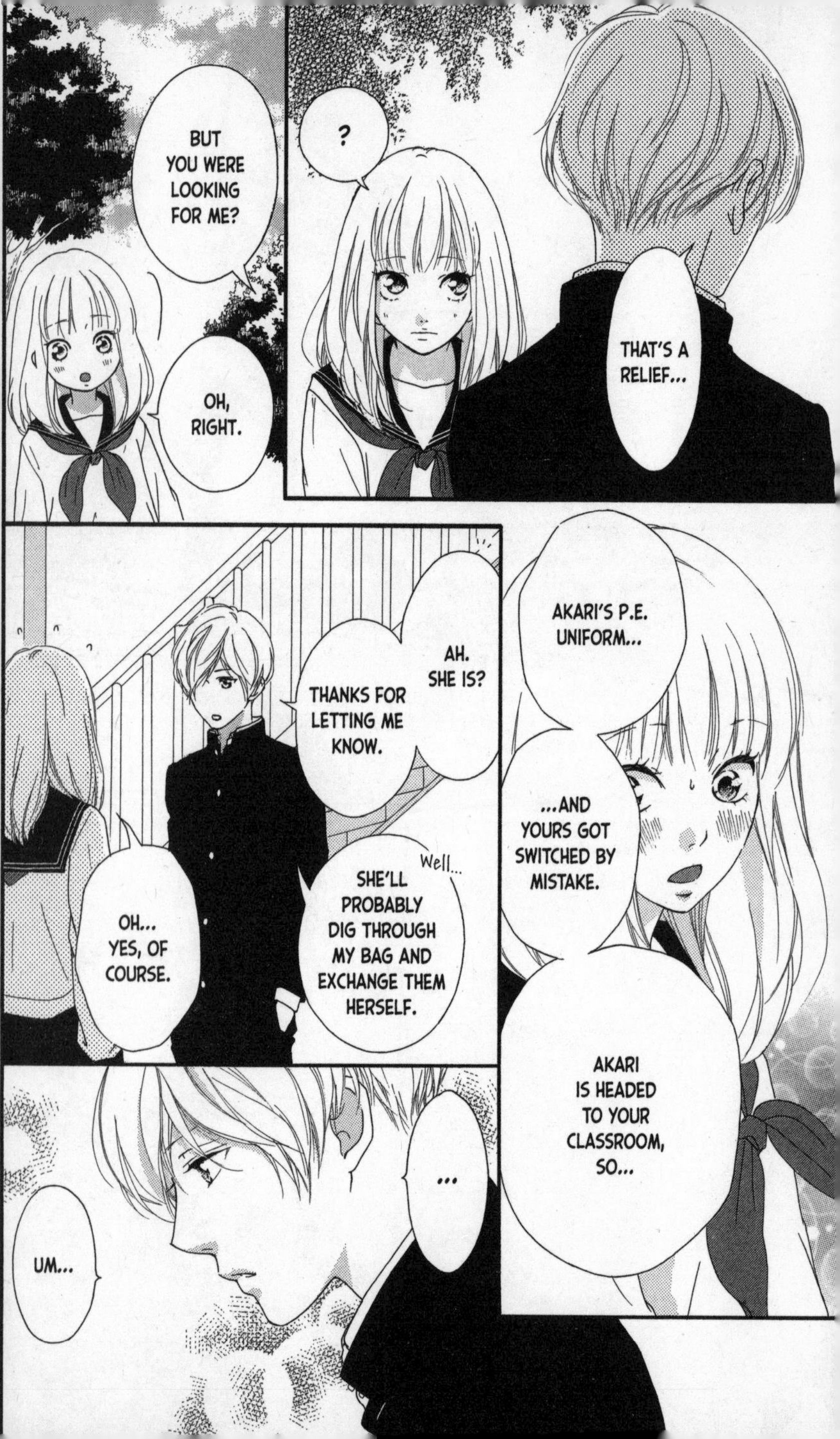
THAT'S A RELIEF...
?
BUT YOU WERE LOOKING FOR ME?
OH, RIGHT.
AKARI'S P.E. UNIFORM...
...AND YOURS GOT SWITCHED BY MISTAKE.
AKARI IS HEADED TO YOUR CLASSROOM, SO...
AH. SHE IS?
THANKS FOR LETTING ME KNOW.
Well...
SHE'LL PROBABLY DIG THROUGH MY BAG AND EXCHANGE THEM HERSELF.
OH... YES, OF COURSE.
...
UM...

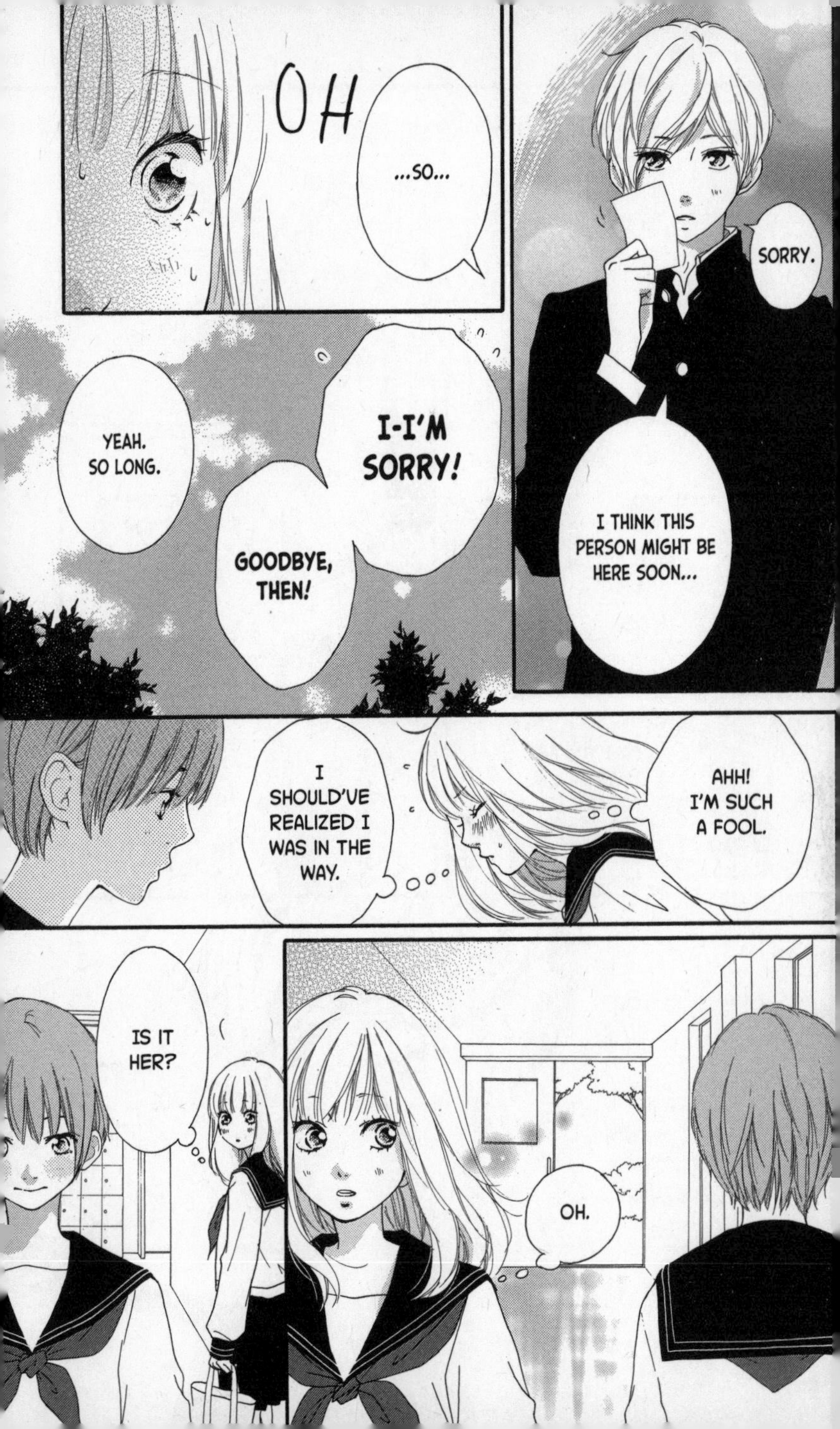
SORRY.
I THINK THIS PERSON MIGHT BE HERE SOON...
OH
...SO...
I-I'M SORRY!
GOODBYE, THEN!
YEAH. SO LONG.
AHH! I'M SUCH A FOOL.
I SHOULD'VE REALIZED I WAS IN THE WAY.
OH.
IS IT HER?

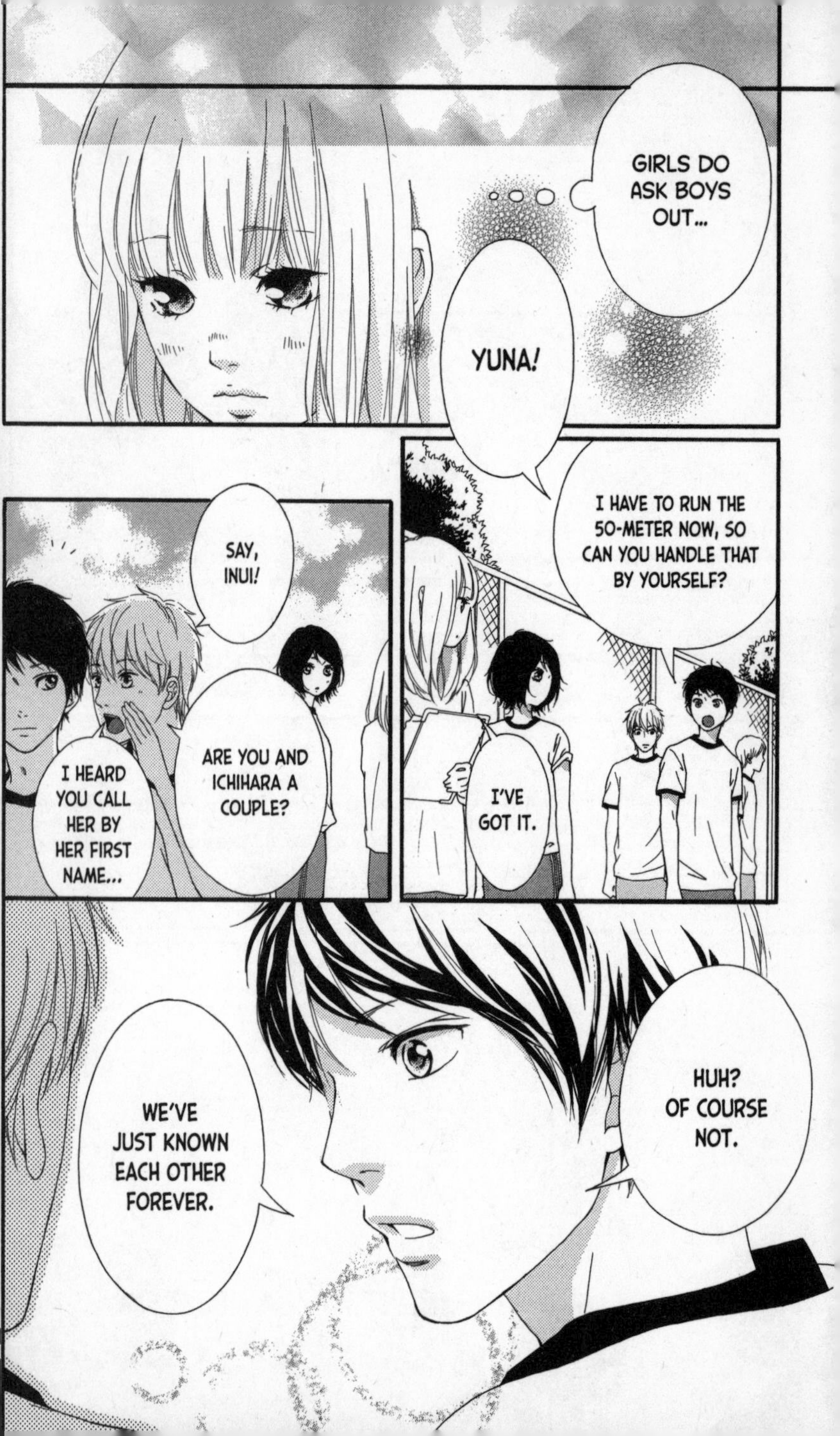
GIRLS DO ASK BOYS OUT...
YUNA!
I HAVE TO RUN THE 50-METER NOW, SO CAN YOU HANDLE THAT BY YOURSELF?
I'VE GOT IT.
SAY, INUI!
ARE YOU AND ICHIHARA A COUPLE?
I HEARD YOU CALL HER BY HER FIRST NAME...
HUH? OF COURSE NOT.
WE'VE JUST KNOWN EACH OTHER FOREVER.

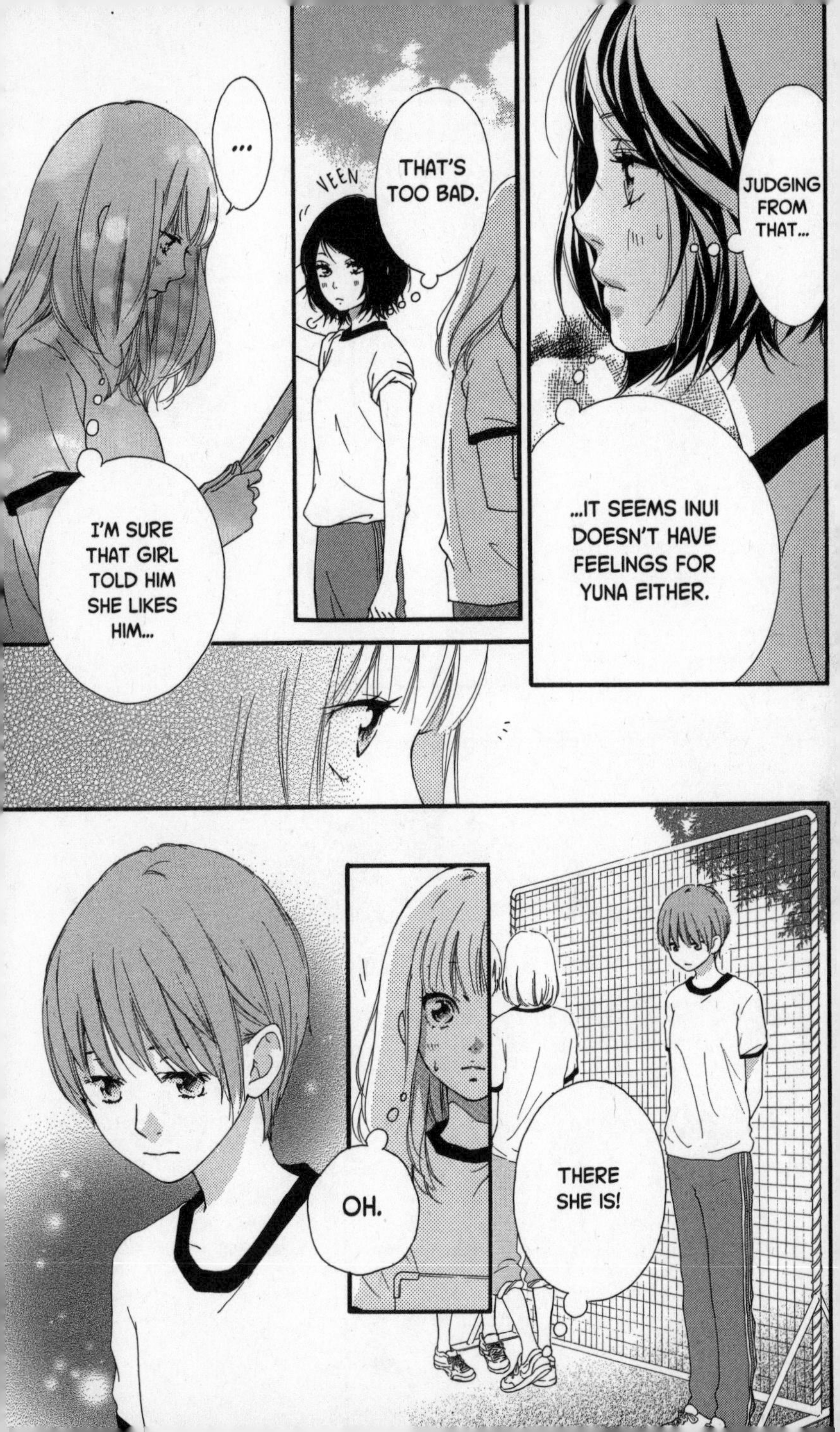
JUDGING FROM THAT...
...IT SEEMS INUI DOESN'T HAVE FEELINGS FOR YUNA EITHER.
VEEN
THAT'S TOO BAD.
...
I'M SURE THAT GIRL TOLD HIM SHE LIKES HIM...
THERE SHE IS!
OH.

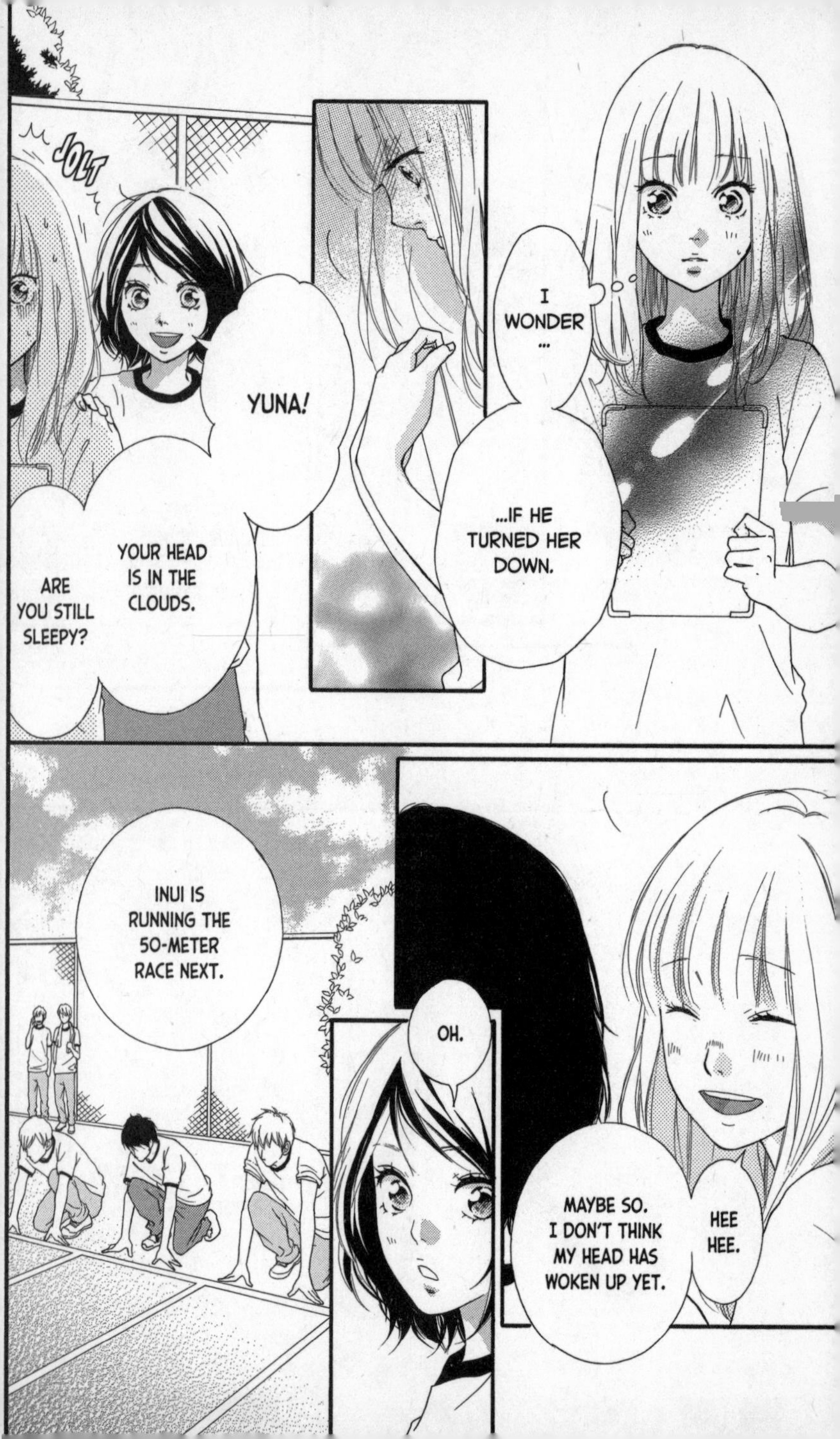
I WONDER ...
...IF HE TURNED HER DOWN.
JOLT
YUNA!
YOUR HEAD IS IN THE CLOUDS.
ARE YOU STILL SLEEPY?
MAYBE SO. I DON'T THINK MY HEAD HAS WOKEN UP YET.
HEE HEE.
OH.
INUI IS RUNNING THE 50-METER RACE NEXT.

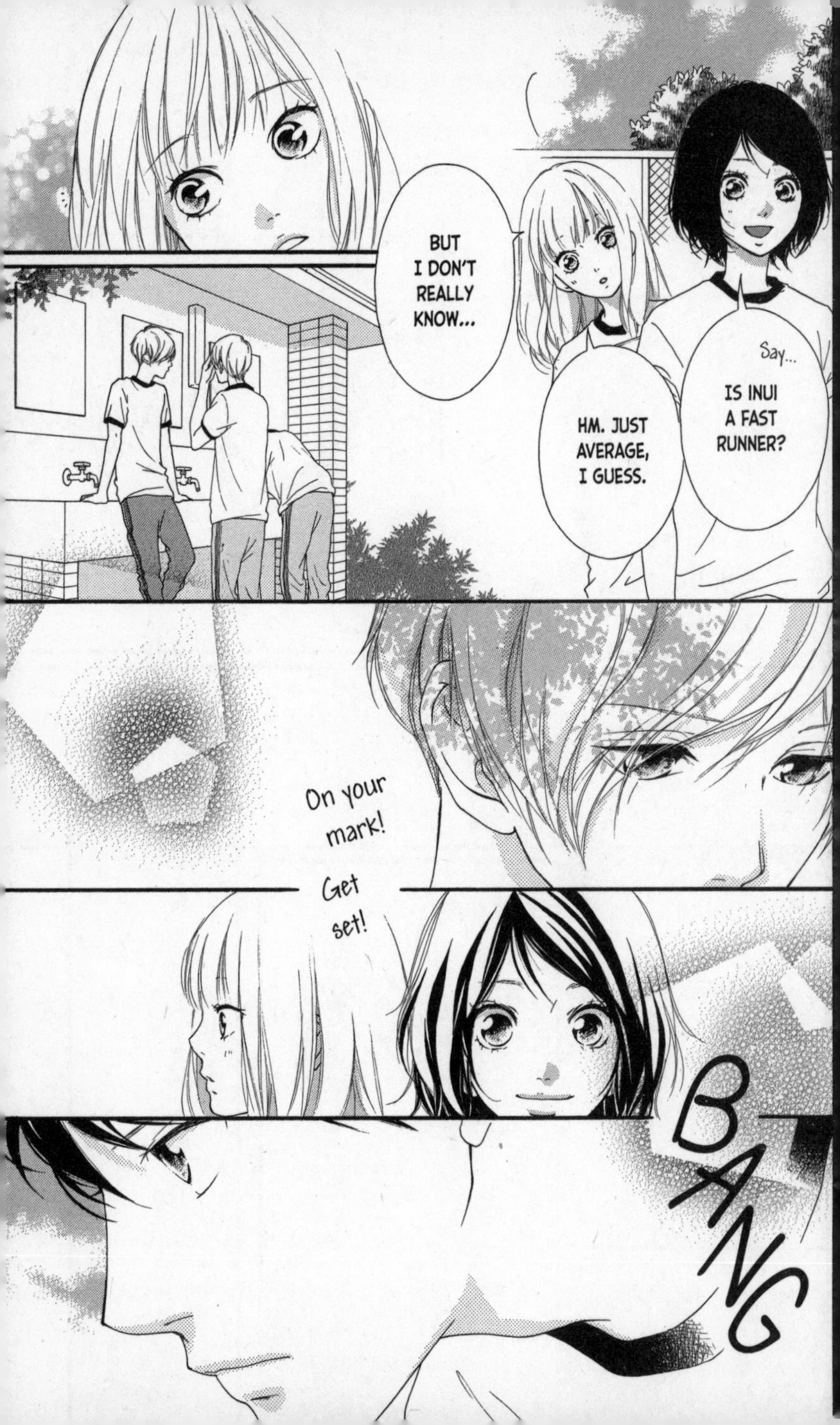
Say... IS INUI A FAST RUNNER?
HM. JUST AVERAGE, I GUESS.
BUT I DON'T REALLY KNOW...
On your mark!
Get set!
BANG

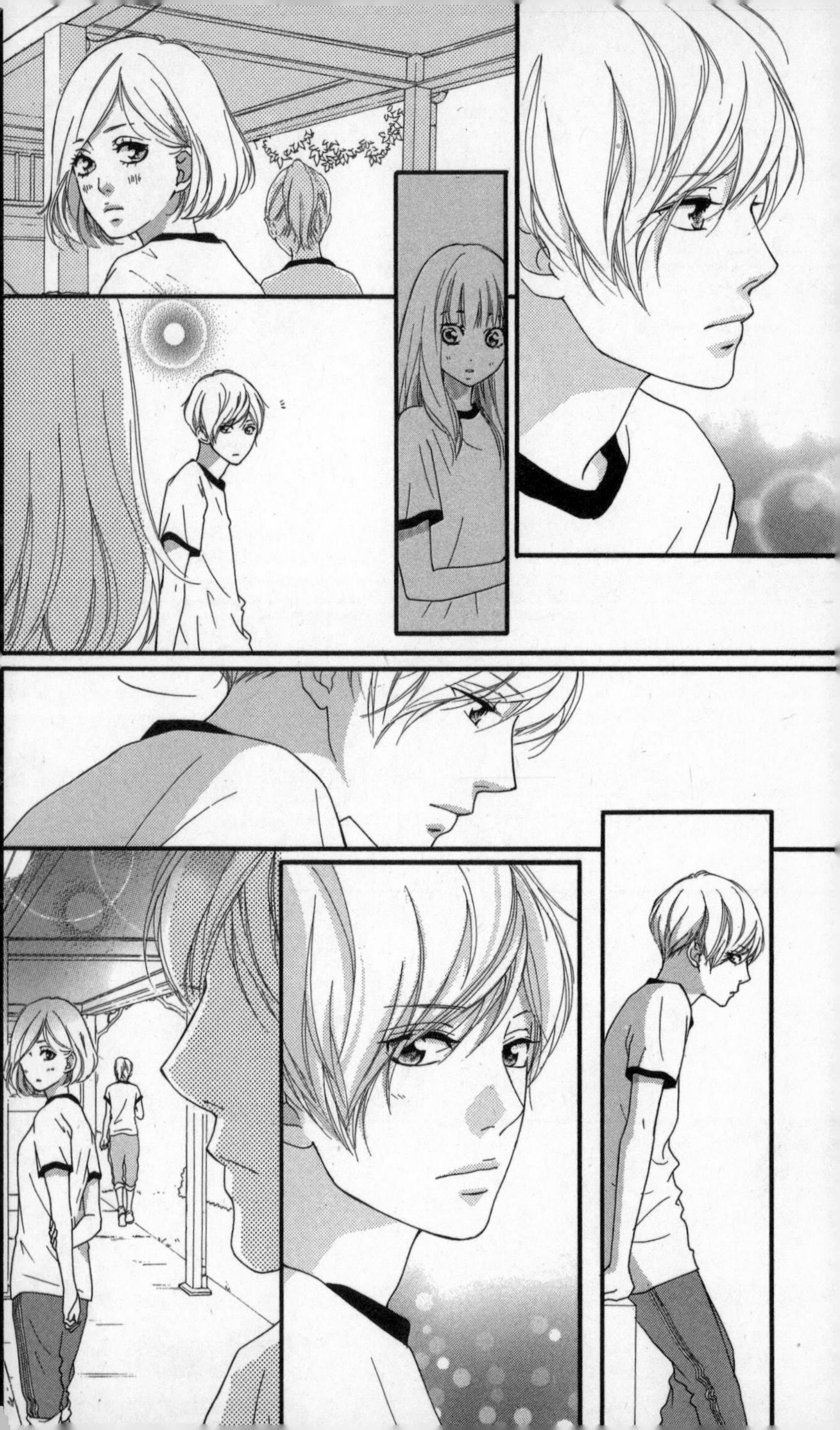

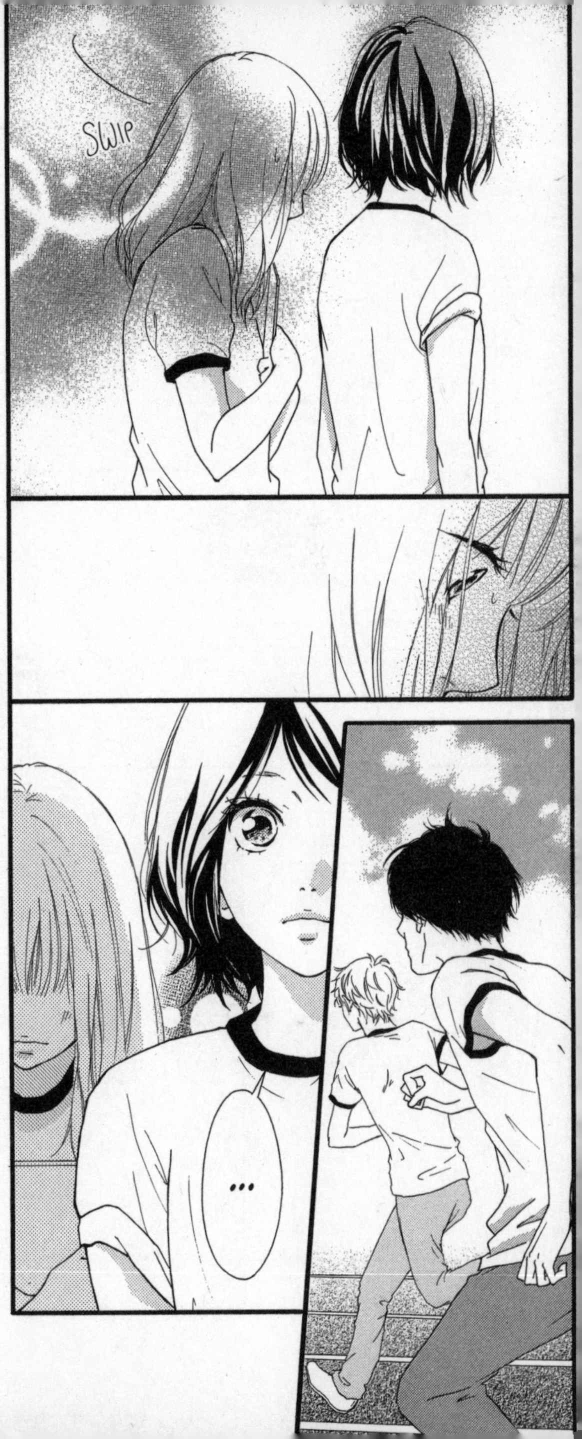
SWIP
...

The manga *A-E-I-O-U All Right* that Yuna is reading in the first chapter was originally a song. However, you won't find it anywhere on the internet. That's because it was a song written and composed by Natsumi Kaizaki (who writes for *Bessatsu Friend*) when she was in elementary school. I love her account of how she bribed a little friend with ice cream to sit and listen to her song. It's so cute that he sat there eating his ice cream and listening to her sing. I laughed just imagining that scene. Then I asked her to sing it for me, and it wasn't too bad, but it made me laugh wildly. I had imagined a weirder melody...

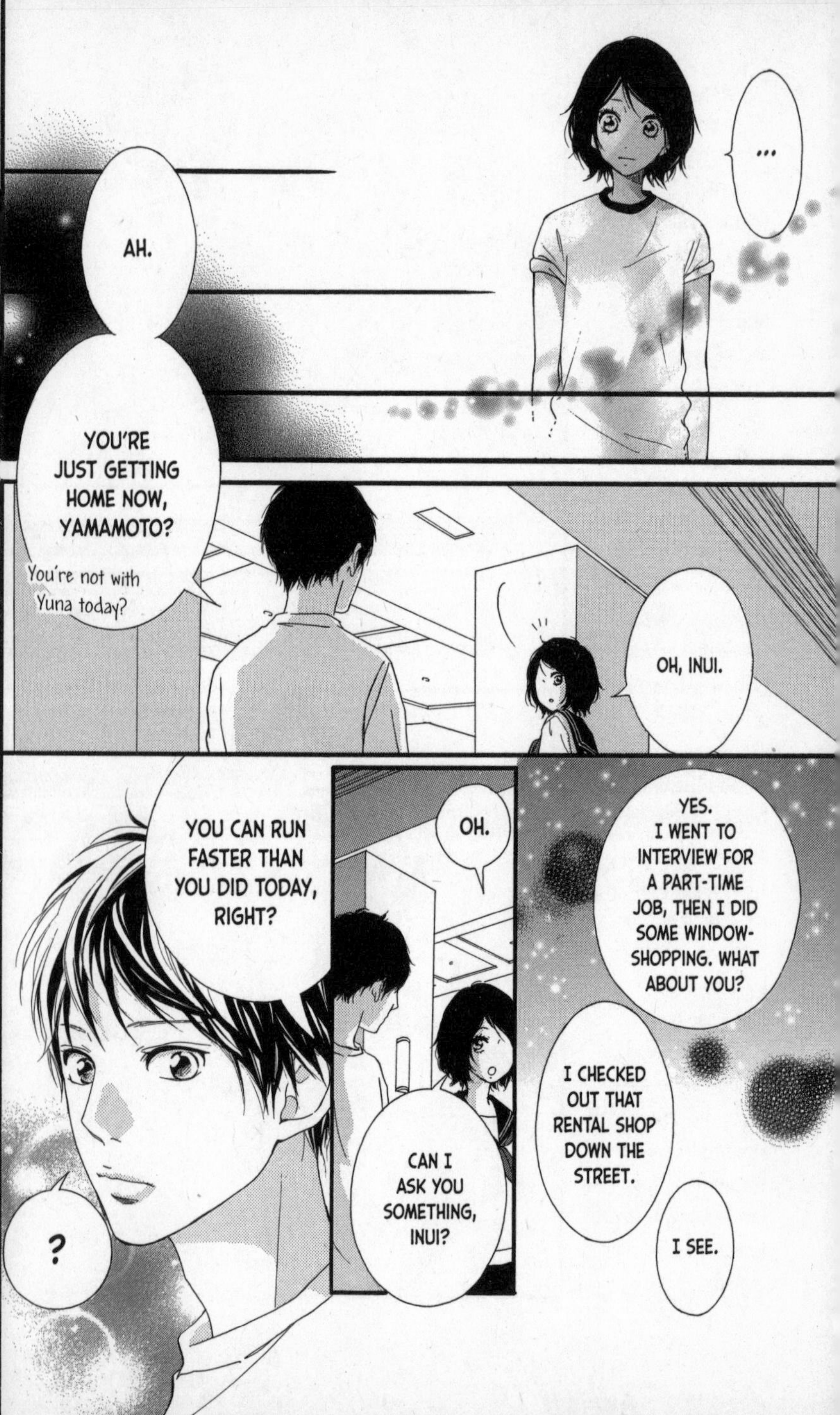
...
AH.
YOU'RE JUST GETTING HOME NOW, YAMAMOTO?
You're not with Yuna today?
OH, INUI.
YES. I WENT TO INTERVIEW FOR A PART-TIME JOB, THEN I DID SOME WINDOW-SHOPPING. WHAT ABOUT YOU?
I CHECKED OUT THAT RENTAL SHOP DOWN THE STREET.
I SEE.
OH.
CAN I ASK YOU SOMETHING, INUI?
YOU CAN RUN FASTER THAN YOU DID TODAY, RIGHT?
?

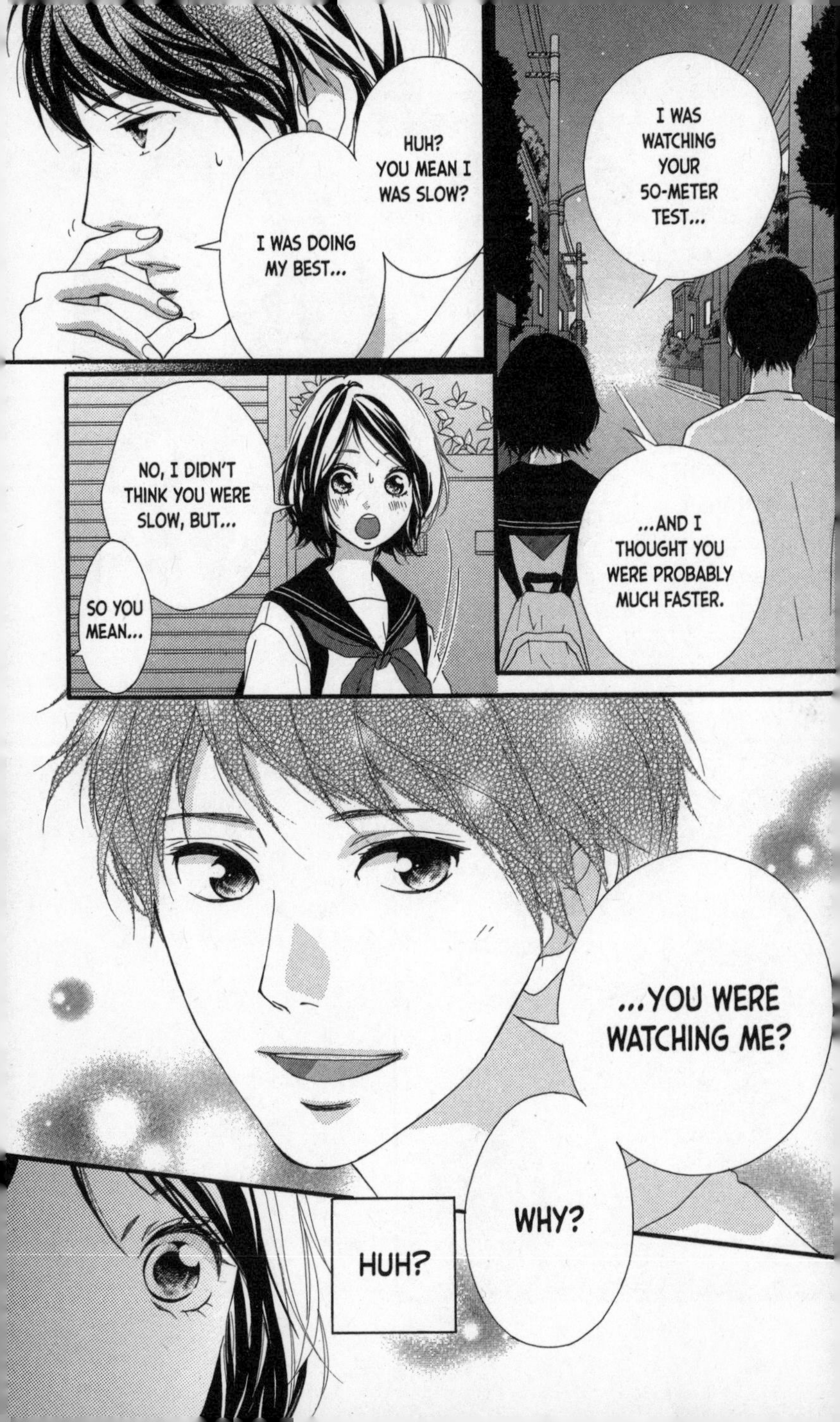
I WAS WATCHING YOUR 50-METER TEST...
...AND I THOUGHT YOU WERE PROBABLY MUCH FASTER.
HUH? YOU MEAN I WAS SLOW?
I WAS DOING MY BEST...
NO, I DIDN'T THINK YOU WERE SLOW, BUT...
SO YOU MEAN...
...YOU WERE WATCHING ME?
WHY?
HUH?

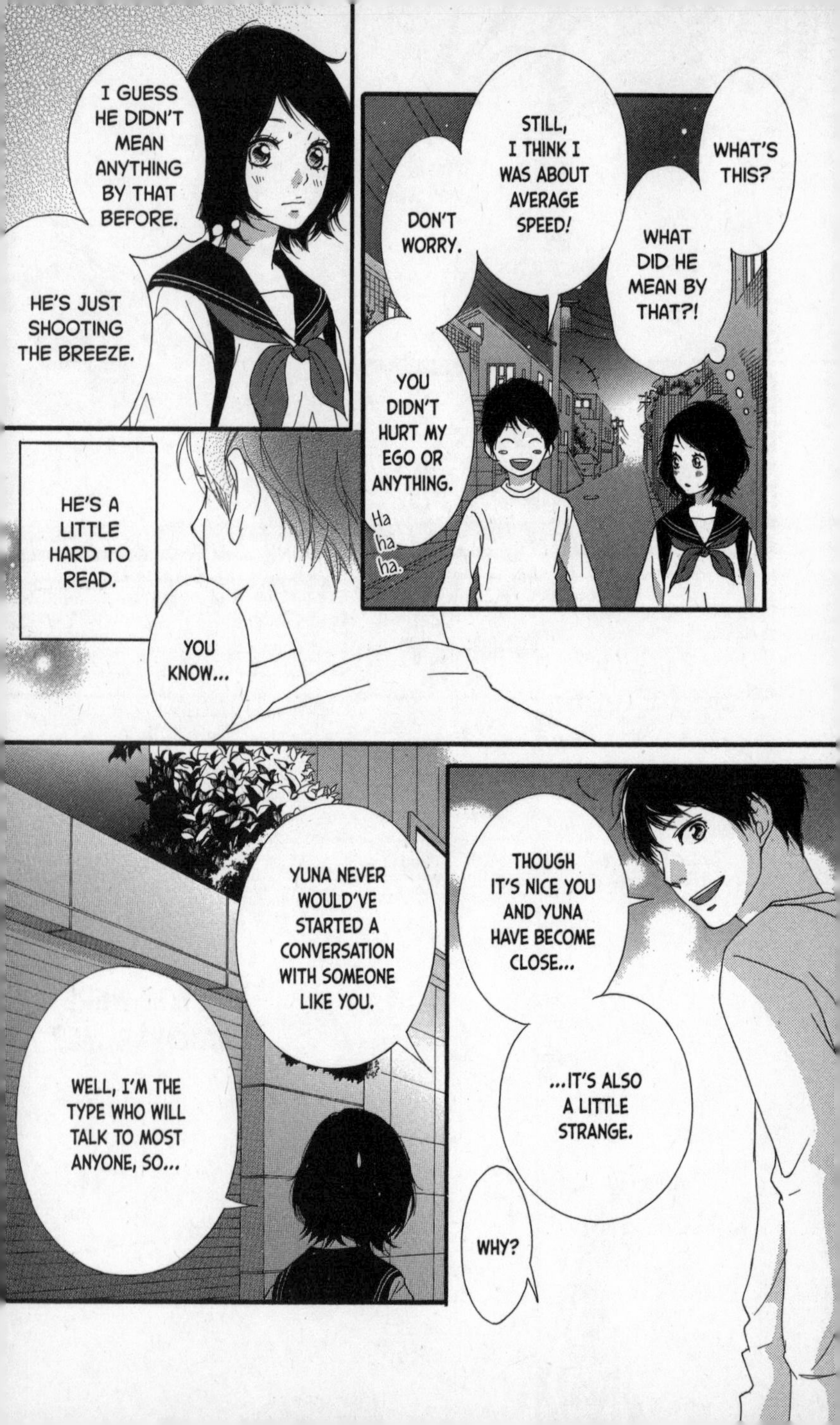
WHAT'S THIS?
WHAT DID HE MEAN BY THAT?!
STILL, I THINK I WAS ABOUT AVERAGE SPEED!
DON'T WORRY.
YOU DIDN'T HURT MY EGO OR ANYTHING.
Ha ha ha.
I GUESS HE DIDN'T MEAN ANYTHING BY THAT BEFORE.
HE'S JUST SHOOTING THE BREEZE.
YOU KNOW...
HE'S A LITTLE HARD TO READ.
THOUGH IT'S NICE YOU AND YUNA HAVE BECOME CLOSE...
...IT'S ALSO A LITTLE STRANGE.
WHY?
YUNA NEVER WOULD'VE STARTED A CONVERSATION WITH SOMEONE LIKE YOU.
WELL, I'M THE TYPE WHO WILL TALK TO MOST ANYONE, SO...

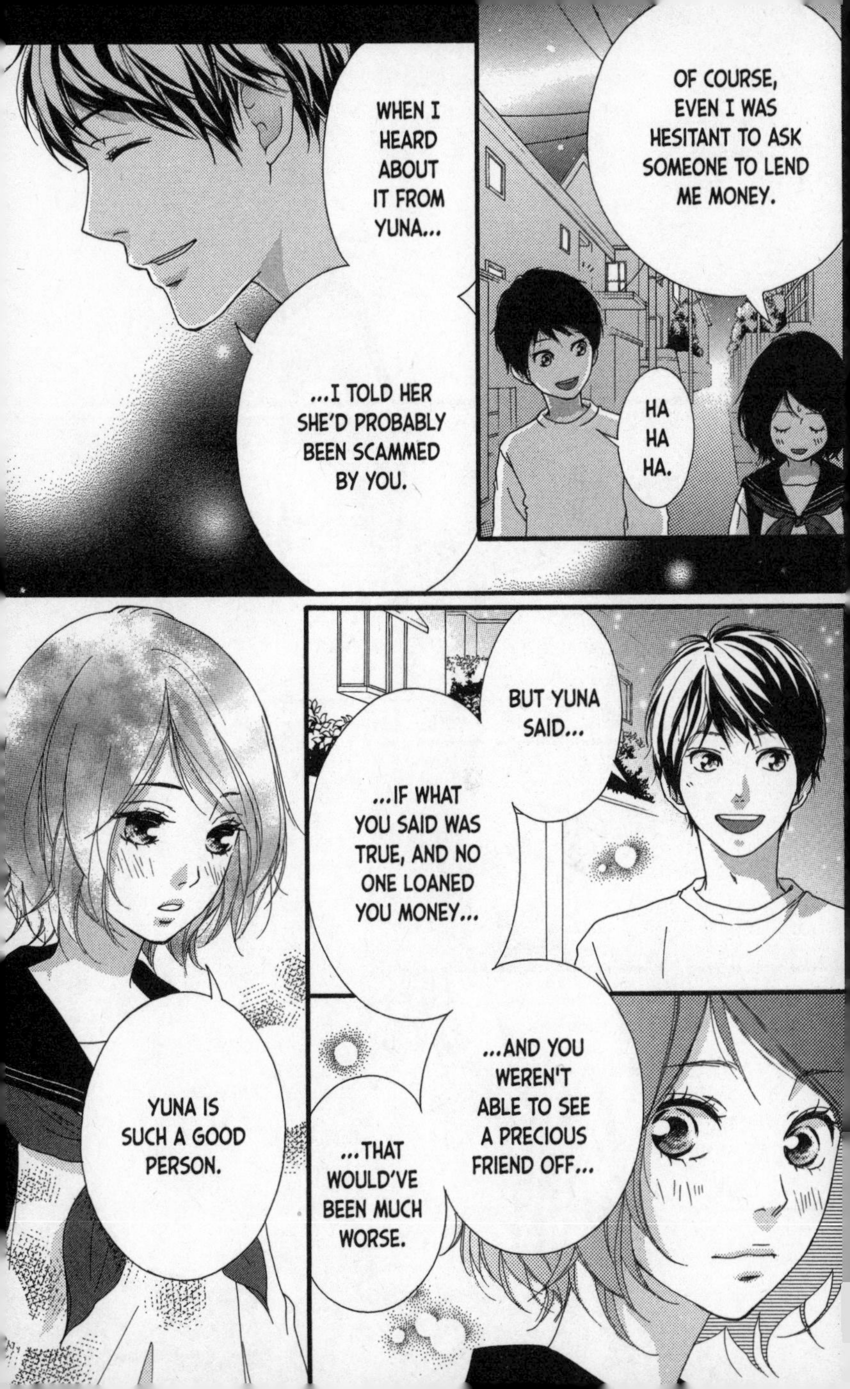
OF COURSE, EVEN I WAS HESITANT TO ASK SOMEONE TO LEND ME MONEY.
HA HA HA.
WHEN I HEARD ABOUT IT FROM YUNA...
...I TOLD HER SHE'D PROBABLY BEEN SCAMMED BY YOU.
BUT YUNA SAID...
...IF WHAT YOU SAID WAS TRUE, AND NO ONE LOANED YOU MONEY...
...AND YOU WEREN'T ABLE TO SEE A PRECIOUS FRIEND OFF...
...THAT WOULD'VE BEEN MUCH WORSE.
YUNA IS SUCH A GOOD PERSON.

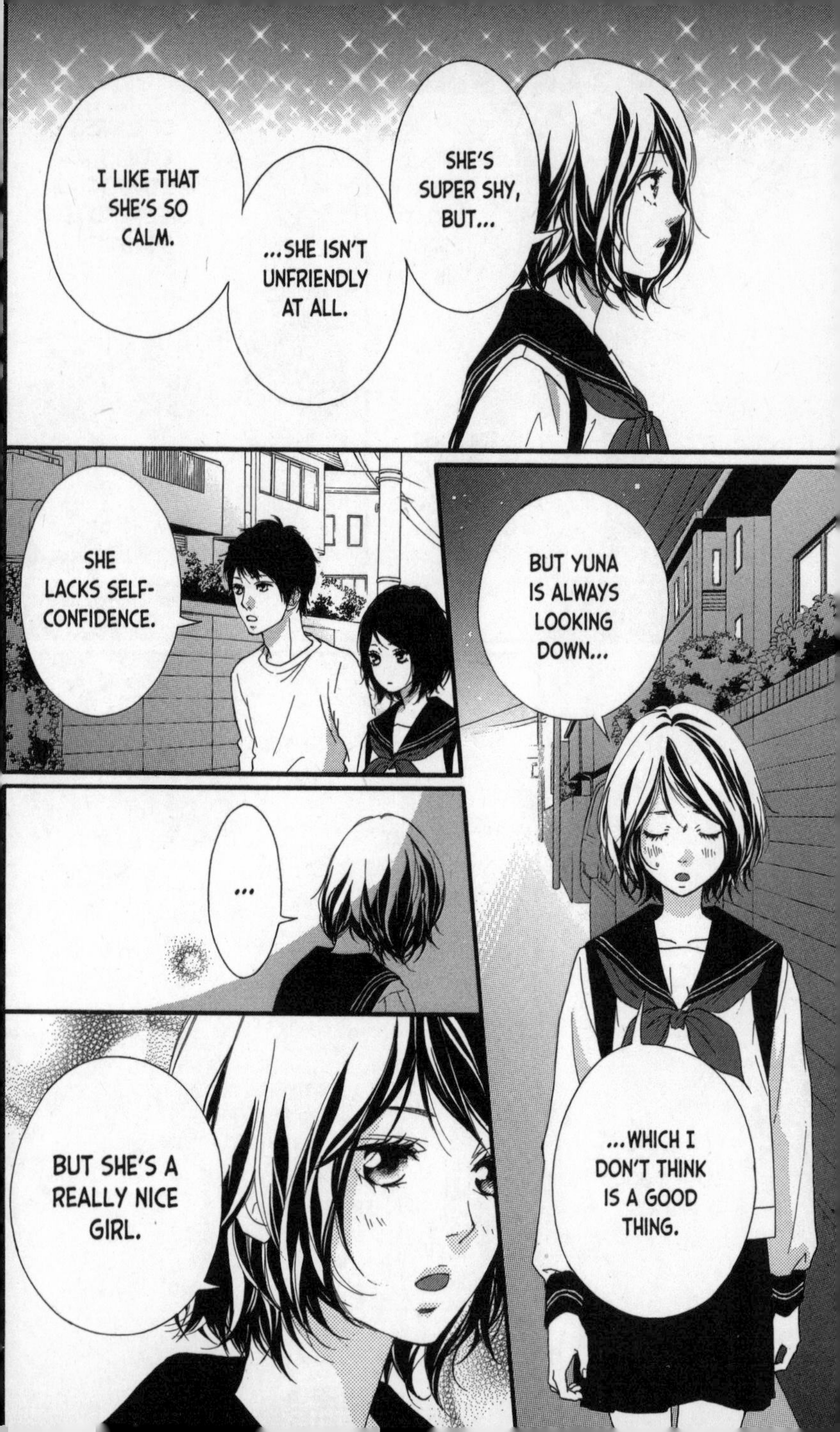
SHE'S SUPER SHY, BUT...
...SHE ISN'T UNFRIENDLY AT ALL.
I LIKE THAT SHE'S SO CALM.
BUT YUNA IS ALWAYS LOOKING DOWN...
...WHICH I DON'T THINK IS A GOOD THING.
SHE LACKS SELF-CONFIDENCE.
...
BUT SHE'S A REALLY NICE GIRL.

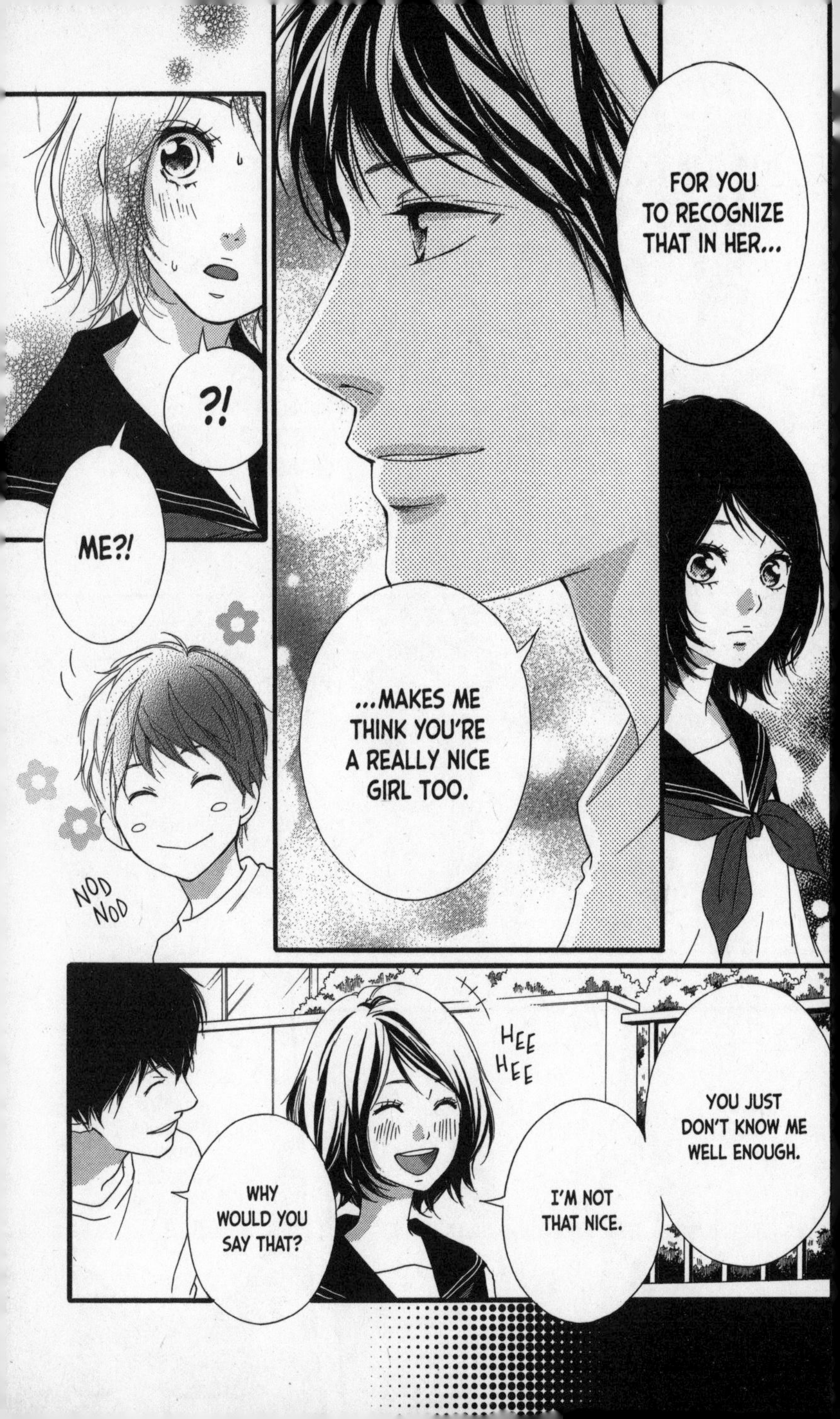
FOR YOU TO RECOGNIZE THAT IN HER...
...MAKES ME THINK YOU'RE A REALLY NICE GIRL TOO.
?!
ME?!
NOD NOD
YOU JUST DON'T KNOW ME WELL ENOUGH.
HEE HEE
I'M NOT THAT NICE.
WHY WOULD YOU SAY THAT?

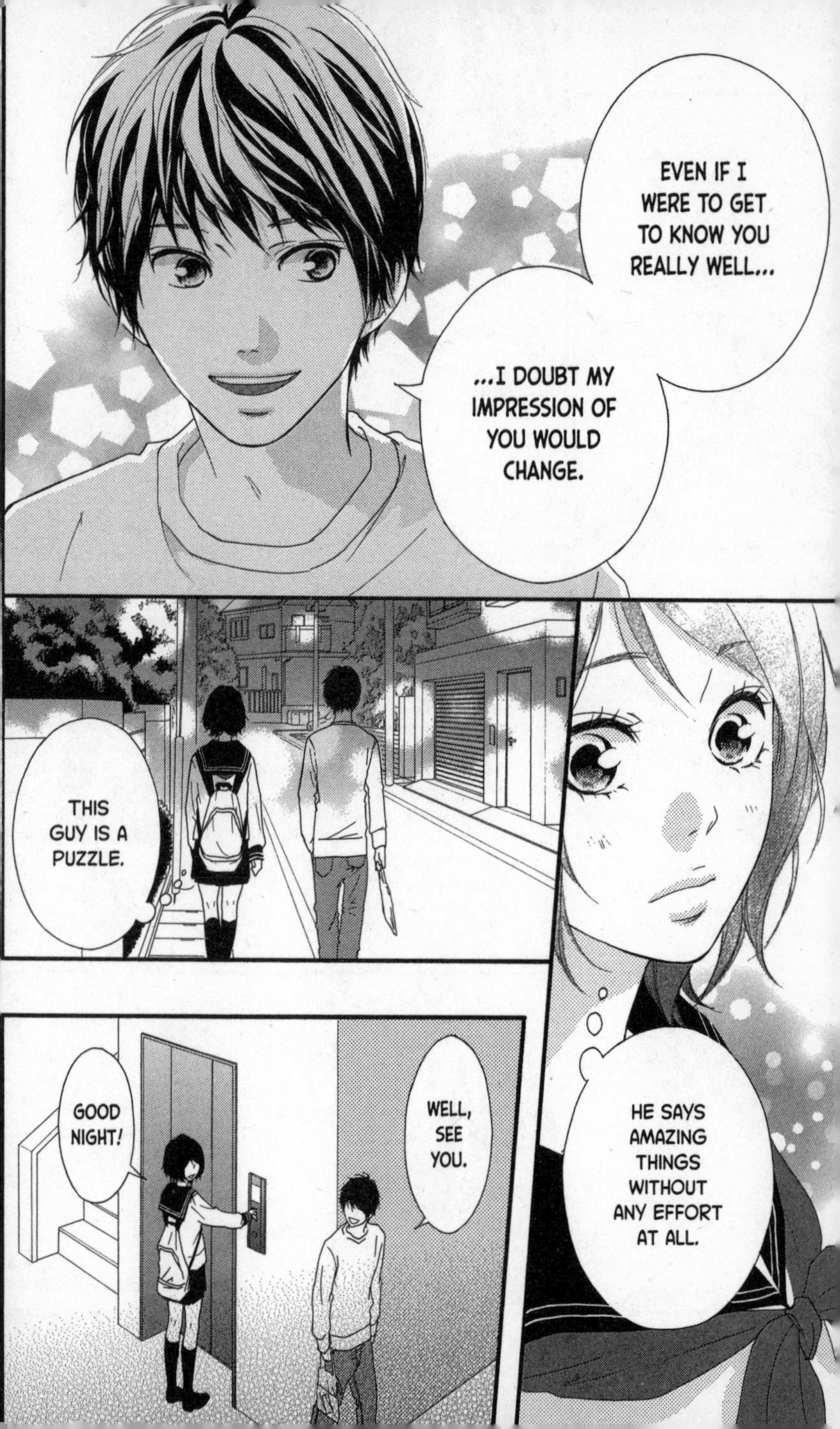
EVEN IF I WERE TO GET TO KNOW YOU REALLY WELL...
...I DOUBT MY IMPRESSION OF YOU WOULD CHANGE.
HE SAYS AMAZING THINGS WITHOUT ANY EFFORT AT ALL.
THIS GUY IS A PUZZLE.
WELL, SEE YOU.
GOOD NIGHT!

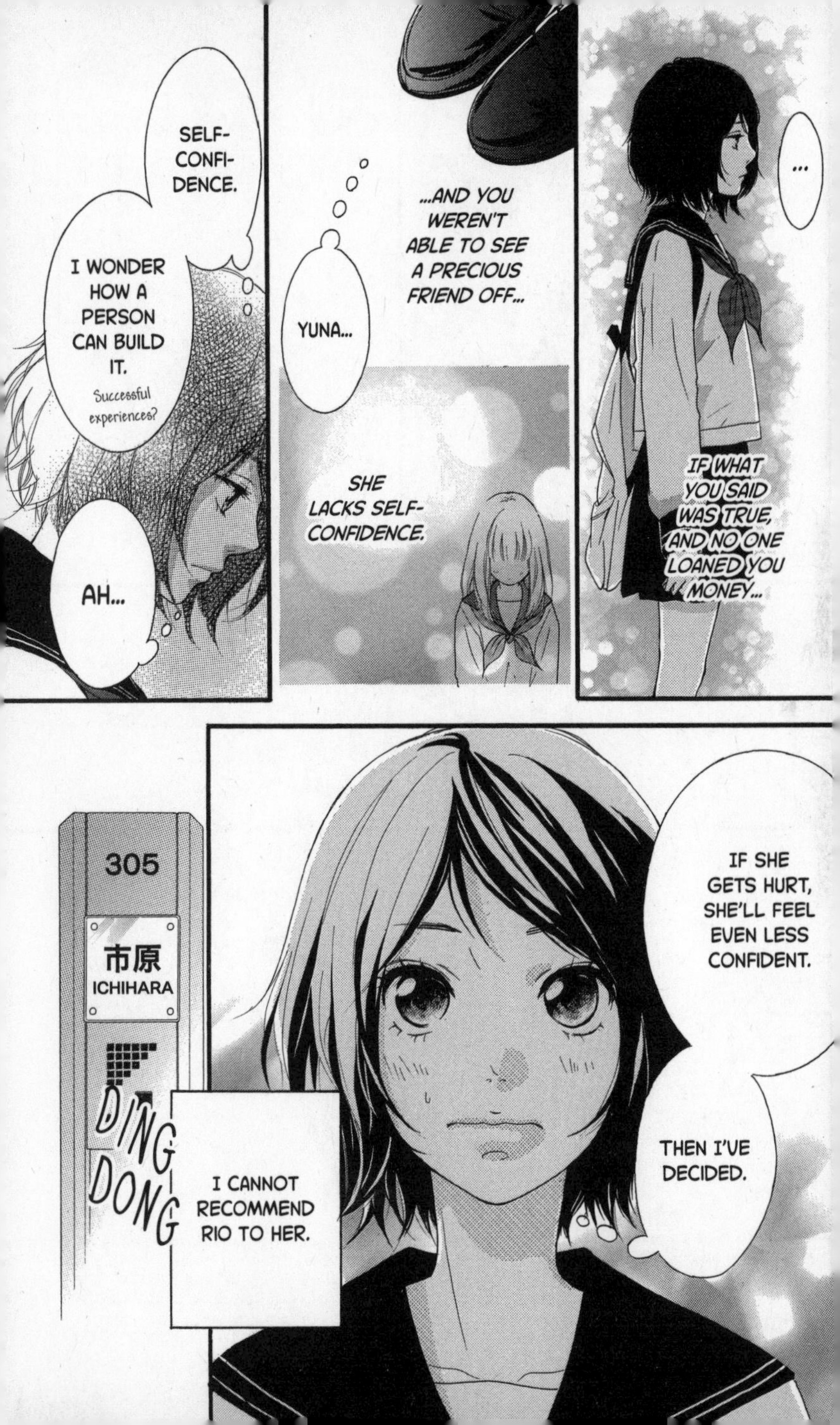
...
IF WHAT YOU SAID WAS TRUE, AND NO ONE LOANED YOU MONEY...
...AND YOU WEREN'T ABLE TO SEE A PRECIOUS FRIEND OFF...
YUNA...
SHE LACKS SELF-CONFIDENCE.
SELF-CONFIDENCE.
I WONDER HOW A PERSON CAN BUILD IT.
Successful experiences?
AH...
IF SHE GETS HURT, SHE'LL FEEL EVEN LESS CONFIDENT.
THEN I'VE DECIDED.
I CANNOT RECOMMEND RIO TO HER.
305
市原
ICHIHARA
DING DONG

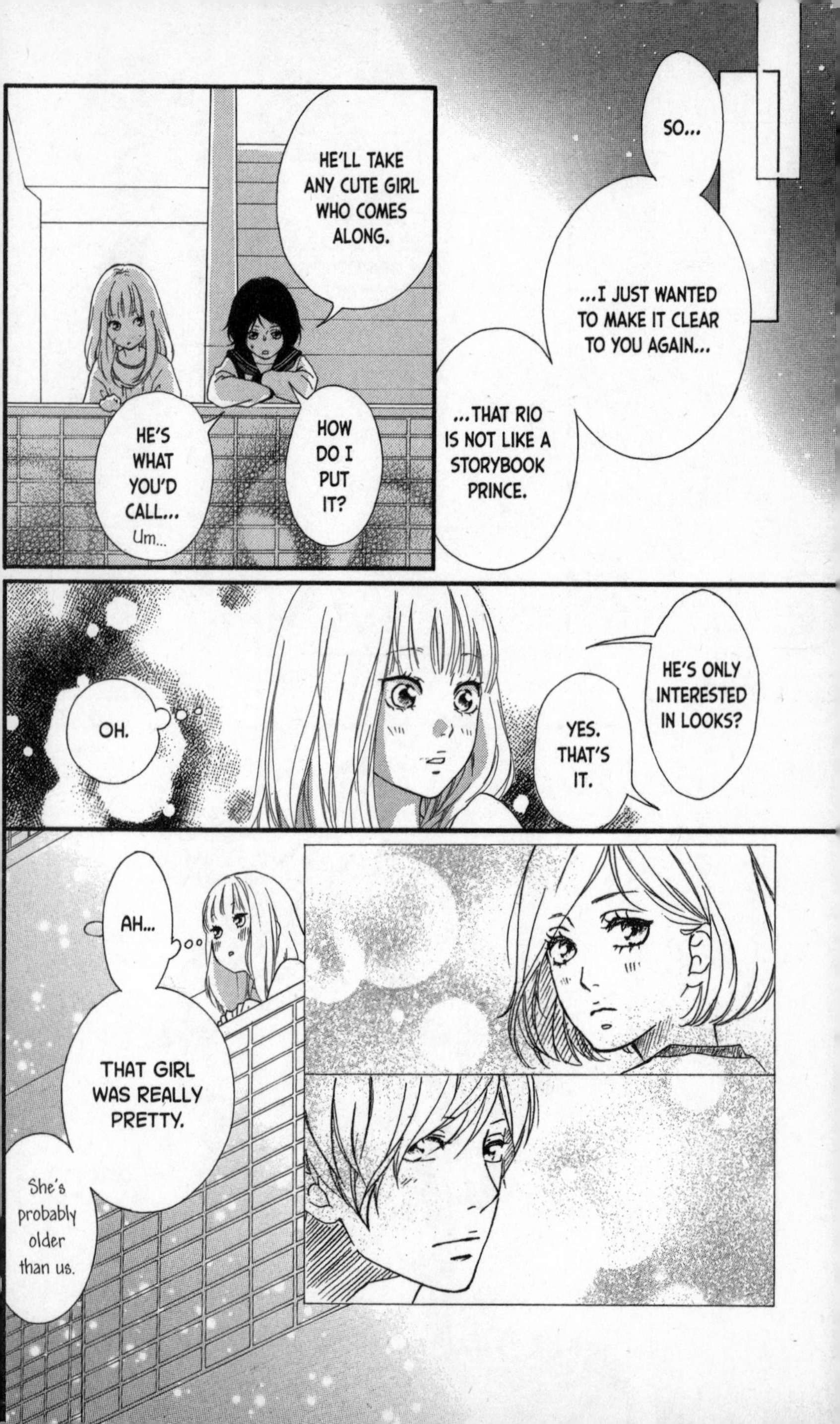
SO...
...I JUST WANTED TO MAKE IT CLEAR TO YOU AGAIN...
...THAT RIO IS NOT LIKE A STORYBOOK PRINCE.
HE'LL TAKE ANY CUTE GIRL WHO COMES ALONG.
HOW DO I PUT IT?
HE'S WHAT YOU'D CALL... Um...
HE'S ONLY INTERESTED IN LOOKS?
YES. THAT'S IT.
OH.
AH...
THAT GIRL WAS REALLY PRETTY.
She's probably older than us.

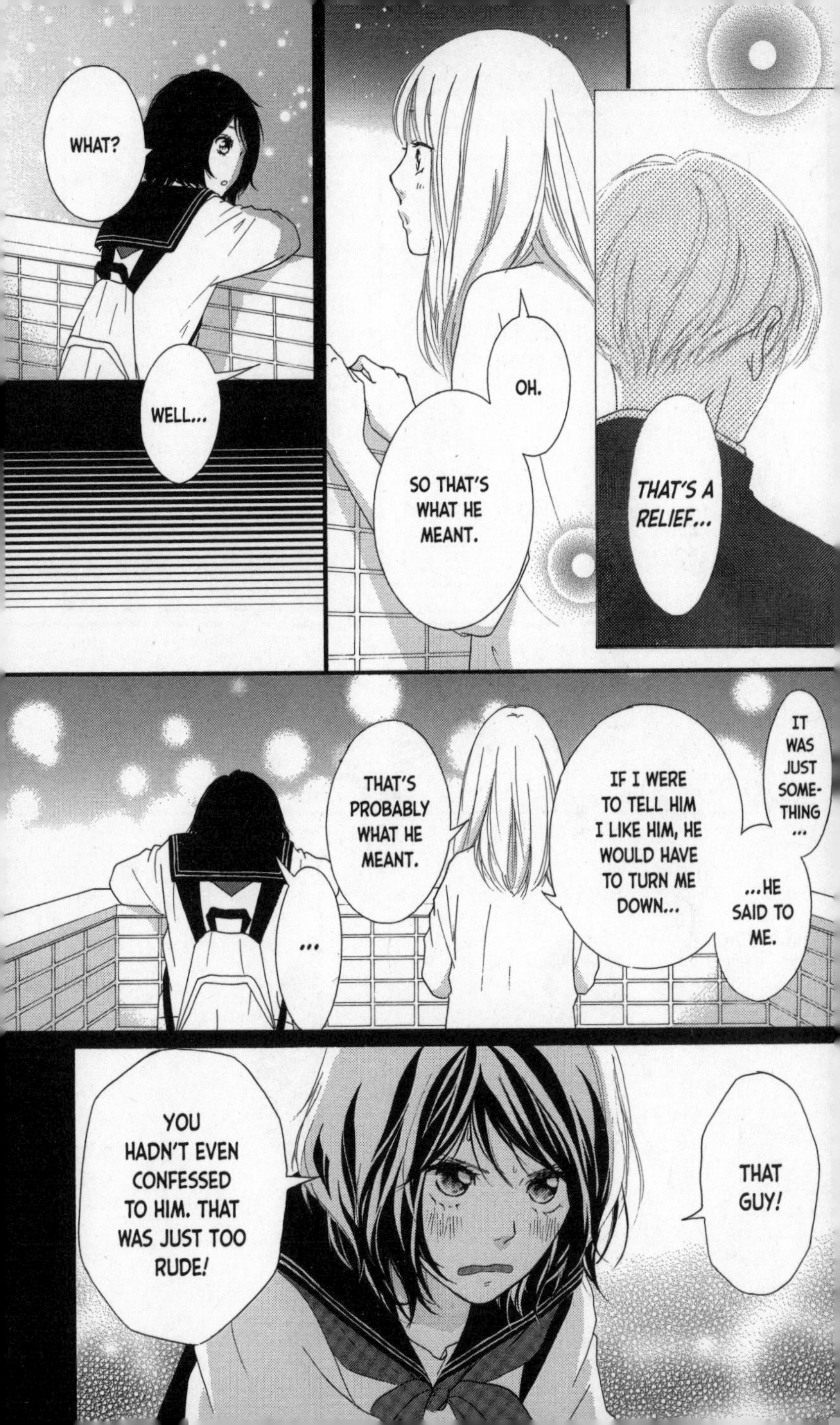
THAT'S A RELIEF...
OH.
SO THAT'S WHAT HE MEANT.
WHAT?
WELL...
IT WAS JUST SOME-THING...
...HE SAID TO ME.
IF I WERE TO TELL HIM I LIKE HIM, HE WOULD HAVE TO TURN ME DOWN...
THAT'S PROBABLY WHAT HE MEANT.
...
THAT GUY!
YOU HADN'T EVEN CONFESSED TO HIM. THAT WAS JUST TOO RUDE!

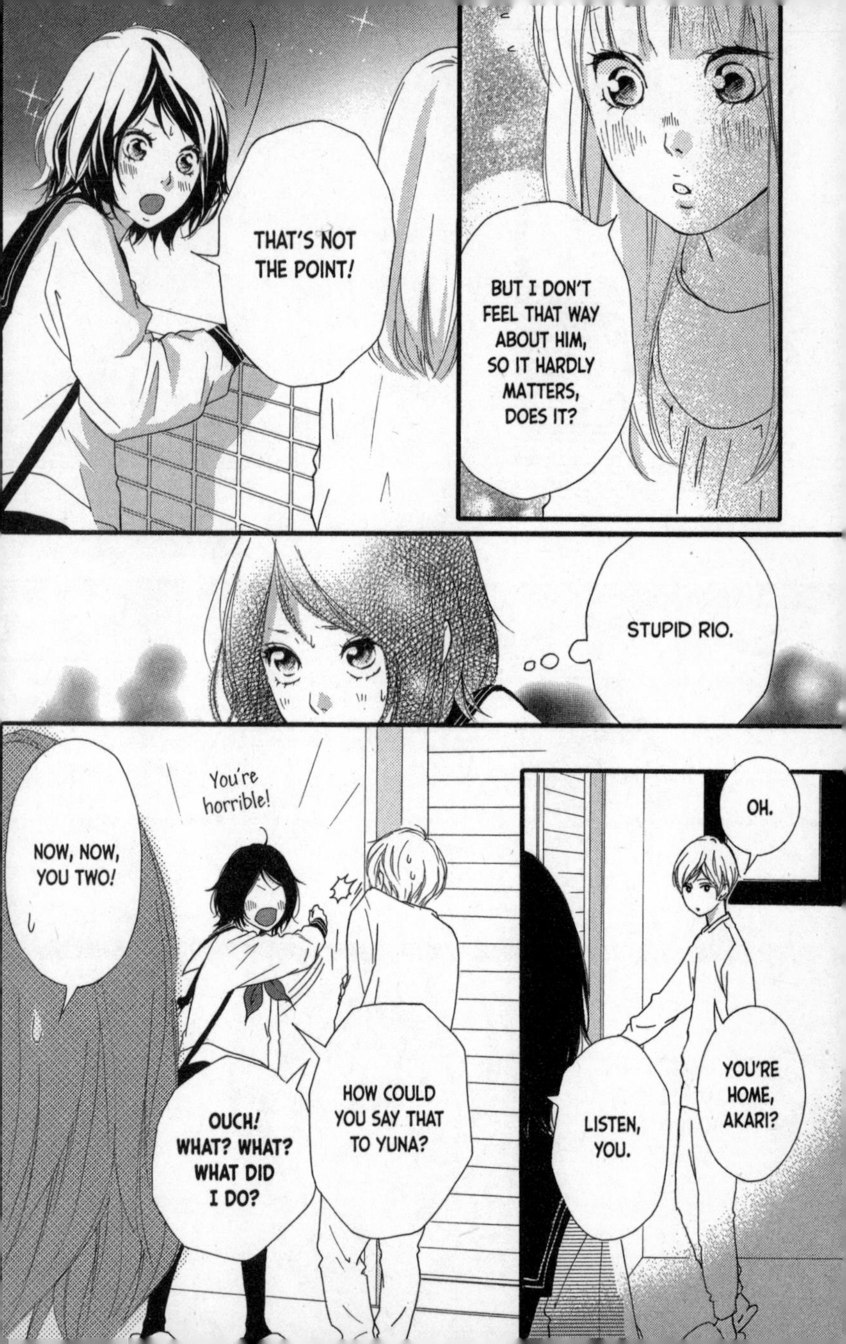
BUT I DON'T FEEL THAT WAY ABOUT HIM, SO IT HARDLY MATTERS, DOES IT?
THAT'S NOT THE POINT!
STUPID RIO.
OH.
YOU'RE HOME, AKARI?
LISTEN, YOU.
You're horrible!
NOW, NOW, YOU TWO!
HOW COULD YOU SAY THAT TO YUNA?
OUCH! WHAT? WHAT? WHAT DID I DO?

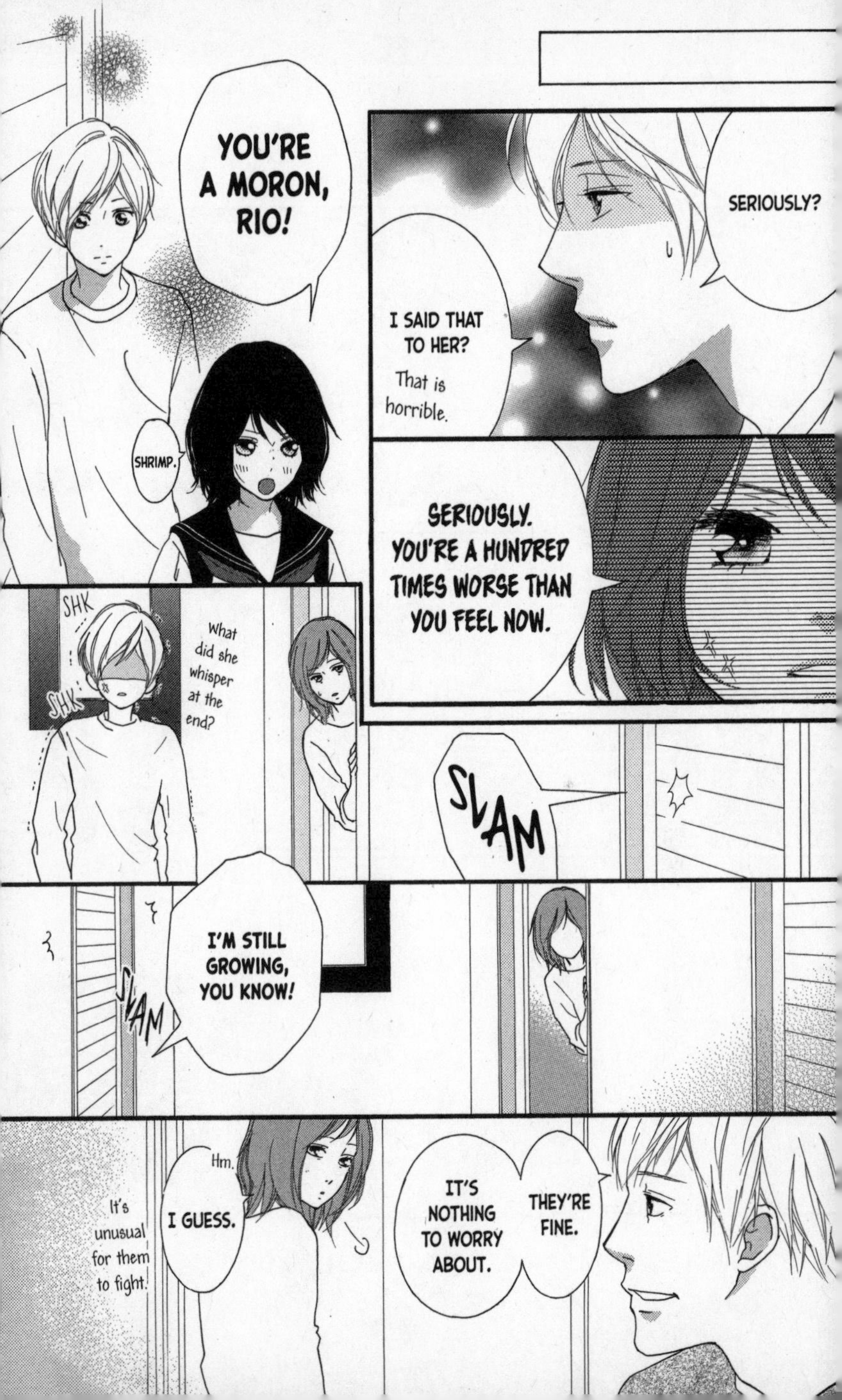
SERIOUSLY?
I SAID THAT TO HER?
That is horrible.
SERIOUSLY. YOU'RE A HUNDRED TIMES WORSE THAN YOU FEEL NOW.
YOU'RE A MORON, RIO!
SHRIMP.
SLAM
SHK
SHK
What did she whisper at the end?
I'M STILL GROWING, YOU KNOW!
SLAM
THEY'RE FINE.
IT'S NOTHING TO WORRY ABOUT.
Hm.
I GUESS.
It's unusual for them to fight.

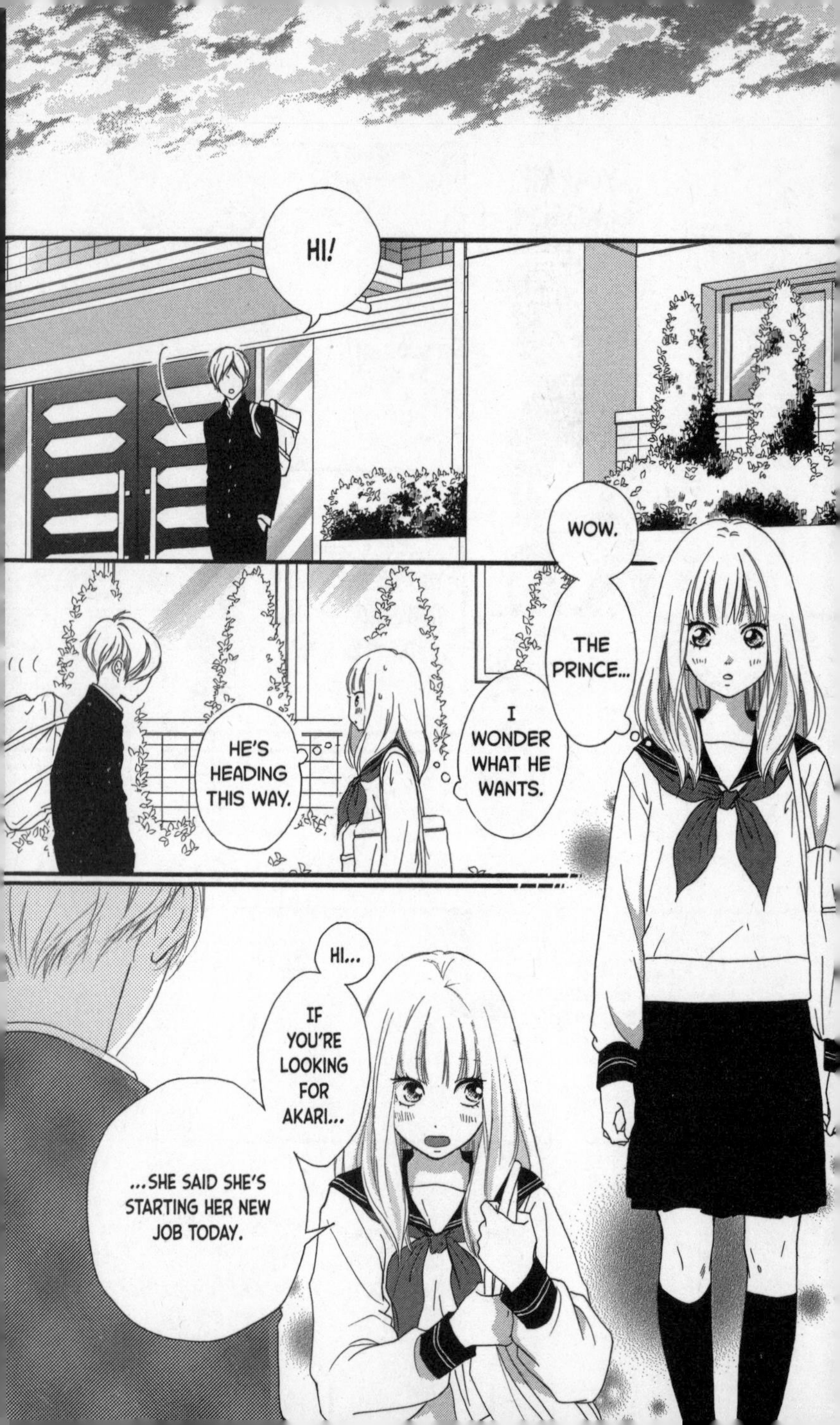
HI!
WOW. THE PRINCE...
I WONDER WHAT HE WANTS.
HE'S HEADING THIS WAY.
HI...
IF YOU'RE LOOKING FOR AKARI...
...SHE SAID SHE'S STARTING HER NEW JOB TODAY.

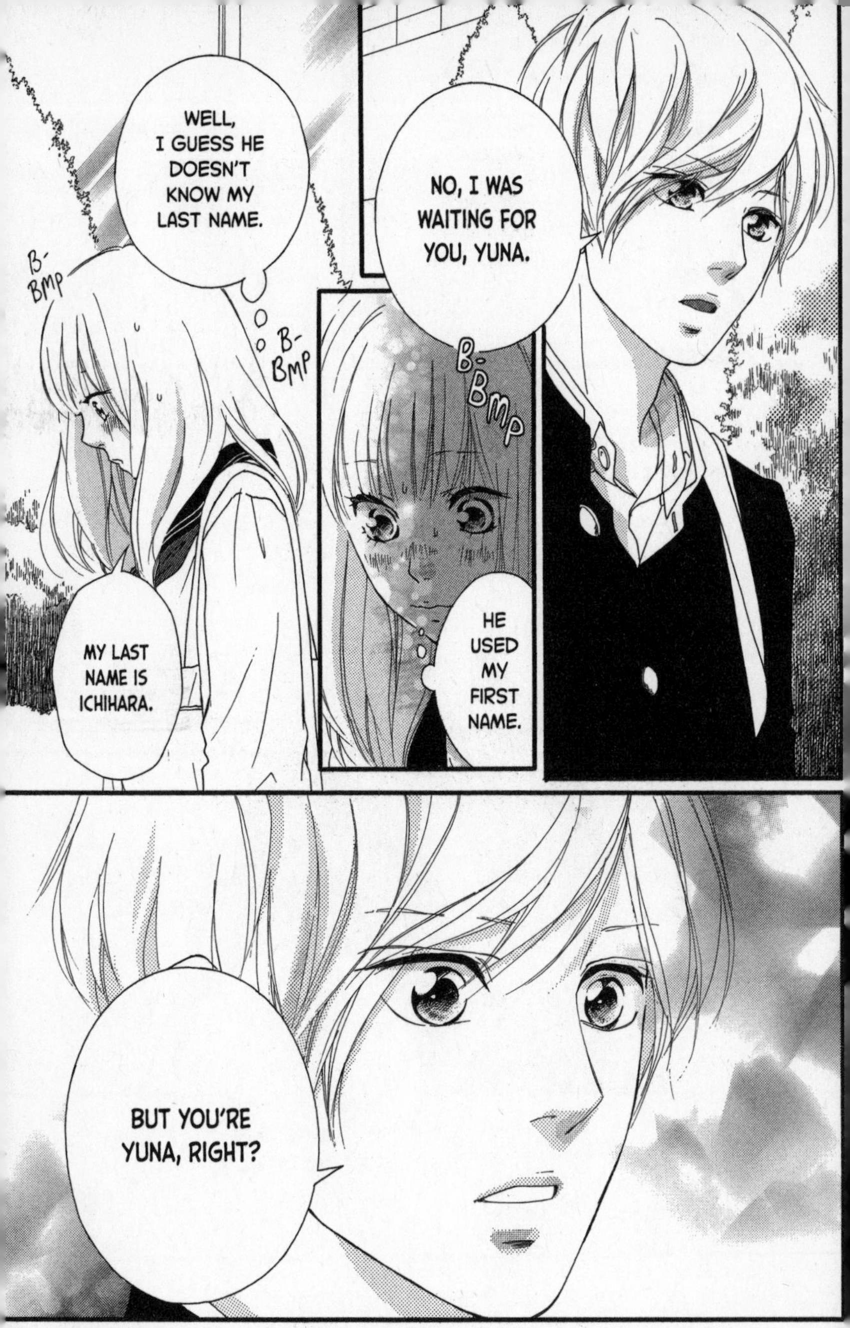
NO, I WAS WAITING FOR YOU, YUNA.
B-BMP
HE USED MY FIRST NAME.
B-BMP
WELL, I GUESS HE DOESN'T KNOW MY LAST NAME.
B-BMP
MY LAST NAME IS ICHIHARA.
BUT YOU'RE YUNA, RIGHT?

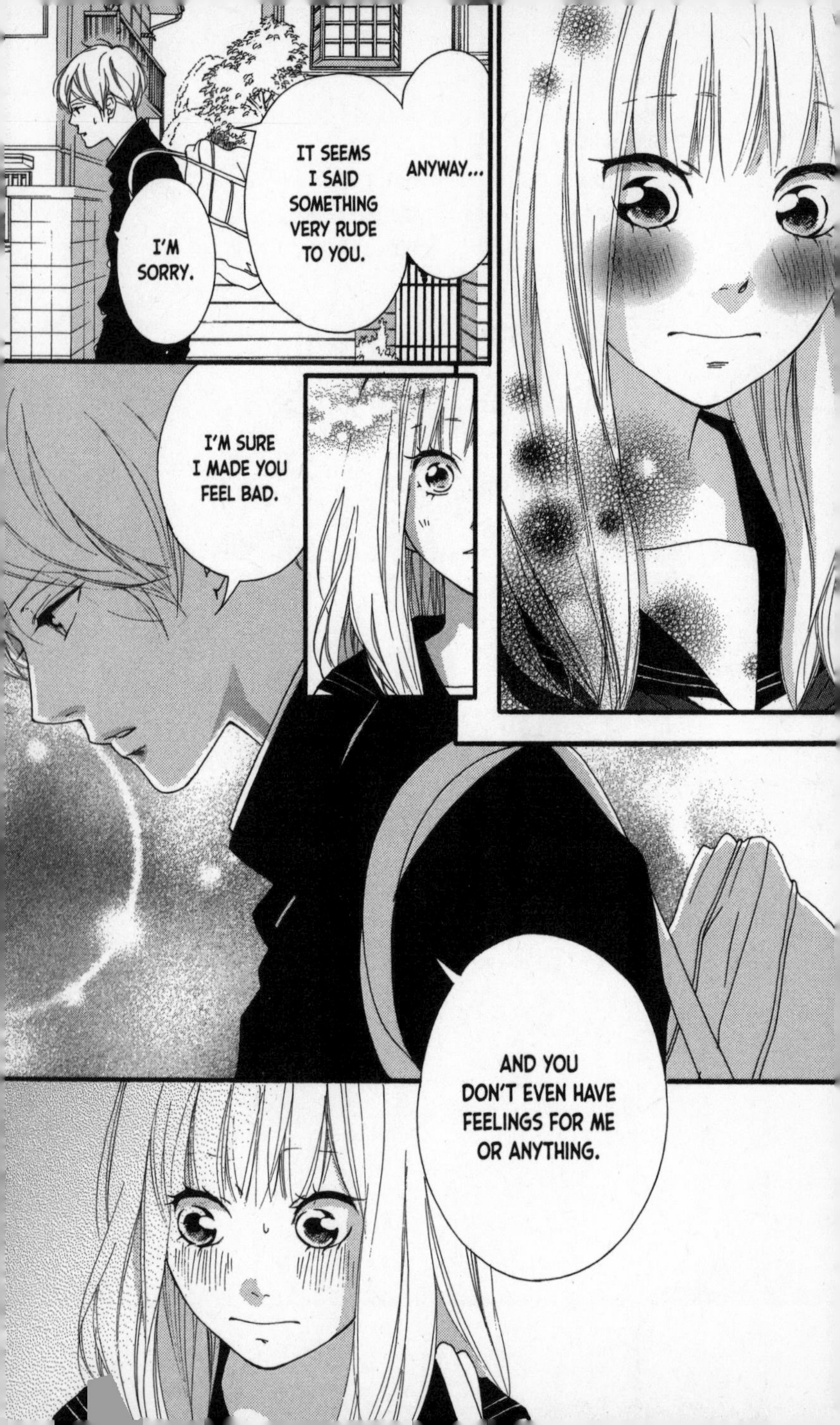
ANYWAY...
IT SEEMS I SAID SOMETHING VERY RUDE TO YOU.
I'M SORRY.
I'M SURE I MADE YOU FEEL BAD.
AND YOU DON'T EVEN HAVE FEELINGS FOR ME OR ANYTHING.

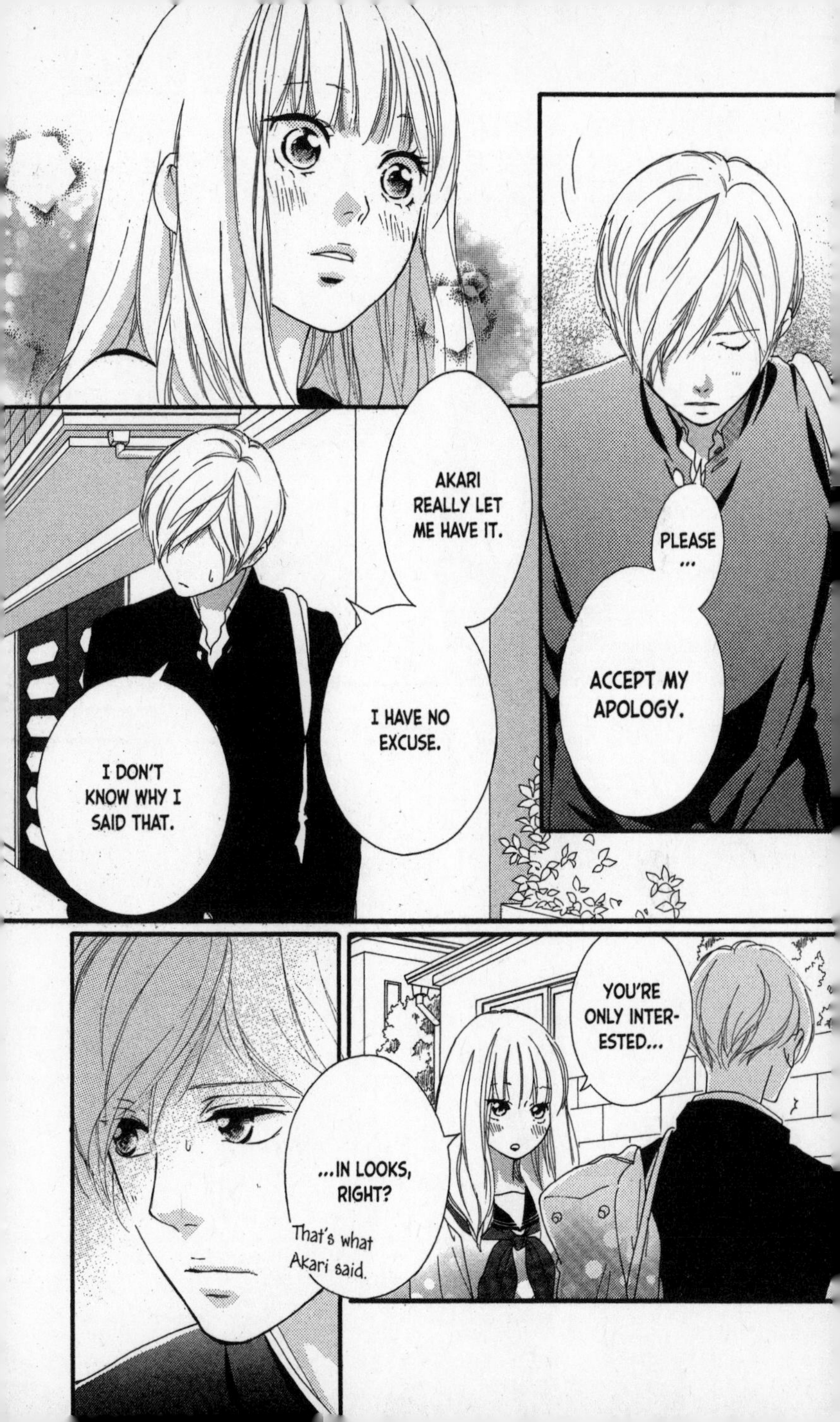
PLEASE...
ACCEPT MY APOLOGY.
AKARI REALLY LET ME HAVE IT.
I HAVE NO EXCUSE.
I DON'T KNOW WHY I SAID THAT.
YOU'RE ONLY INTER-ESTED...
...IN LOOKS, RIGHT?
That's what Akari said.

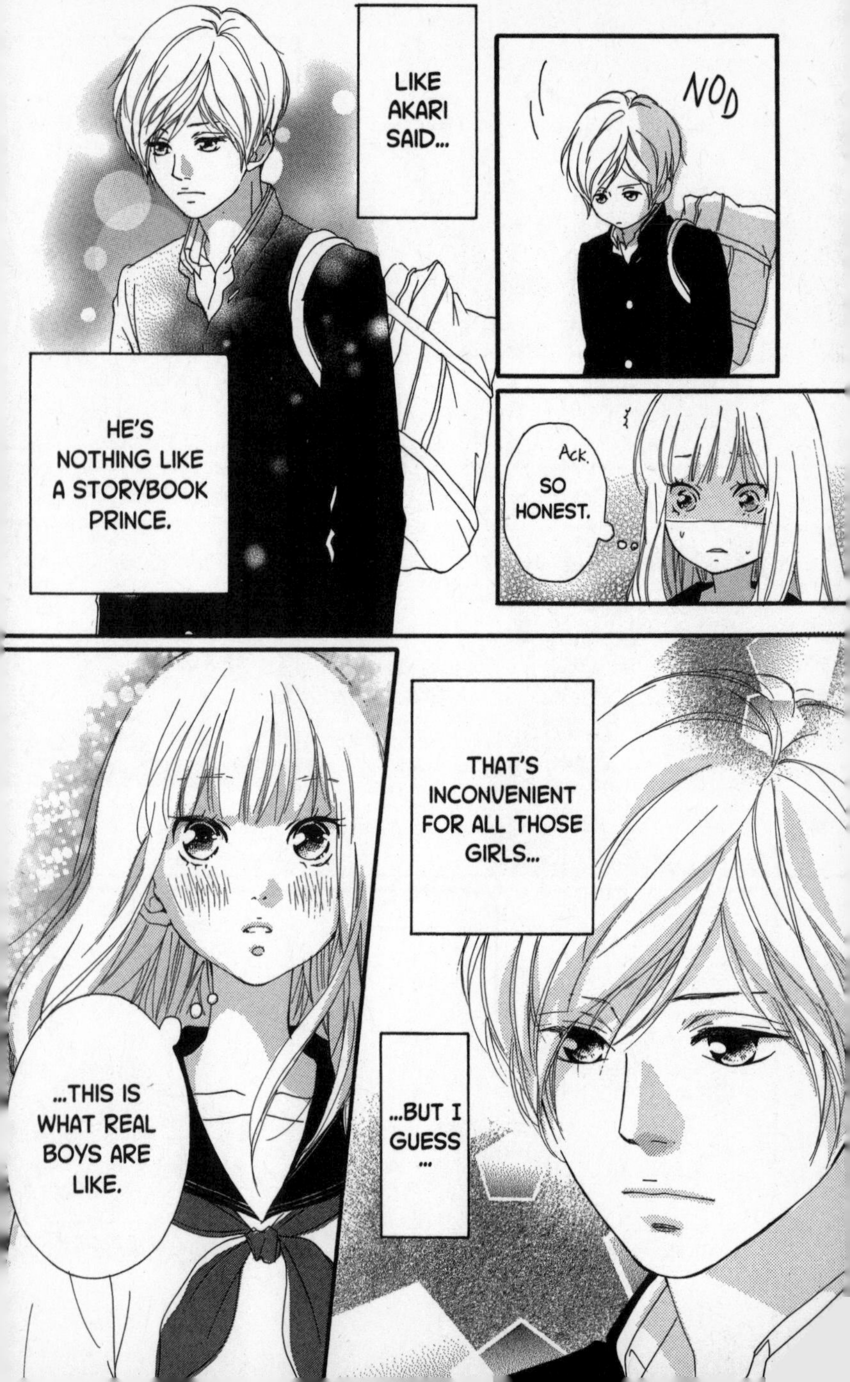
NOD
Ack.
SO HONEST.
LIKE AKARI SAID...
HE'S NOTHING LIKE A STORYBOOK PRINCE.
THAT'S INCONVENIENT FOR ALL THOSE GIRLS...
...BUT I GUESS...
...THIS IS WHAT REAL BOYS ARE LIKE.

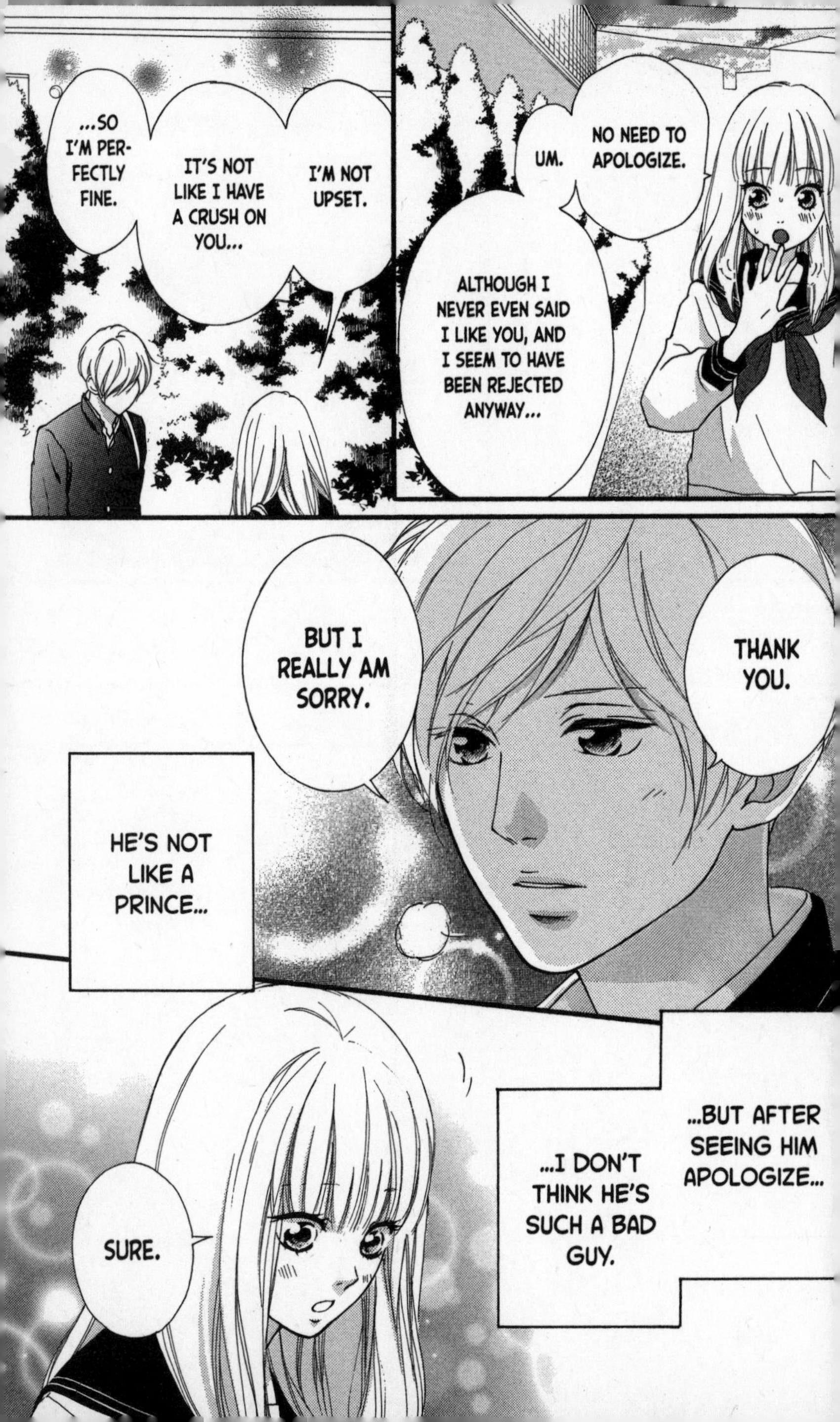
NO NEED TO APOLOGIZE.
UM.
ALTHOUGH I NEVER EVEN SAID I LIKE YOU, AND I SEEM TO HAVE BEEN REJECTED ANYWAY...
I'M NOT UPSET.
IT'S NOT LIKE I HAVE A CRUSH ON YOU...
...SO I'M PER-FECTLY FINE.
THANK YOU.
BUT I REALLY AM SORRY.
HE'S NOT LIKE A PRINCE...
...BUT AFTER SEEING HIM APOLOGIZE...
...I DON'T THINK HE'S SUCH A BAD GUY.
SURE.

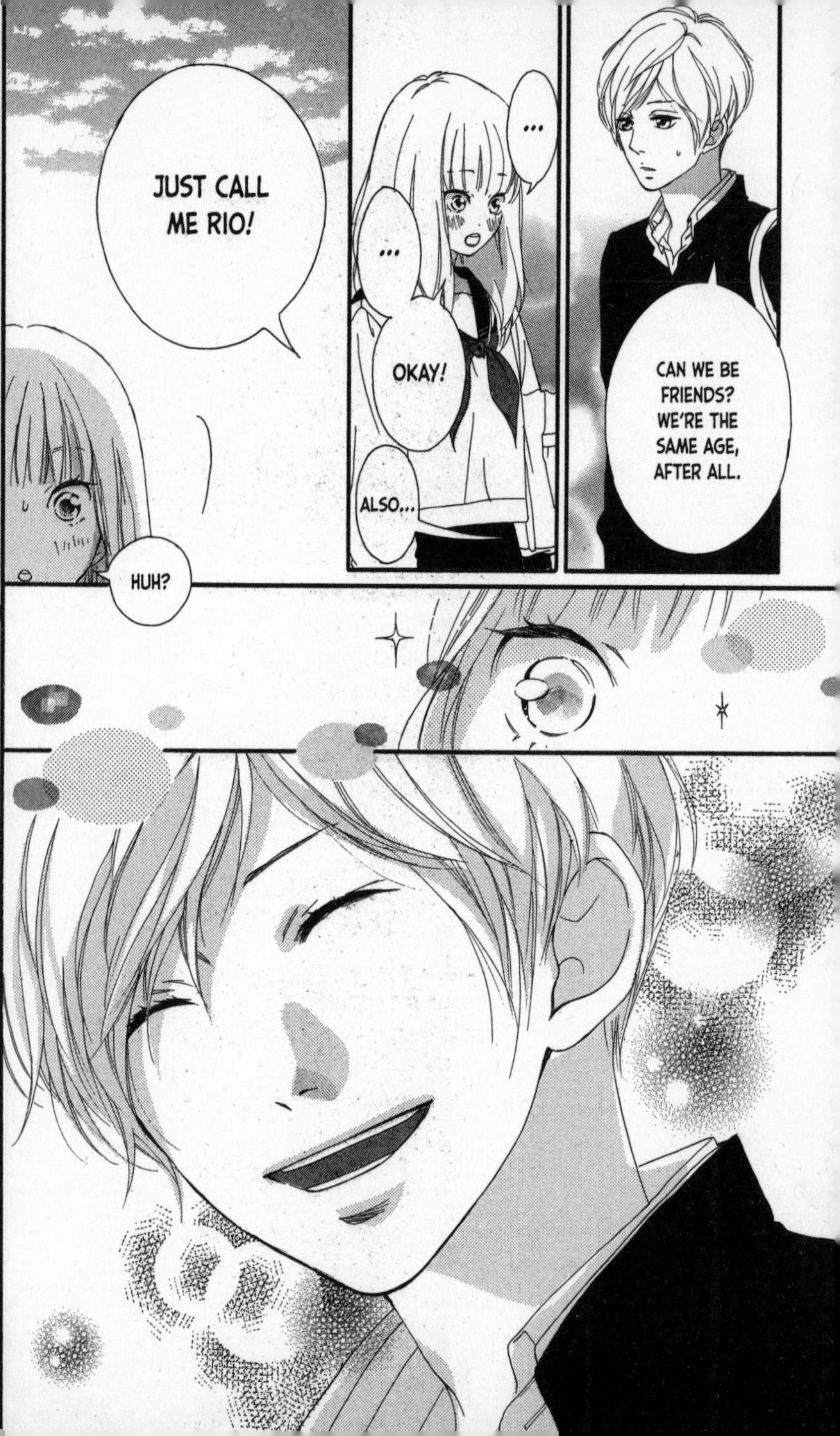
CAN WE BE FRIENDS? WE'RE THE SAME AGE, AFTER ALL.
...
...
OKAY!
ALSO...
JUST CALL ME RIO!
HUH?

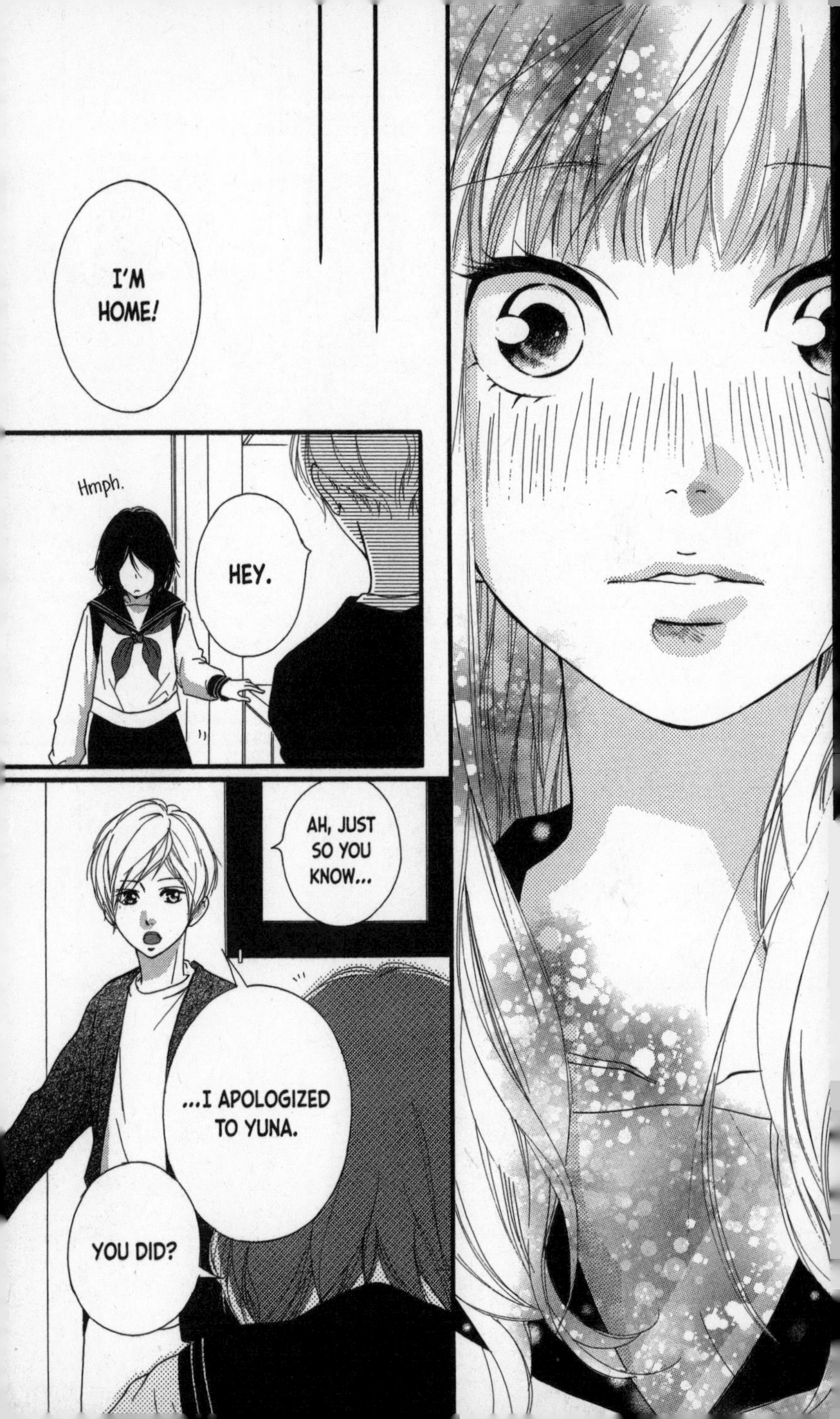
I'M HOME!
HEY.
Hmph.
AH, JUST SO YOU KNOW...
...I APOLOGIZED TO YUNA.
YOU DID?

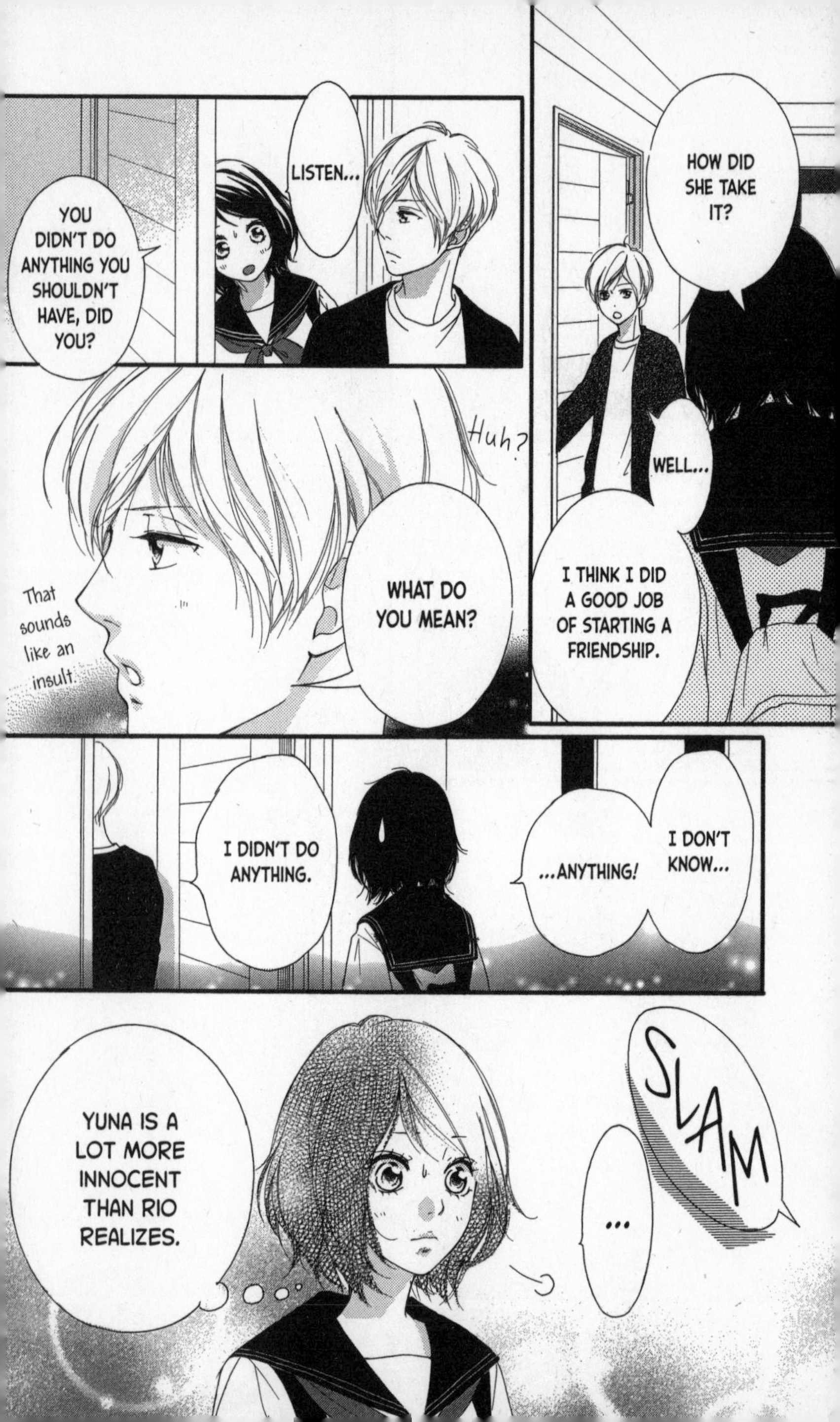
HOW DID SHE TAKE IT?
WELL...
I THINK I DID A GOOD JOB OF STARTING A FRIENDSHIP.
LISTEN...
YOU DIDN'T DO ANYTHING YOU SHOULDN'T HAVE, DID YOU?
Huh?
WHAT DO YOU MEAN?
That sounds like an insult.
I DON'T KNOW...
...ANYTHING!
I DIDN'T DO ANYTHING.
SLAM
...
YUNA IS A LOT MORE INNOCENT THAN RIO REALIZES.

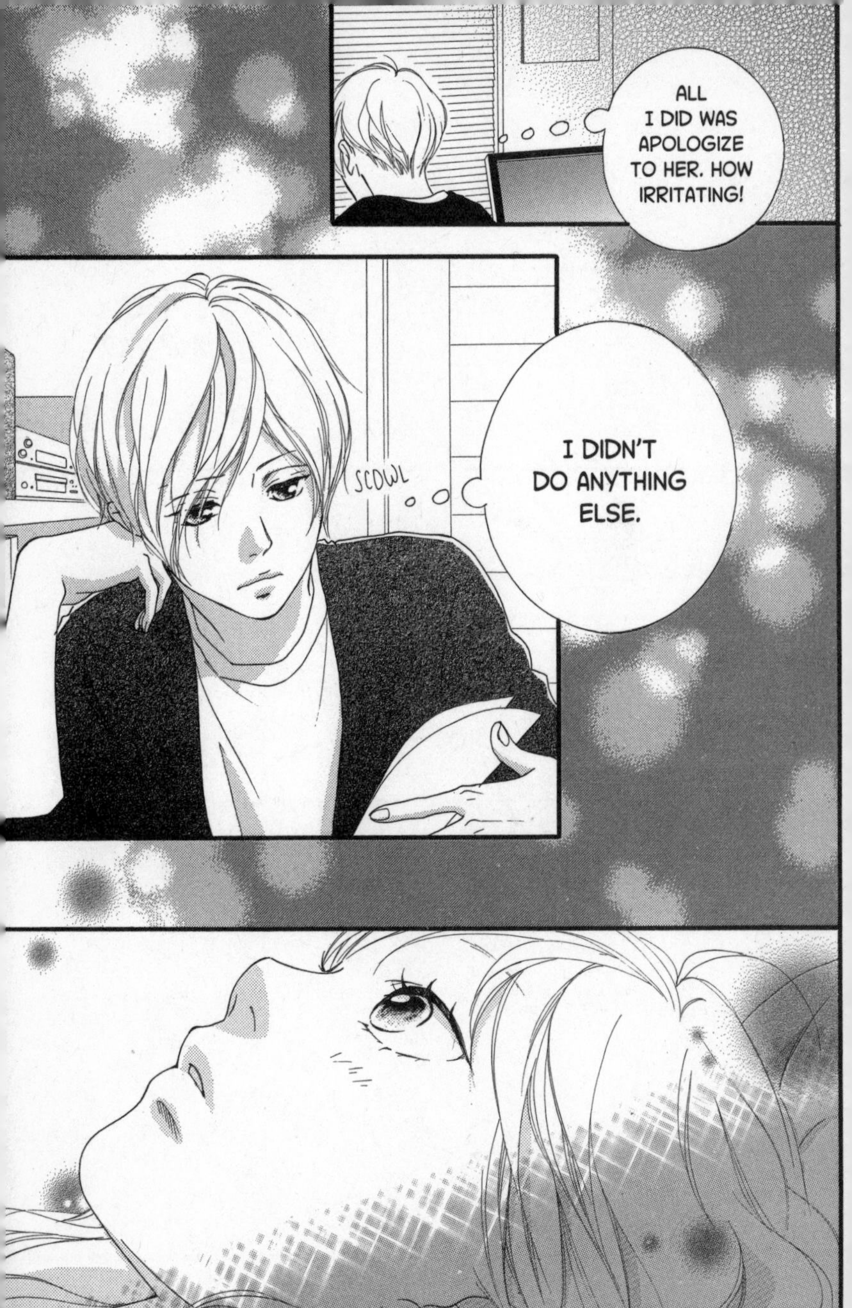
ALL I DID WAS APOLOGIZE TO HER. HOW IRRITATING!
I DIDN'T DO ANYTHING ELSE.
SCOWL

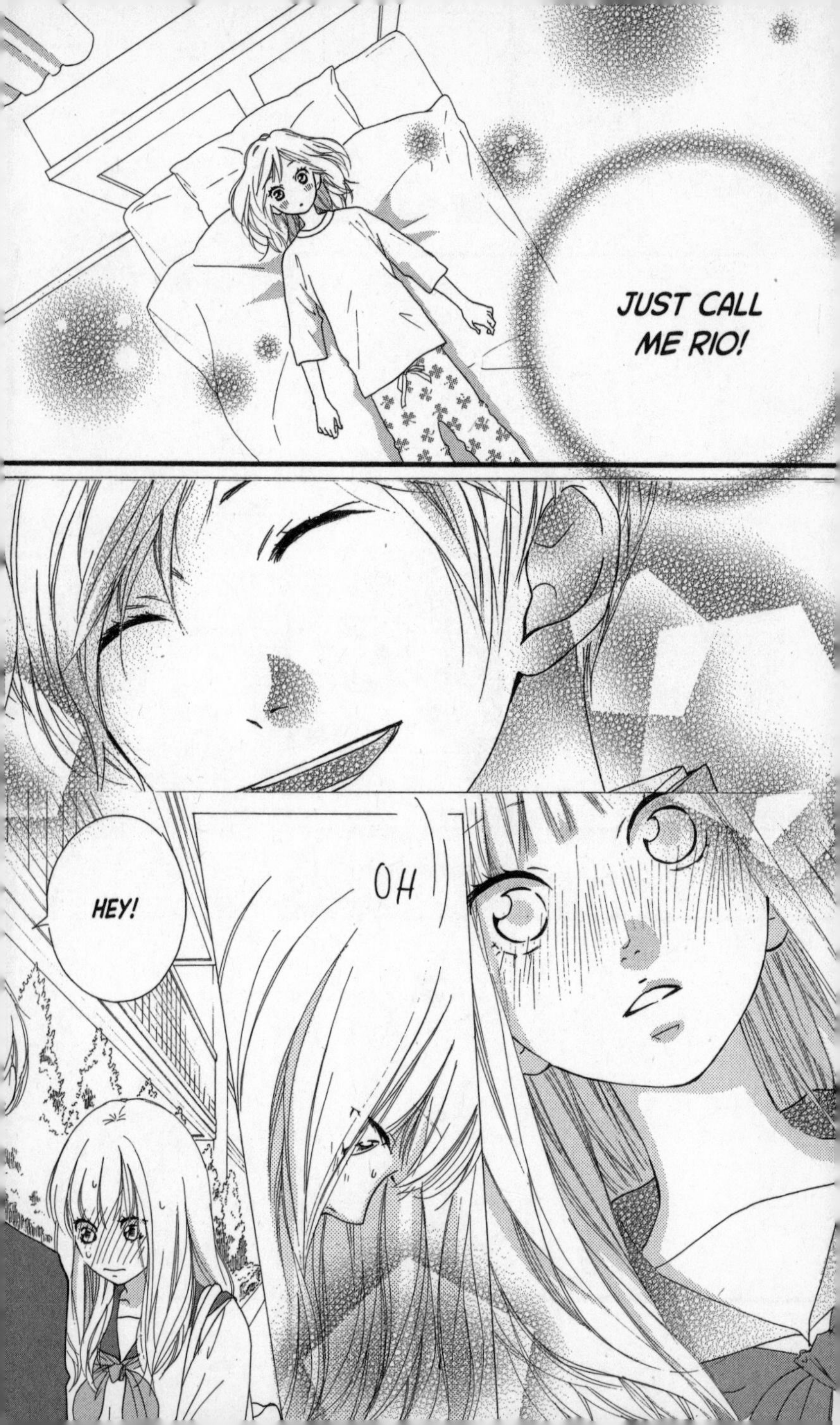
JUST CALL ME RIO!
OH
HEY!

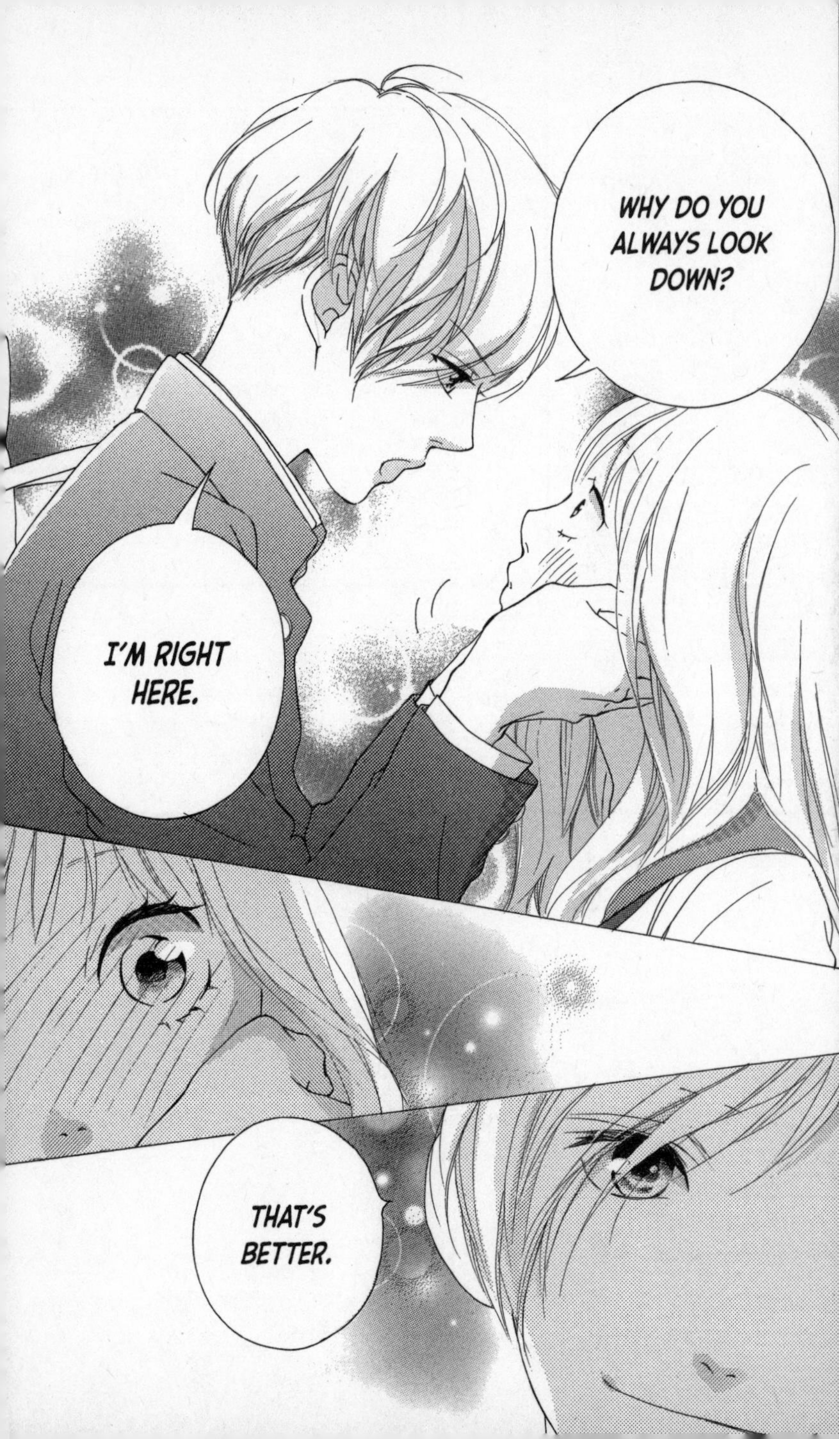
WHY DO YOU ALWAYS LOOK DOWN?
I'M RIGHT HERE.
THAT'S BETTER.

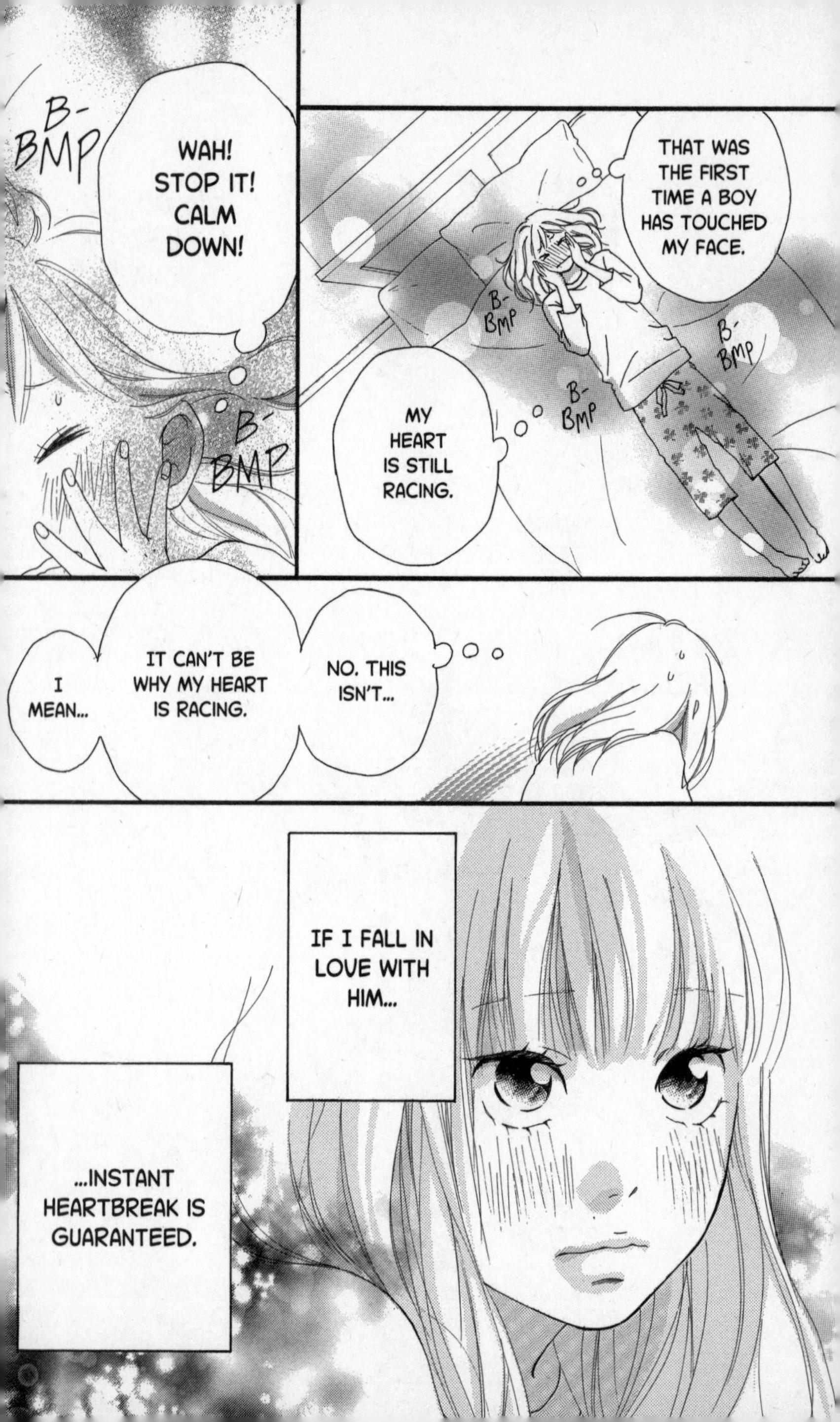
THAT WAS THE FIRST TIME A BOY HAS TOUCHED MY FACE.
B-BMP
B-BMP
B-BMP
MY HEART IS STILL RACING.
B-BMP
WAH! STOP IT! CALM DOWN!
B-BMP
NO. THIS ISN'T...
IT CAN'T BE WHY MY HEART IS RACING.
I MEAN...
IF I FALL IN LOVE WITH HIM...
...INSTANT HEARTBREAK IS GUARANTEED.

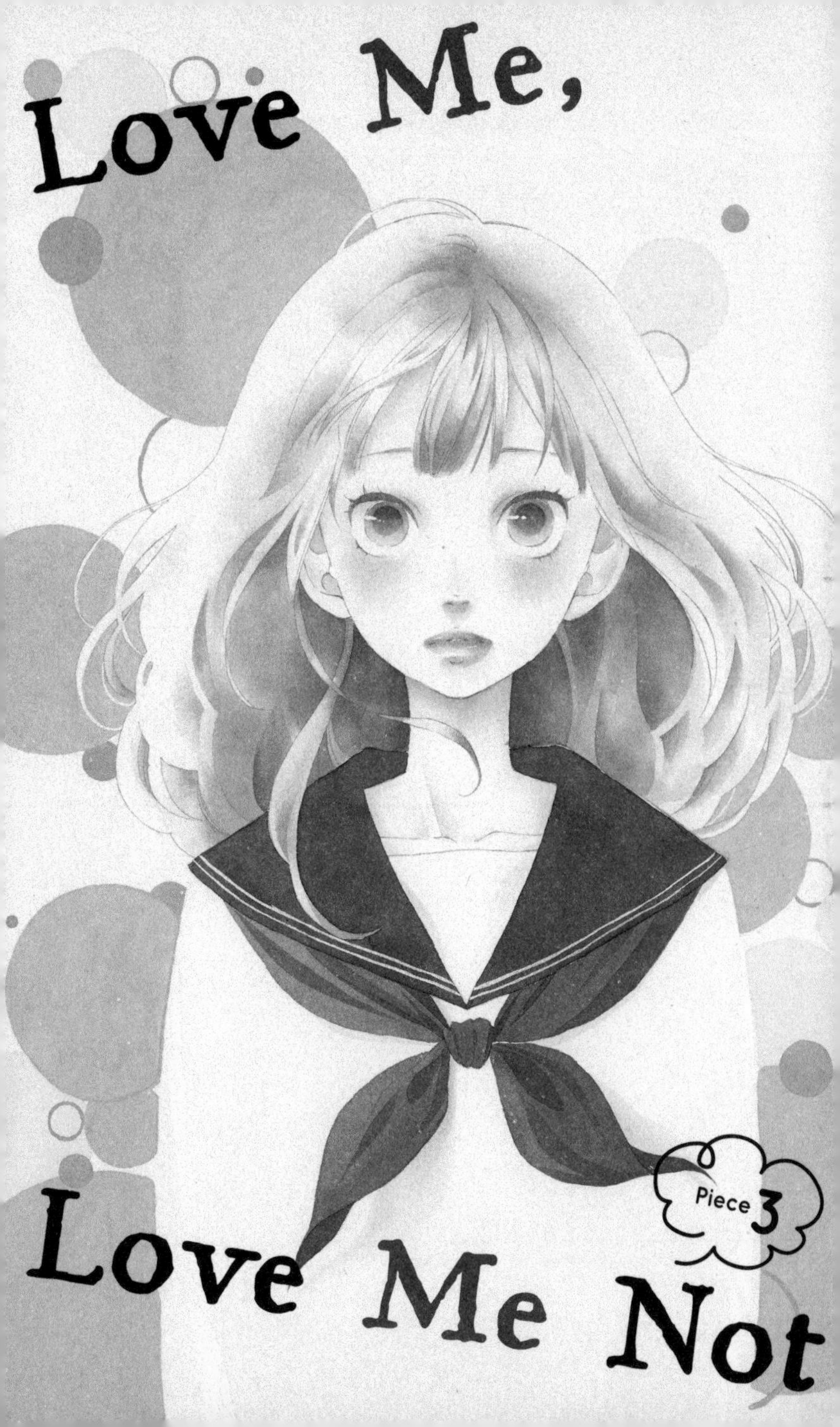
Love Me,
Love Me Not
Piece 3

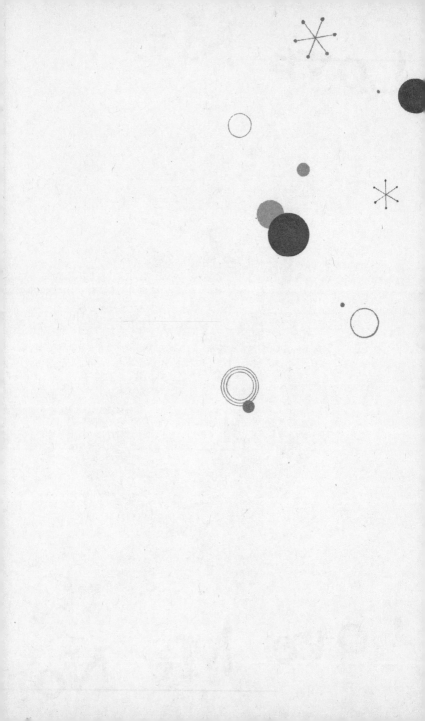

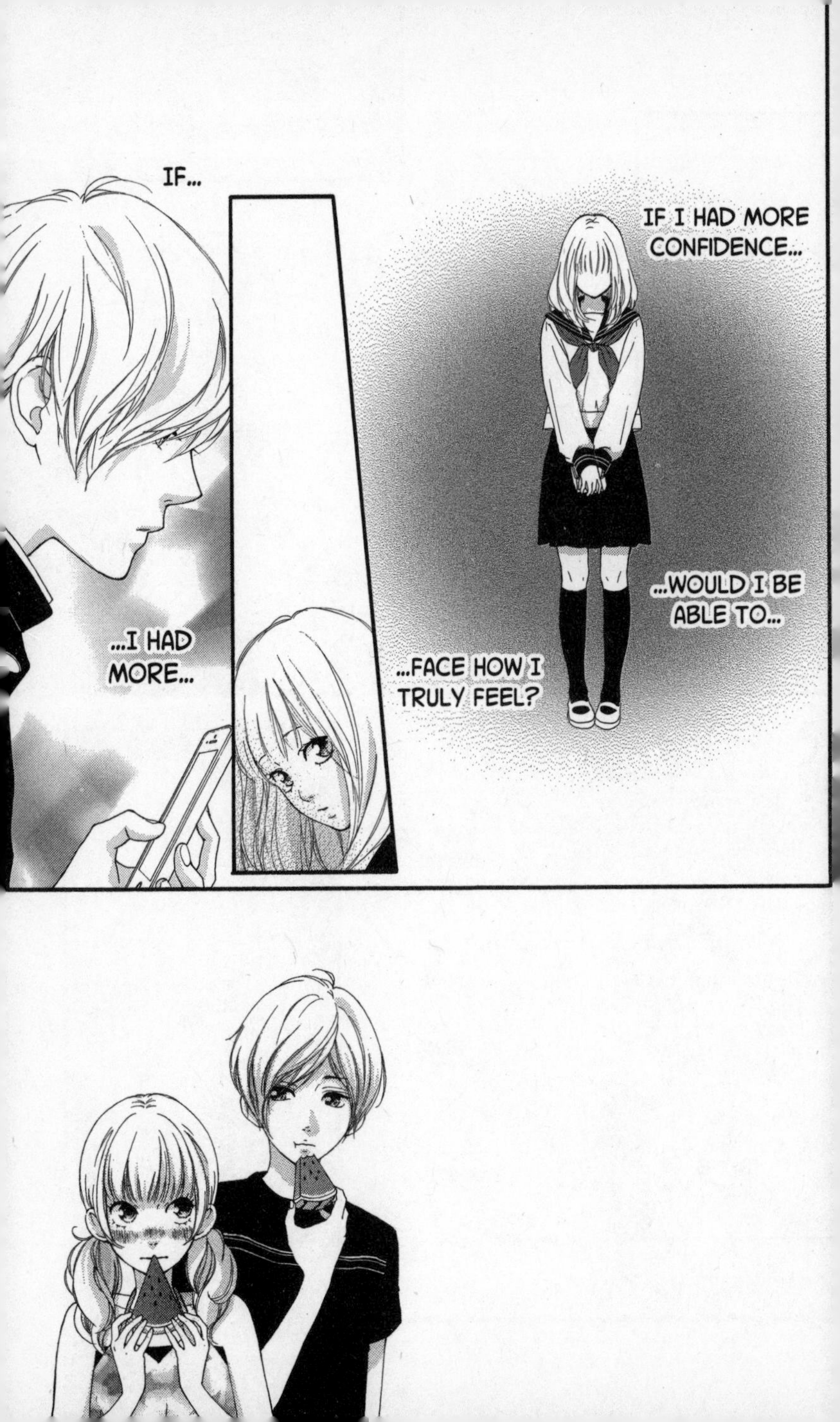
IF I HAD MORE CONFIDENCE...
...WOULD I BE ABLE TO...
...FACE HOW I TRULY FEEL?
IF...
...I HAD MORE...

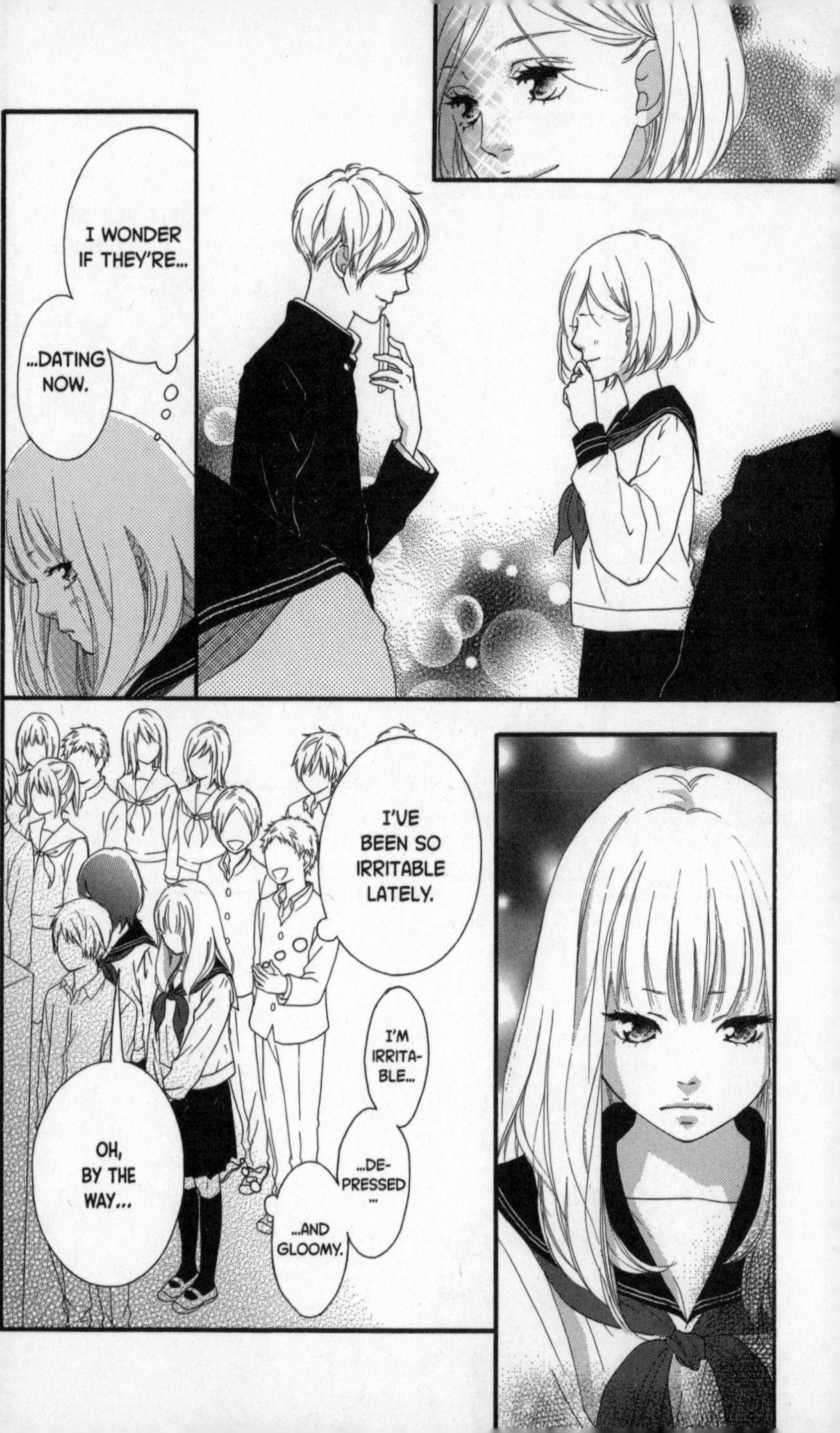
I WONDER IF THEY'RE...
...DATING NOW.
I'VE BEEN SO IRRITABLE LATELY.
I'M IRRITA-BLE...
...DE-PRESSED...
...AND GLOOMY.
OH, BY THE WAY...

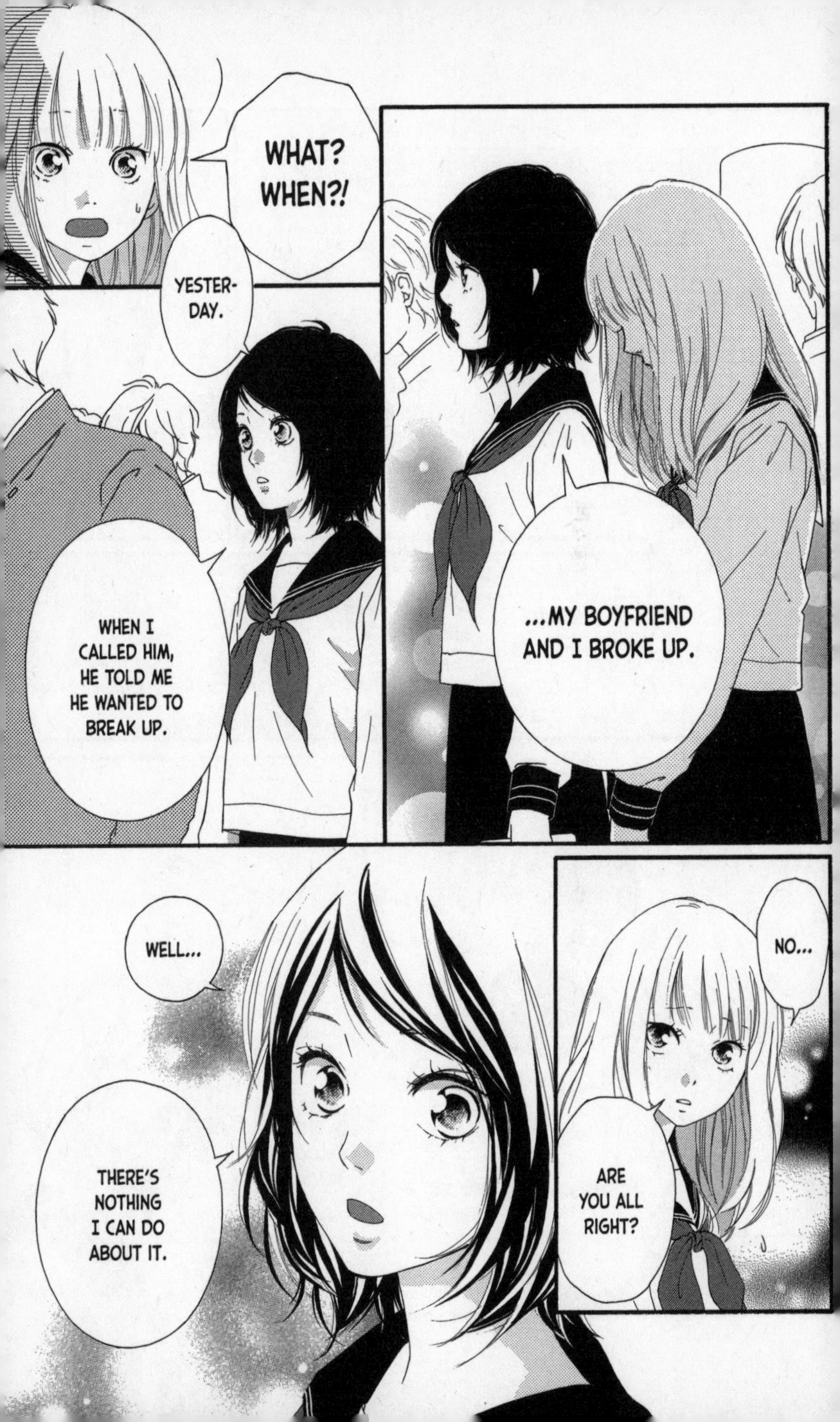
...MY BOYFRIEND AND I BROKE UP.
WHAT? WHEN?!
YESTER-DAY.
WHEN I CALLED HIM, HE TOLD ME HE WANTED TO BREAK UP.
NO...
ARE YOU ALL RIGHT?
WELL...
THERE'S NOTHING I CAN DO ABOUT IT.

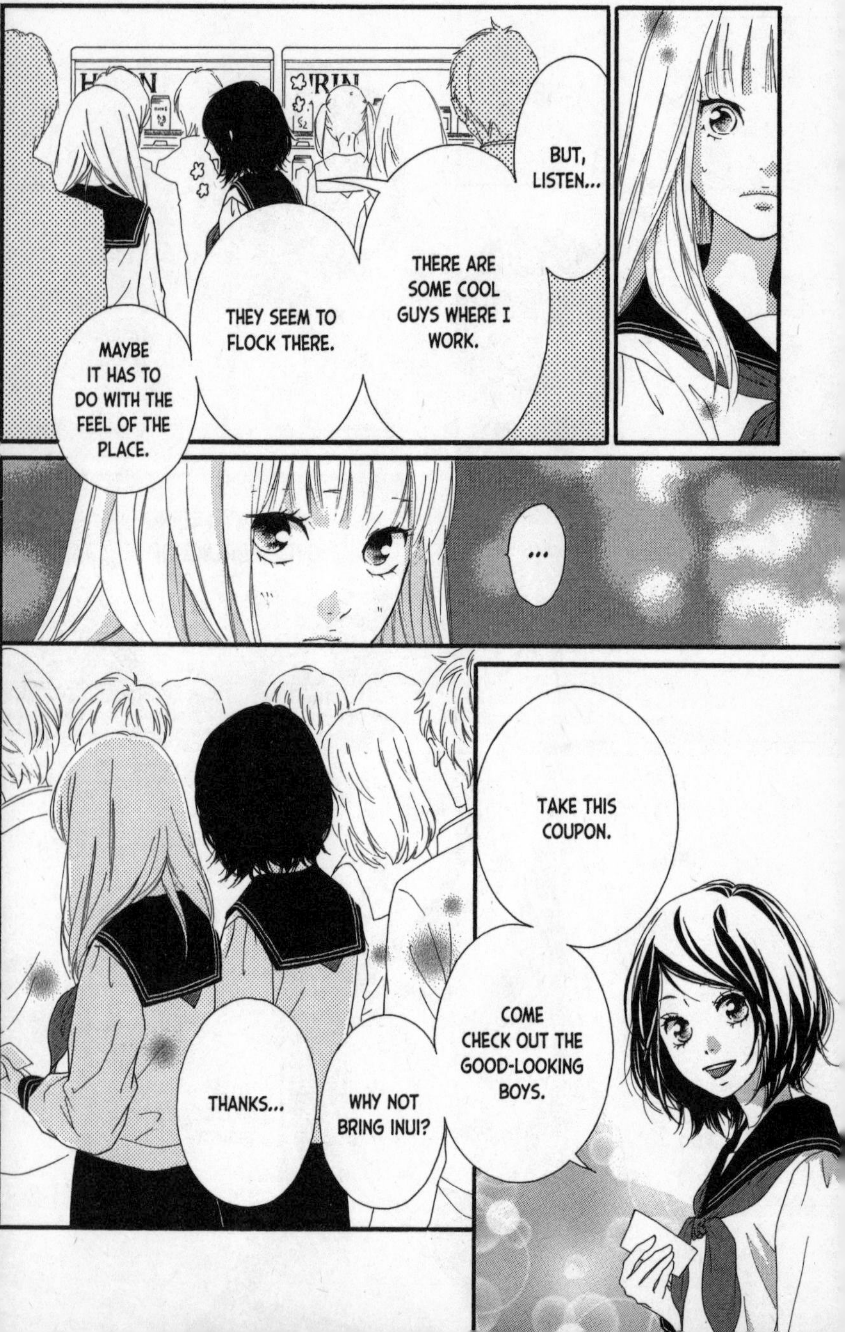
BUT, LISTEN...
THERE ARE SOME COOL GUYS WHERE I WORK.
THEY SEEM TO FLOCK THERE.
MAYBE IT HAS TO DO WITH THE FEEL OF THE PLACE.
...
TAKE THIS COUPON.
COME CHECK OUT THE GOOD-LOOKING BOYS.
WHY NOT BRING INUI?
THANKS...

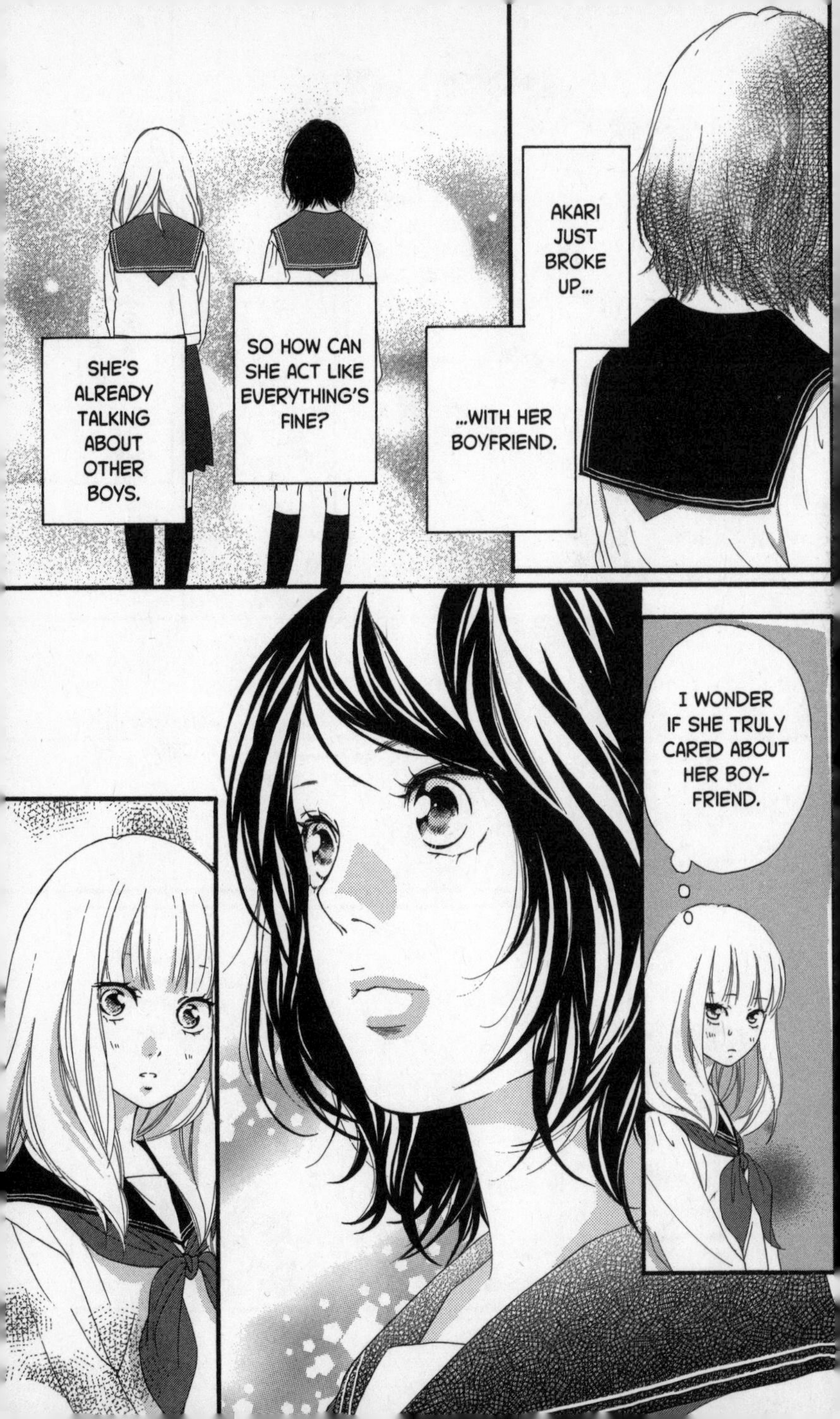
AKARI JUST BROKE UP...
...WITH HER BOYFRIEND.
SO HOW CAN SHE ACT LIKE EVERYTHING'S FINE?
SHE'S ALREADY TALKING ABOUT OTHER BOYS.
I WONDER IF SHE TRULY CARED ABOUT HER BOY-FRIEND.

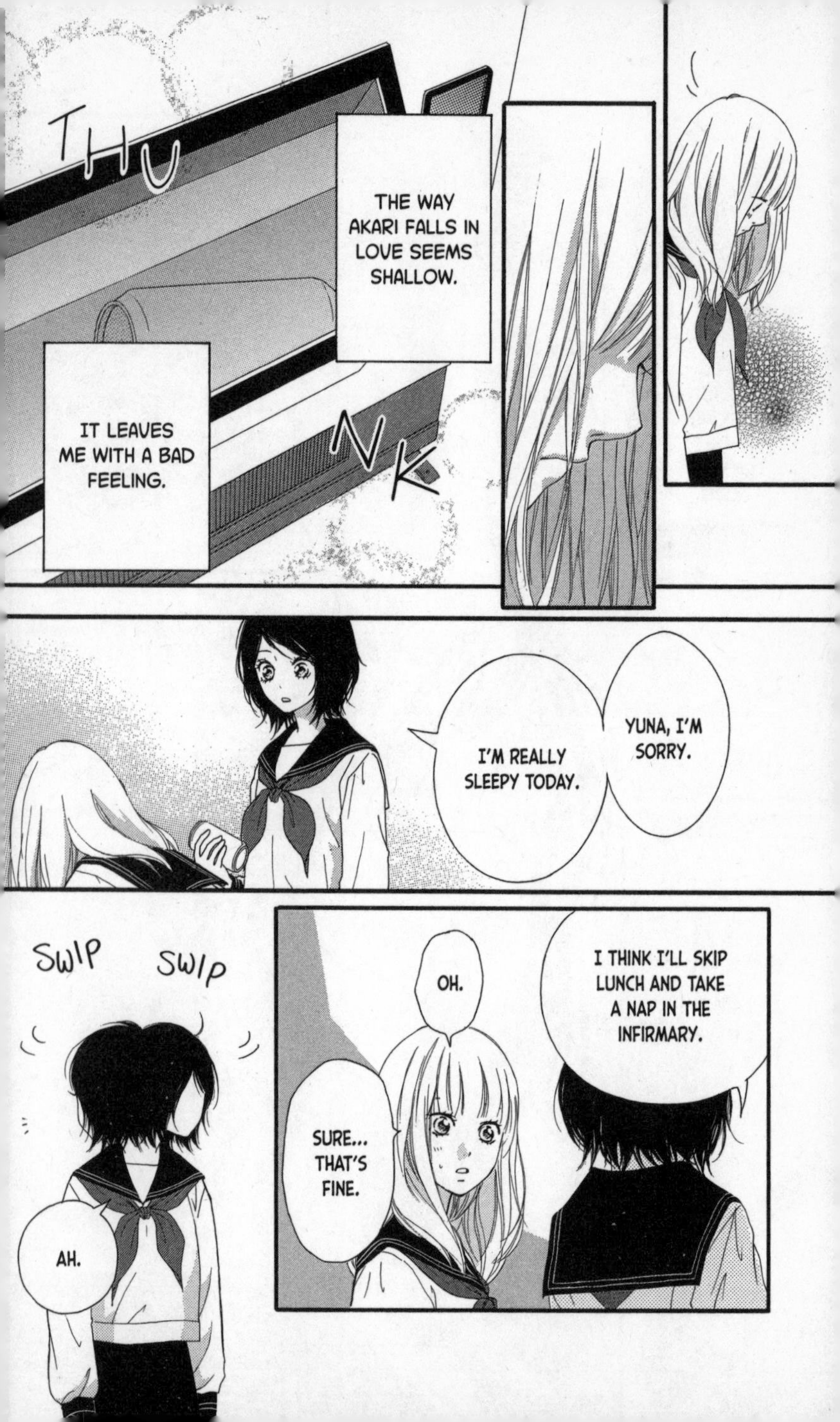
THE WAY AKARI FALLS IN LOVE SEEMS SHALLOW.
THUNK
IT LEAVES ME WITH A BAD FEELING.
YUNA, I'M SORRY.
I'M REALLY SLEEPY TODAY.
I THINK I'LL SKIP LUNCH AND TAKE A NAP IN THE INFIRMARY.
OH.
SURE... THAT'S FINE.
SWIP SWIP
AH.

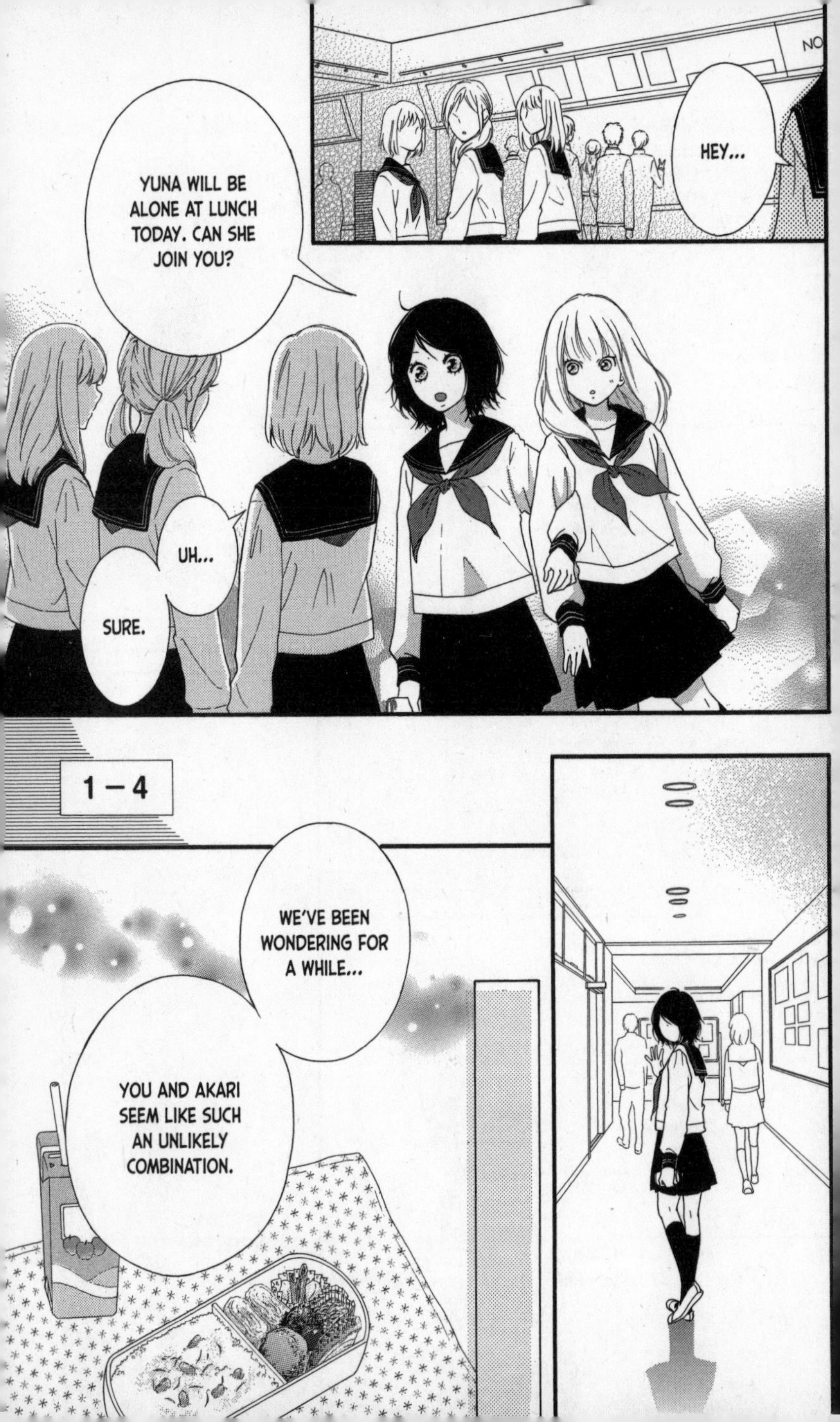
NO
HEY...
YUNA WILL BE ALONE AT LUNCH TODAY. CAN SHE JOIN YOU?
UH...
SURE.
1-4
WE'VE BEEN WONDERING FOR A WHILE...
YOU AND AKARI SEEM LIKE SUCH AN UNLIKELY COMBINATION.

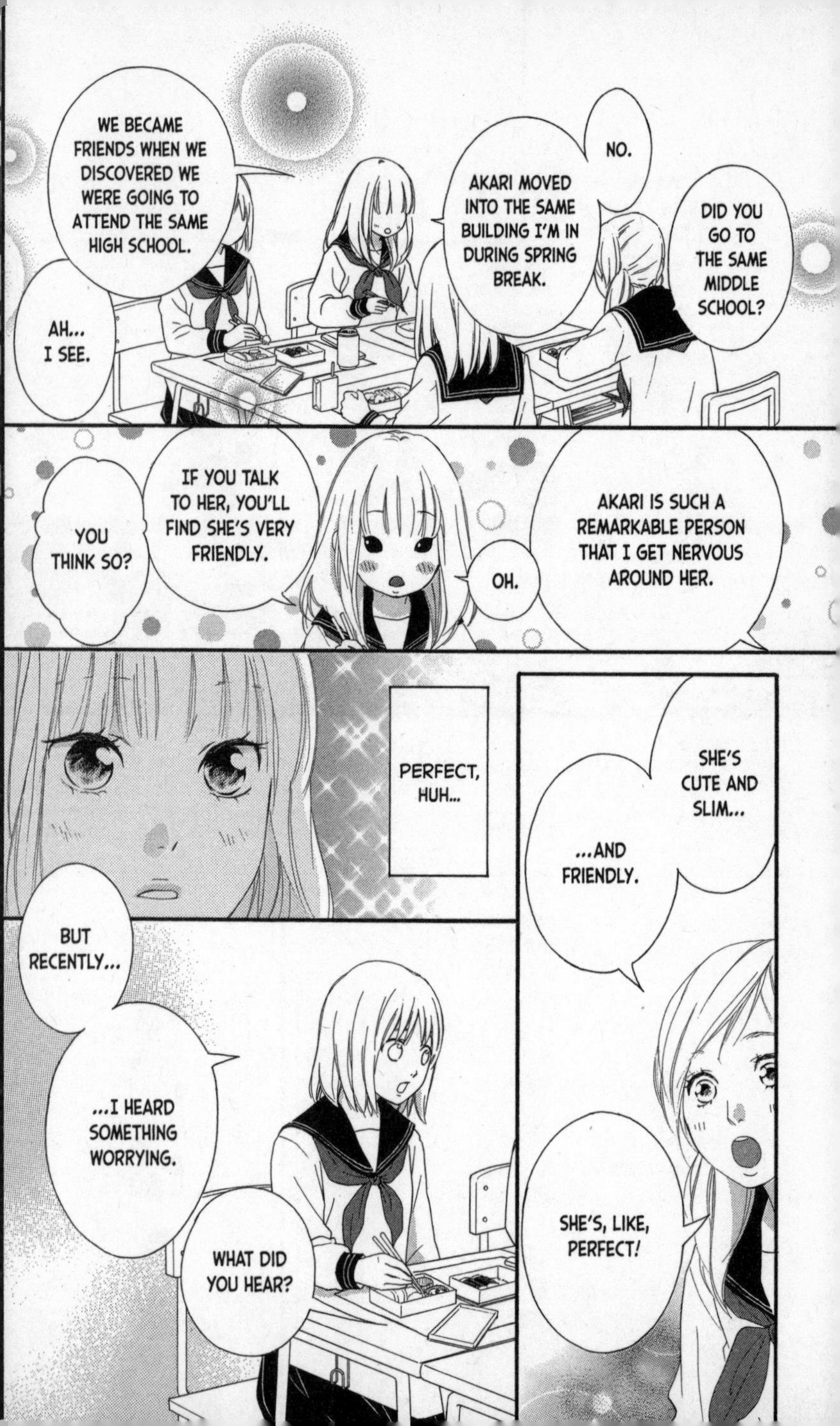
DID YOU GO TO THE SAME MIDDLE SCHOOL?
NO.
AKARI MOVED INTO THE SAME BUILDING I'M IN DURING SPRING BREAK.
WE BECAME FRIENDS WHEN WE DISCOVERED WE WERE GOING TO ATTEND THE SAME HIGH SCHOOL.
AH... I SEE.
AKARI IS SUCH A REMARKABLE PERSON THAT I GET NERVOUS AROUND HER.
OH.
IF YOU TALK TO HER, YOU'LL FIND SHE'S VERY FRIENDLY.
YOU THINK SO?
SHE'S CUTE AND SLIM...
...AND FRIENDLY.
SHE'S, LIKE, PERFECT!
PERFECT, HUH...
BUT RECENTLY...
...I HEARD SOMETHING WORRYING.
WHAT DID YOU HEAR?

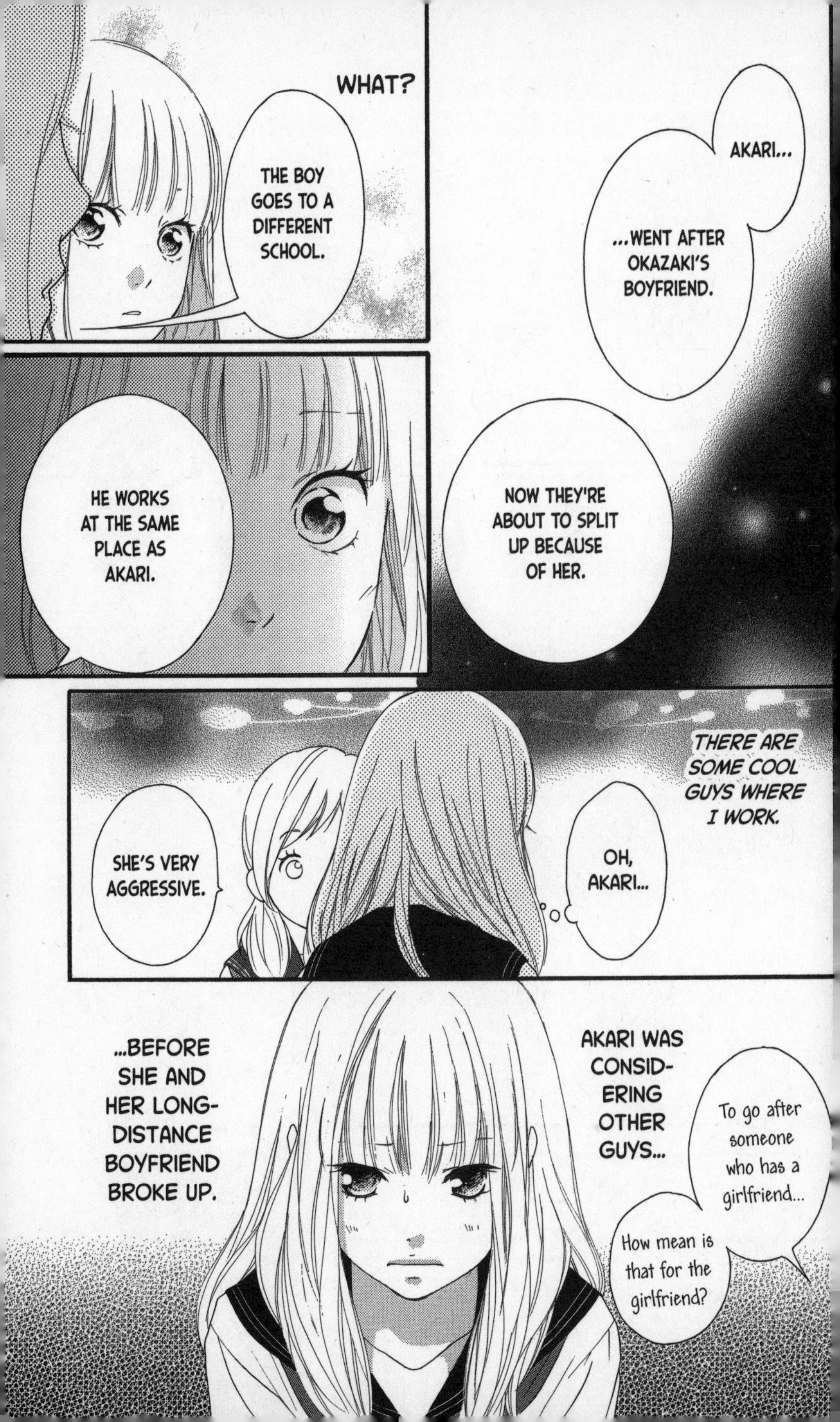
AKARI...
...WENT AFTER OKAZAKI'S BOYFRIEND.
NOW THEY'RE ABOUT TO SPLIT UP BECAUSE OF HER.
WHAT?
THE BOY GOES TO A DIFFERENT SCHOOL.
HE WORKS AT THE SAME PLACE AS AKARI.
THERE ARE SOME COOL GUYS WHERE I WORK.
OH, AKARI...
SHE'S VERY AGGRESSIVE.
AKARI WAS CONSID-ERING OTHER GUYS...
To go after someone who has a girlfriend...
How mean is that for the girlfriend?
...BEFORE SHE AND HER LONG-DISTANCE BOYFRIEND BROKE UP.

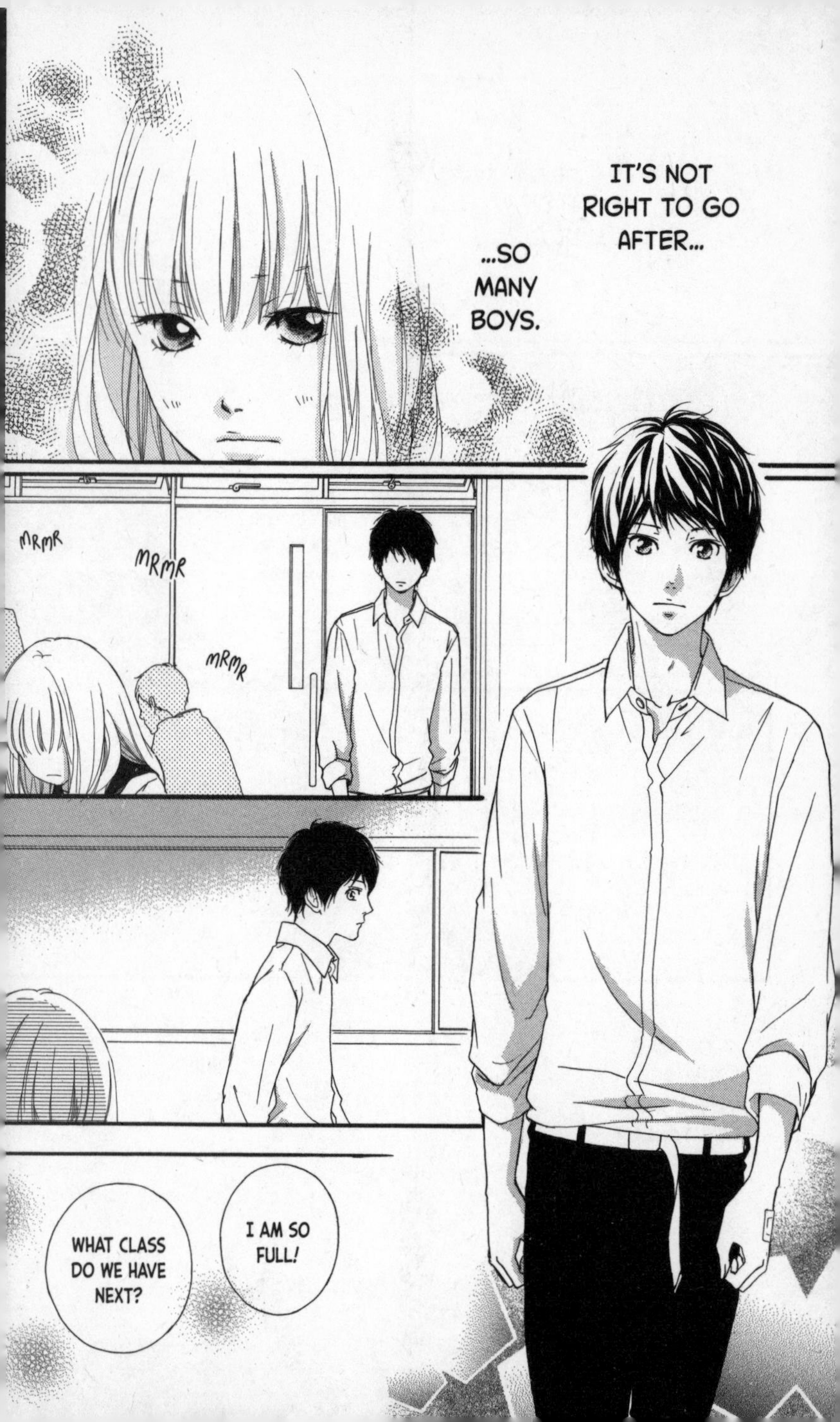
IT'S NOT RIGHT TO GO AFTER...
...SO MANY BOYS.
MRMR
MRMR
MRMR
I AM SO FULL!
WHAT CLASS DO WE HAVE NEXT?

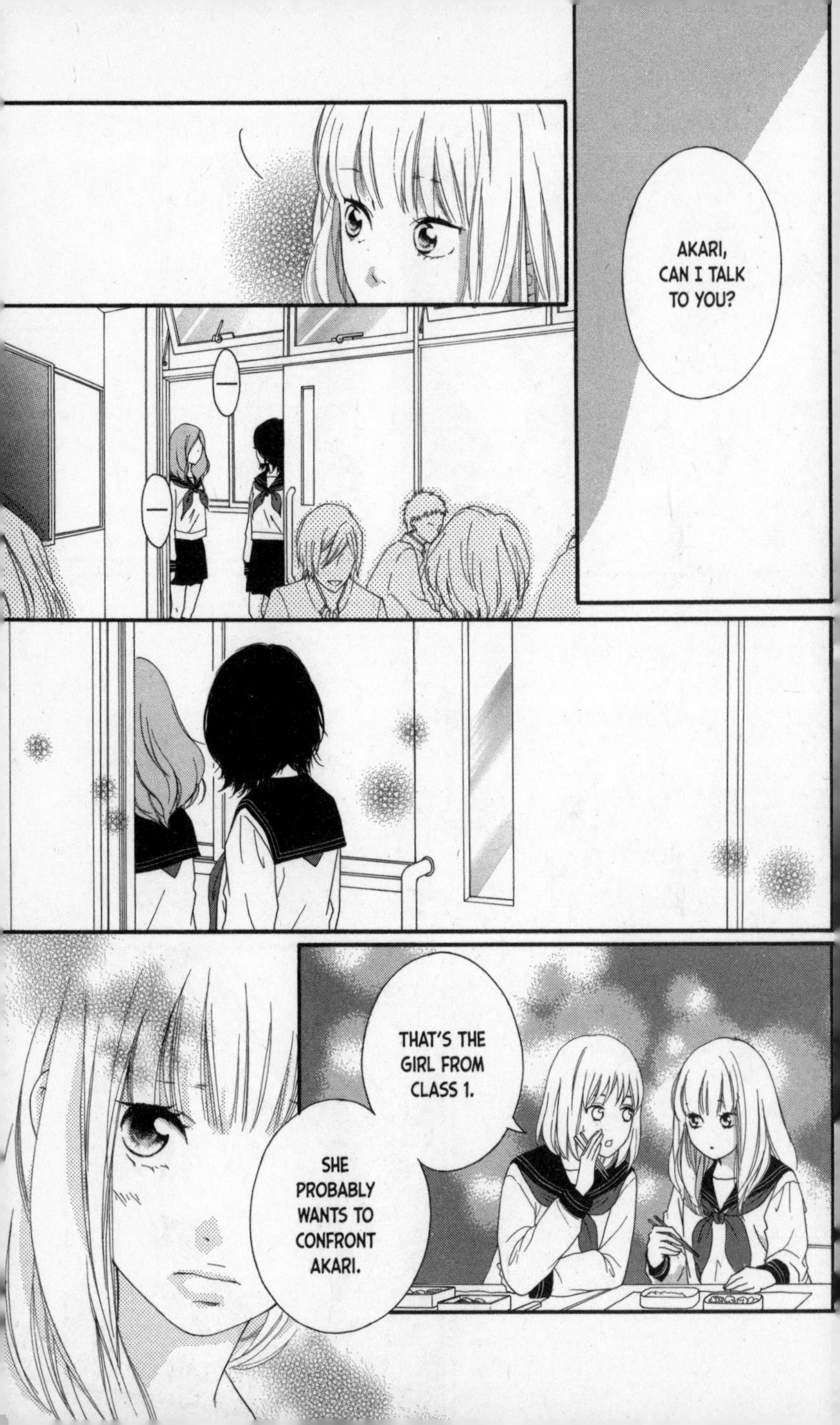
AKARI, CAN I TALK TO YOU?
THAT'S THE GIRL FROM CLASS 1.
SHE PROBABLY WANTS TO CONFRONT AKARI.

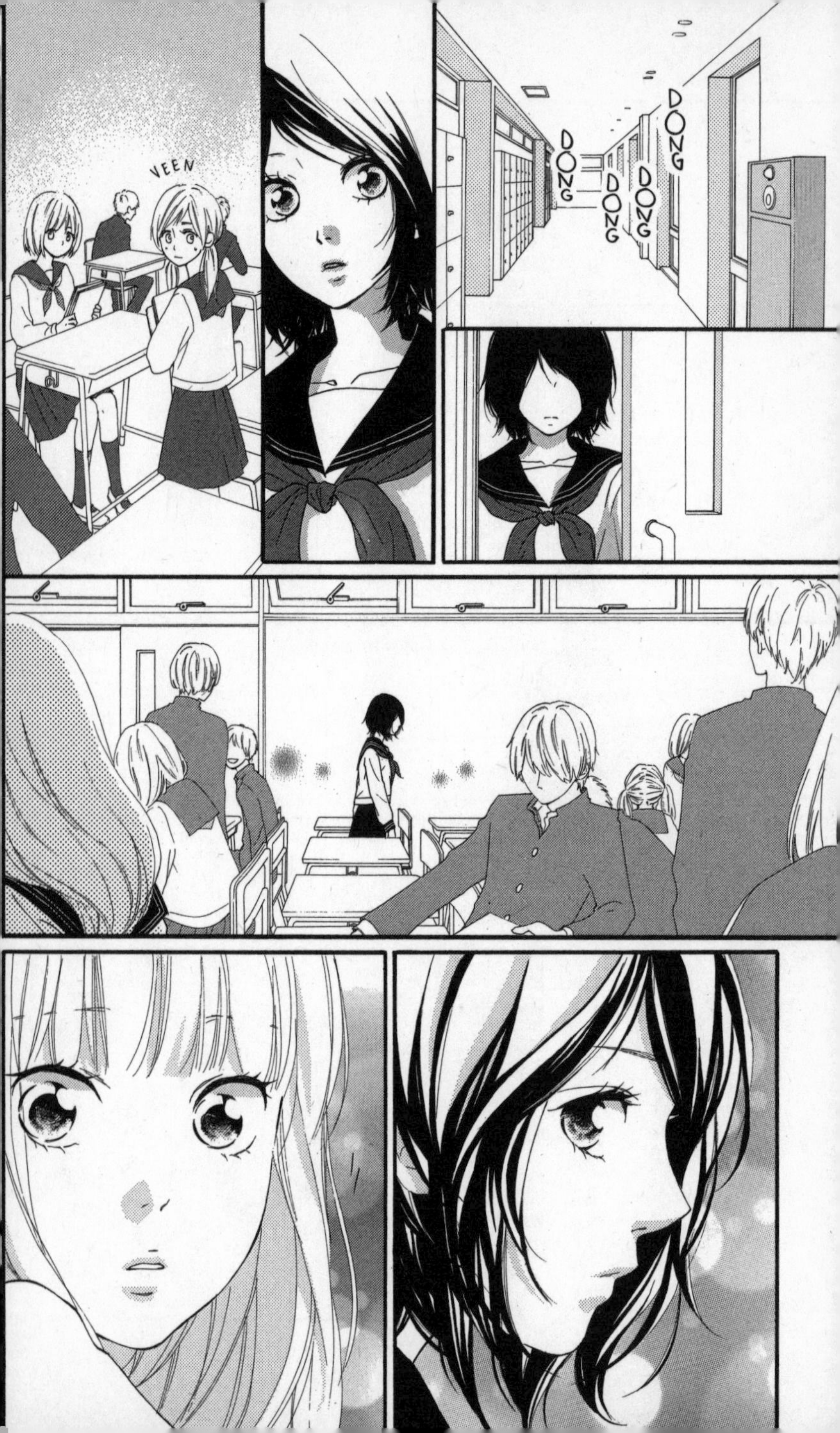
DONG
DONG
DONG
DONG
VEEN

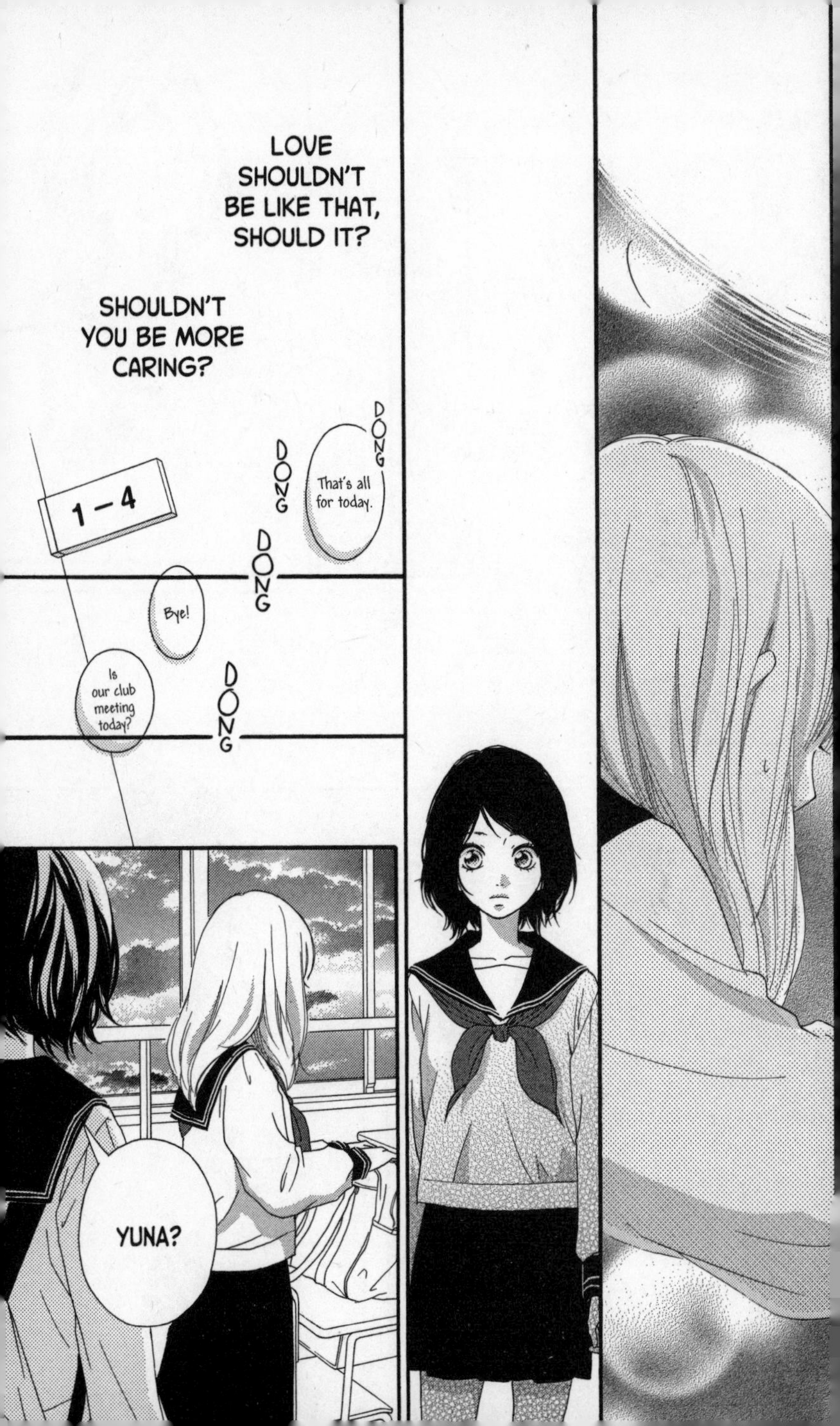
LOVE SHOULDN'T BE LIKE THAT, SHOULD IT?
SHOULDN'T YOU BE MORE CARING?
DONG
That's all for today.
DONG
1-4
DONG
Bye!
DONG
Is our club meeting today?
YUNA?

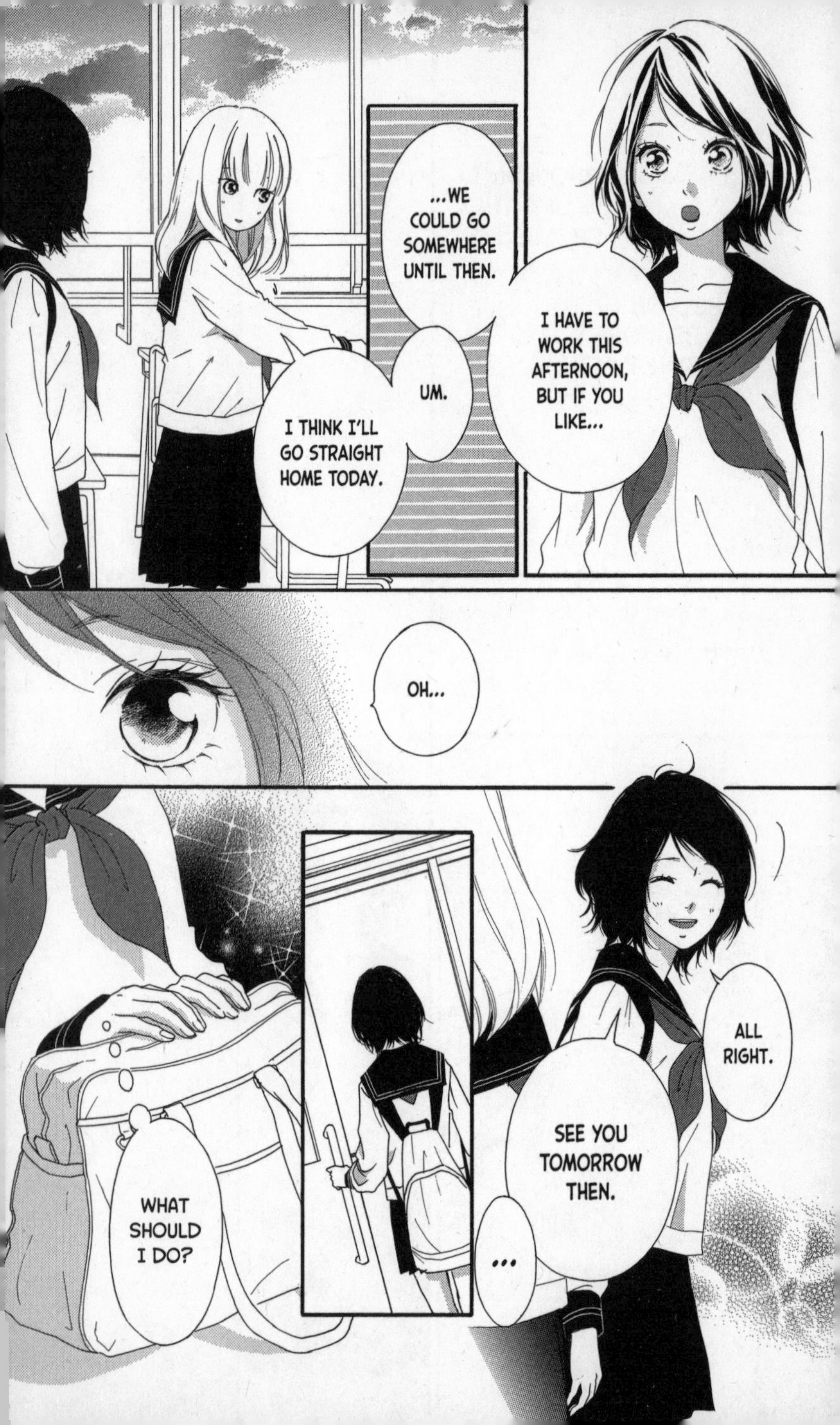
I HAVE TO WORK THIS AFTERNOON, BUT IF YOU LIKE...
...WE COULD GO SOMEWHERE UNTIL THEN.
UM.
I THINK I'LL GO STRAIGHT HOME TODAY.
OH...
ALL RIGHT.
SEE YOU TOMORROW THEN.
...
WHAT SHOULD I DO?

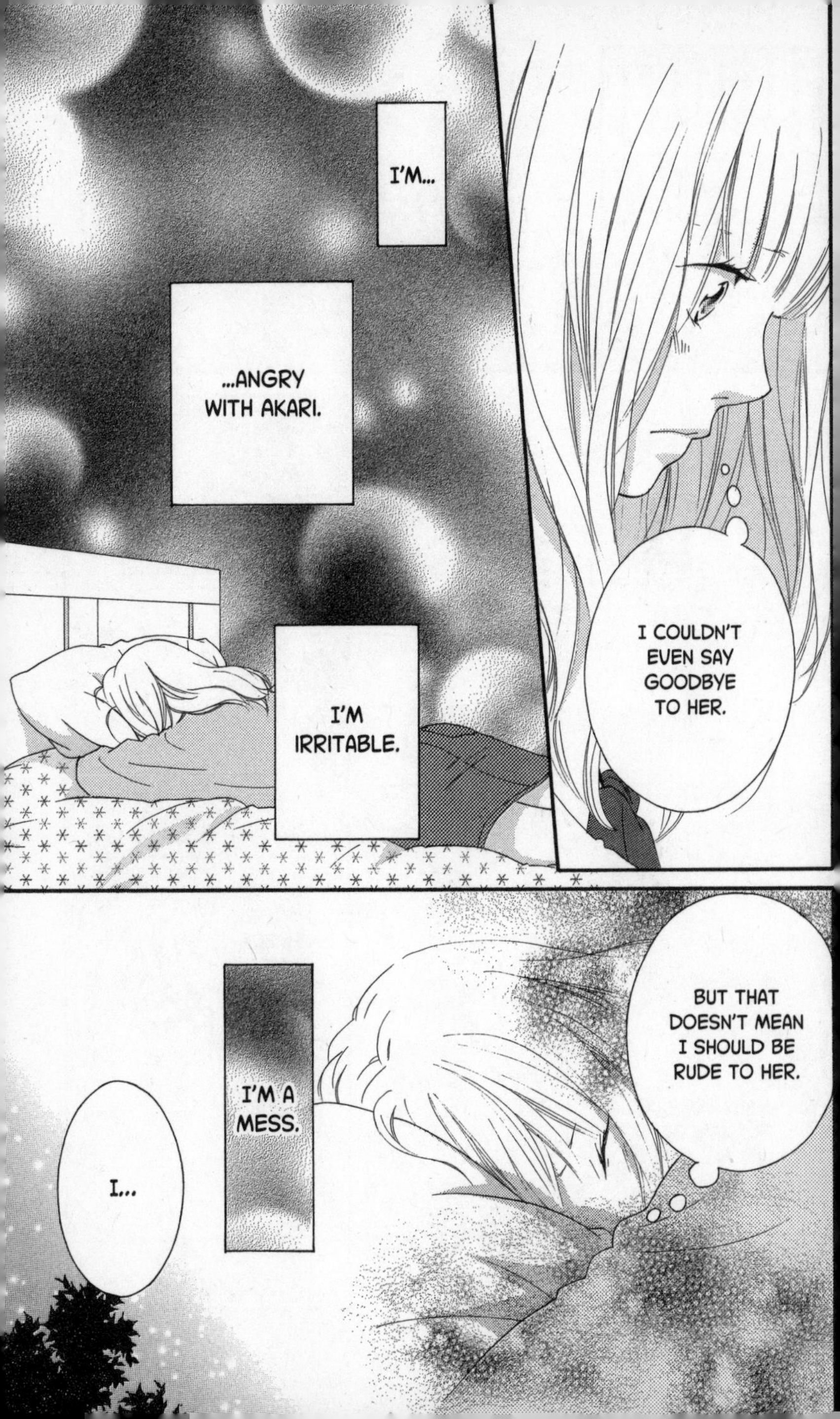
I COULDN'T EVEN SAY GOODBYE TO HER.
I'M...
...ANGRY WITH AKARI.
I'M IRRITABLE.
BUT THAT DOESN'T MEAN I SHOULD BE RUDE TO HER.
I'M A MESS.
I...

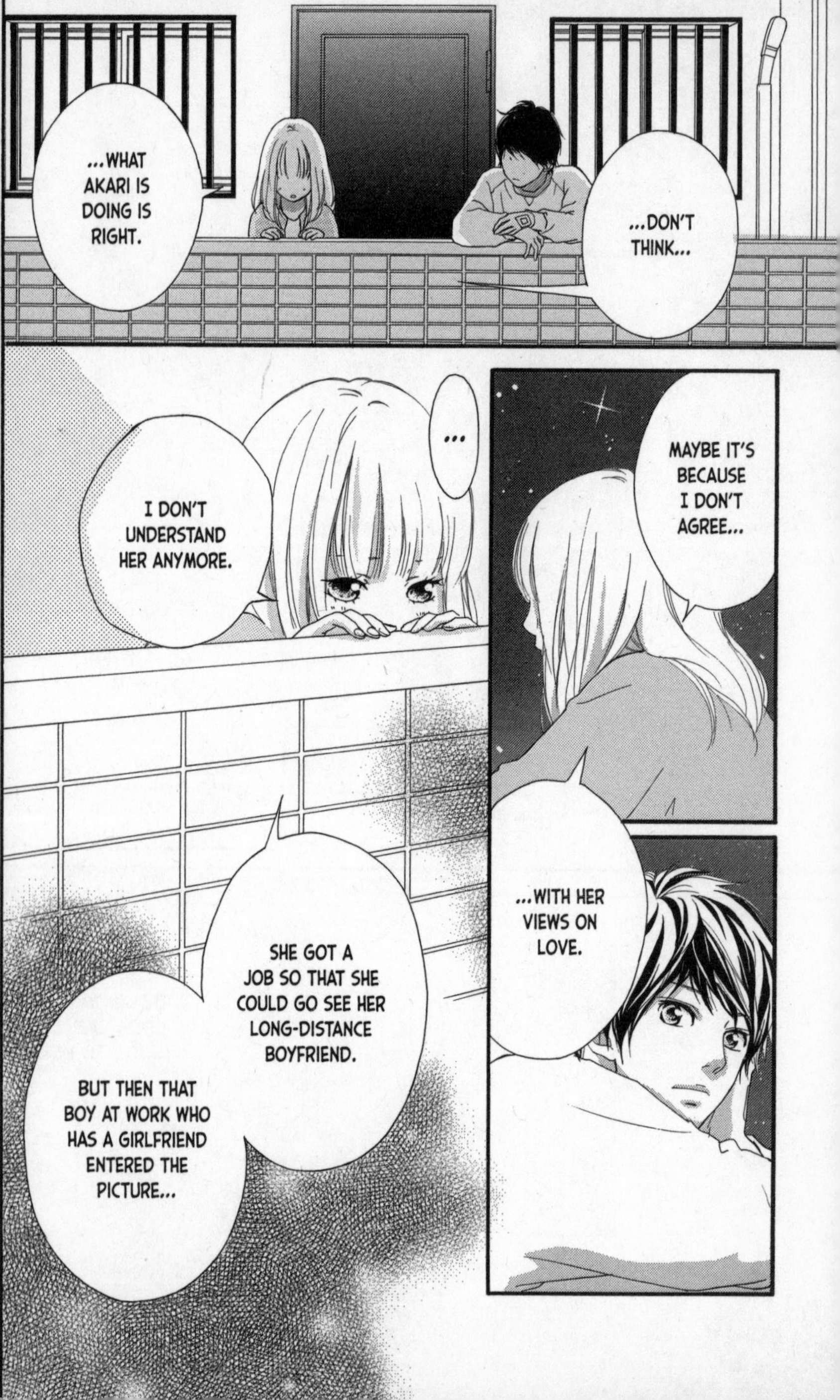
...DON'T THINK...
...WHAT AKARI IS DOING IS RIGHT.
MAYBE IT'S BECAUSE I DON'T AGREE...
...WITH HER VIEWS ON LOVE.
...
I DON'T UNDERSTAND HER ANYMORE.
SHE GOT A JOB SO THAT SHE COULD GO SEE HER LONG-DISTANCE BOYFRIEND.
BUT THEN THAT BOY AT WORK WHO HAS A GIRLFRIEND ENTERED THE PICTURE...

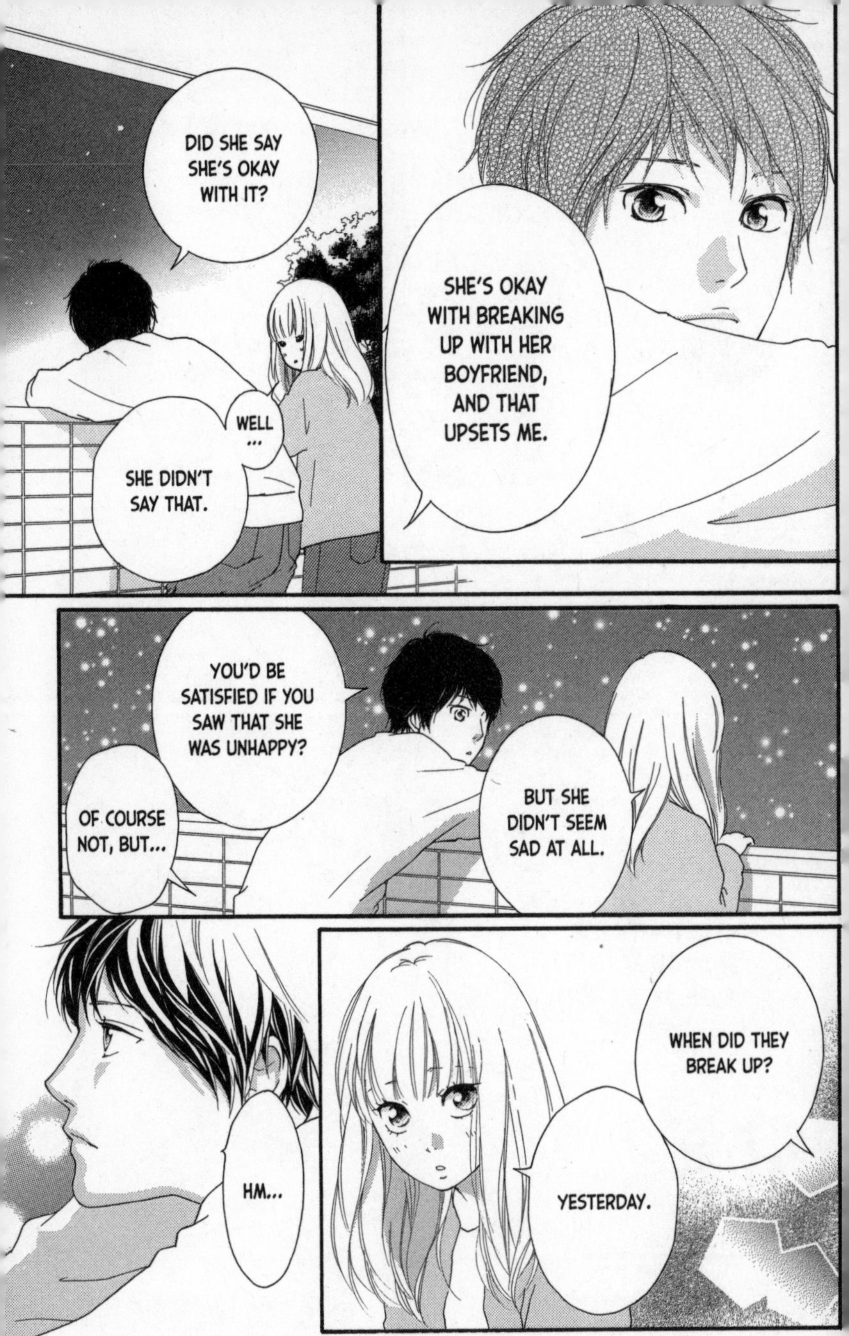
SHE'S OKAY WITH BREAKING UP WITH HER BOYFRIEND, AND THAT UPSETS ME.
DID SHE SAY SHE'S OKAY WITH IT?
WELL...
SHE DIDN'T SAY THAT.
BUT SHE DIDN'T SEEM SAD AT ALL.
YOU'D BE SATISFIED IF YOU SAW THAT SHE WAS UNHAPPY?
OF COURSE NOT, BUT...
WHEN DID THEY BREAK UP?
YESTERDAY.
HM...

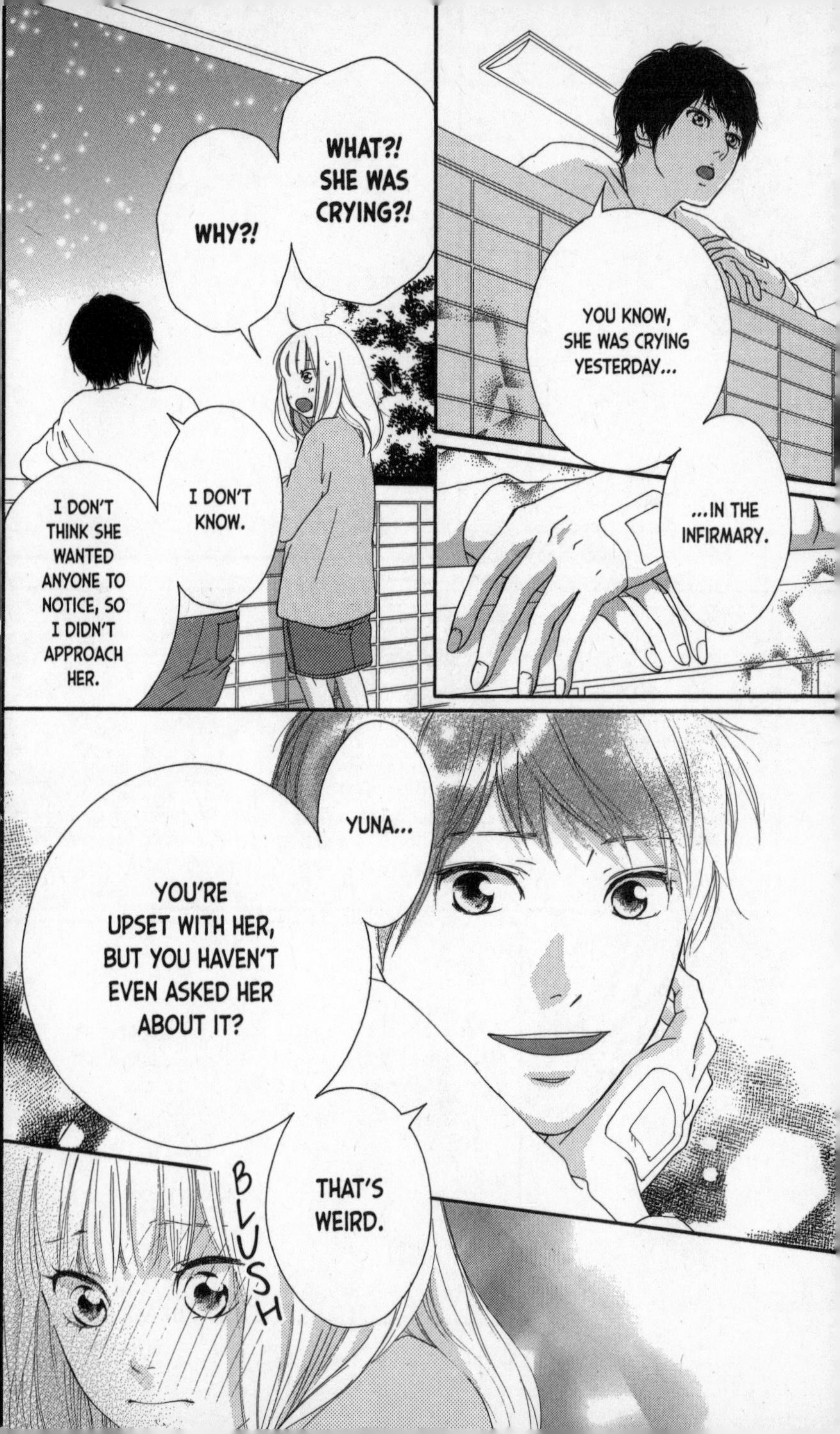
YOU KNOW, SHE WAS CRYING YESTERDAY...
...IN THE INFIRMARY.
WHAT?! SHE WAS CRYING?!
WHY?!
I DON'T KNOW.
I DON'T THINK SHE WANTED ANYONE TO NOTICE, SO I DIDN'T APPROACH HER.
YUNA...
YOU'RE UPSET WITH HER, BUT YOU HAVEN'T EVEN ASKED HER ABOUT IT?
THAT'S WEIRD.
BLUSH

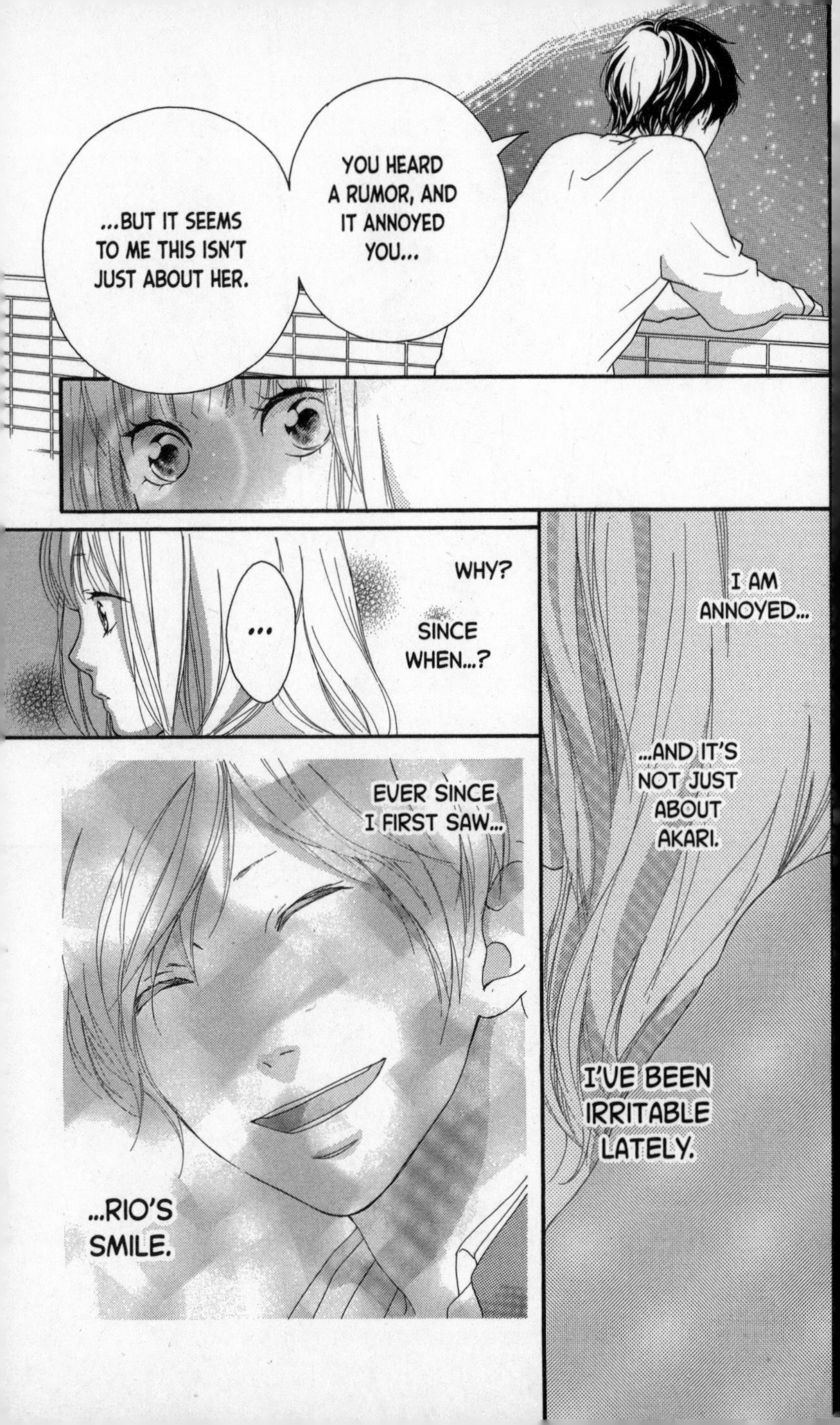
YOU HEARD A RUMOR, AND IT ANNOYED YOU...
...BUT IT SEEMS TO ME THIS ISN'T JUST ABOUT HER.
I AM ANNOYED...
...AND IT'S NOT JUST ABOUT AKARI.
I'VE BEEN IRRITABLE LATELY.
WHY?
SINCE WHEN...?
...
EVER SINCE I FIRST SAW...
...RIO'S SMILE.

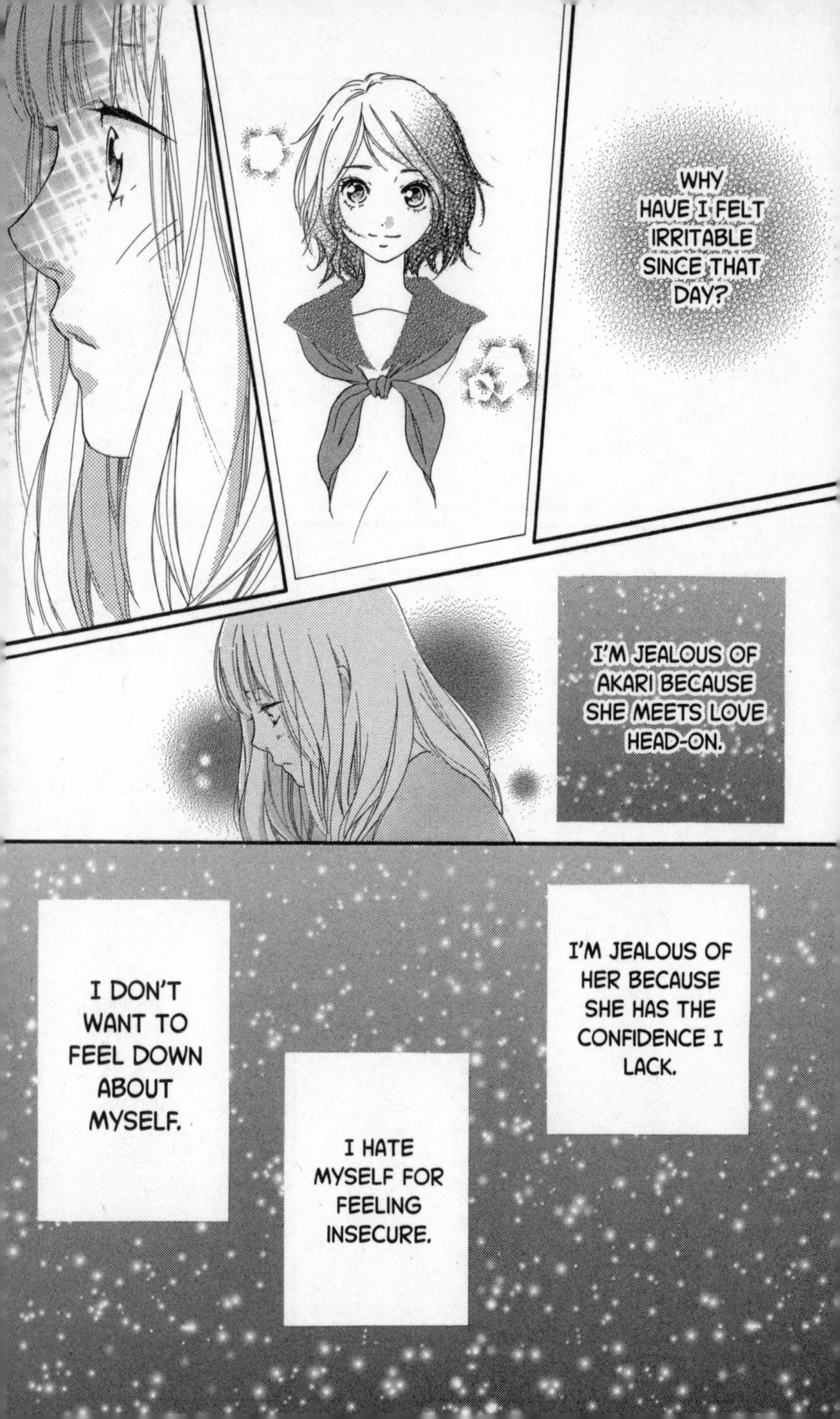
WHY HAVE I FELT IRRITABLE SINCE THAT DAY?
I'M JEALOUS OF AKARI BECAUSE SHE MEETS LOVE HEAD-ON.
I'M JEALOUS OF HER BECAUSE SHE HAS THE CONFIDENCE I LACK.
I HATE MYSELF FOR FEELING INSECURE.
I DON'T WANT TO FEEL DOWN ABOUT MYSELF.

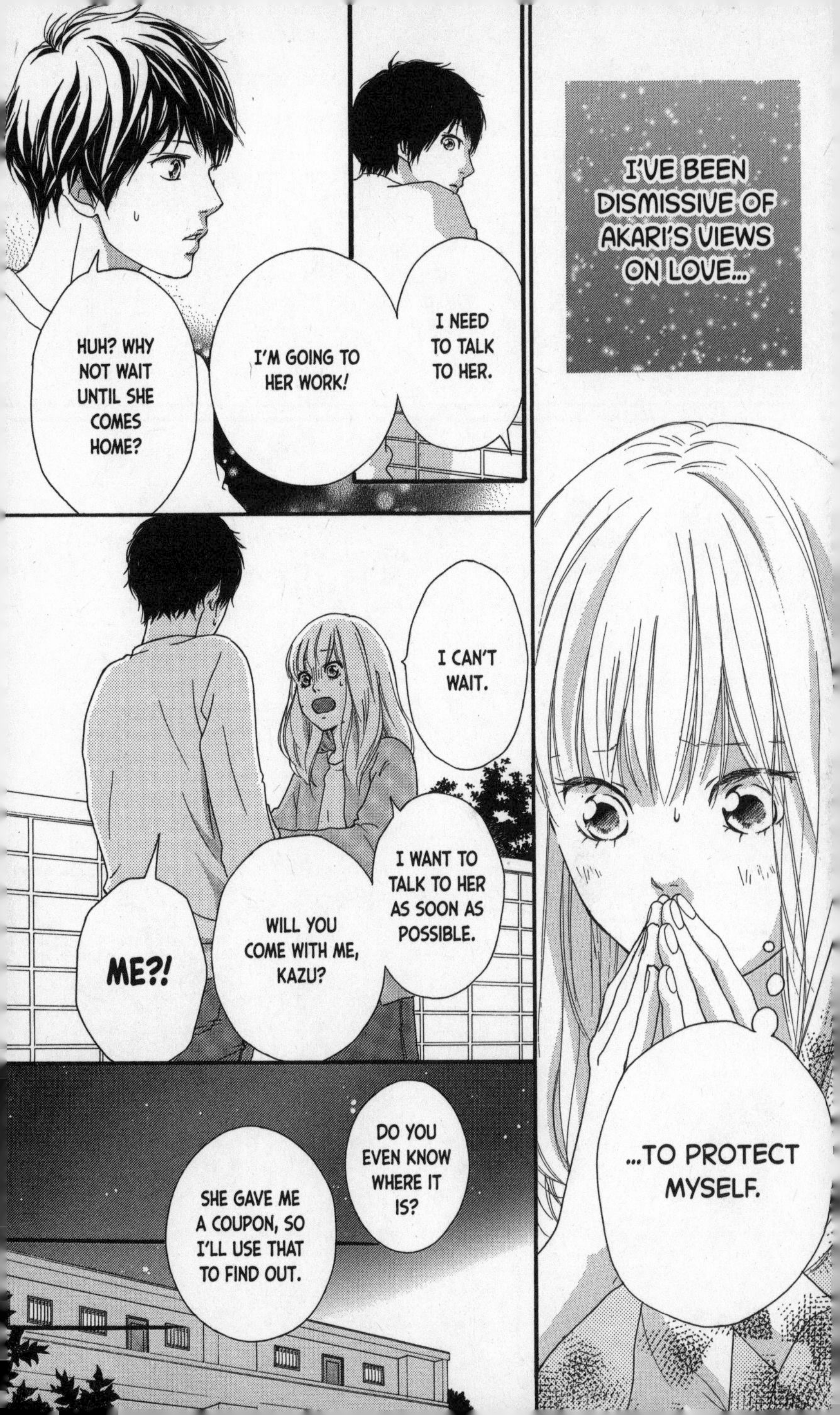
I'VE BEEN DISMISSIVE OF AKARI'S VIEWS ON LOVE...
...TO PROTECT MYSELF.
I NEED TO TALK TO HER.
I'M GOING TO HER WORK!
HUH? WHY NOT WAIT UNTIL SHE COMES HOME?
I CAN'T WAIT.
I WANT TO TALK TO HER AS SOON AS POSSIBLE.
WILL YOU COME WITH ME, KAZU?
ME?!
DO YOU EVEN KNOW WHERE IT IS?
SHE GAVE ME A COUPON, SO I'LL USE THAT TO FIND OUT.

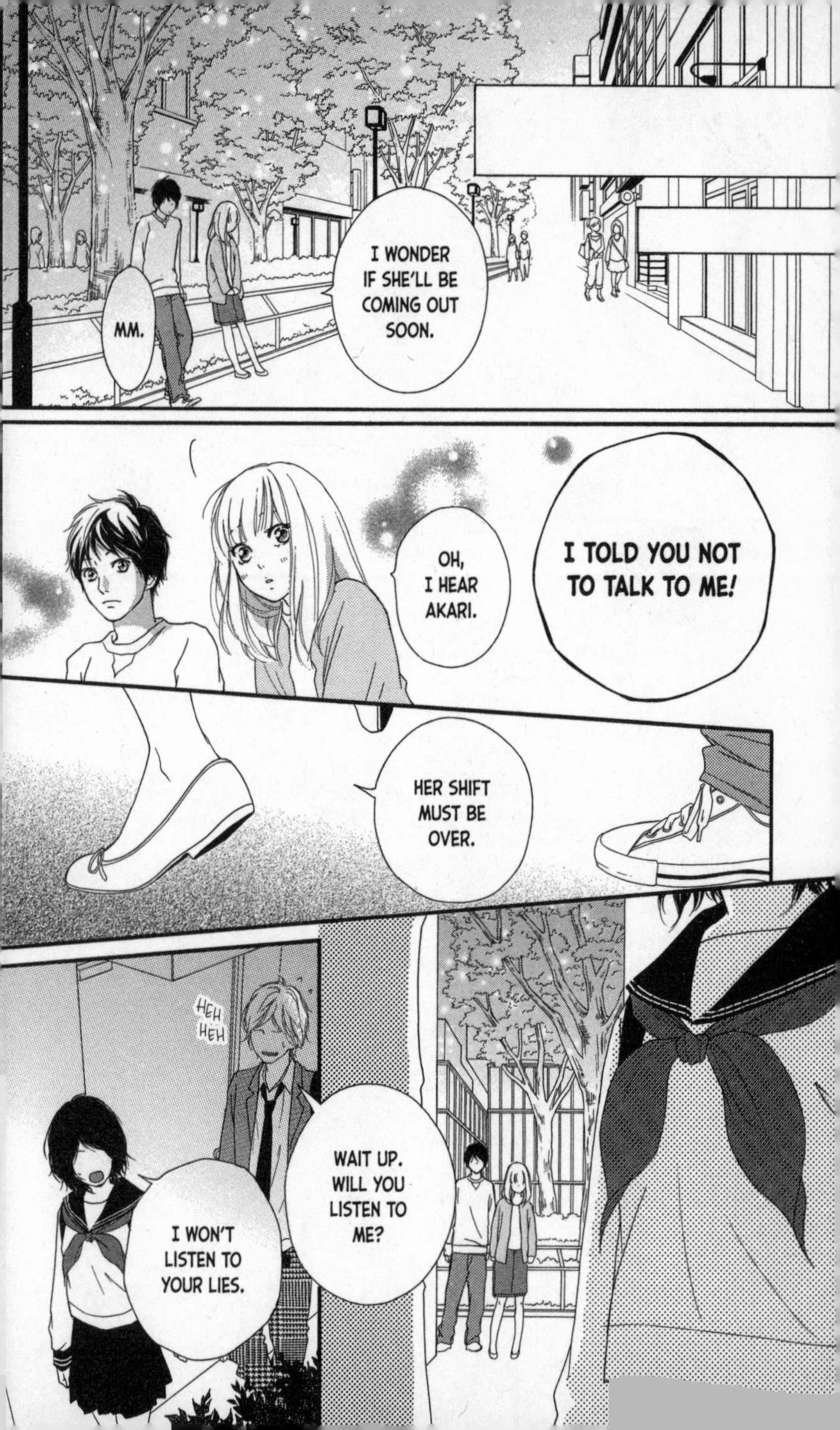
I WONDER IF SHE'LL BE COMING OUT SOON.
MM.
I TOLD YOU NOT TO TALK TO ME!
OH, I HEAR AKARI.
HER SHIFT MUST BE OVER.
HEH HEH
WAIT UP. WILL YOU LISTEN TO ME?
I WON'T LISTEN TO YOUR LIES.

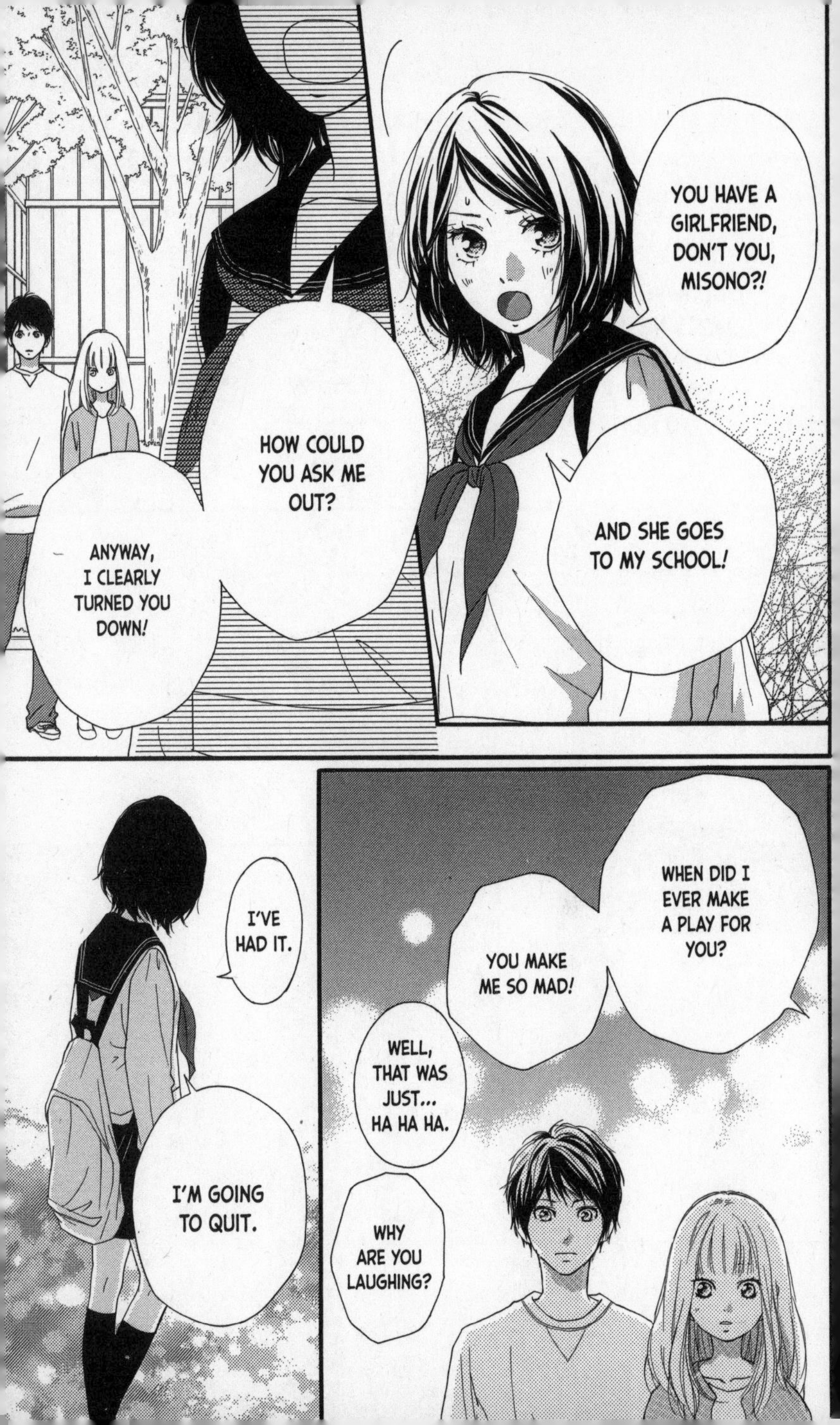
YOU HAVE A GIRLFRIEND, DON'T YOU, MISONO?!
AND SHE GOES TO MY SCHOOL!
HOW COULD YOU ASK ME OUT?
ANYWAY, I CLEARLY TURNED YOU DOWN!
WHEN DID I EVER MAKE A PLAY FOR YOU?
YOU MAKE ME SO MAD!
WELL, THAT WAS JUST... HA HA HA.
WHY ARE YOU LAUGHING?
I'VE HAD IT.
I'M GOING TO QUIT.

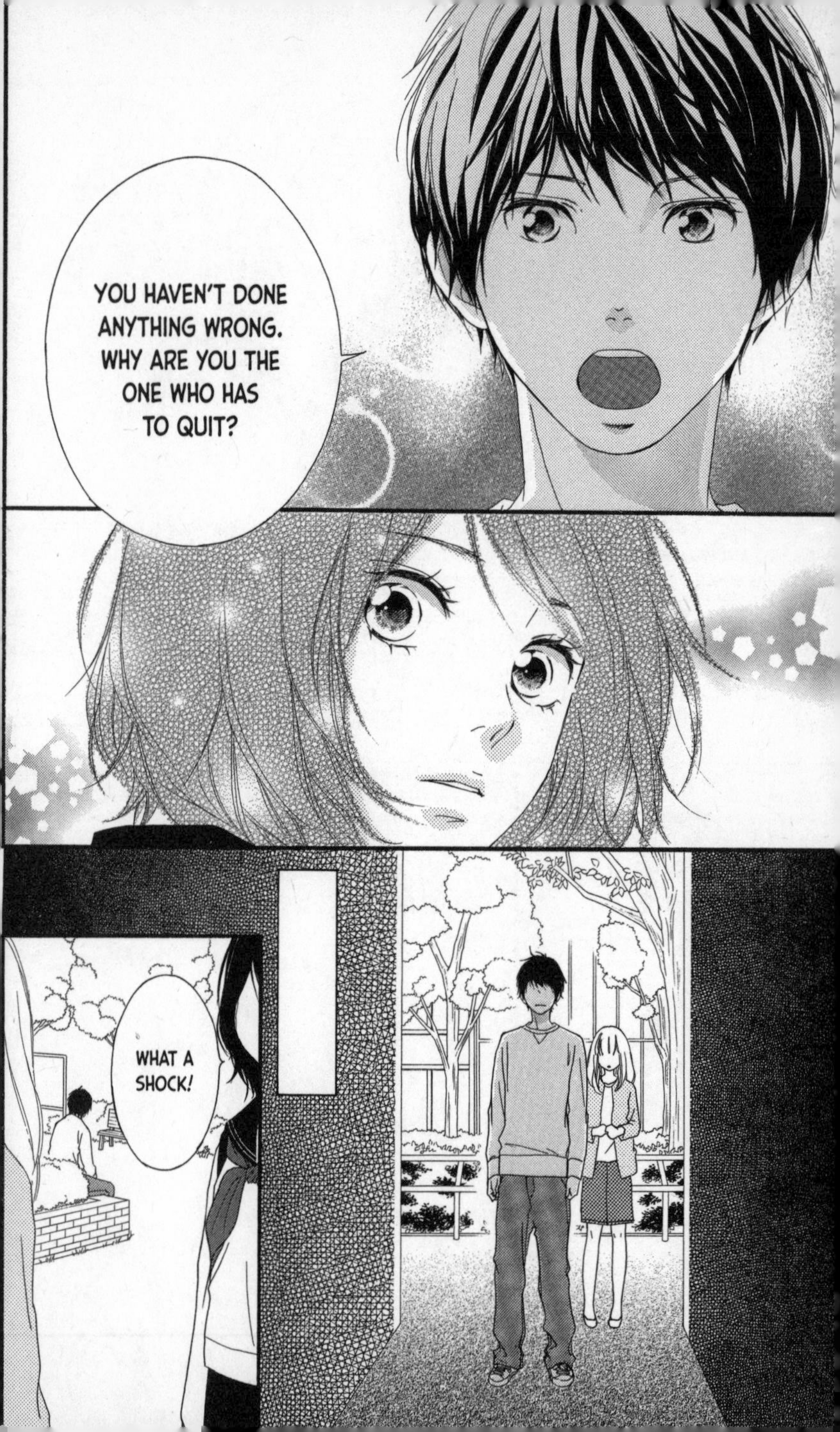
YOU HAVEN'T DONE ANYTHING WRONG. WHY ARE YOU THE ONE WHO HAS TO QUIT?
WHAT A SHOCK!

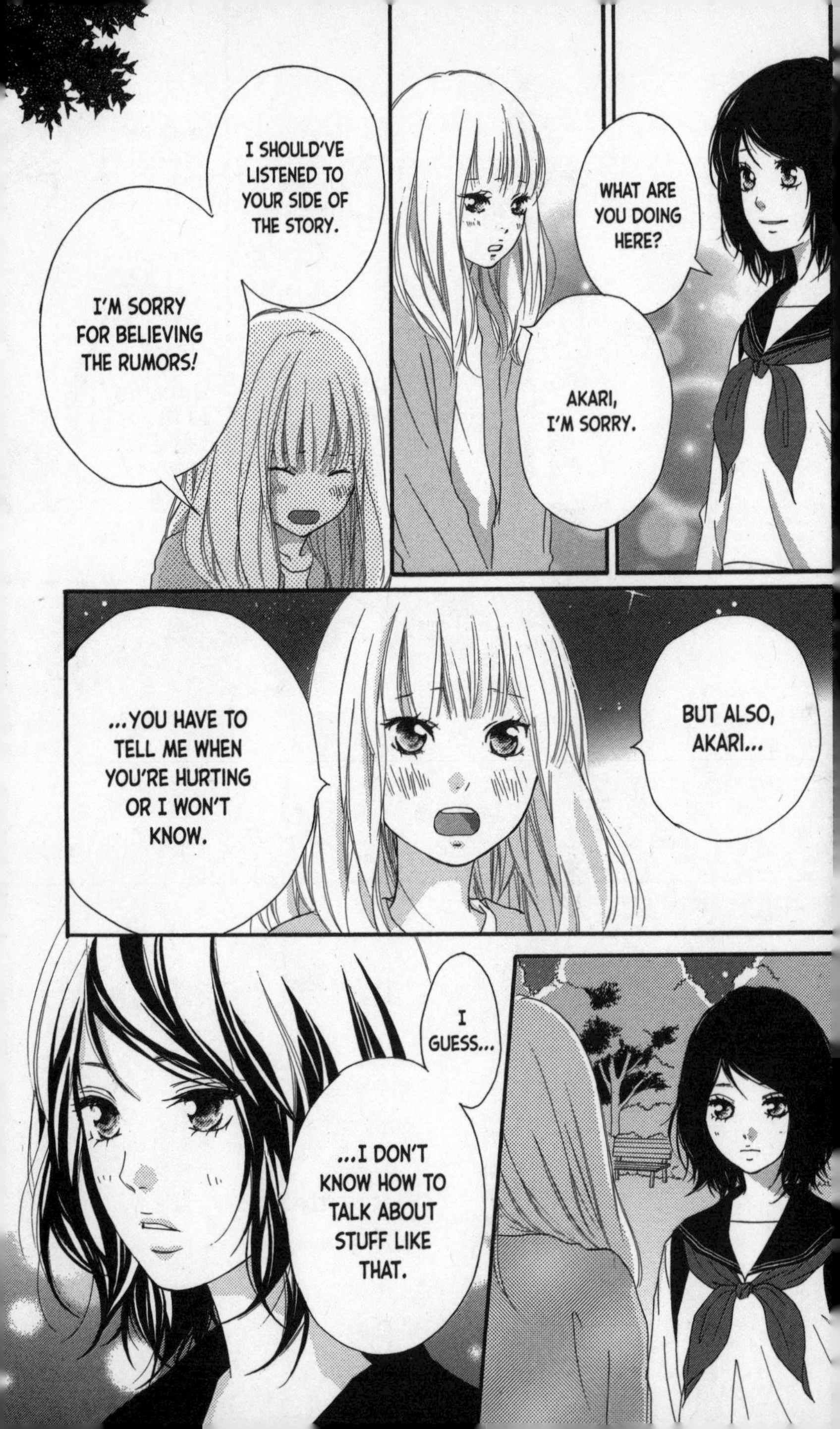
WHAT ARE YOU DOING HERE?
AKARI, I'M SORRY.
I SHOULD'VE LISTENED TO YOUR SIDE OF THE STORY.
I'M SORRY FOR BELIEVING THE RUMORS!
BUT ALSO, AKARI...
...YOU HAVE TO TELL ME WHEN YOU'RE HURTING OR I WON'T KNOW.
I GUESS...
...I DON'T KNOW HOW TO TALK ABOUT STUFF LIKE THAT.

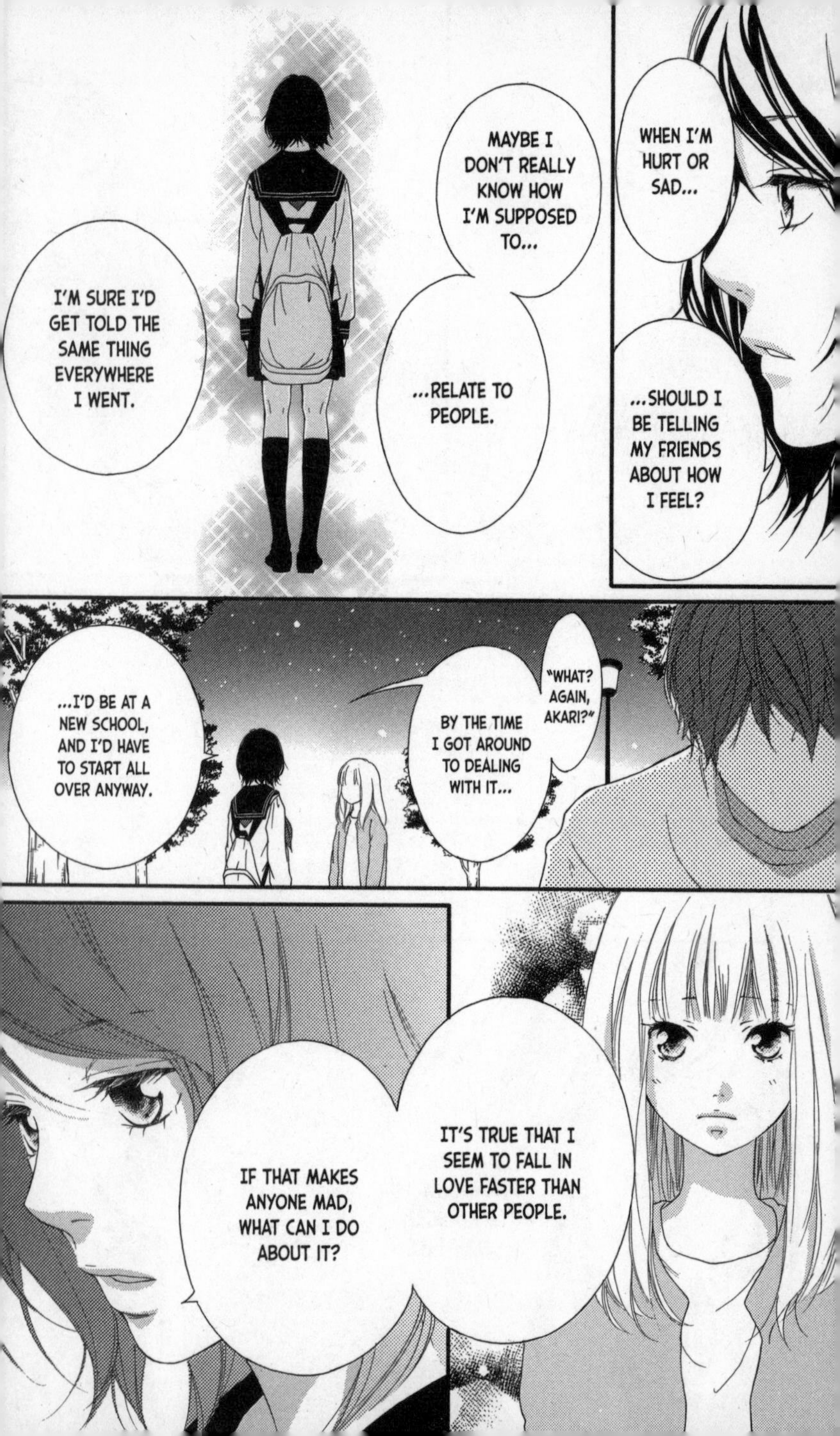
WHEN I'M HURT OR SAD...
...SHOULD I BE TELLING MY FRIENDS ABOUT HOW I FEEL?
MAYBE I DON'T REALLY KNOW HOW I'M SUPPOSED TO...
...RELATE TO PEOPLE.
I'M SURE I'D GET TOLD THE SAME THING EVERYWHERE I WENT.
"WHAT? AGAIN, AKARI?"
BY THE TIME I GOT AROUND TO DEALING WITH IT...
...I'D BE AT A NEW SCHOOL, AND I'D HAVE TO START ALL OVER ANYWAY.
IT'S TRUE THAT I SEEM TO FALL IN LOVE FASTER THAN OTHER PEOPLE.
IF THAT MAKES ANYONE MAD, WHAT CAN I DO ABOUT IT?

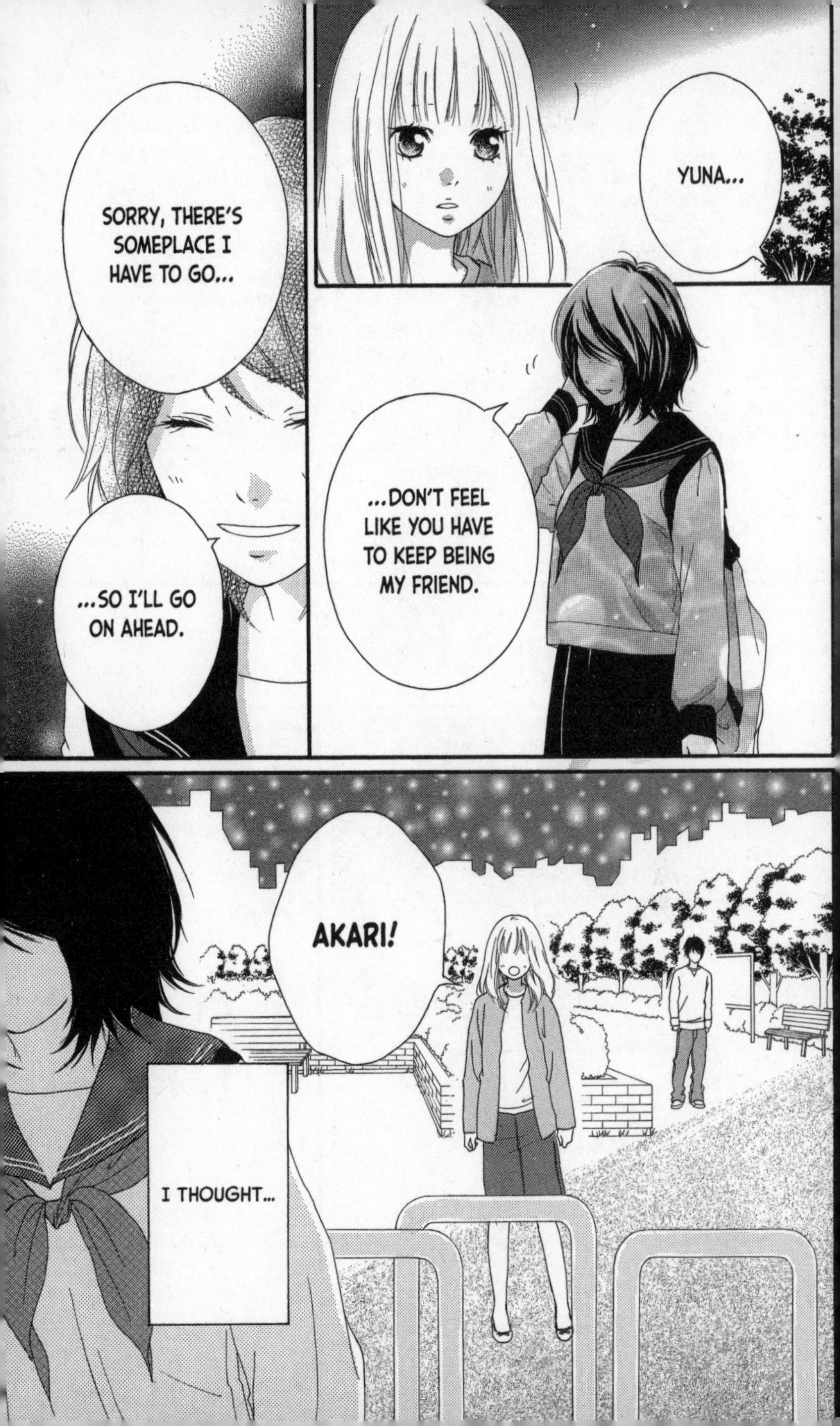
YUNA...
...DON'T FEEL LIKE YOU HAVE TO KEEP BEING MY FRIEND.
SORRY, THERE'S SOMEPLACE I HAVE TO GO...
...SO I'LL GO ON AHEAD.
AKARI!
I THOUGHT...

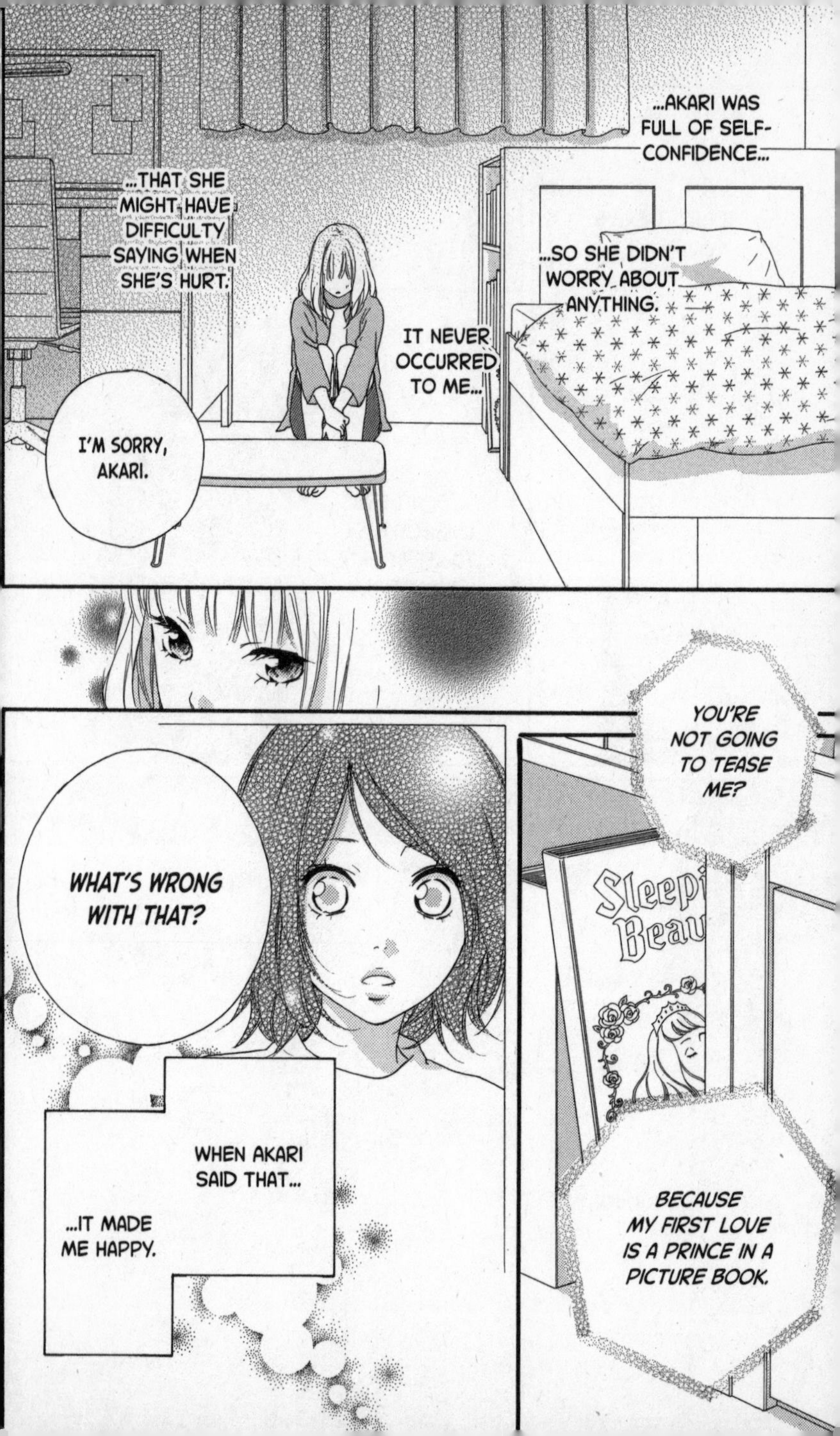

...AKARI WAS FULL OF SELF-CONFIDENCE...
...SO SHE DIDN'T WORRY ABOUT ANYTHING.
IT NEVER OCCURRED TO ME...
...THAT SHE MIGHT HAVE DIFFICULTY SAYING WHEN SHE'S HURT.
I'M SORRY, AKARI.
YOU'RE NOT GOING TO TEASE ME?
BECAUSE MY FIRST LOVE IS A PRINCE IN A PICTURE BOOK.
WHAT'S WRONG WITH THAT?
WHEN AKARI SAID THAT...
...IT MADE ME HAPPY.

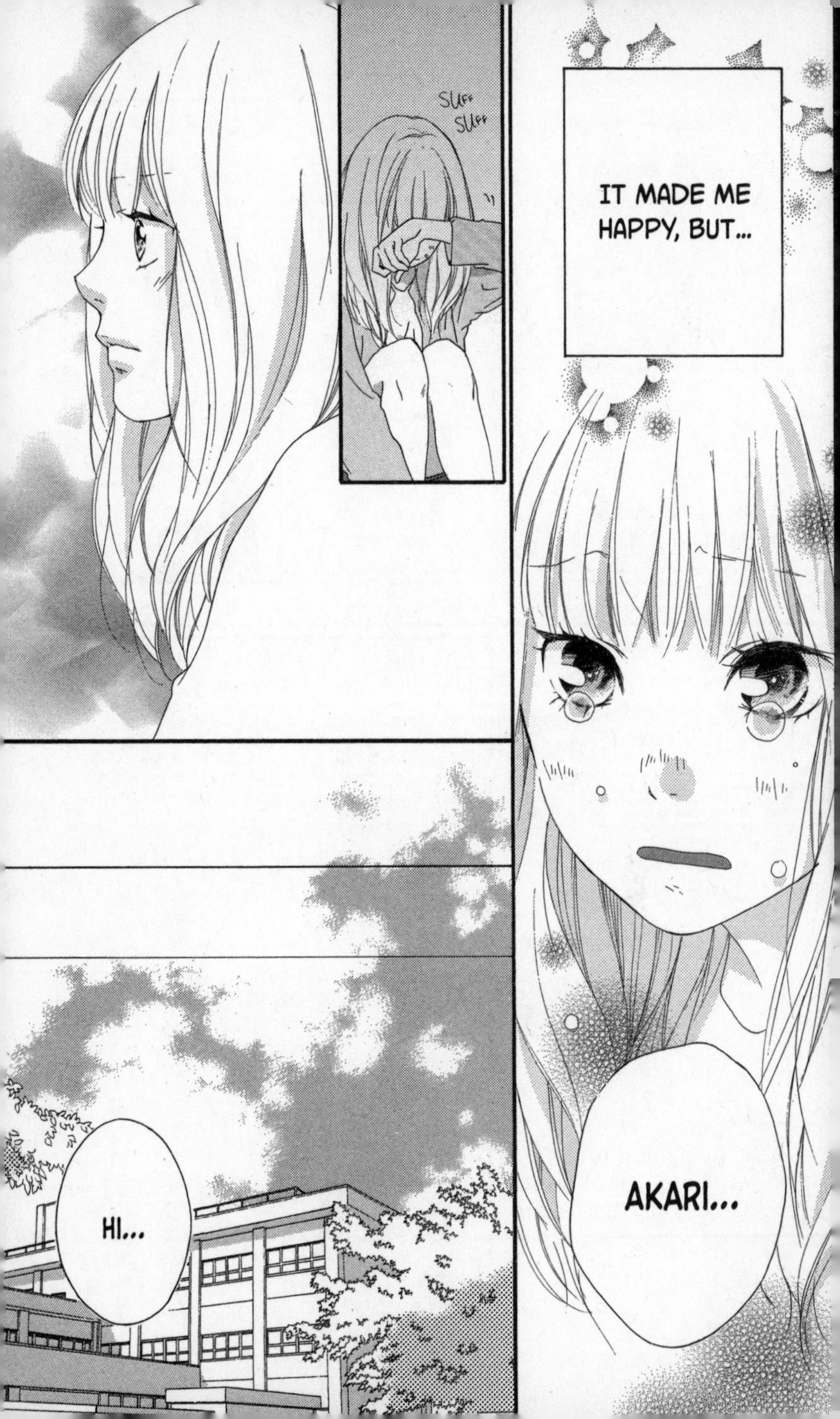
IT MADE ME HAPPY, BUT...
AKARI...
SUFF SUFF
HI...

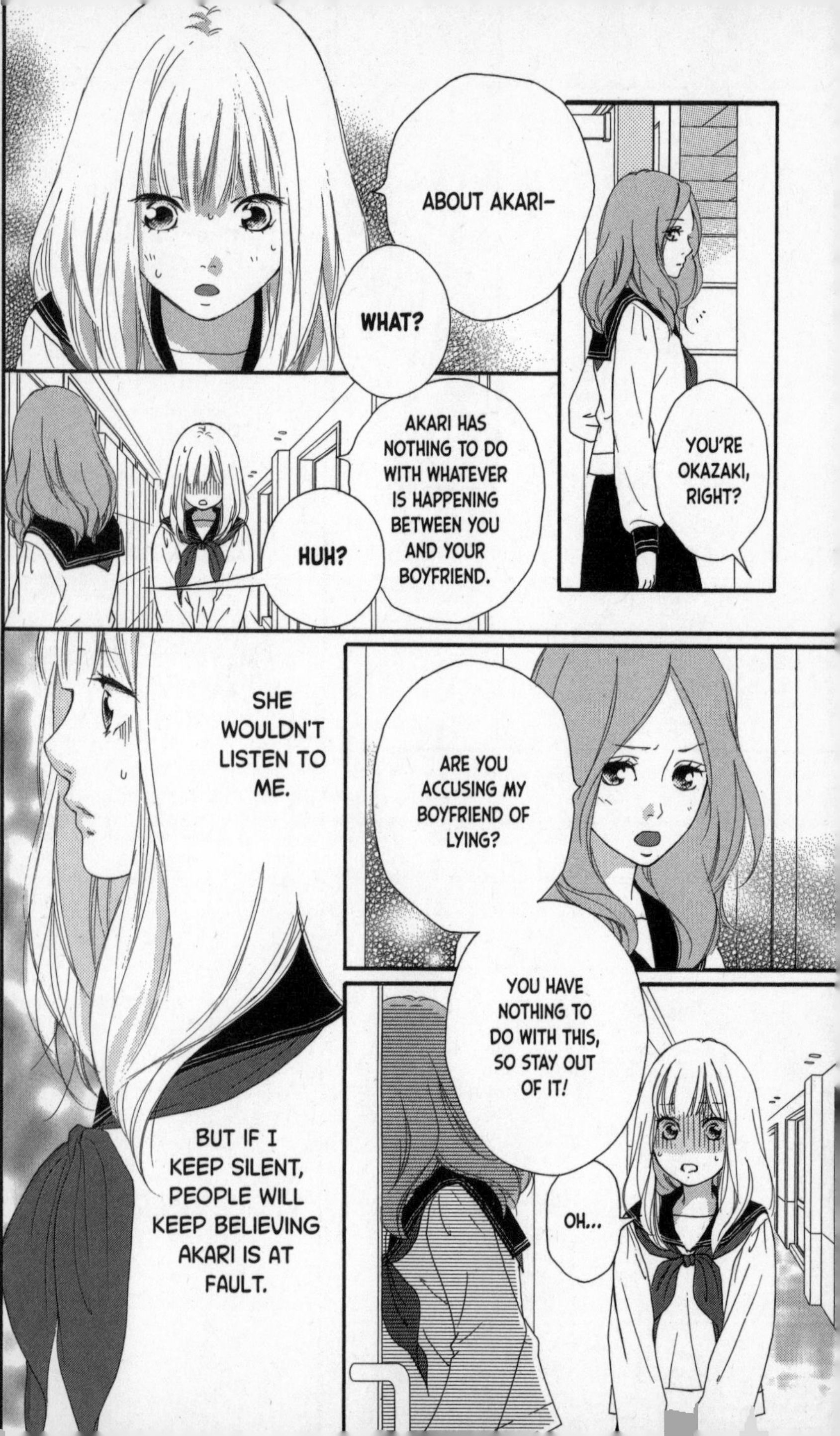
YOU'RE OKAZAKI, RIGHT?
ABOUT AKARI–
WHAT?
AKARI HAS NOTHING TO DO WITH WHATEVER IS HAPPENING BETWEEN YOU AND YOUR BOYFRIEND.
HUH?
ARE YOU ACCUSING MY BOYFRIEND OF LYING?
YOU HAVE NOTHING TO DO WITH THIS, SO STAY OUT OF IT!
OH...
SHE WOULDN'T LISTEN TO ME.
BUT IF I KEEP SILENT, PEOPLE WILL KEEP BELIEVING AKARI IS AT FAULT.

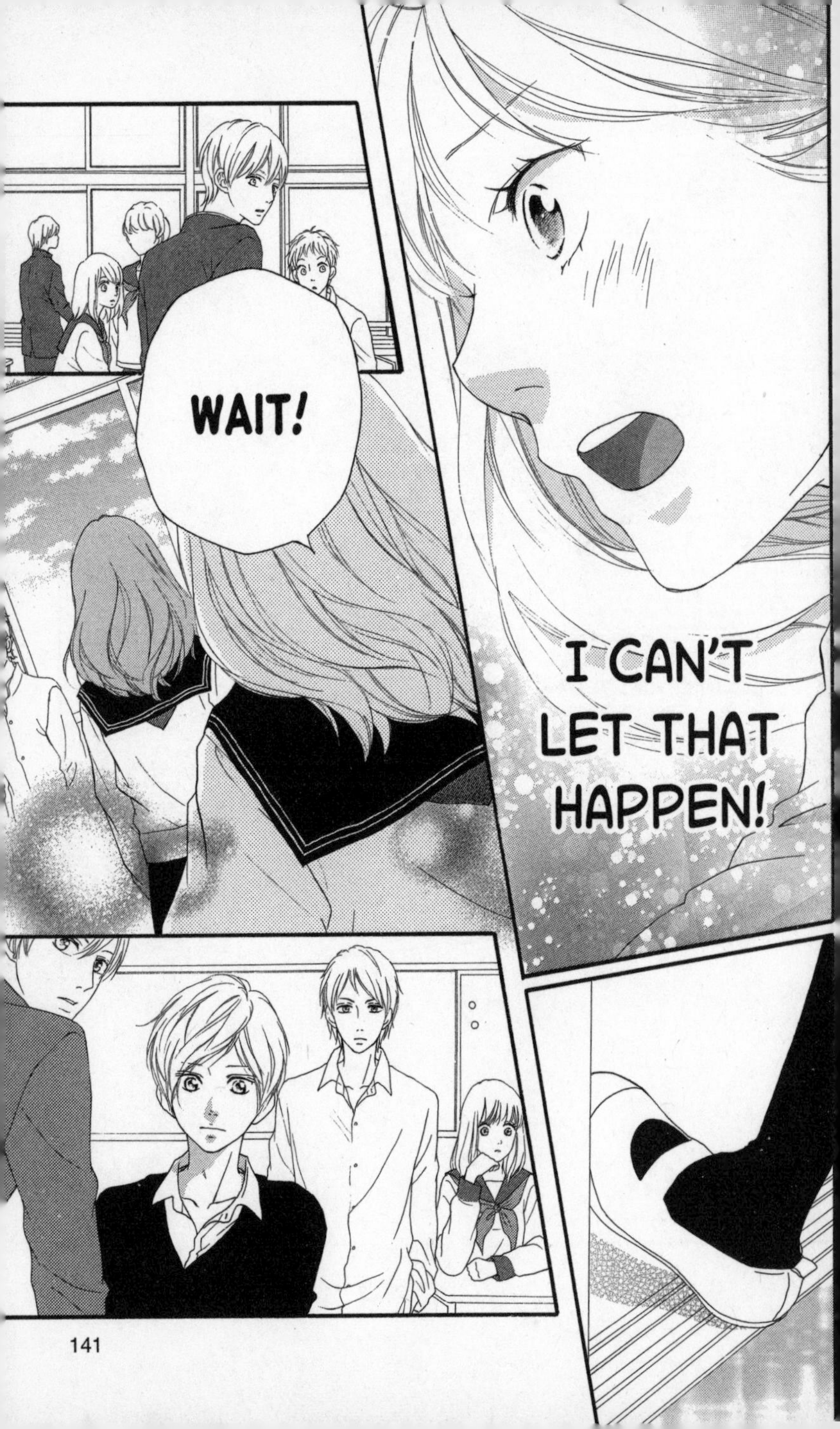
I CAN'T LET THAT HAPPEN!
WAIT!

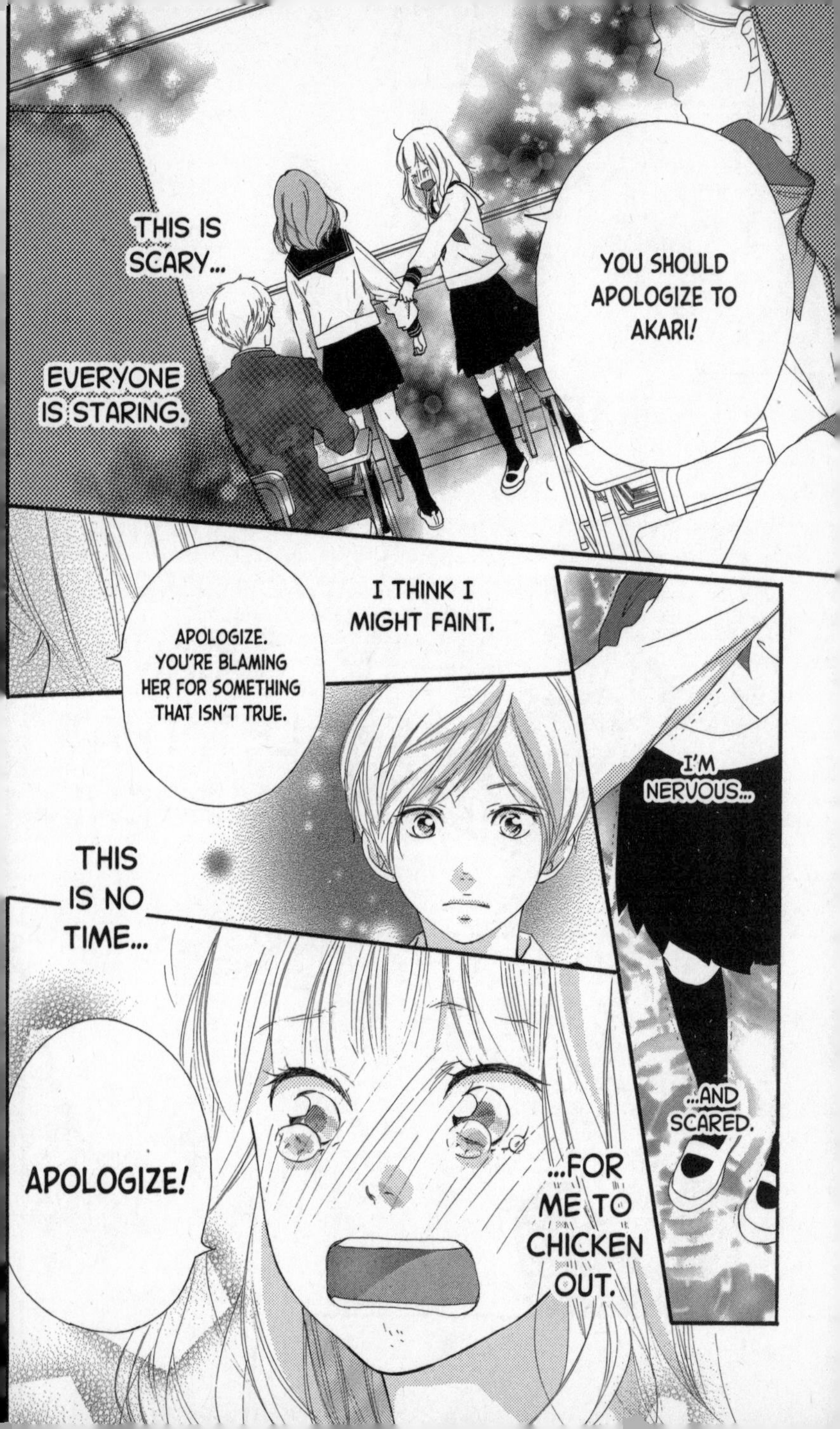
YOU SHOULD APOLOGIZE TO AKARI!
THIS IS SCARY...
EVERYONE IS STARING.
I'M NERVOUS...
...AND SCARED.
I THINK I MIGHT FAINT.
APOLOGIZE. YOU'RE BLAMING HER FOR SOMETHING THAT ISN'T TRUE.
THIS IS NO TIME...
...FOR ME TO CHICKEN OUT.
APOLOGIZE!

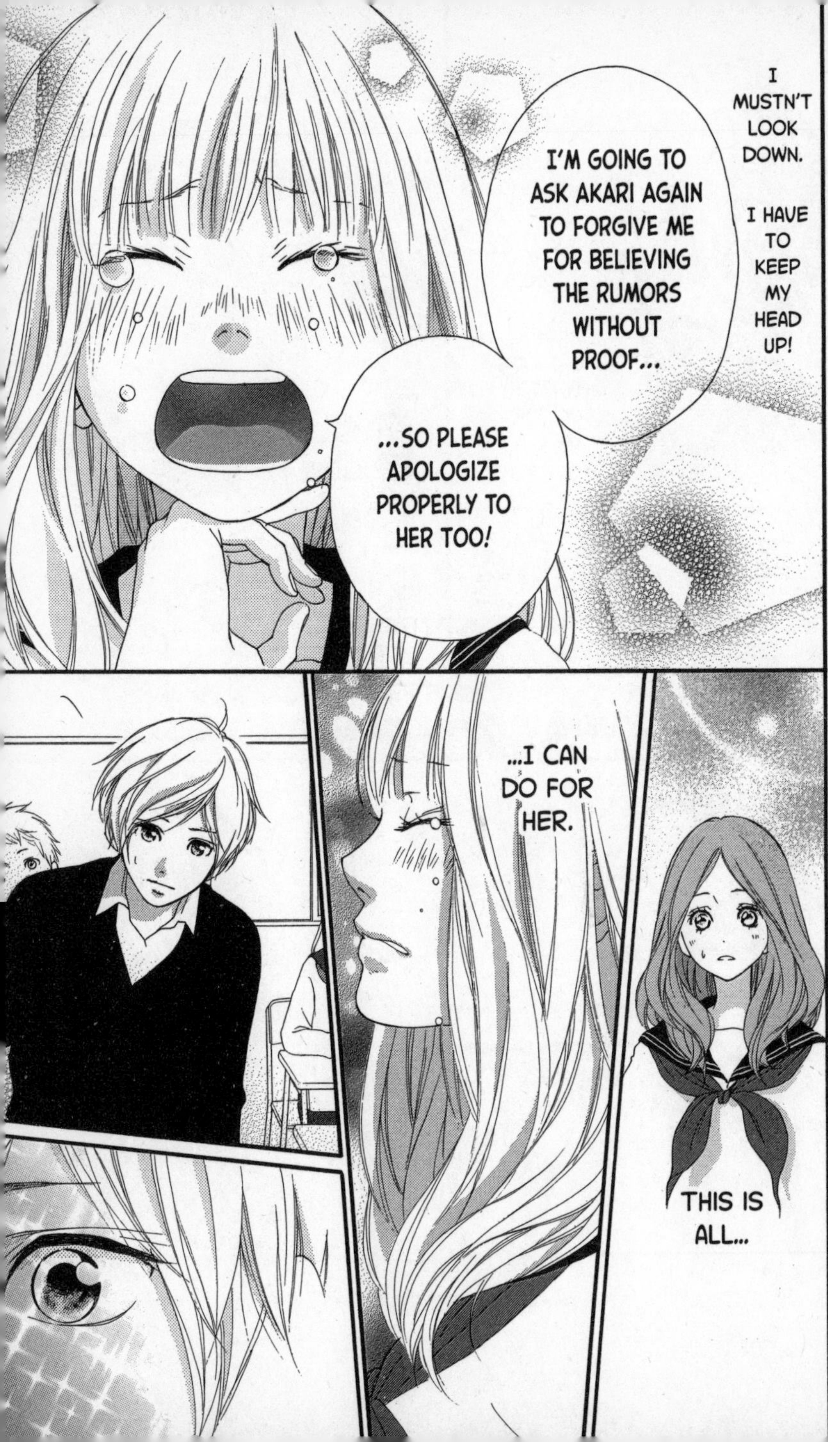
I MUSTN'T LOOK DOWN.
I HAVE TO KEEP MY HEAD UP!
I'M GOING TO ASK AKARI AGAIN TO FORGIVE ME FOR BELIEVING THE RUMORS WITHOUT PROOF...
...SO PLEASE APOLOGIZE PROPERLY TO HER TOO!
THIS IS ALL...
...I CAN DO FOR HER.

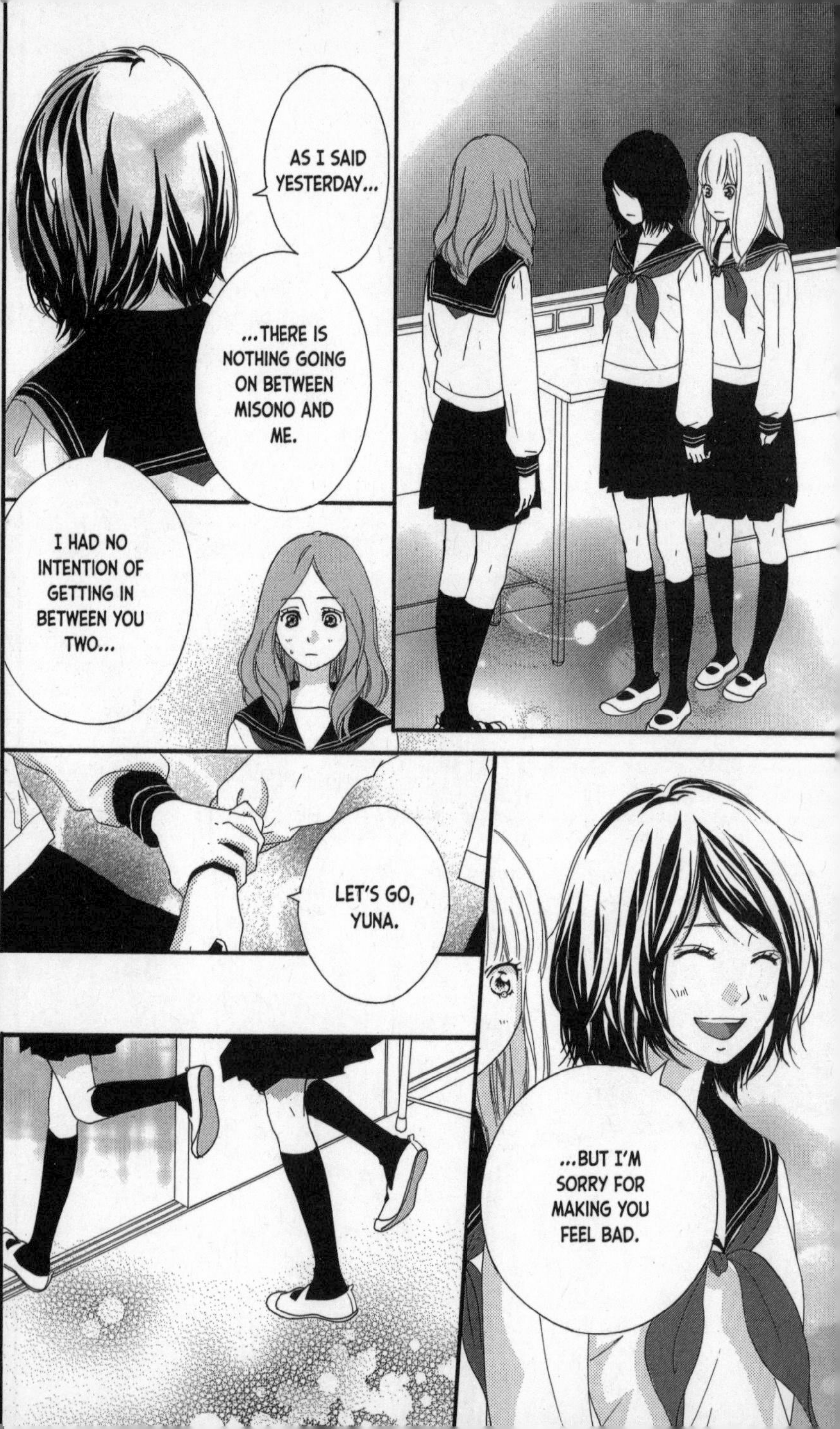
AS I SAID YESTERDAY...
...THERE IS NOTHING GOING ON BETWEEN MISONO AND ME.
I HAD NO INTENTION OF GETTING IN BETWEEN YOU TWO...
...BUT I'M SORRY FOR MAKING YOU FEEL BAD.
LET'S GO, YUNA.

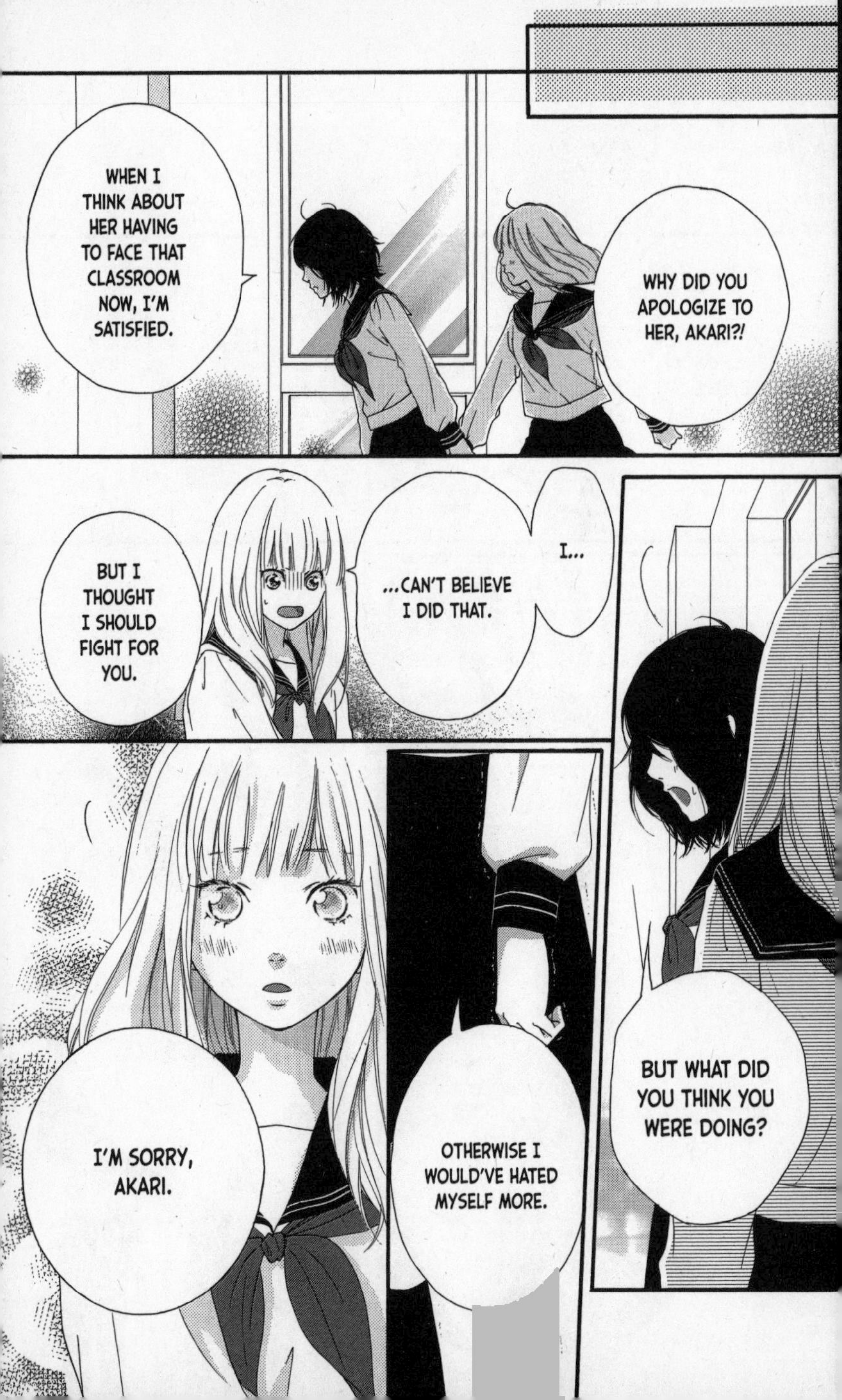
WHY DID YOU APOLOGIZE TO HER, AKARI?!
WHEN I THINK ABOUT HER HAVING TO FACE THAT CLASSROOM NOW, I'M SATISFIED.
BUT WHAT DID YOU THINK YOU WERE DOING?
I...
...CAN'T BELIEVE I DID THAT.
BUT I THOUGHT I SHOULD FIGHT FOR YOU.
OTHERWISE I WOULD'VE HATED MYSELF MORE.
I'M SORRY, AKARI.

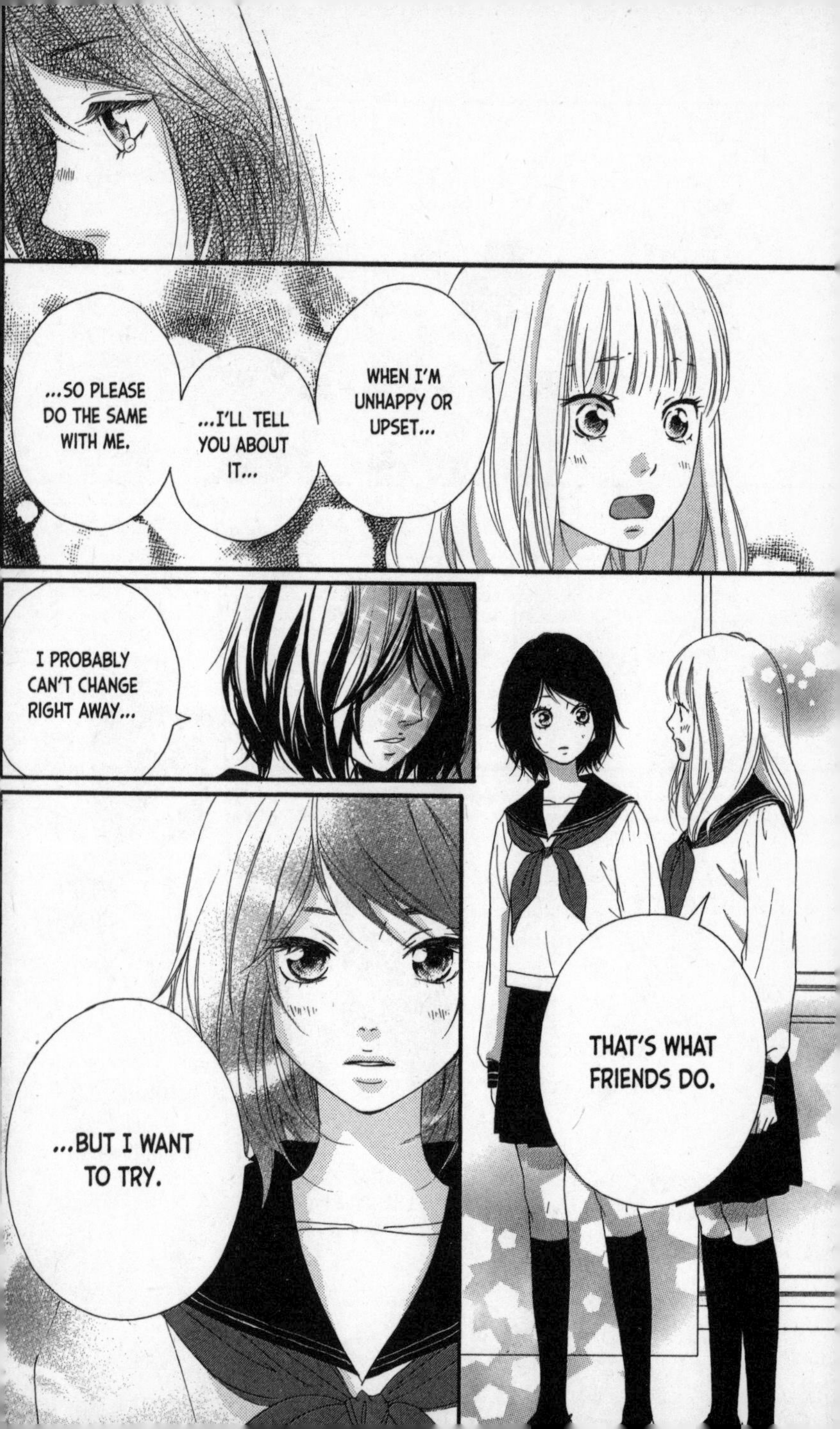
WHEN I'M UNHAPPY OR UPSET...
...I'LL TELL YOU ABOUT IT...
...SO PLEASE DO THE SAME WITH ME.
THAT'S WHAT FRIENDS DO.
I PROBABLY CAN'T CHANGE RIGHT AWAY...
...BUT I WANT TO TRY.

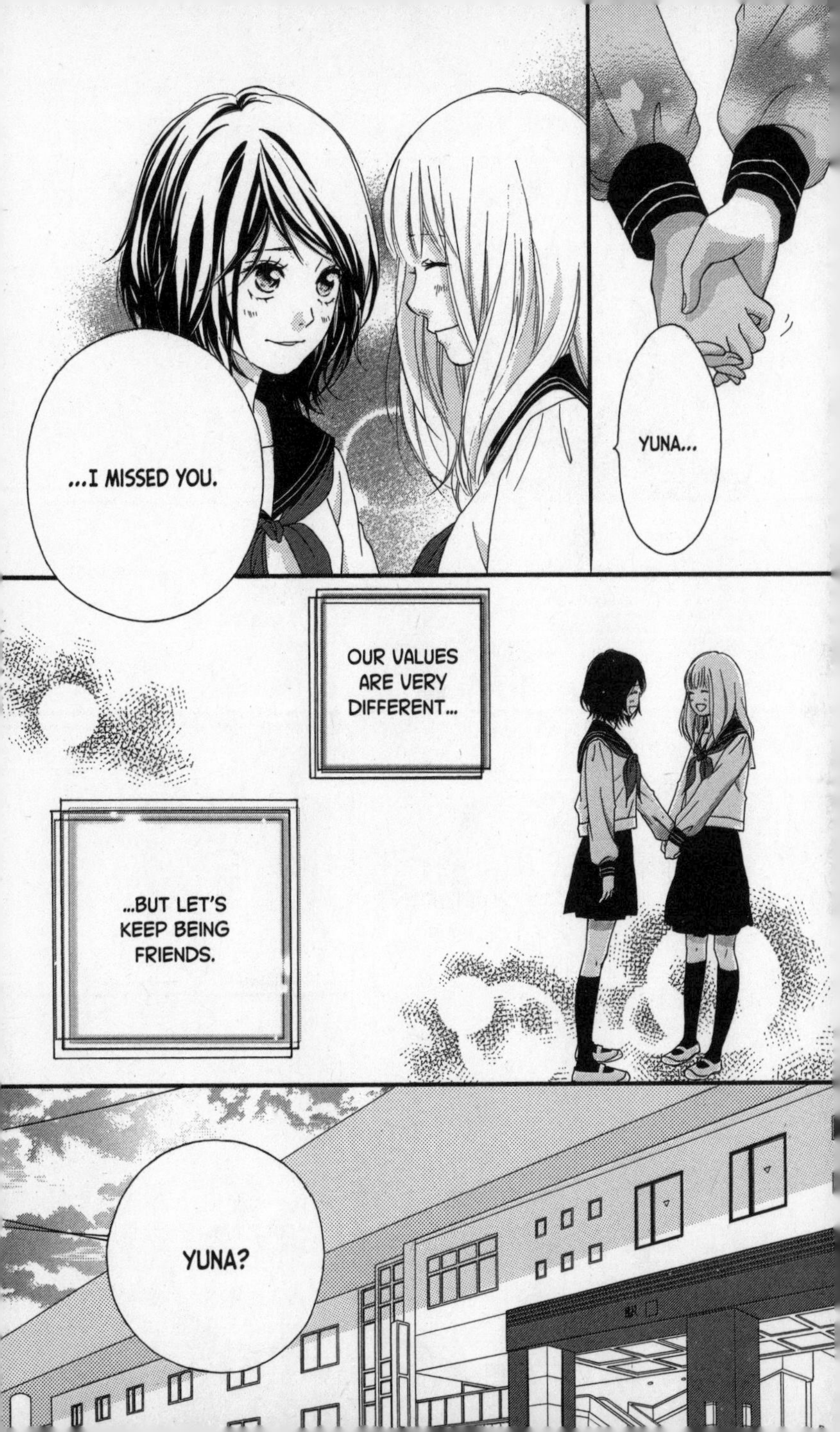
YUNA...
...I MISSED YOU.
OUR VALUES ARE VERY DIFFERENT...
...BUT LET'S KEEP BEING FRIENDS.
YUNA?

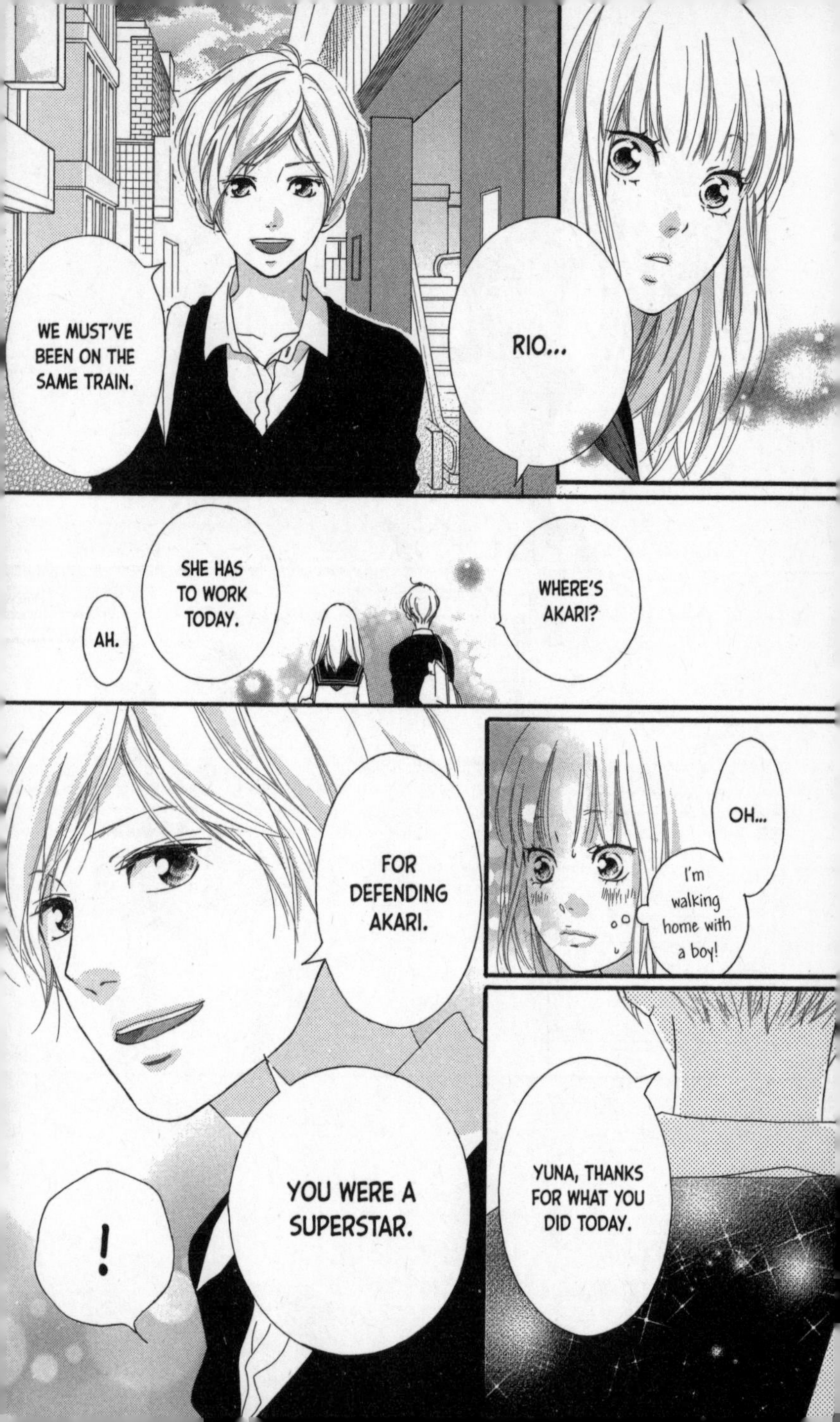
RIO...
WE MUST'VE BEEN ON THE SAME TRAIN.
WHERE'S AKARI?
SHE HAS TO WORK TODAY.
AH.
OH...
I'm walking home with a boy!
YUNA, THANKS FOR WHAT YOU DID TODAY.
FOR DEFENDING AKARI.
YOU WERE A SUPERSTAR.
!

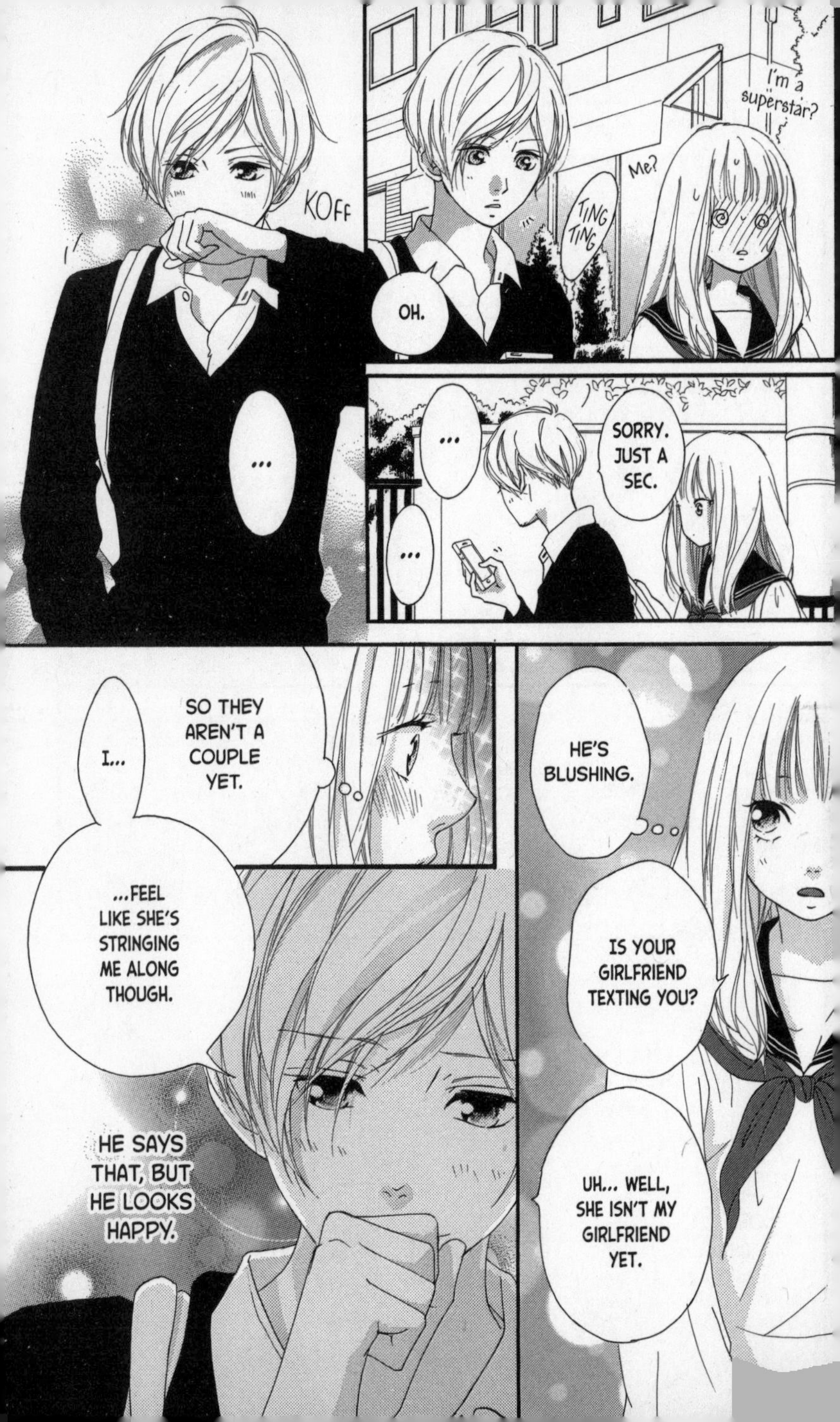
I'm a superstar?
Me?
TING TING
OH.
SORRY. JUST A SEC.
...
...
KOFF
...
HE'S BLUSHING.
IS YOUR GIRLFRIEND TEXTING YOU?
UH... WELL, SHE ISN'T MY GIRLFRIEND YET.
SO THEY AREN'T A COUPLE YET.
I...
...FEEL LIKE SHE'S STRINGING ME ALONG THOUGH.
HE SAYS THAT, BUT HE LOOKS HAPPY.

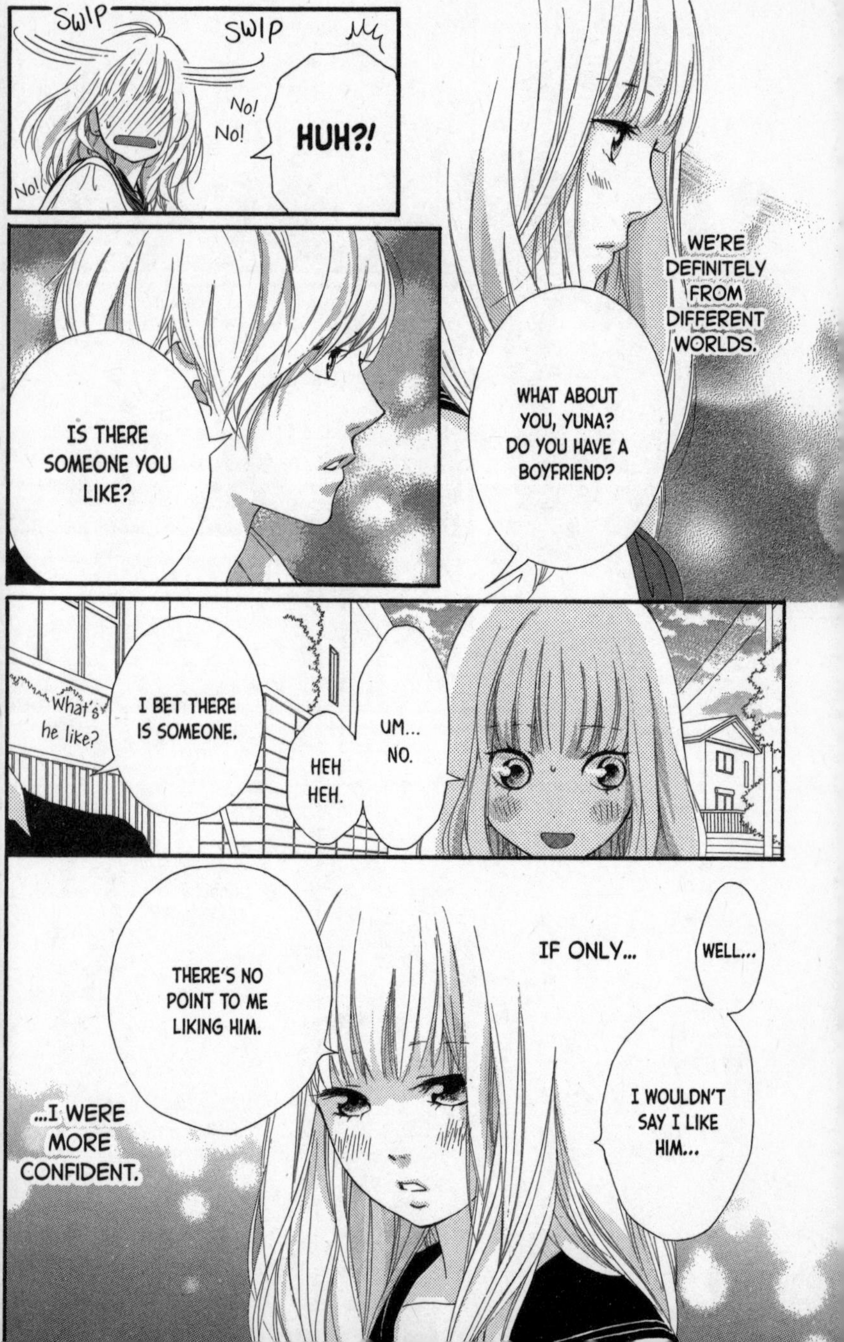
WE'RE DEFINITELY FROM DIFFERENT WORLDS.
WHAT ABOUT YOU, YUNA? DO YOU HAVE A BOYFRIEND?
HUH?!
No!
No!
SWIP
SWIP
No!
IS THERE SOMEONE YOU LIKE?
UM... NO.
HEH HEH.
I BET THERE IS SOMEONE.
What's he like?
WELL...
IF ONLY...
I WOULDN'T SAY I LIKE HIM...
THERE'S NO POINT TO ME LIKING HIM.
...I WERE MORE CONFIDENT.

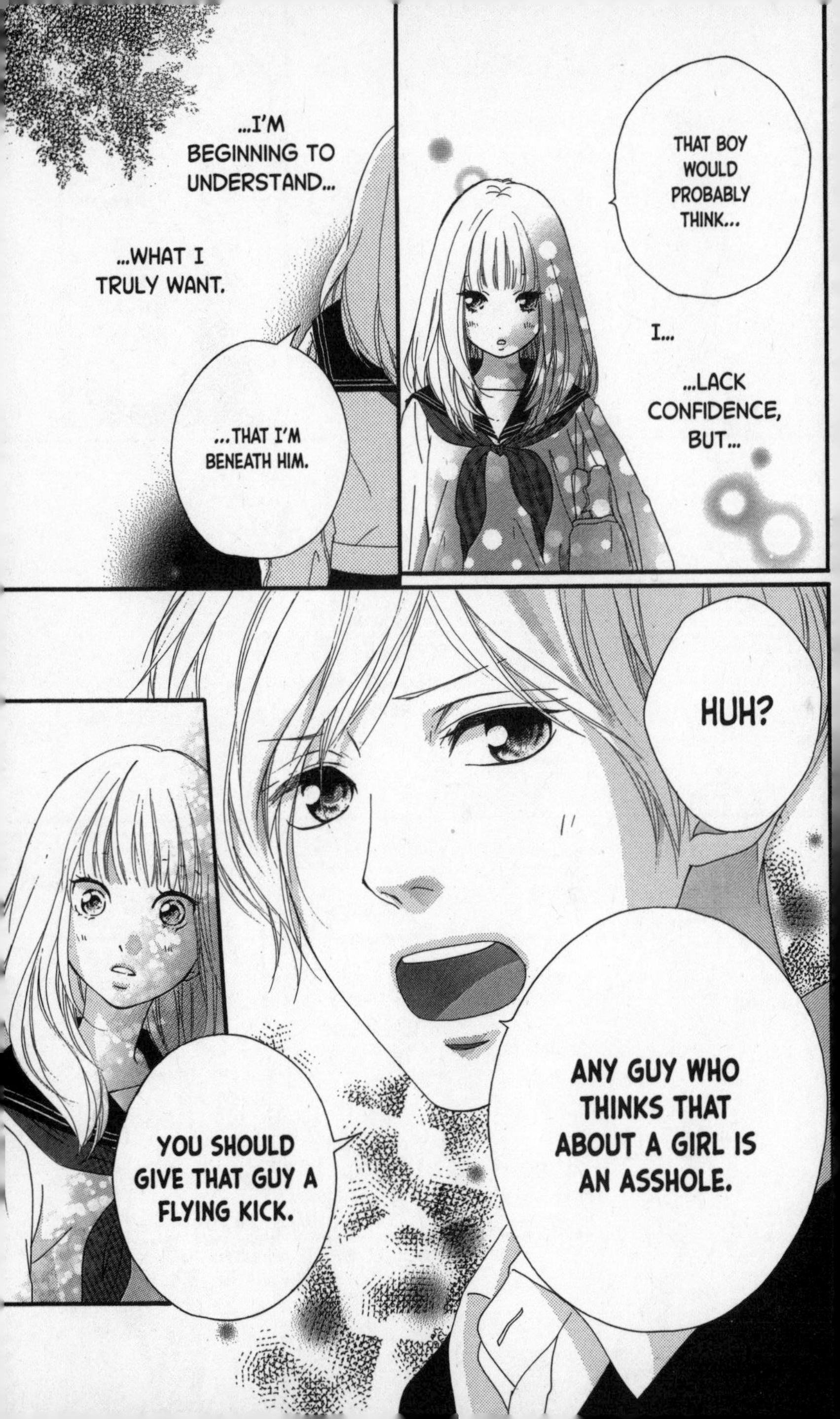
THAT BOY WOULD PROBABLY THINK...
I...
...LACK CONFIDENCE, BUT...
...I'M BEGINNING TO UNDERSTAND...
...WHAT I TRULY WANT.
...THAT I'M BENEATH HIM.
HUH?
ANY GUY WHO THINKS THAT ABOUT A GIRL IS AN ASSHOLE.
YOU SHOULD GIVE THAT GUY A FLYING KICK.

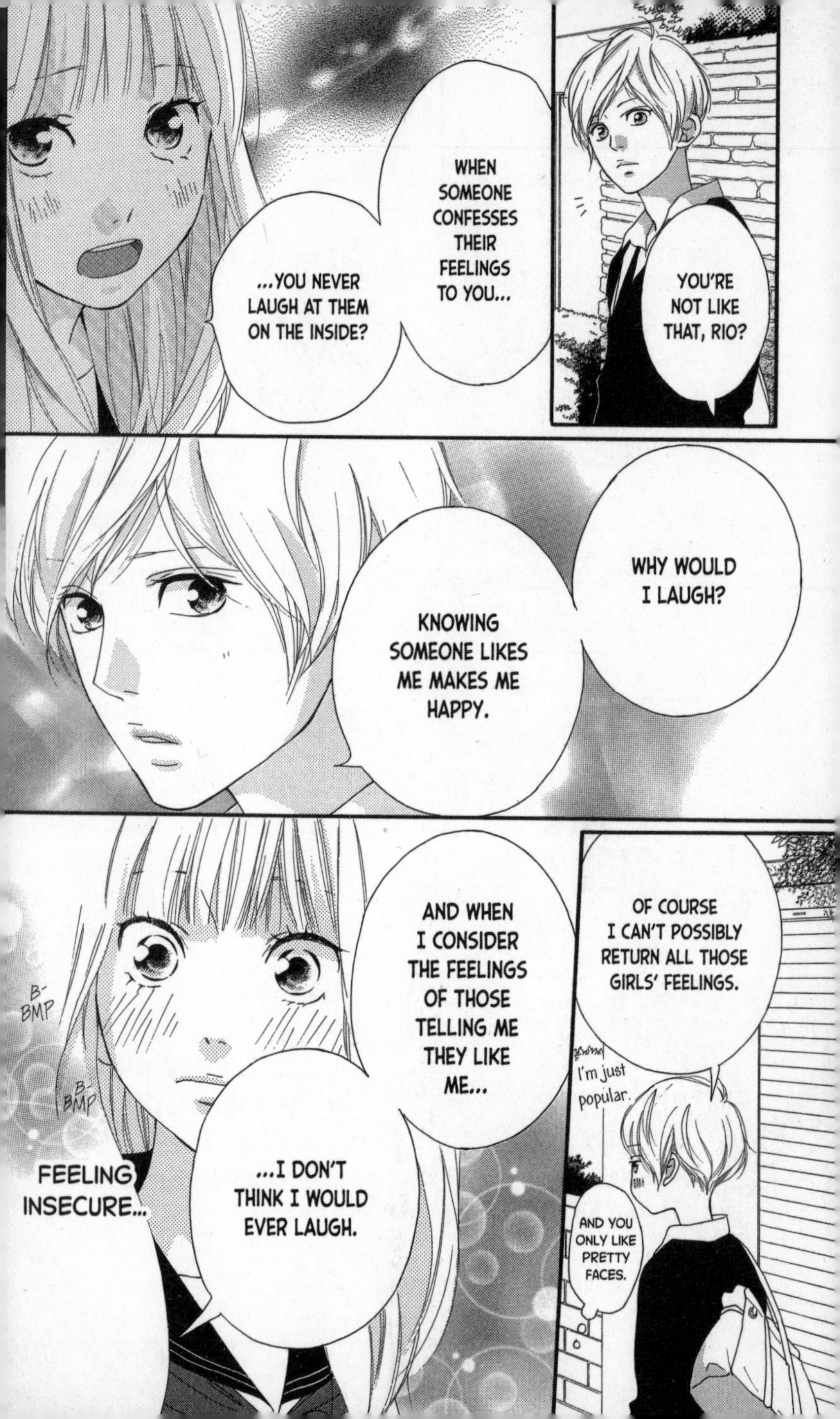
YOU'RE NOT LIKE THAT, RIO?
WHEN SOMEONE CONFESSES THEIR FEELINGS TO YOU...
...YOU NEVER LAUGH AT THEM ON THE INSIDE?
WHY WOULD I LAUGH?
KNOWING SOMEONE LIKES ME MAKES ME HAPPY.
OF COURSE I CAN'T POSSIBLY RETURN ALL THOSE GIRLS' FEELINGS.
I'm just popular.
AND YOU ONLY LIKE PRETTY FACES.
AND WHEN I CONSIDER THE FEELINGS OF THOSE TELLING ME THEY LIKE ME...
B-BMP
B-BMP
FEELING INSECURE...
...I DON'T THINK I WOULD EVER LAUGH.

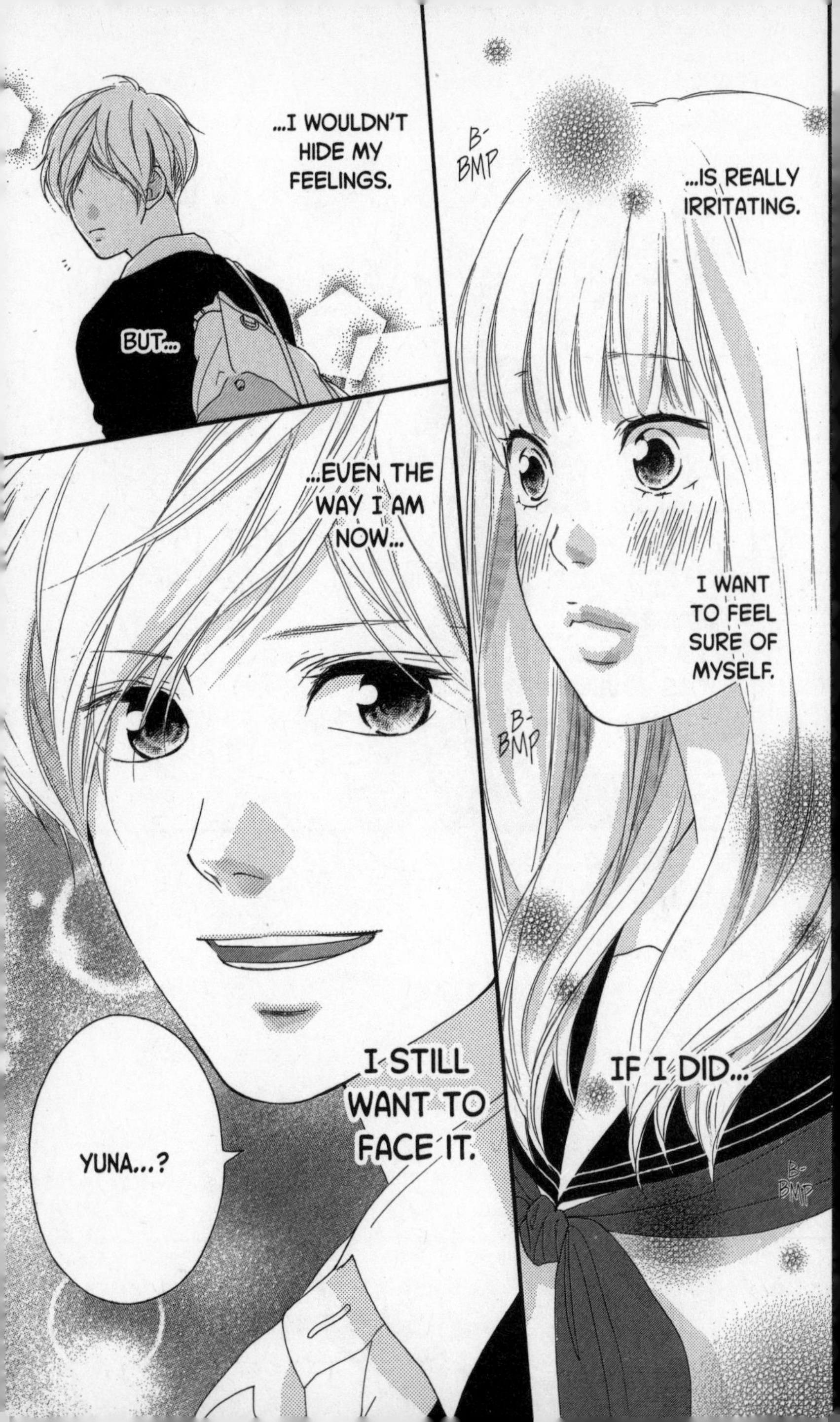
B-BMP
...IS REALLY IRRITATING.
I WANT TO FEEL SURE OF MYSELF.
B-BMP
IF I DID...
B-BMP
...I WOULDN'T HIDE MY FEELINGS.
BUT...
...EVEN THE WAY I AM NOW...
I STILL WANT TO FACE IT.
YUNA...?

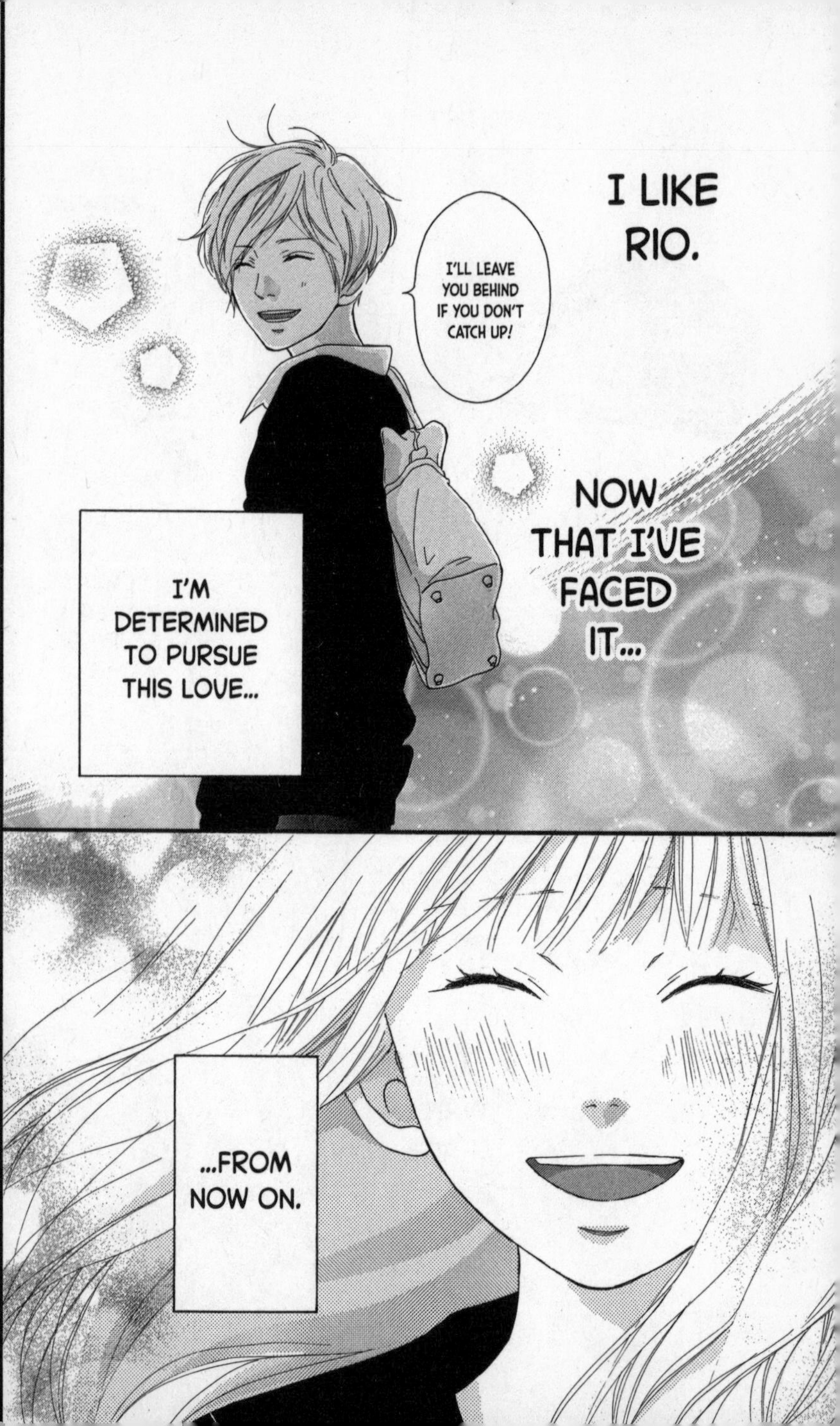
I LIKE RIO.
I'LL LEAVE YOU BEHIND IF YOU DON'T CATCH UP!
NOW THAT I'VE FACED IT...
I'M DETERMINED TO PURSUE THIS LOVE...
...FROM NOW ON.

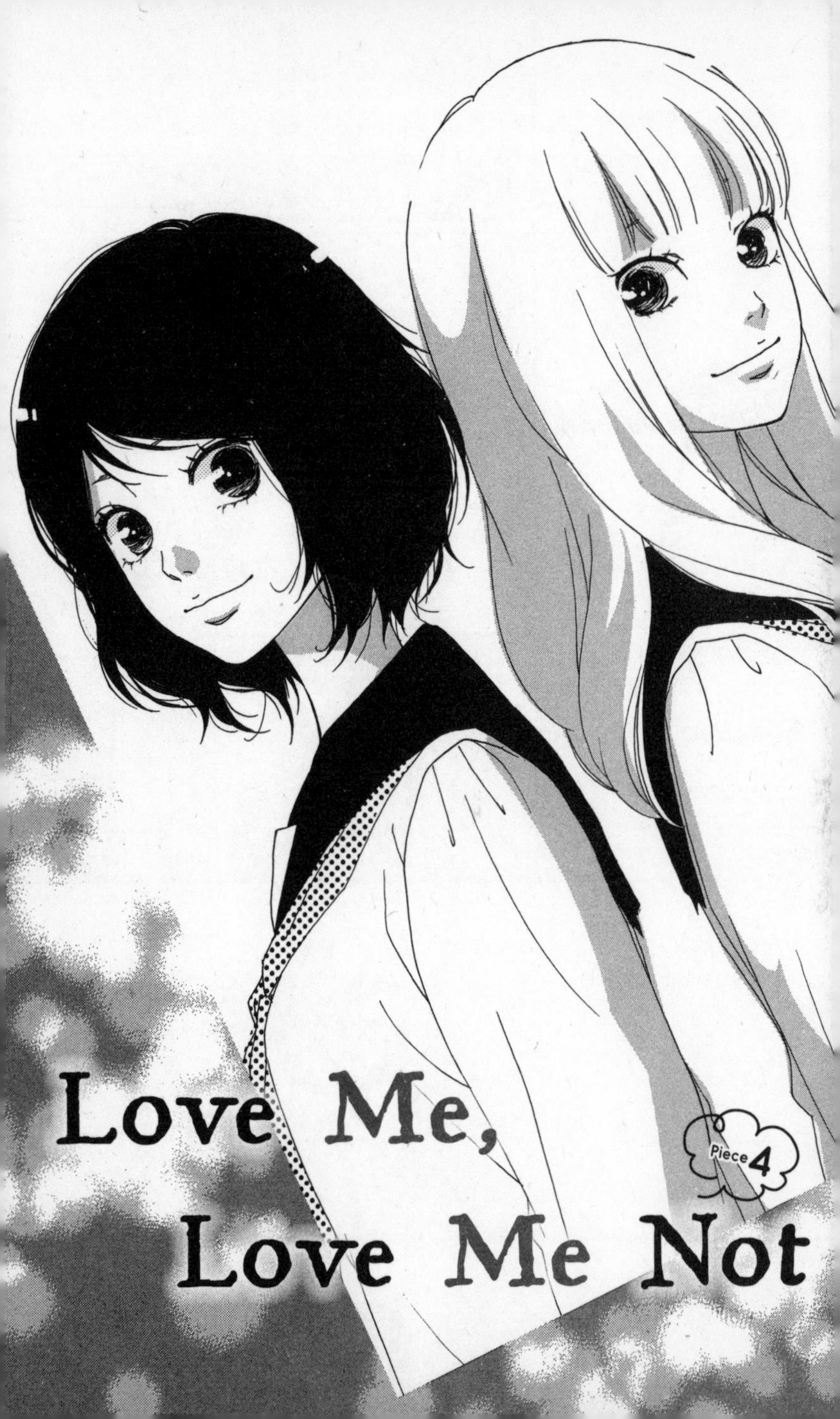
Love Me,
Love Me Not
Piece 4

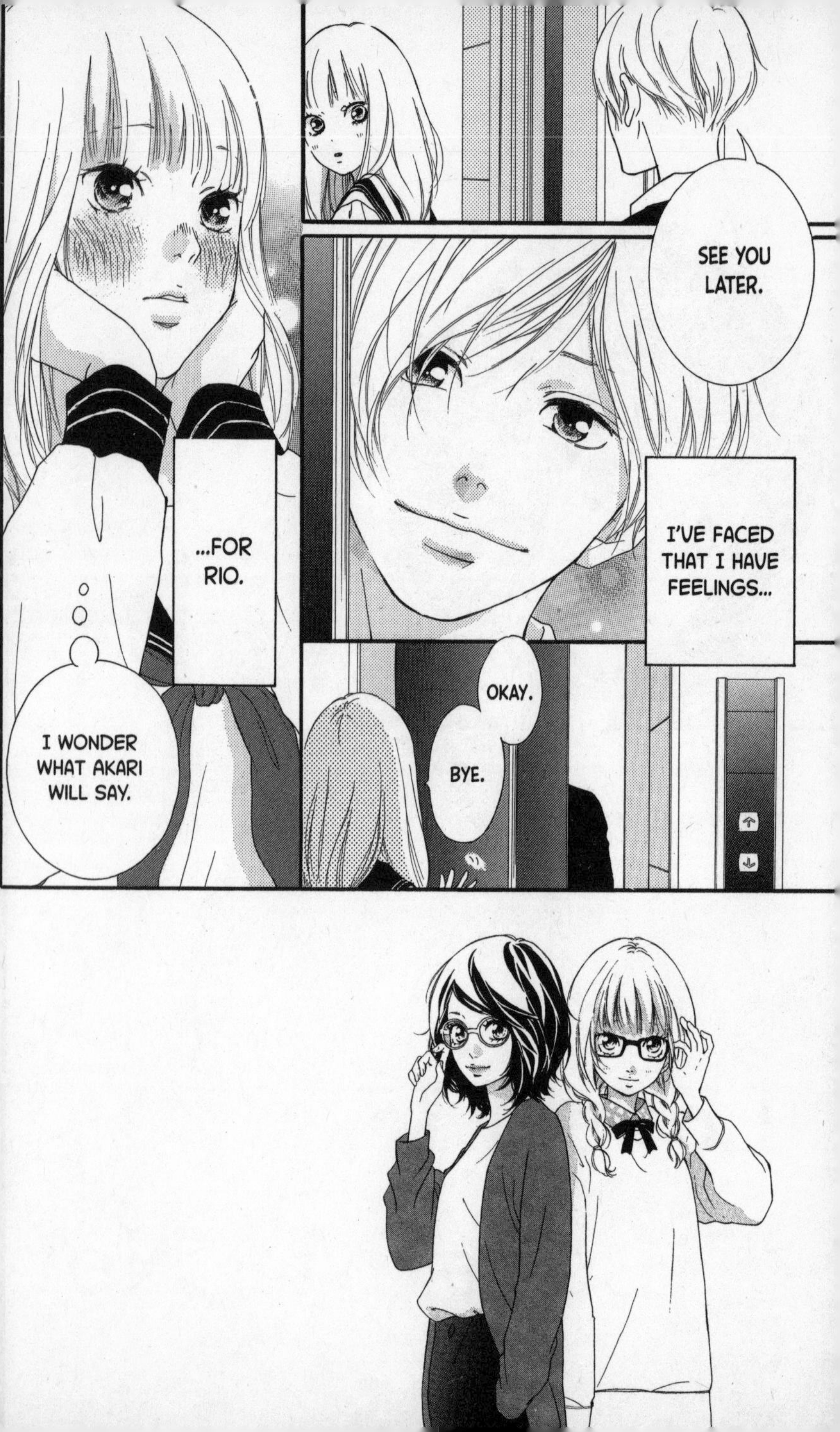
SEE YOU LATER.
I'VE FACED THAT I HAVE FEELINGS...
OKAY.
BYE.
...FOR RIO.
I WONDER WHAT AKARI WILL SAY.

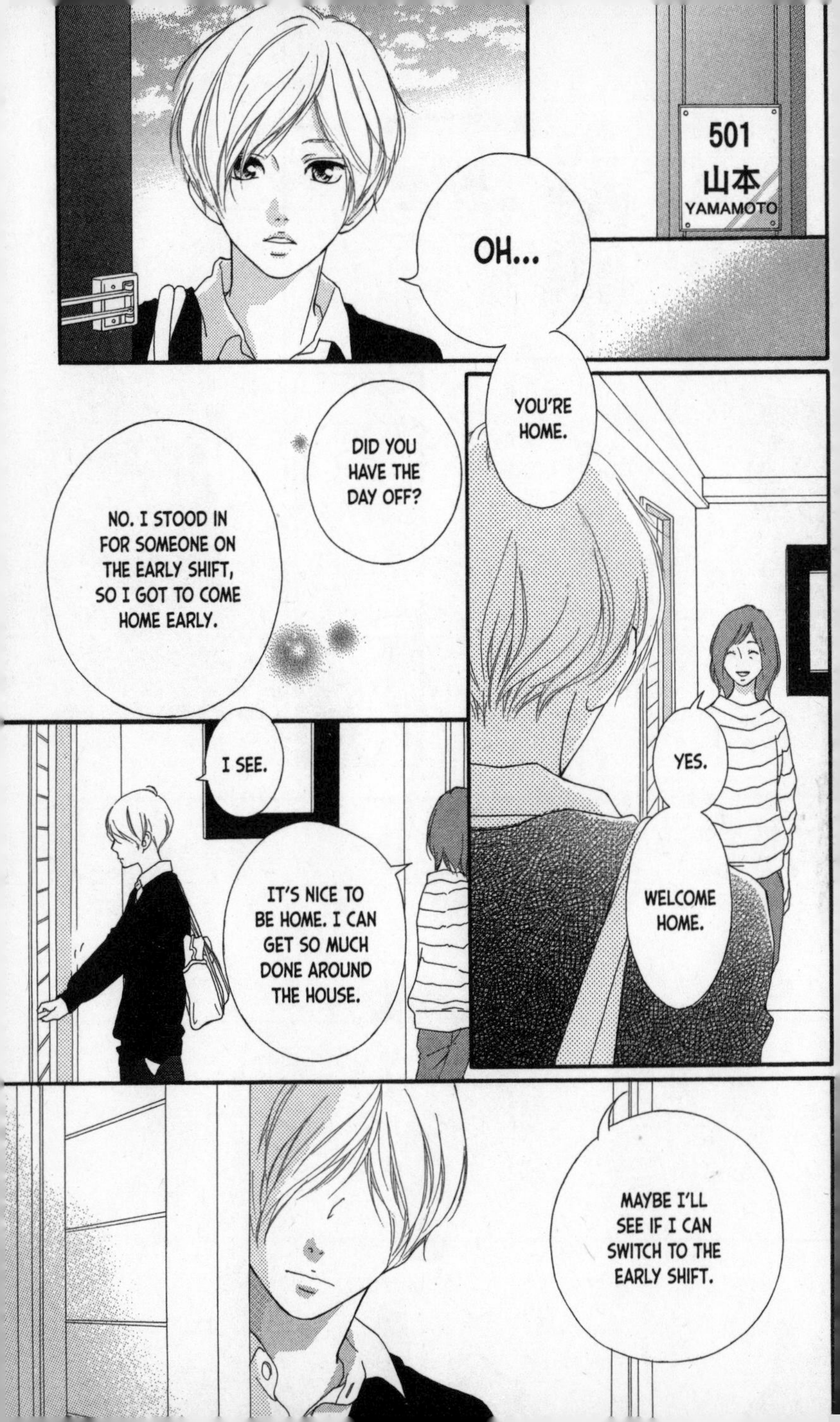

501
山本
YAMAMOTO
OH...
YOU'RE HOME.
YES.
WELCOME HOME.
DID YOU HAVE THE DAY OFF?
NO. I STOOD IN FOR SOMEONE ON THE EARLY SHIFT, SO I GOT TO COME HOME EARLY.
I SEE.
IT'S NICE TO BE HOME. I CAN GET SO MUCH DONE AROUND THE HOUSE.
MAYBE I'LL SEE IF I CAN SWITCH TO THE EARLY SHIFT.

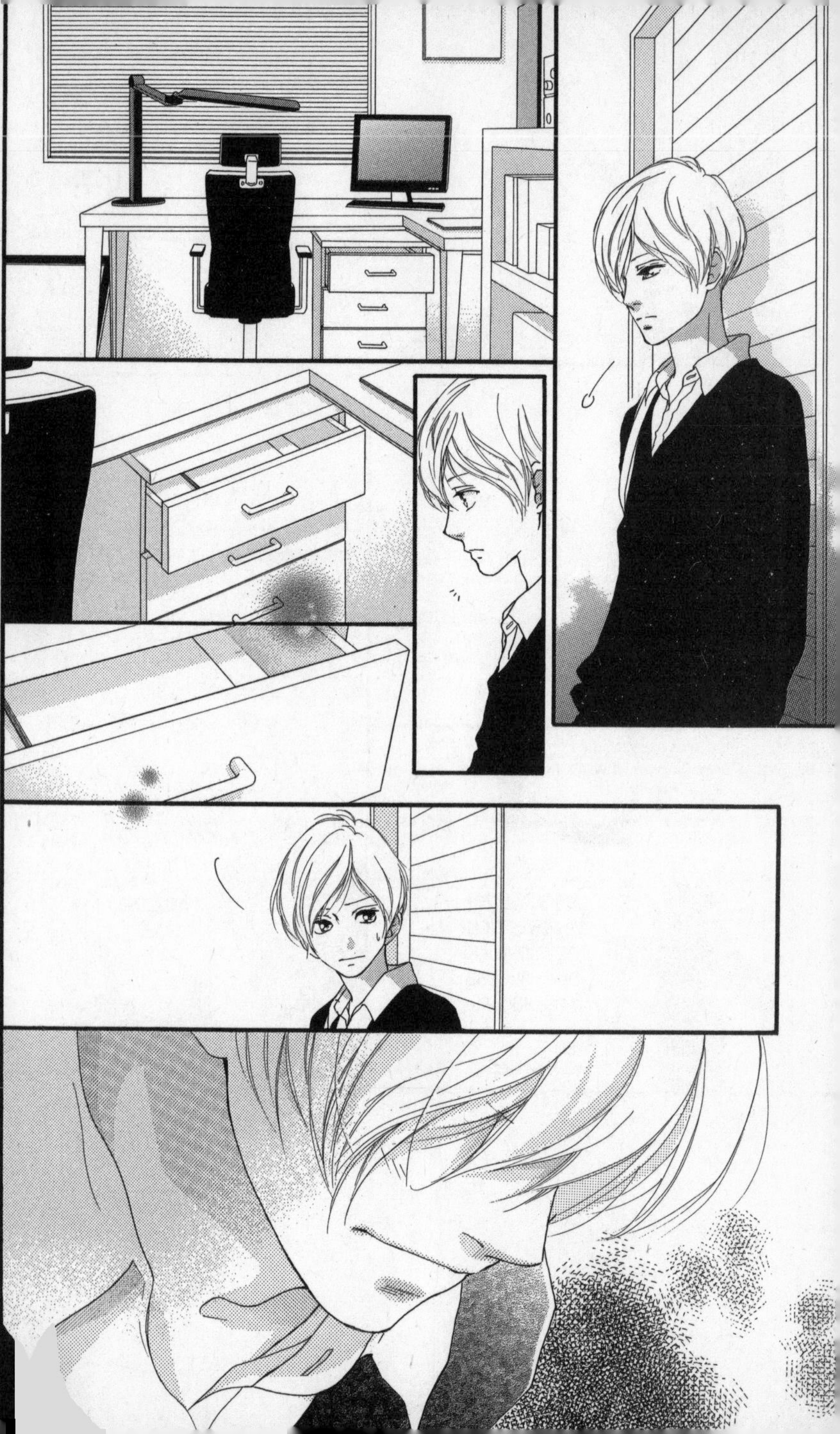

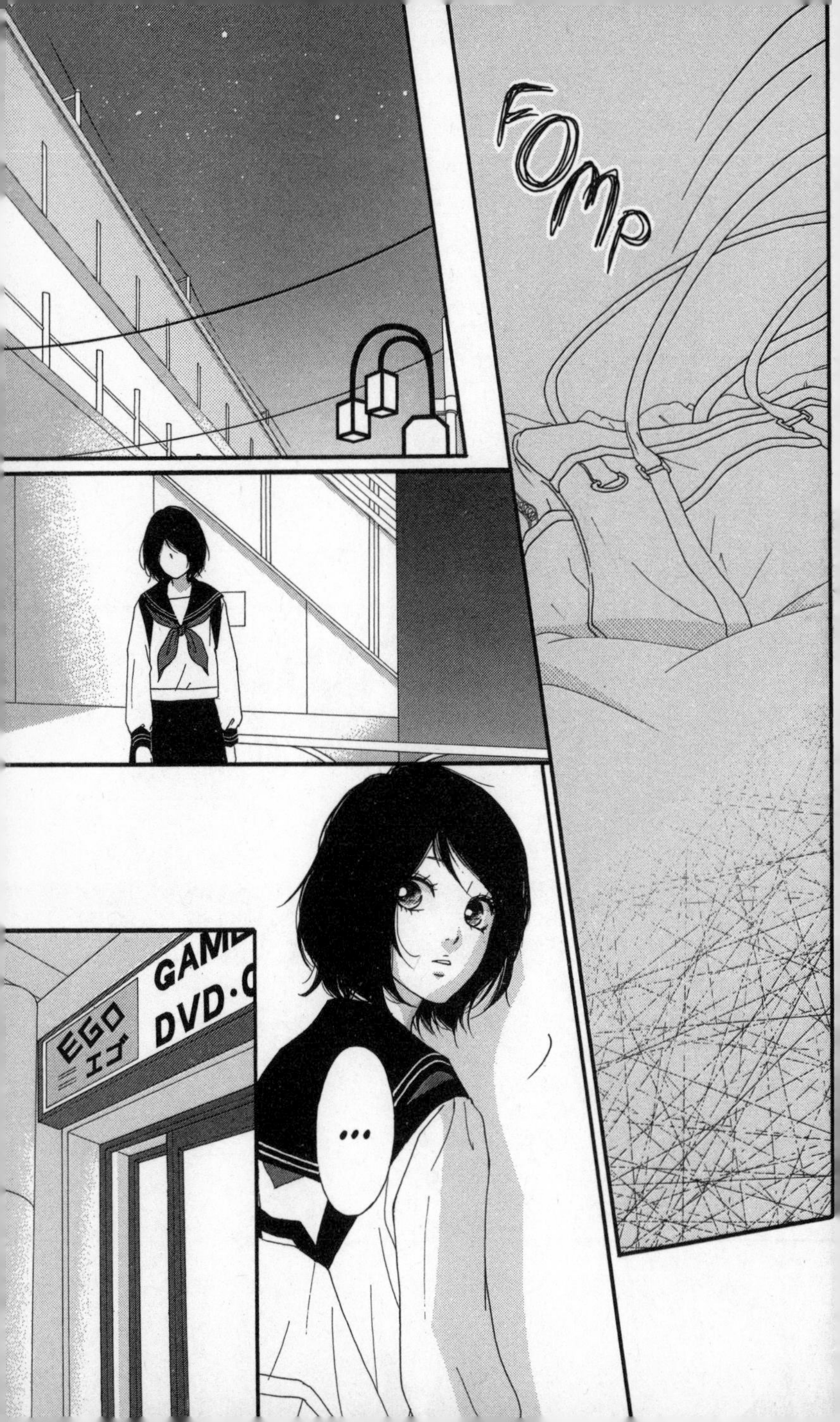
FOMP
EGO
エゴ
GAM
DVD・
...

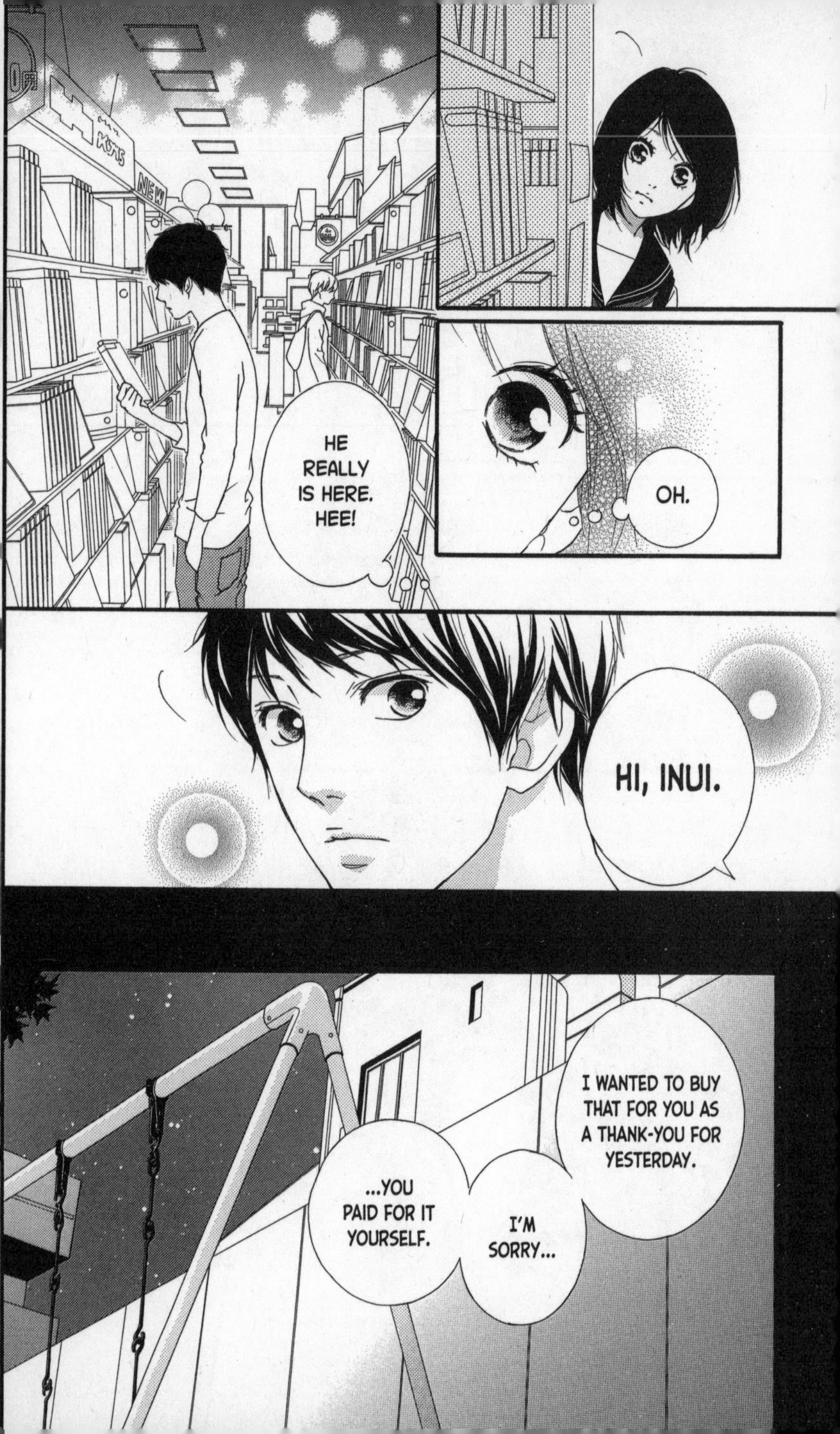
OH.
HE REALLY IS HERE. HEE!
HI, INUI.
I WANTED TO BUY THAT FOR YOU AS A THANK-YOU FOR YESTERDAY.
I'M SORRY...
...YOU PAID FOR IT YOURSELF.

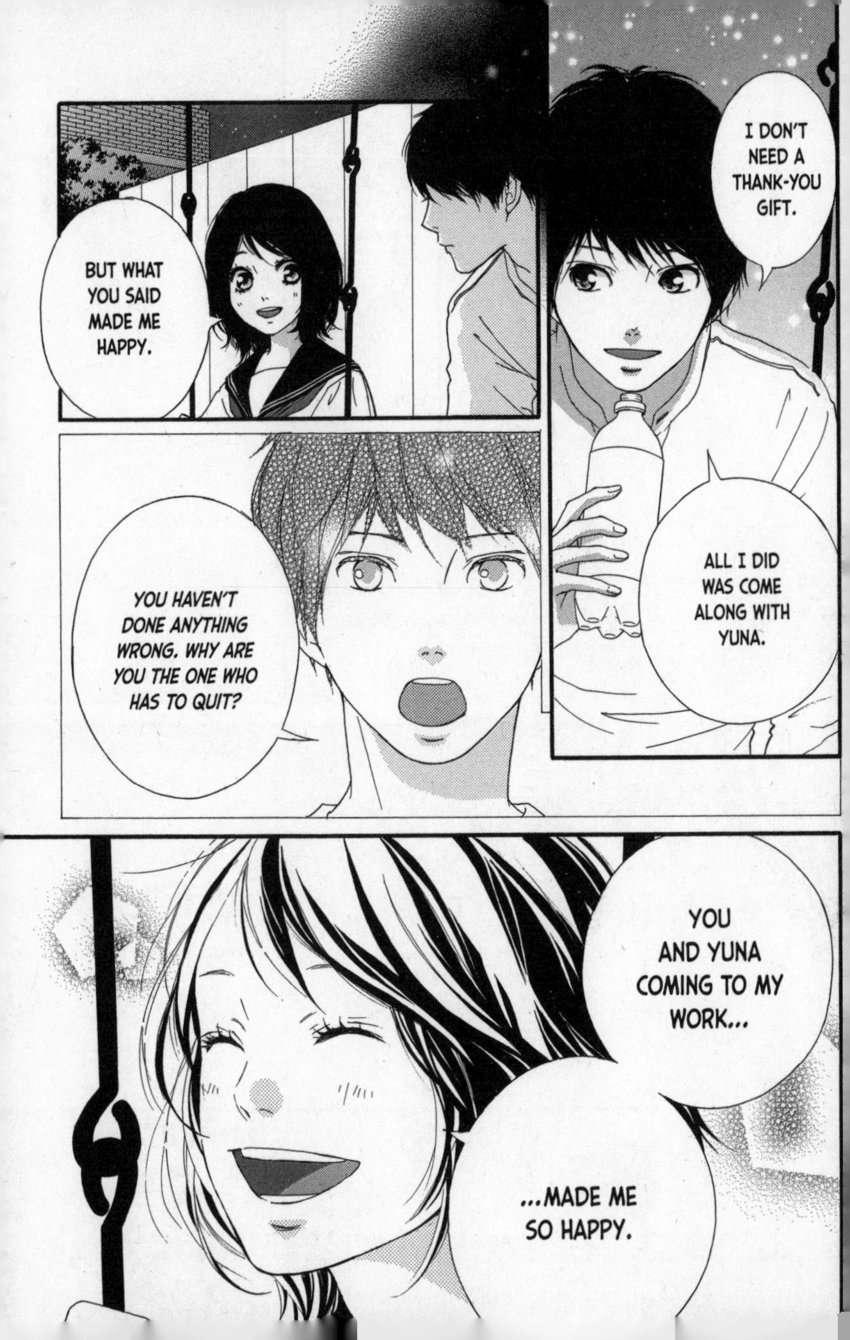
I DON'T NEED A THANK-YOU GIFT.
ALL I DID WAS COME ALONG WITH YUNA.
BUT WHAT YOU SAID MADE ME HAPPY.
YOU HAVEN'T DONE ANYTHING WRONG. WHY ARE YOU THE ONE WHO HAS TO QUIT?
YOU AND YUNA COMING TO MY WORK...
...MADE ME SO HAPPY.

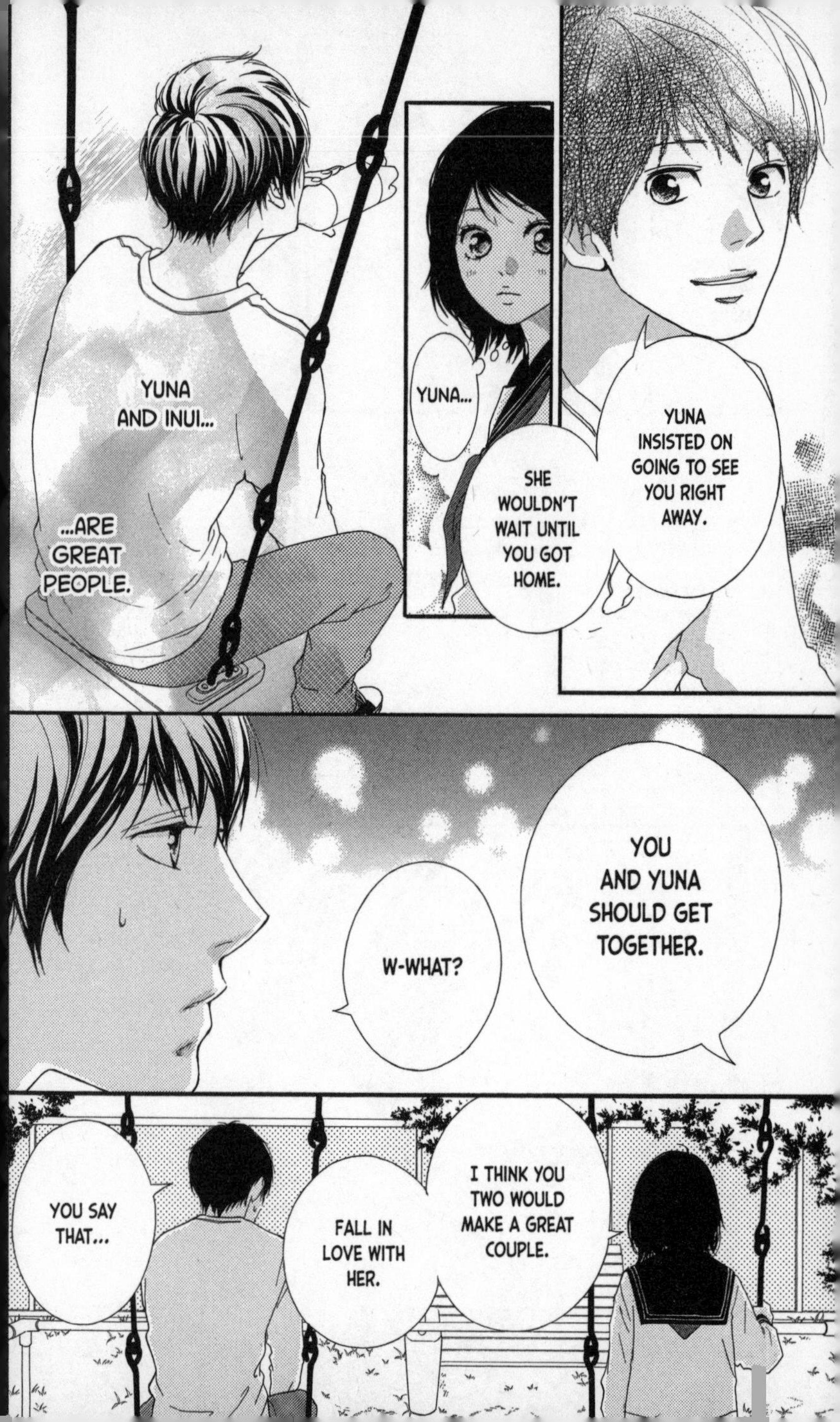
YUNA INSISTED ON GOING TO SEE YOU RIGHT AWAY.
SHE WOULDN'T WAIT UNTIL YOU GOT HOME.
YUNA...
YUNA AND INUI...
...ARE GREAT PEOPLE.
YOU AND YUNA SHOULD GET TOGETHER.
W-WHAT?
I THINK YOU TWO WOULD MAKE A GREAT COUPLE.
FALL IN LOVE WITH HER.
YOU SAY THAT...

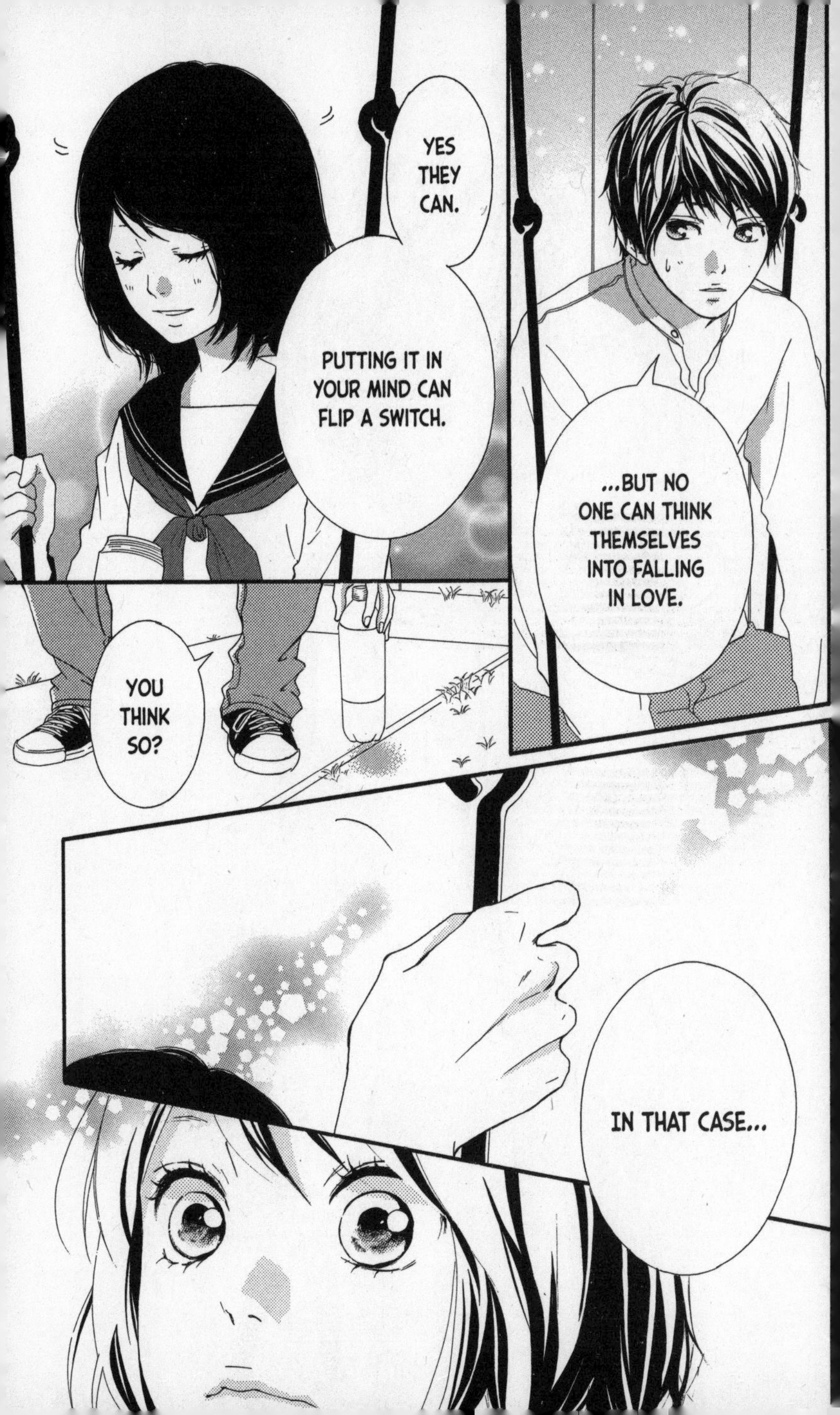
...BUT NO ONE CAN THINK THEMSELVES INTO FALLING IN LOVE.
YES THEY CAN.
PUTTING IT IN YOUR MIND CAN FLIP A SWITCH.
YOU THINK SO?
IN THAT CASE...

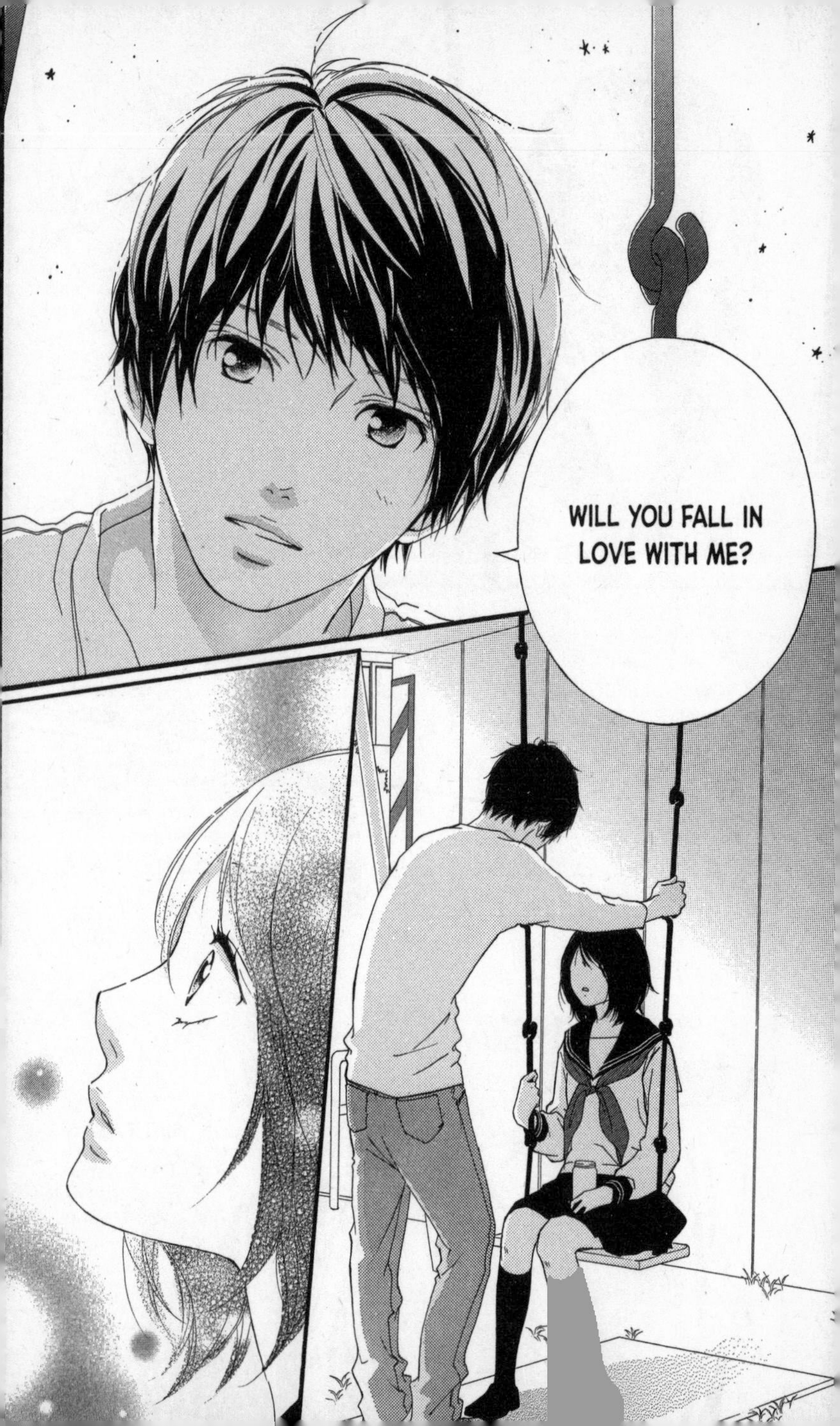
WILL YOU FALL IN LOVE WITH ME?

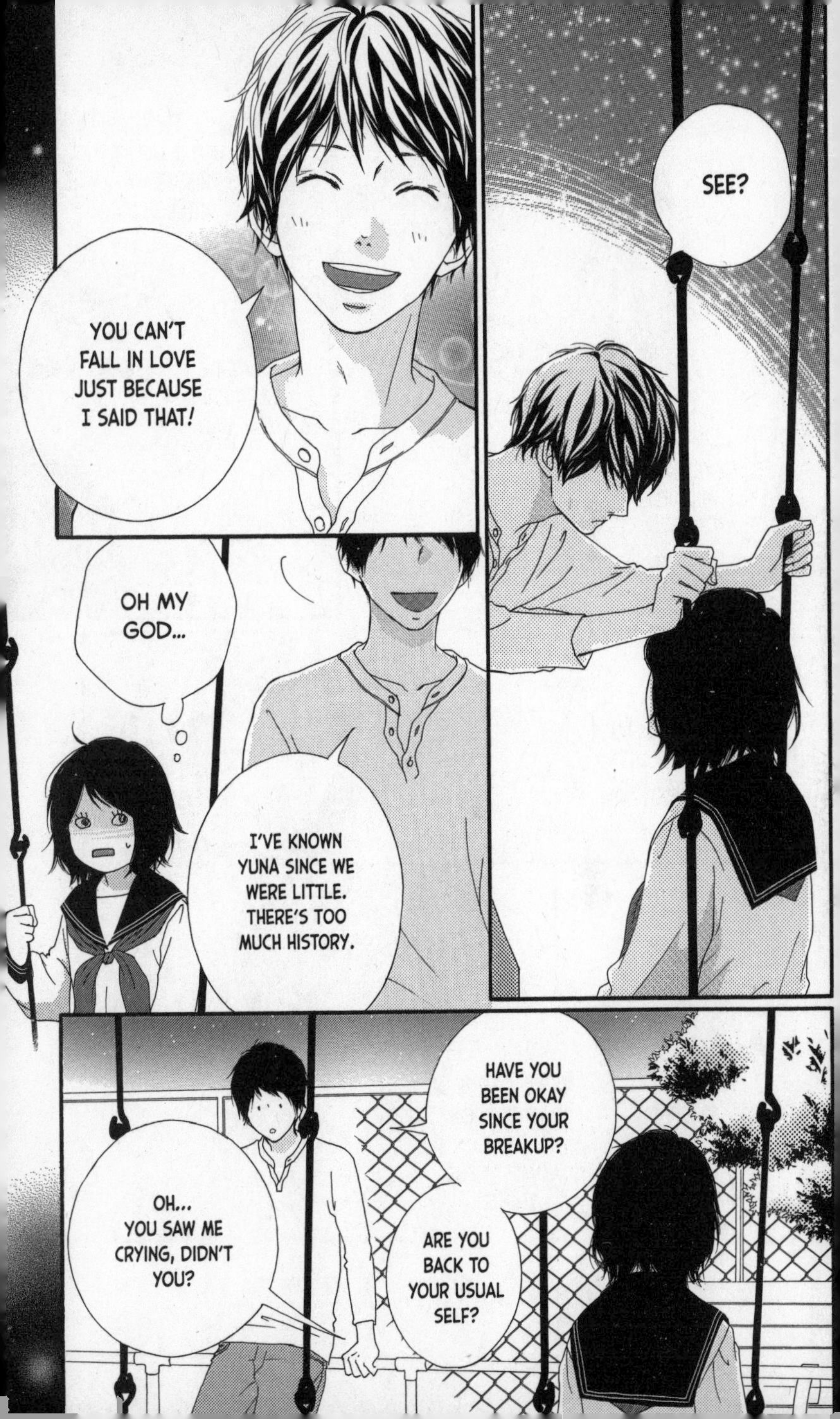
SEE?
YOU CAN'T FALL IN LOVE JUST BECAUSE I SAID THAT!
OH MY GOD...
I'VE KNOWN YUNA SINCE WE WERE LITTLE. THERE'S TOO MUCH HISTORY.
HAVE YOU BEEN OKAY SINCE YOUR BREAKUP?
ARE YOU BACK TO YOUR USUAL SELF?
OH... YOU SAW ME CRYING, DIDN'T YOU?

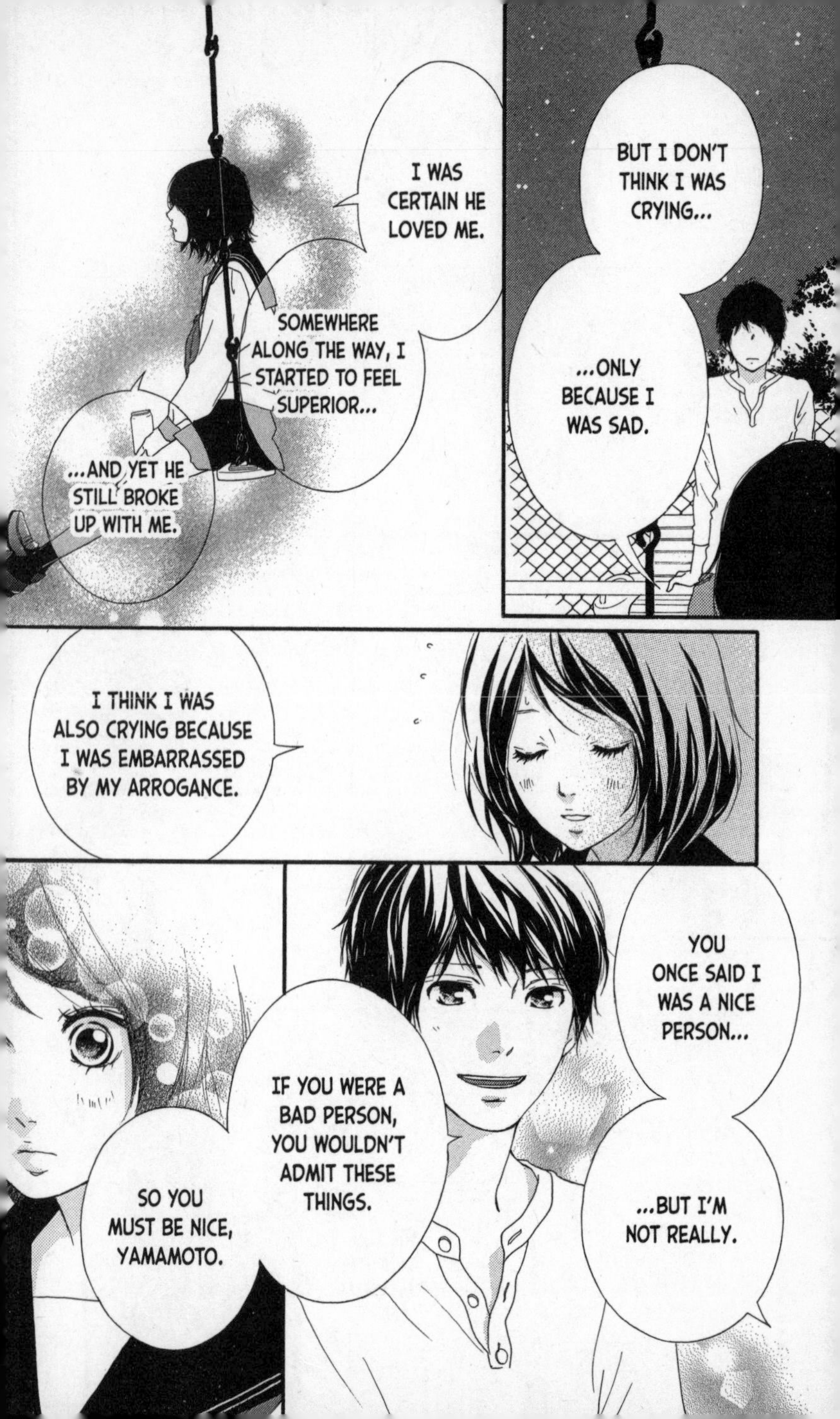
BUT I DON'T THINK I WAS CRYING...
...ONLY BECAUSE I WAS SAD.
I WAS CERTAIN HE LOVED ME.
SOMEWHERE ALONG THE WAY, I STARTED TO FEEL SUPERIOR...
...AND YET HE STILL BROKE UP WITH ME.
I THINK I WAS ALSO CRYING BECAUSE I WAS EMBARRASSED BY MY ARROGANCE.
YOU ONCE SAID I WAS A NICE PERSON...
...BUT I'M NOT REALLY.
IF YOU WERE A BAD PERSON, YOU WOULDN'T ADMIT THESE THINGS.
SO YOU MUST BE NICE, YAMAMOTO.

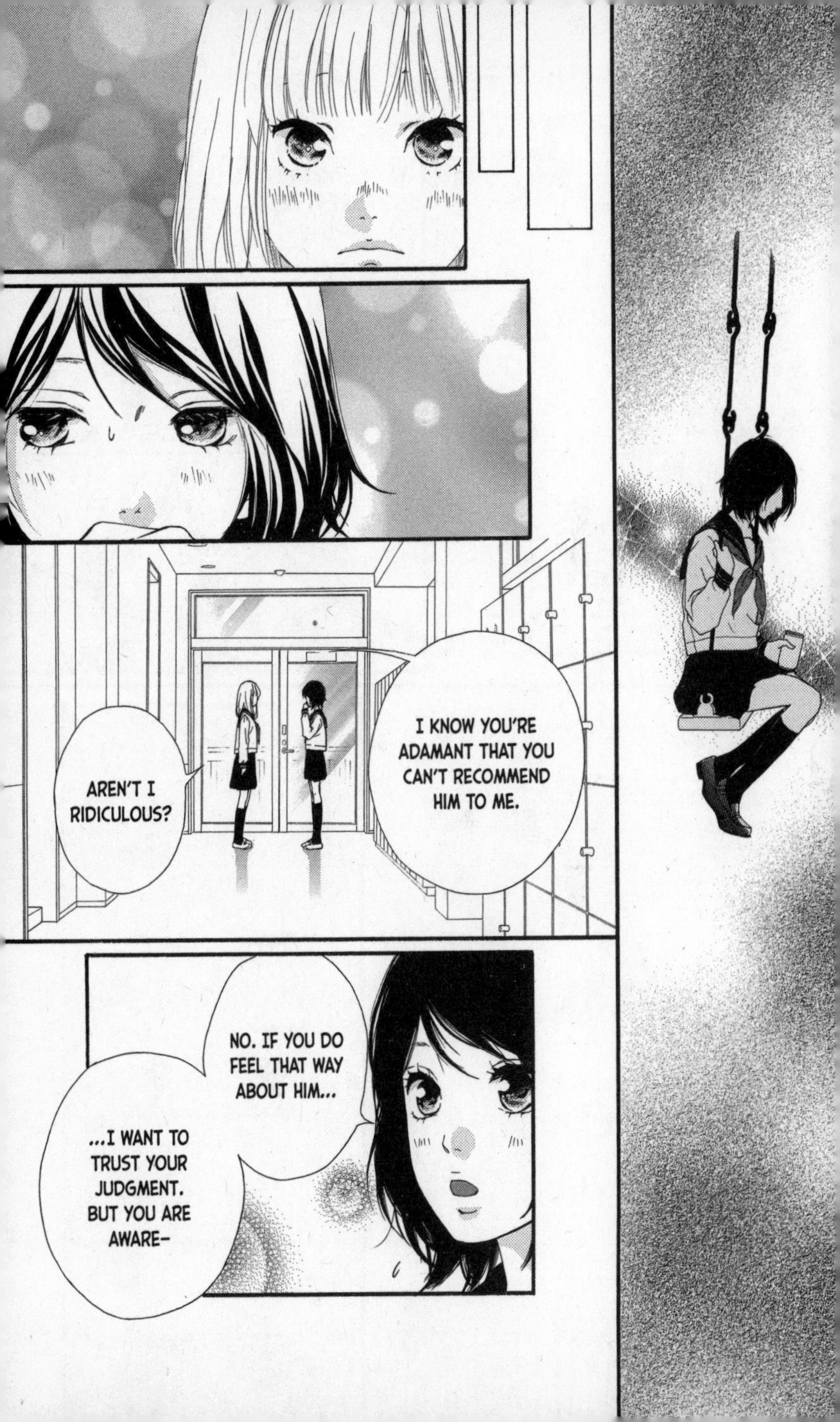
I KNOW YOU'RE ADAMANT THAT YOU CAN'T RECOMMEND HIM TO ME.
AREN'T I RIDICULOUS?
NO. IF YOU DO FEEL THAT WAY ABOUT HIM...
...I WANT TO TRUST YOUR JUDGMENT. BUT YOU ARE AWARE–

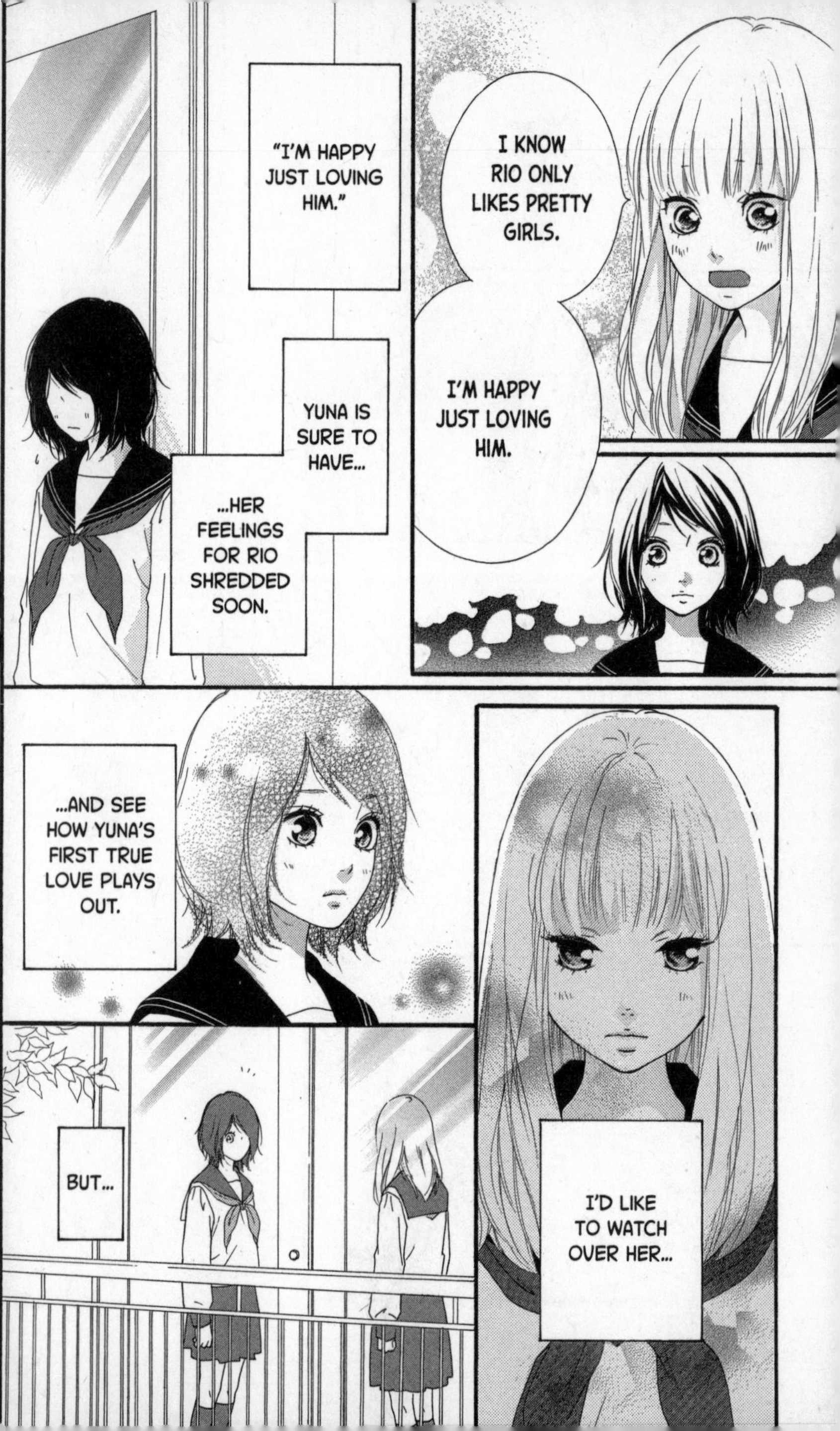
I KNOW RIO ONLY LIKES PRETTY GIRLS.
I'M HAPPY JUST LOVING HIM.
"I'M HAPPY JUST LOVING HIM."
YUNA IS SURE TO HAVE...
...HER FEELINGS FOR RIO SHREDDED SOON.
I'D LIKE TO WATCH OVER HER...
...AND SEE HOW YUNA'S FIRST TRUE LOVE PLAYS OUT.
BUT...

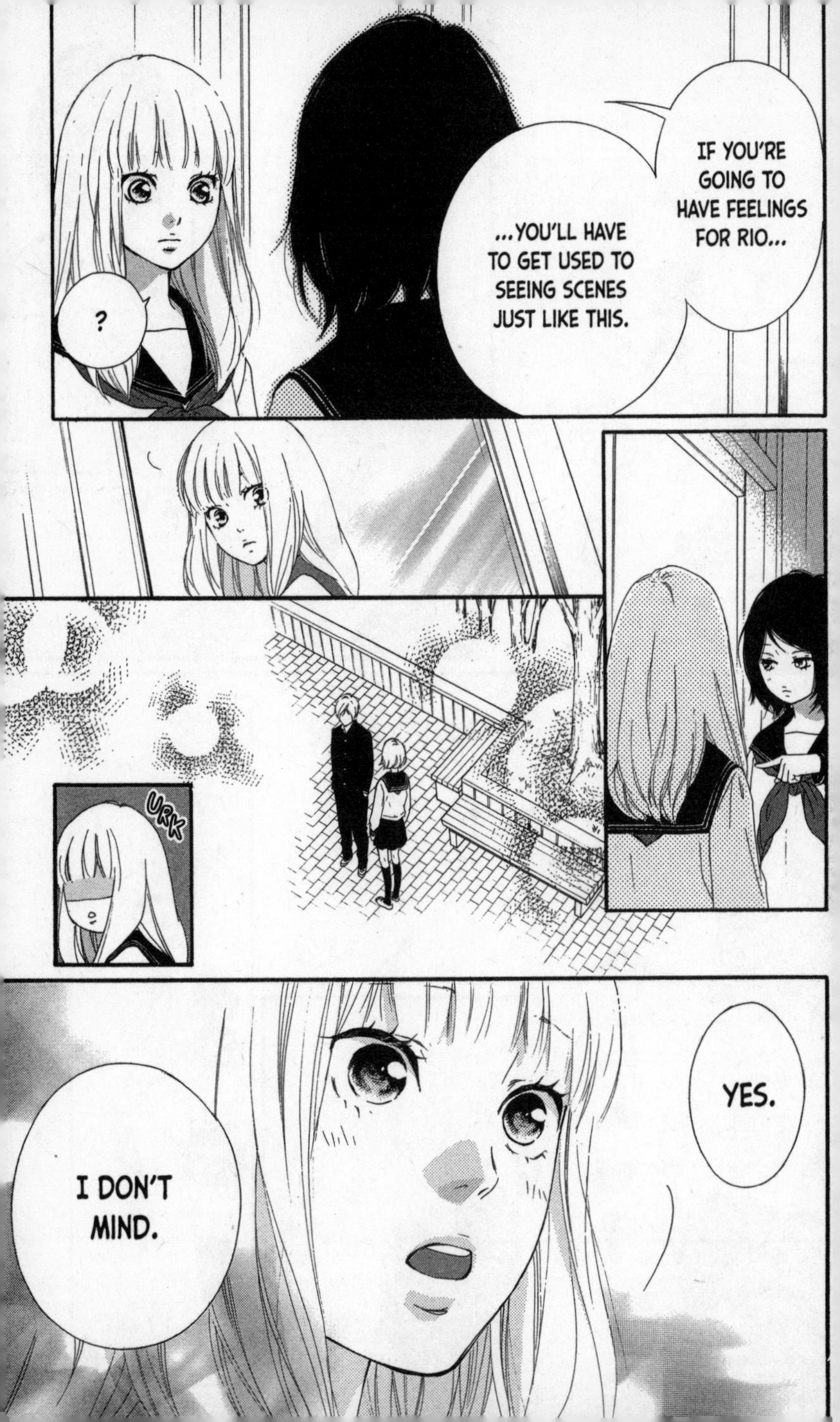

IF YOU'RE GOING TO HAVE FEELINGS FOR RIO...
...YOU'LL HAVE TO GET USED TO SEEING SCENES JUST LIKE THIS.
?
URK
YES.
I DON'T MIND.

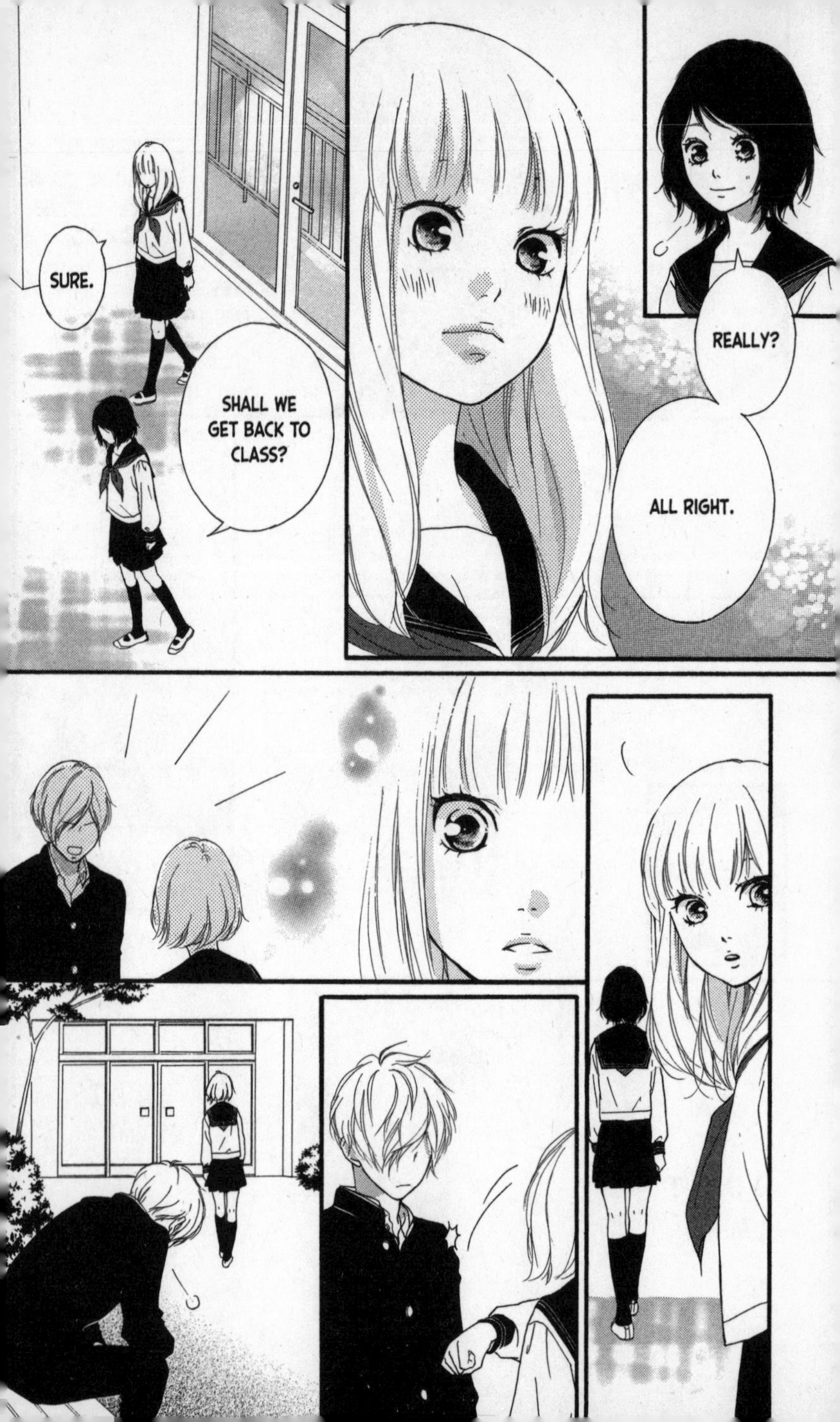
REALLY?
ALL RIGHT.
SHALL WE GET BACK TO CLASS?
SURE.

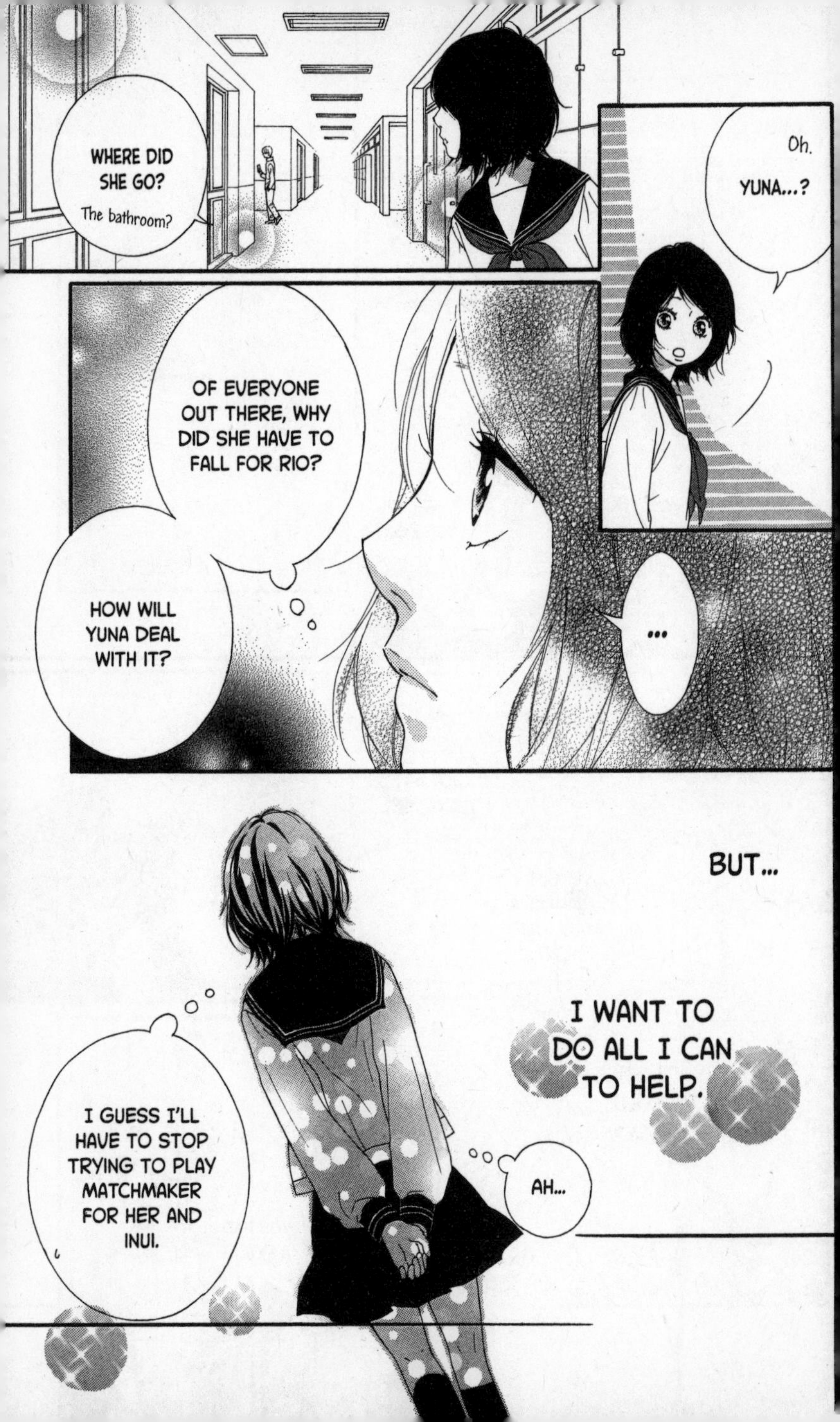
WHERE DID SHE GO?
The bathroom?
Oh.
YUNA...?
...
OF EVERYONE OUT THERE, WHY DID SHE HAVE TO FALL FOR RIO?
HOW WILL YUNA DEAL WITH IT?
AH...
I GUESS I'LL HAVE TO STOP TRYING TO PLAY MATCHMAKER FOR HER AND INUI.
BUT...
I WANT TO DO ALL I CAN TO HELP.

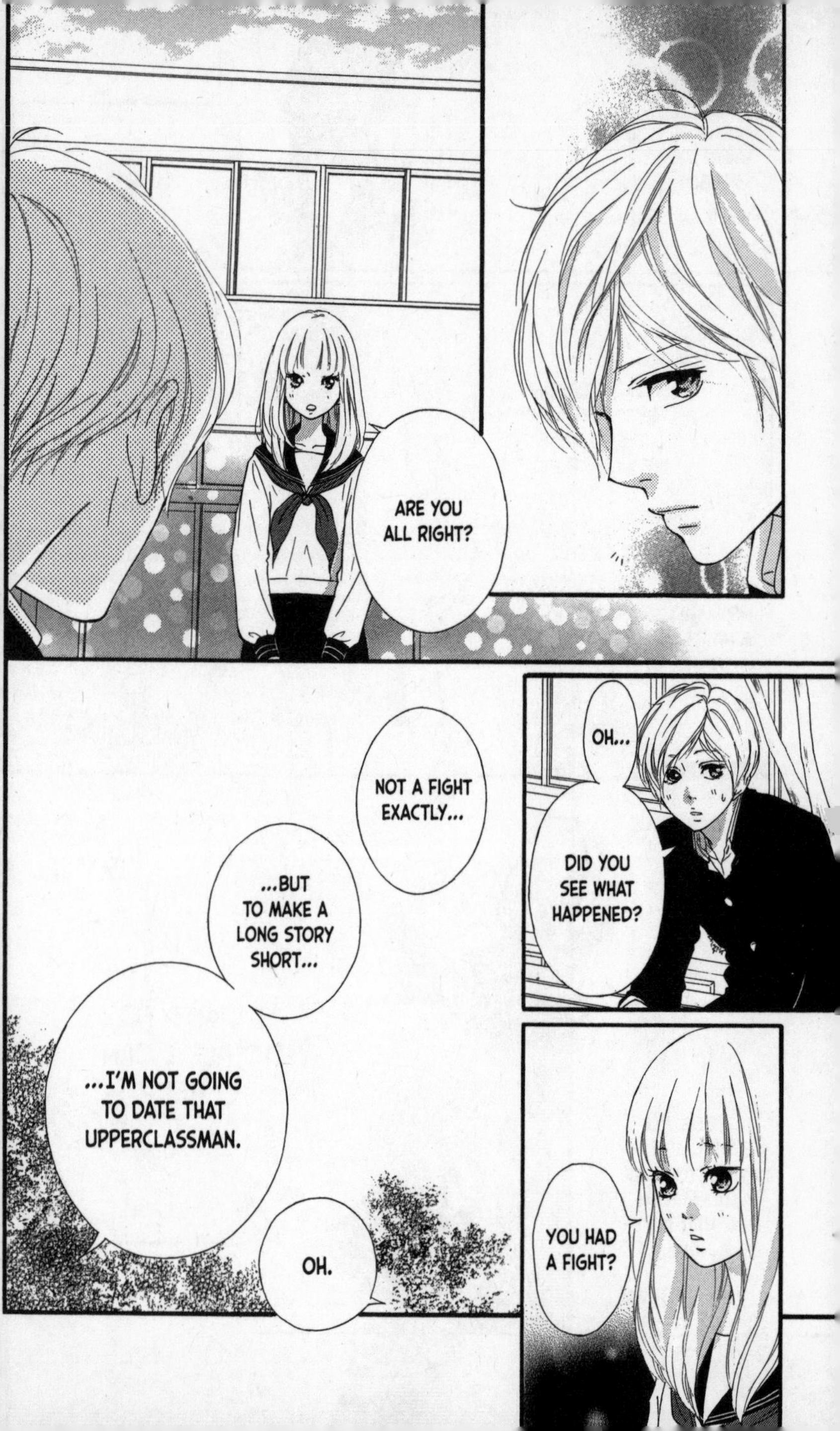
ARE YOU ALL RIGHT?
OH...
DID YOU SEE WHAT HAPPENED?
YOU HAD A FIGHT?
NOT A FIGHT EXACTLY...
...BUT TO MAKE A LONG STORY SHORT...
...I'M NOT GOING TO DATE THAT UPPERCLASSMAN.
OH.

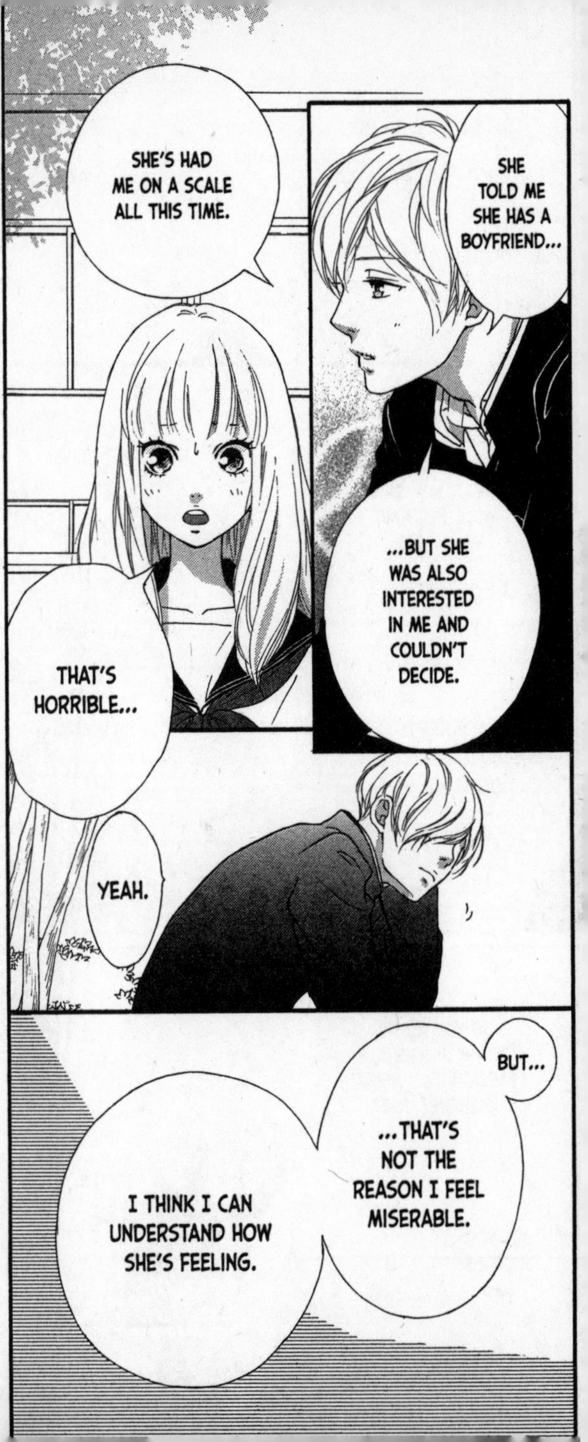
SHE TOLD ME SHE HAS A BOYFRIEND...
...BUT SHE WAS ALSO INTERESTED IN ME AND COULDN'T DECIDE.
SHE'S HAD ME ON A SCALE ALL THIS TIME.
THAT'S HORRIBLE...
YEAH.
BUT...
...THAT'S NOT THE REASON I FEEL MISERABLE.
I THINK I CAN UNDERSTAND HOW SHE'S FEELING.

Early one morning after working all night, I decided to walk to the convenience store for a break. When I left the building, I heard a loud squawking from above. "What? Am I in a jungle?" I thought. Looking up, I saw a small flock of green birds with red beaks above me. Judging from their large size and how they didn't look like birds native to Japan, I thought they might be parrots. I wondered if we have birds like that here, so I looked them up. They are true parrots. They were wild. I never knew parrots grew so large. They look like tropical birds, and yet they survive Japan's cold winters? I guess they're adaptable.

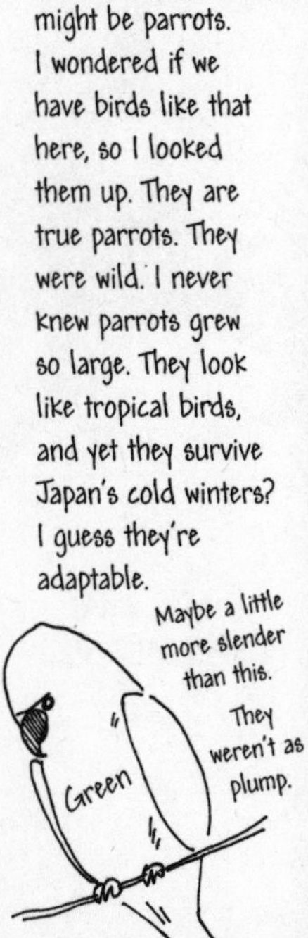
Maybe a little more slender than this.
They weren't as plump.
Green

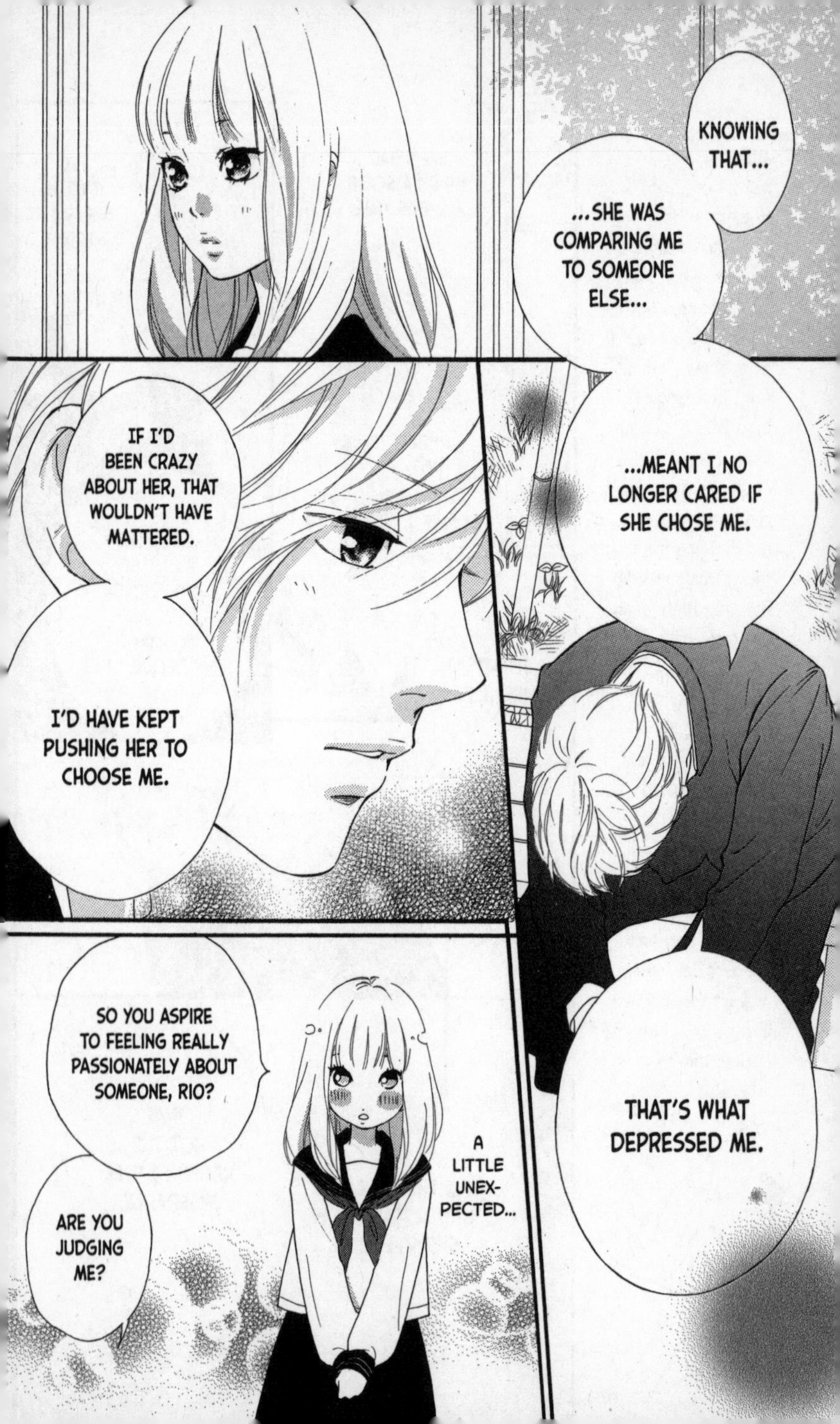
KNOWING THAT...
...SHE WAS COMPARING ME TO SOMEONE ELSE...
...MEANT I NO LONGER CARED IF SHE CHOSE ME.
THAT'S WHAT DEPRESSED ME.
IF I'D BEEN CRAZY ABOUT HER, THAT WOULDN'T HAVE MATTERED.
I'D HAVE KEPT PUSHING HER TO CHOOSE ME.
A LITTLE UNEXPECTED...
SO YOU ASPIRE TO FEELING REALLY PASSIONATELY ABOUT SOMEONE, RIO?
ARE YOU JUDGING ME?

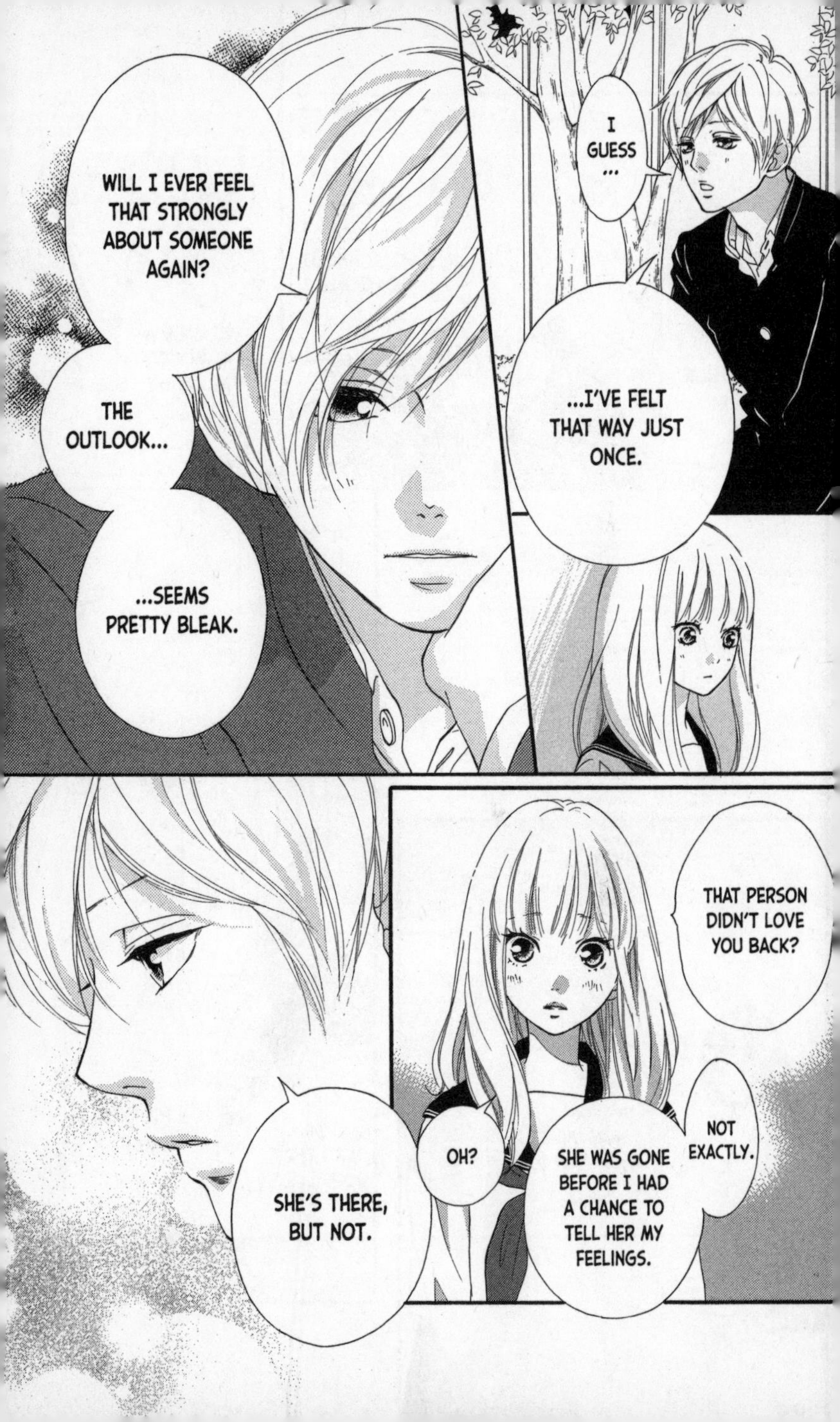
I GUESS...
...I'VE FELT THAT WAY JUST ONCE.
WILL I EVER FEEL THAT STRONGLY ABOUT SOMEONE AGAIN?
THE OUTLOOK...
...SEEMS PRETTY BLEAK.
THAT PERSON DIDN'T LOVE YOU BACK?
NOT EXACTLY.
SHE WAS GONE BEFORE I HAD A CHANCE TO TELL HER MY FEELINGS.
OH?
SHE'S THERE, BUT NOT.

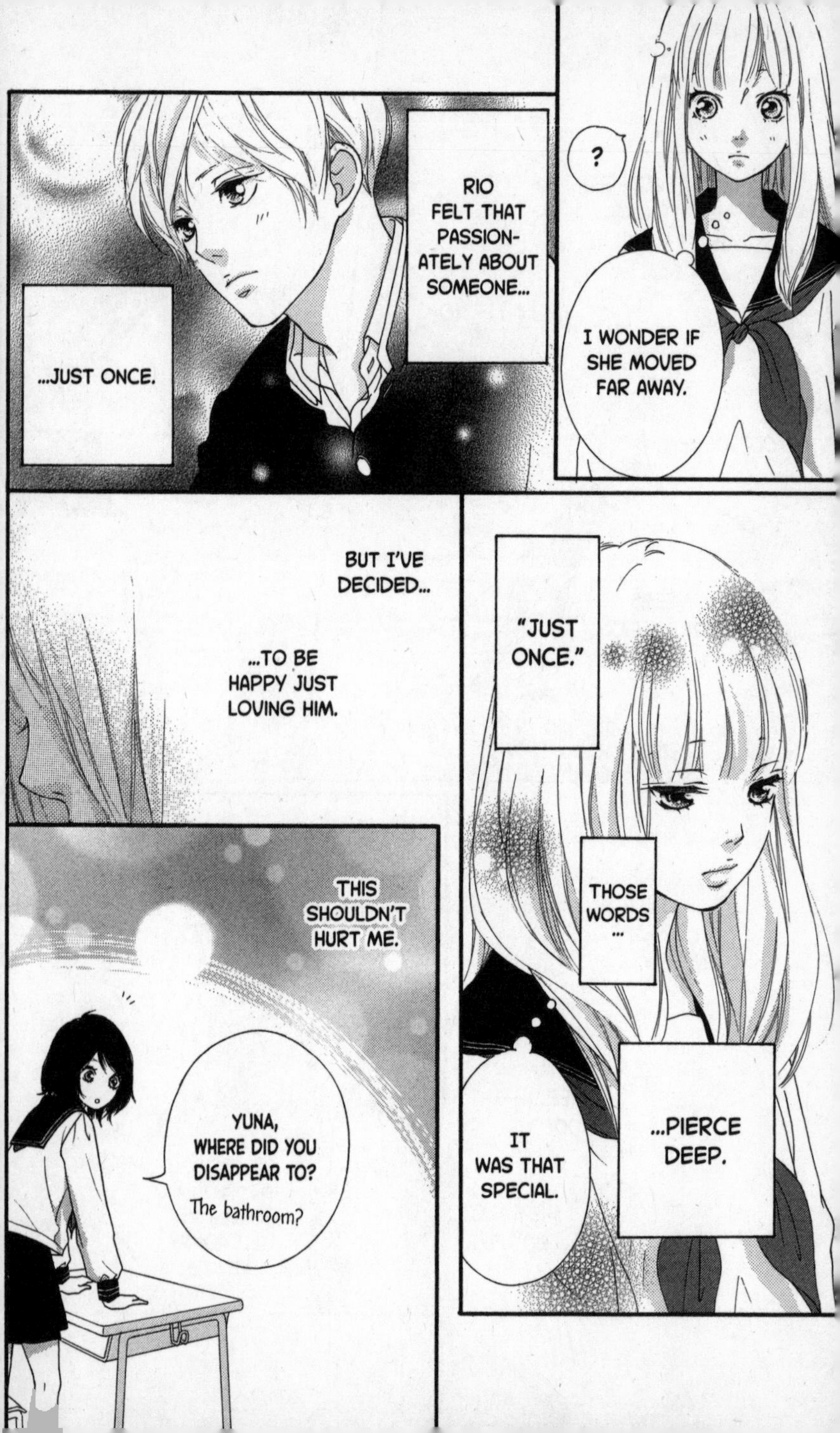
?
I WONDER IF SHE MOVED FAR AWAY.
RIO FELT THAT PASSION-ATELY ABOUT SOMEONE...
...JUST ONCE.
"JUST ONCE."
THOSE WORDS...
...PIERCE DEEP.
IT WAS THAT SPECIAL.
BUT I'VE DECIDED...
...TO BE HAPPY JUST LOVING HIM.
THIS SHOULDN'T HURT ME.
YUNA, WHERE DID YOU DISAPPEAR TO?
The bathroom?

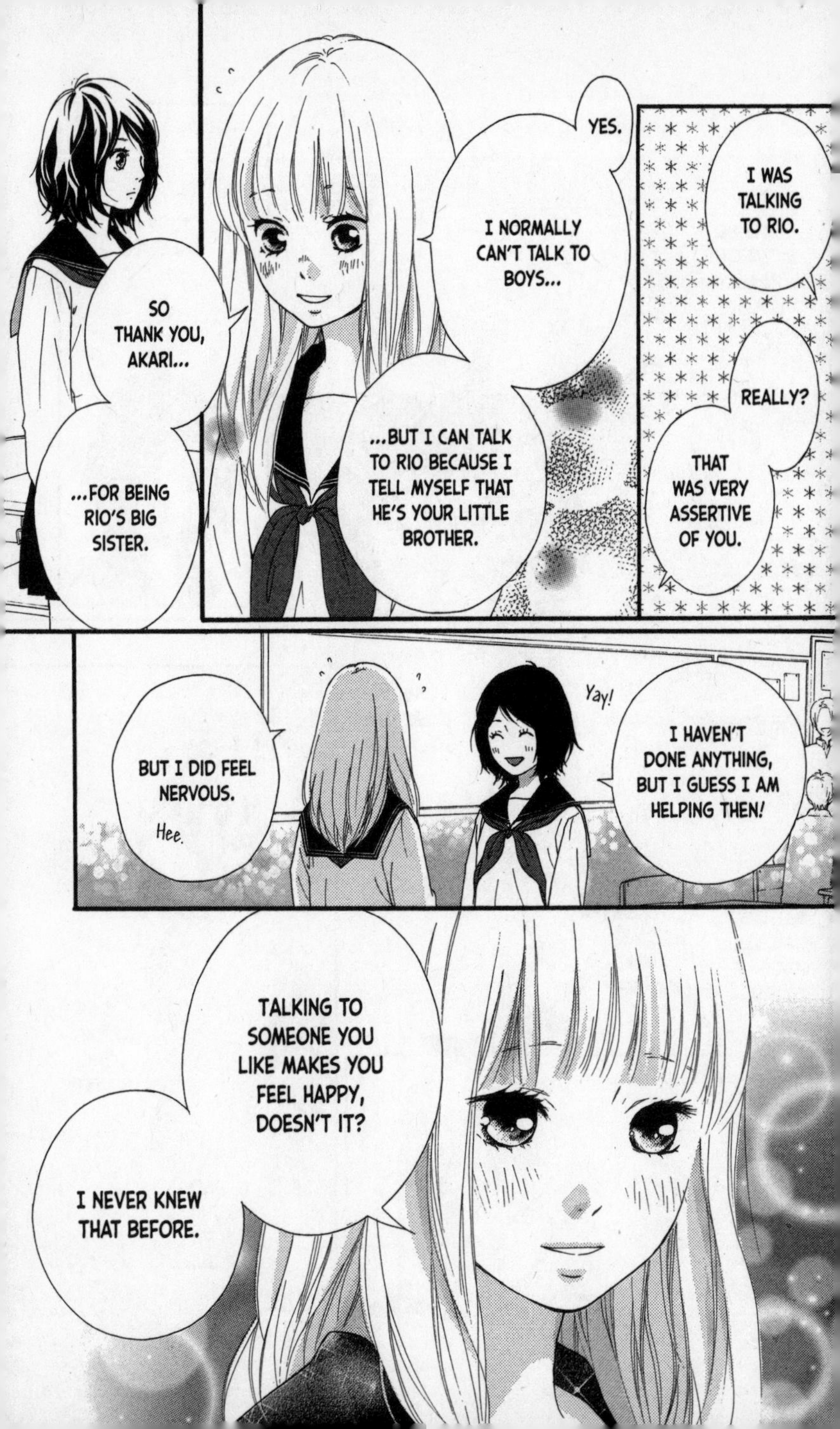
I WAS TALKING TO RIO.
REALLY?
THAT WAS VERY ASSERTIVE OF YOU.
YES.
I NORMALLY CAN'T TALK TO BOYS...
...BUT I CAN TALK TO RIO BECAUSE I TELL MYSELF THAT HE'S YOUR LITTLE BROTHER.
SO THANK YOU, AKARI...
...FOR BEING RIO'S BIG SISTER.
Yay!
I HAVEN'T DONE ANYTHING, BUT I GUESS I AM HELPING THEN!
BUT I DID FEEL NERVOUS.
Hee.
TALKING TO SOMEONE YOU LIKE MAKES YOU FEEL HAPPY, DOESN'T IT?
I NEVER KNEW THAT BEFORE.

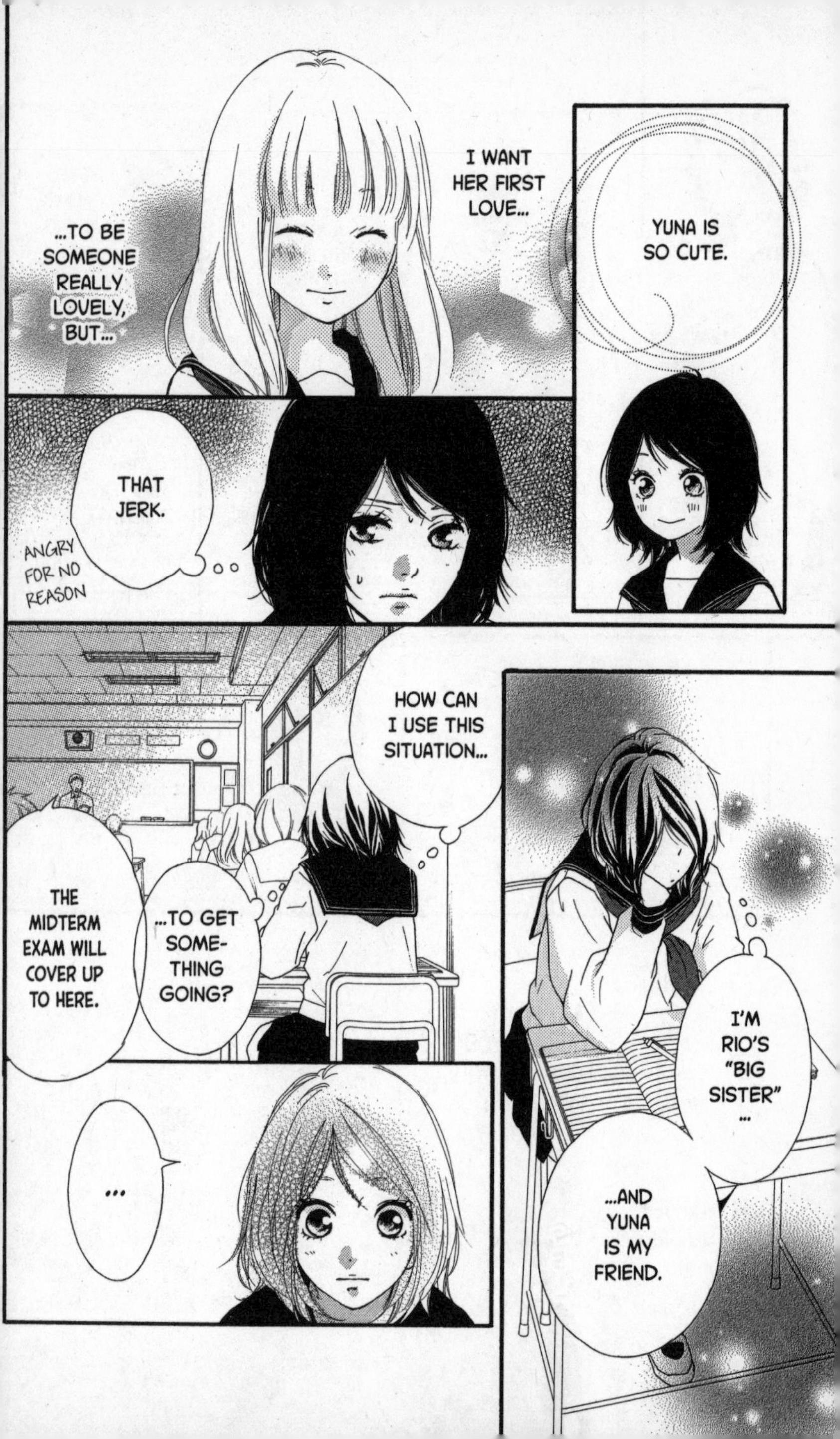
YUNA IS SO CUTE.
I WANT HER FIRST LOVE...
...TO BE SOMEONE REALLY LOVELY, BUT...
THAT JERK.
ANGRY FOR NO REASON
I'M RIO'S "BIG SISTER"...
...AND YUNA IS MY FRIEND.
HOW CAN I USE THIS SITUATION...
...TO GET SOME-THING GOING?
THE MIDTERM EXAM WILL COVER UP TO HERE.
...

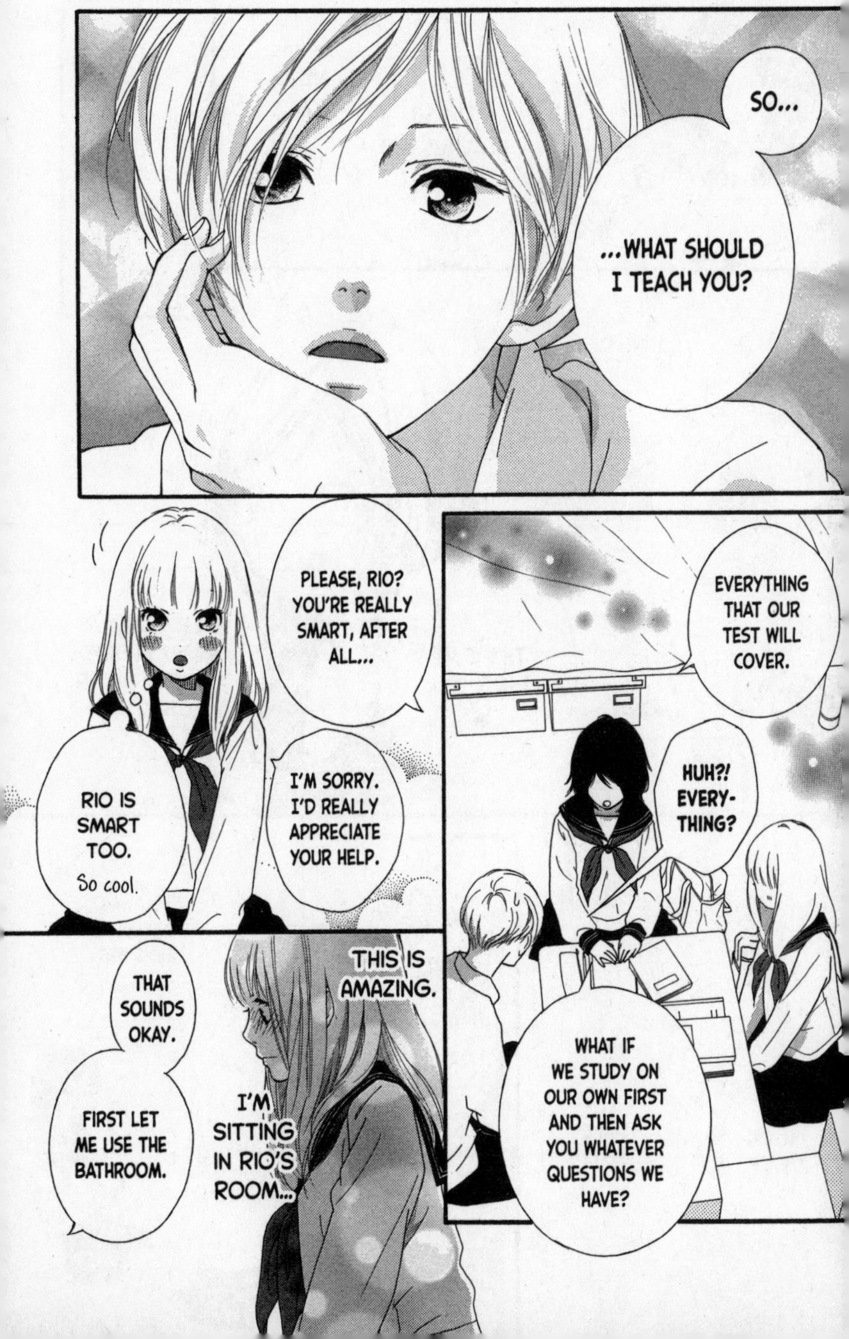
SO...
...WHAT SHOULD I TEACH YOU?
EVERYTHING THAT OUR TEST WILL COVER.
HUH?! EVERY-THING?
WHAT IF WE STUDY ON OUR OWN FIRST AND THEN ASK YOU WHATEVER QUESTIONS WE HAVE?
PLEASE, RIO? YOU'RE REALLY SMART, AFTER ALL...
I'M SORRY. I'D REALLY APPRECIATE YOUR HELP.
RIO IS SMART TOO.
So cool.
THIS IS AMAZING.
I'M SITTING IN RIO'S ROOM...
THAT SOUNDS OKAY.
FIRST LET ME USE THE BATHROOM.

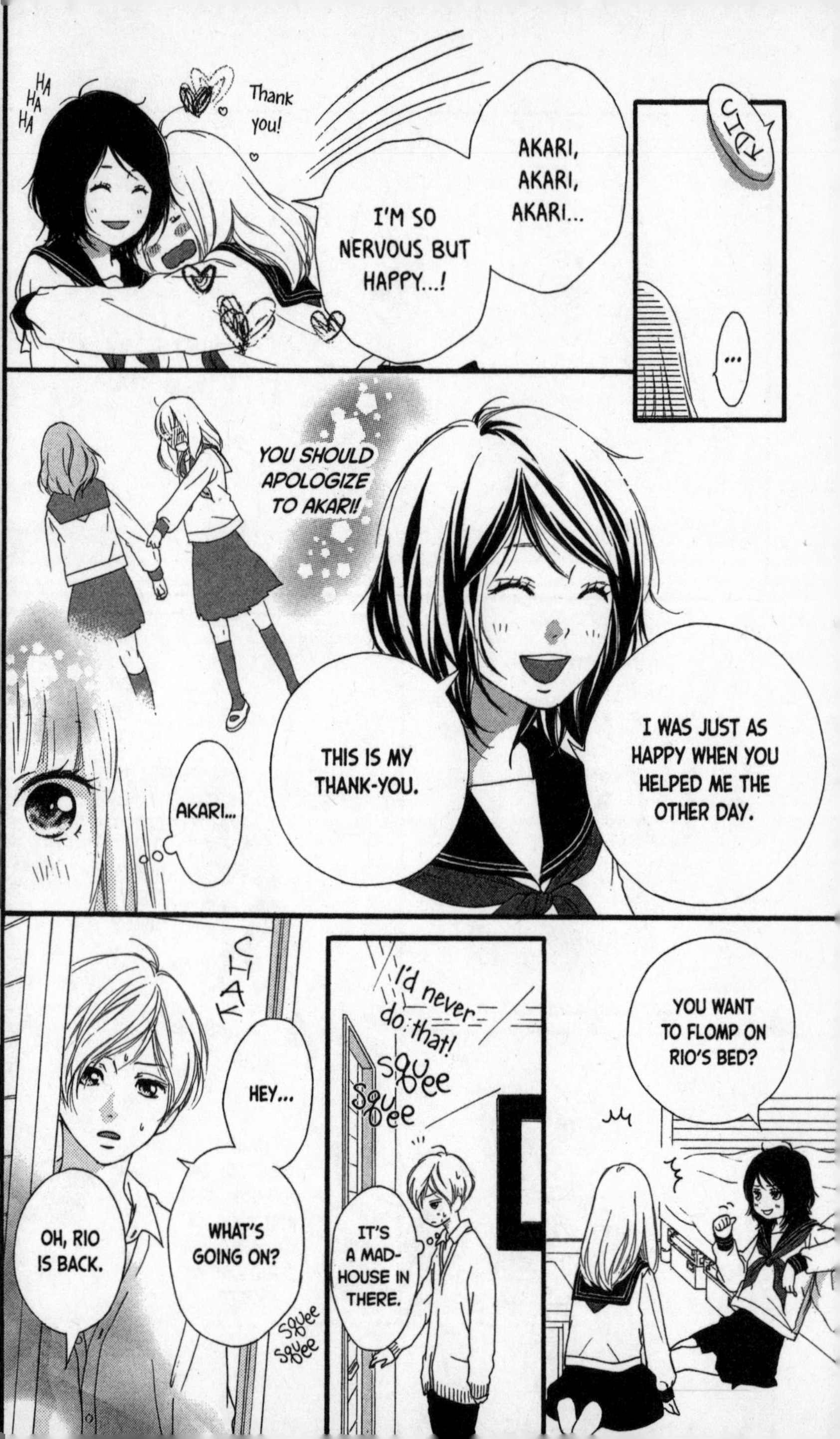
CLICK
...
AKARI, AKARI, AKARI...
I'M SO NERVOUS BUT HAPPY...!
Thank you!
HA HA HA
I WAS JUST AS HAPPY WHEN YOU HELPED ME THE OTHER DAY.
THIS IS MY THANK-YOU.
YOU SHOULD APOLOGIZE TO AKARI!
AKARI...
YOU WANT TO FLOMP ON RIO'S BED?
I'd never do that!
squee squee
IT'S A MAD-HOUSE IN THERE.
HEY...
WHAT'S GOING ON?
OH, RIO IS BACK.
squee squee

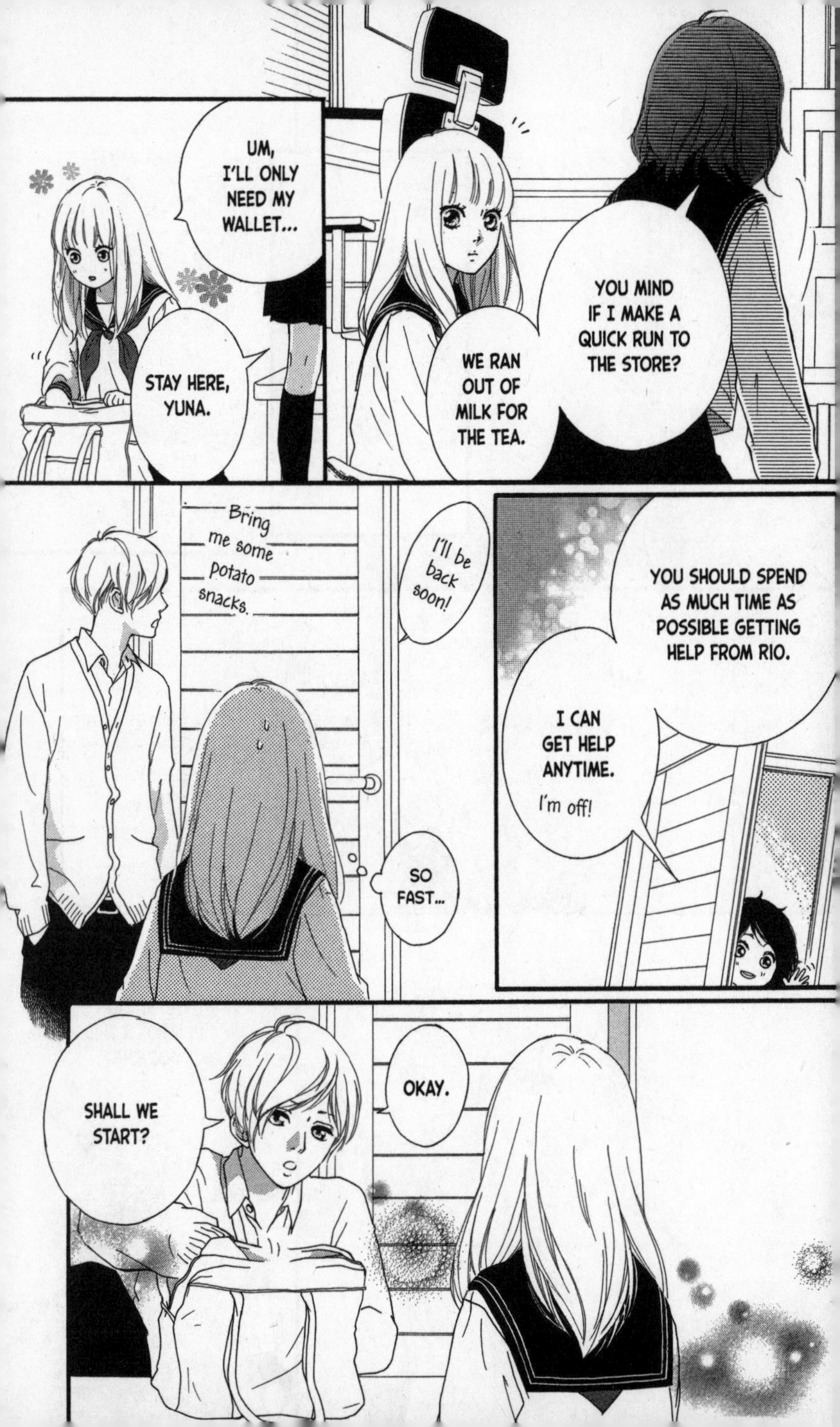
YOU MIND IF I MAKE A QUICK RUN TO THE STORE?
WE RAN OUT OF MILK FOR THE TEA.
UM, I'LL ONLY NEED MY WALLET...
STAY HERE, YUNA.
YOU SHOULD SPEND AS MUCH TIME AS POSSIBLE GETTING HELP FROM RIO.
I CAN GET HELP ANYTIME.
I'm off!
I'll be back soon!
Bring me some potato snacks.
SO FAST...
OKAY.
SHALL WE START?

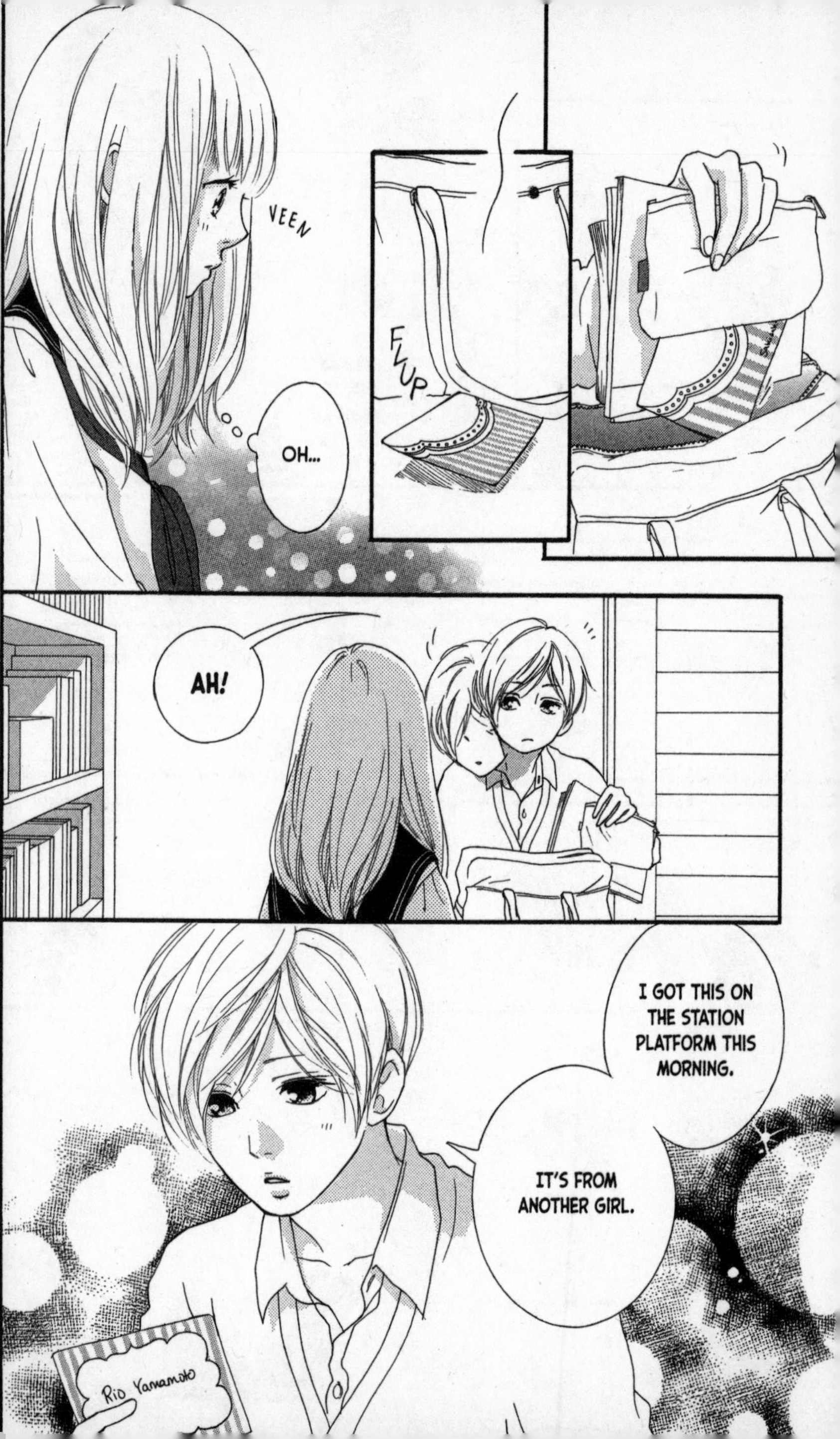
FLUP
VEEN
OH...
AH!
I GOT THIS ON THE STATION PLATFORM THIS MORNING.
IT'S FROM ANOTHER GIRL.
Rio Yamamoto

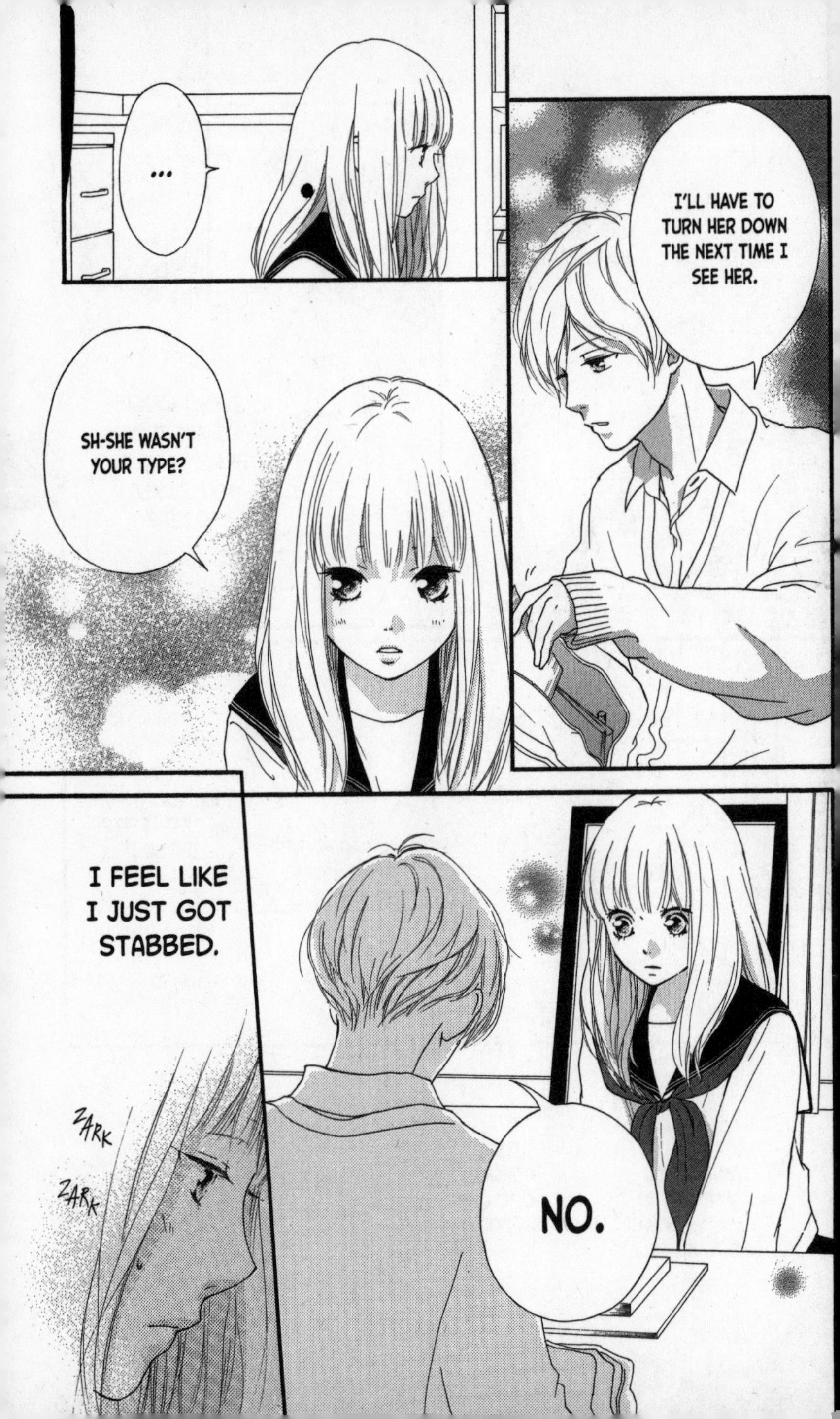
...
I'LL HAVE TO TURN HER DOWN THE NEXT TIME I SEE HER.
SH-SHE WASN'T YOUR TYPE?
NO.
I FEEL LIKE I JUST GOT STABBED.
ZARK
ZARK

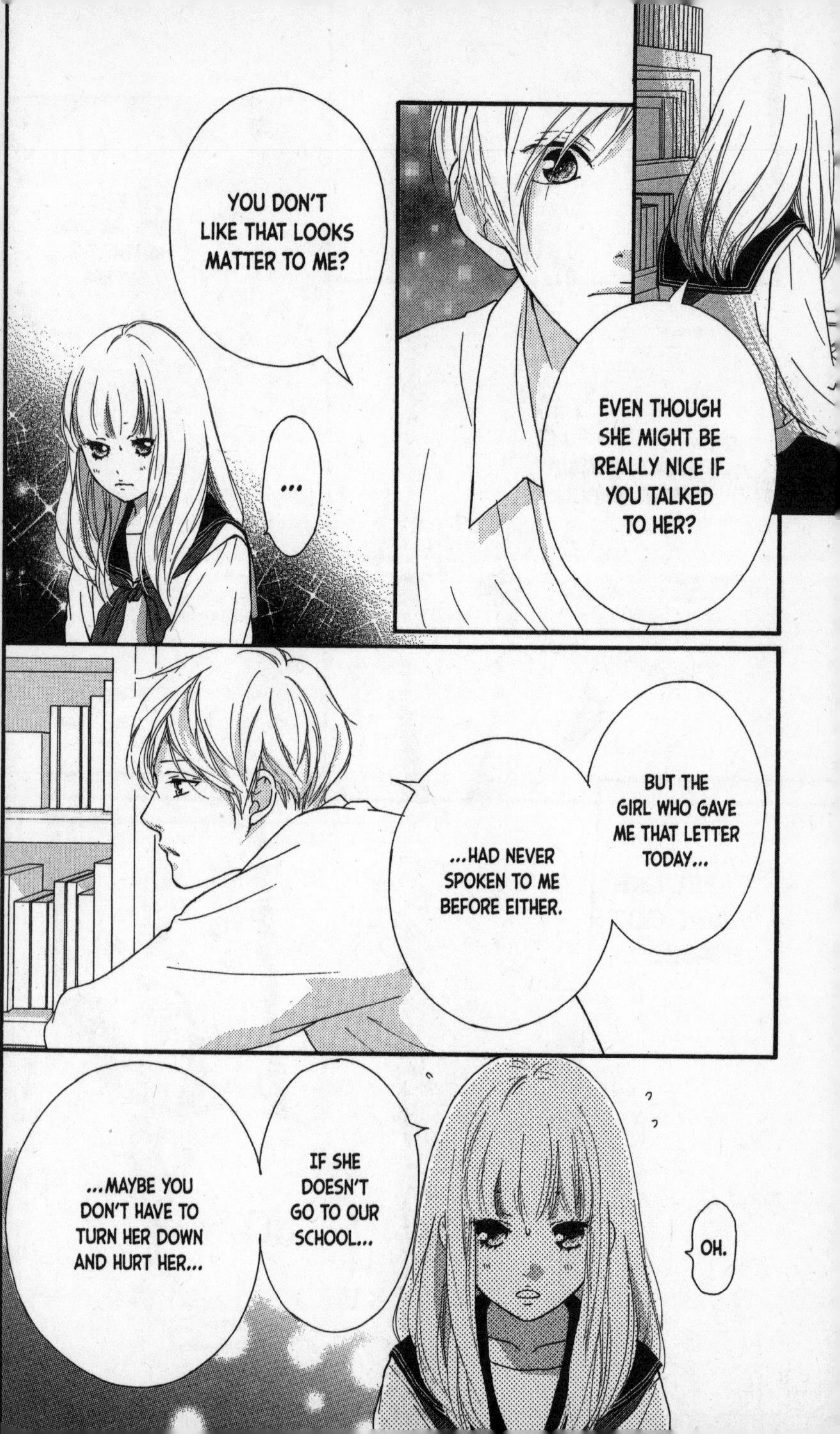
EVEN THOUGH SHE MIGHT BE REALLY NICE IF YOU TALKED TO HER?
YOU DON'T LIKE THAT LOOKS MATTER TO ME?
...
BUT THE GIRL WHO GAVE ME THAT LETTER TODAY...
...HAD NEVER SPOKEN TO ME BEFORE EITHER.
OH.
IF SHE DOESN'T GO TO OUR SCHOOL...
...MAYBE YOU DON'T HAVE TO TURN HER DOWN AND HURT HER...

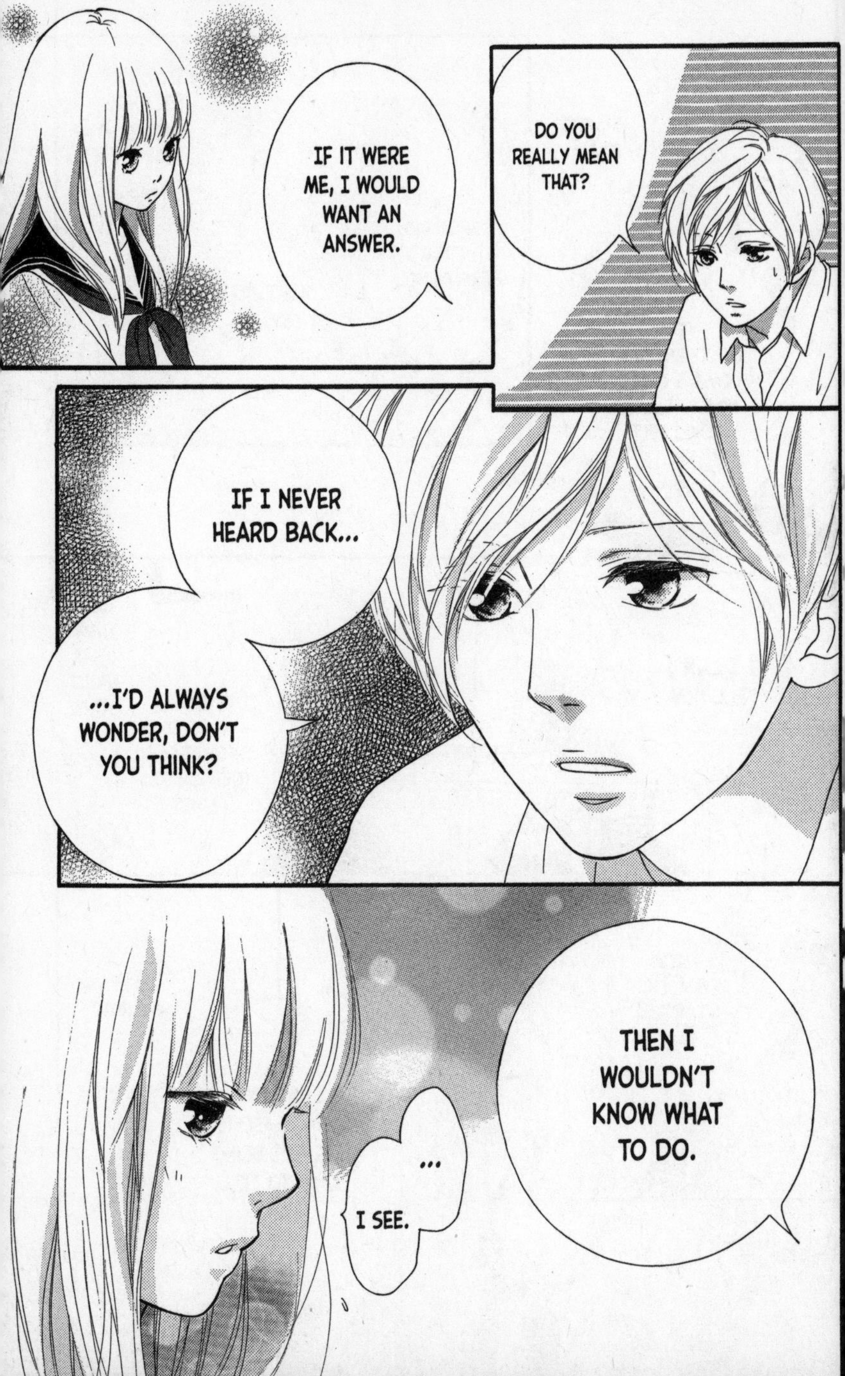
DO YOU REALLY MEAN THAT?
IF IT WERE ME, I WOULD WANT AN ANSWER.
IF I NEVER HEARD BACK...
...I'D ALWAYS WONDER, DON'T YOU THINK?
THEN I WOULDN'T KNOW WHAT TO DO.
...
I SEE.

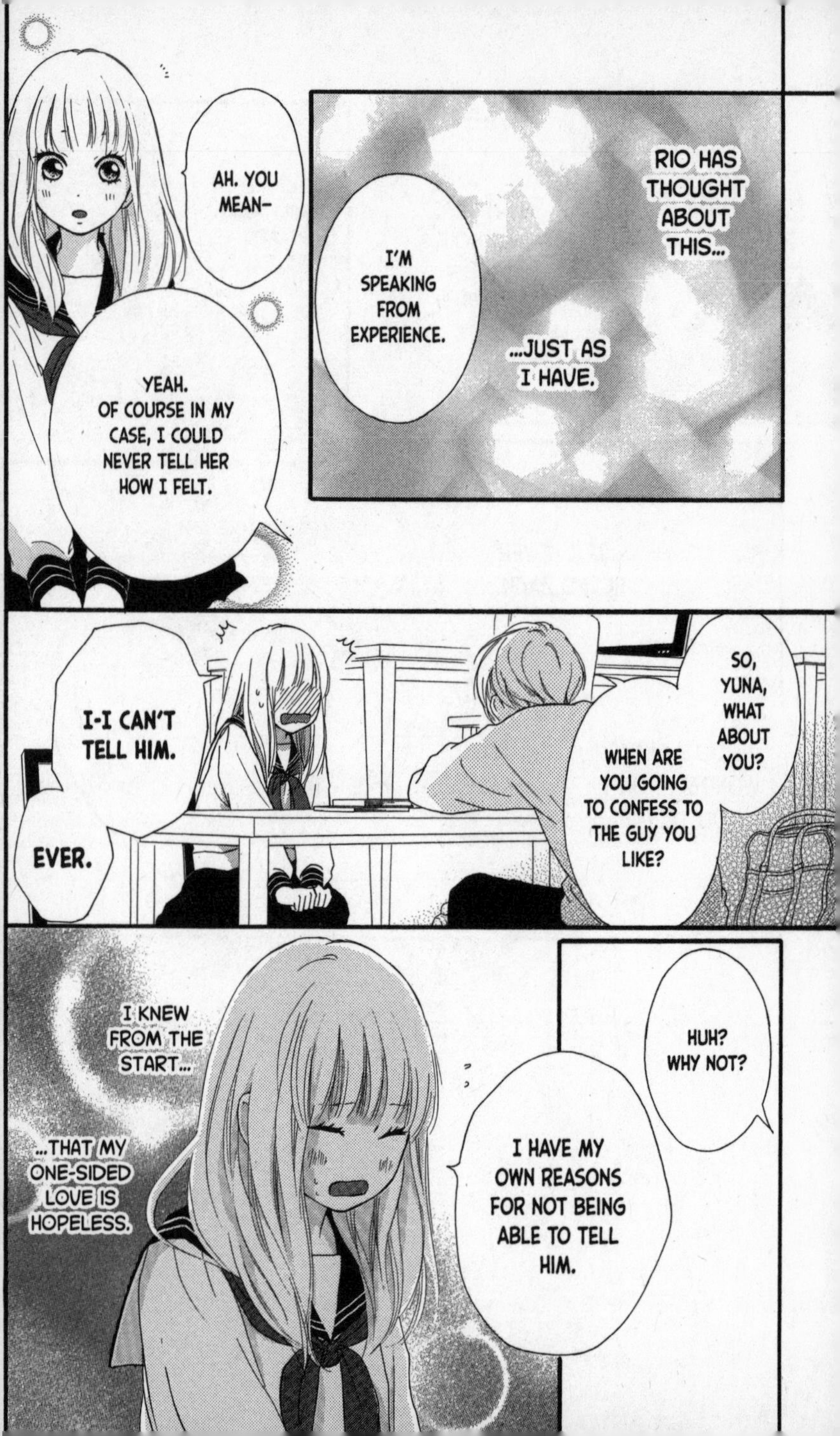
RIO HAS THOUGHT ABOUT THIS...
I'M SPEAKING FROM EXPERIENCE.
...JUST AS I HAVE.
AH. YOU MEAN—
YEAH. OF COURSE IN MY CASE, I COULD NEVER TELL HER HOW I FELT.
SO, YUNA, WHAT ABOUT YOU?
WHEN ARE YOU GOING TO CONFESS TO THE GUY YOU LIKE?
I-I CAN'T TELL HIM.
EVER.
HUH? WHY NOT?
I HAVE MY OWN REASONS FOR NOT BEING ABLE TO TELL HIM.
I KNEW FROM THE START...
...THAT MY ONE-SIDED LOVE IS HOPELESS.

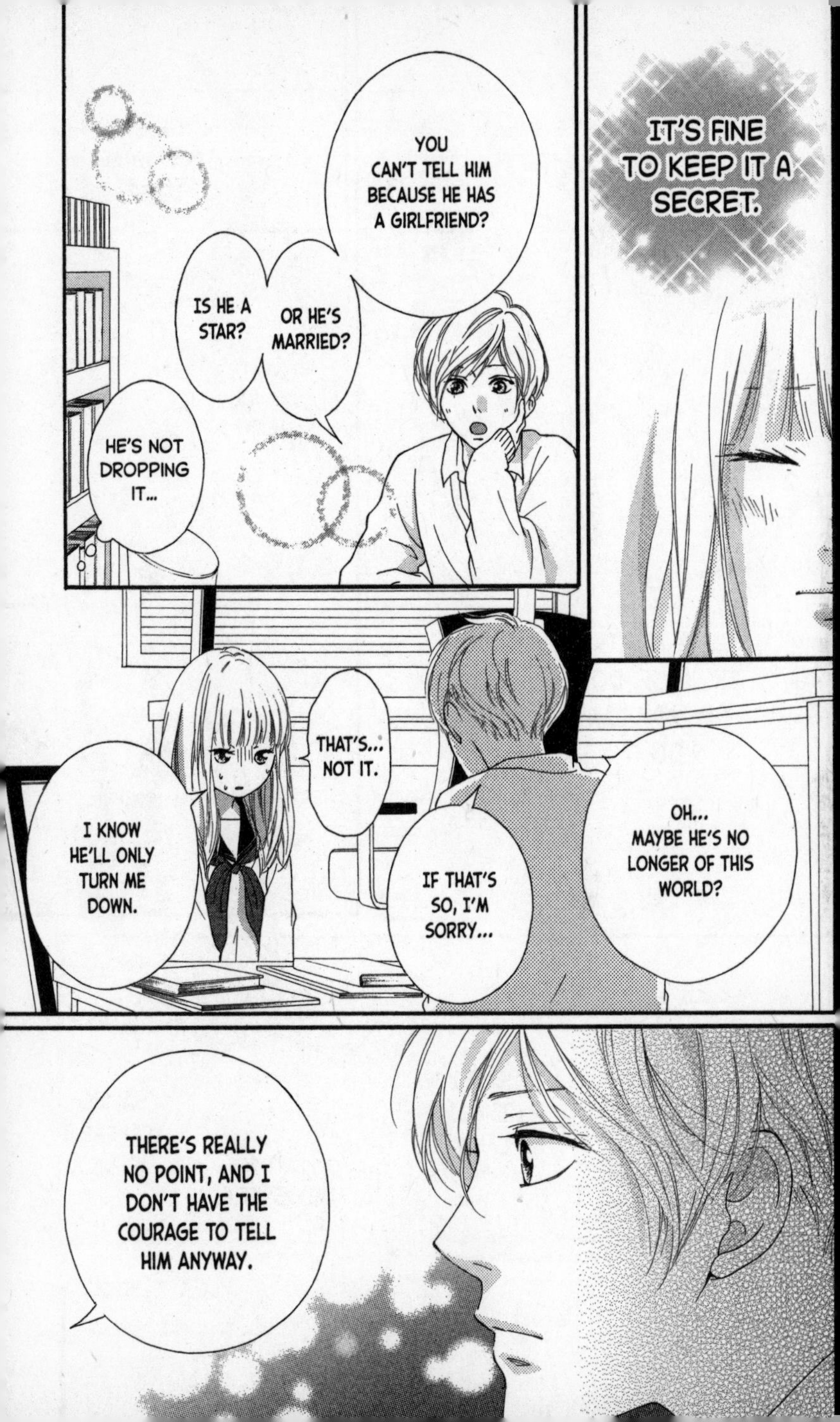
IT'S FINE TO KEEP IT A SECRET.
YOU CAN'T TELL HIM BECAUSE HE HAS A GIRLFRIEND?
OR HE'S MARRIED?
IS HE A STAR?
HE'S NOT DROPPING IT...
OH... MAYBE HE'S NO LONGER OF THIS WORLD?
IF THAT'S SO, I'M SORRY...
THAT'S... NOT IT.
I KNOW HE'LL ONLY TURN ME DOWN.
THERE'S REALLY NO POINT, AND I DON'T HAVE THE COURAGE TO TELL HIM ANYWAY.

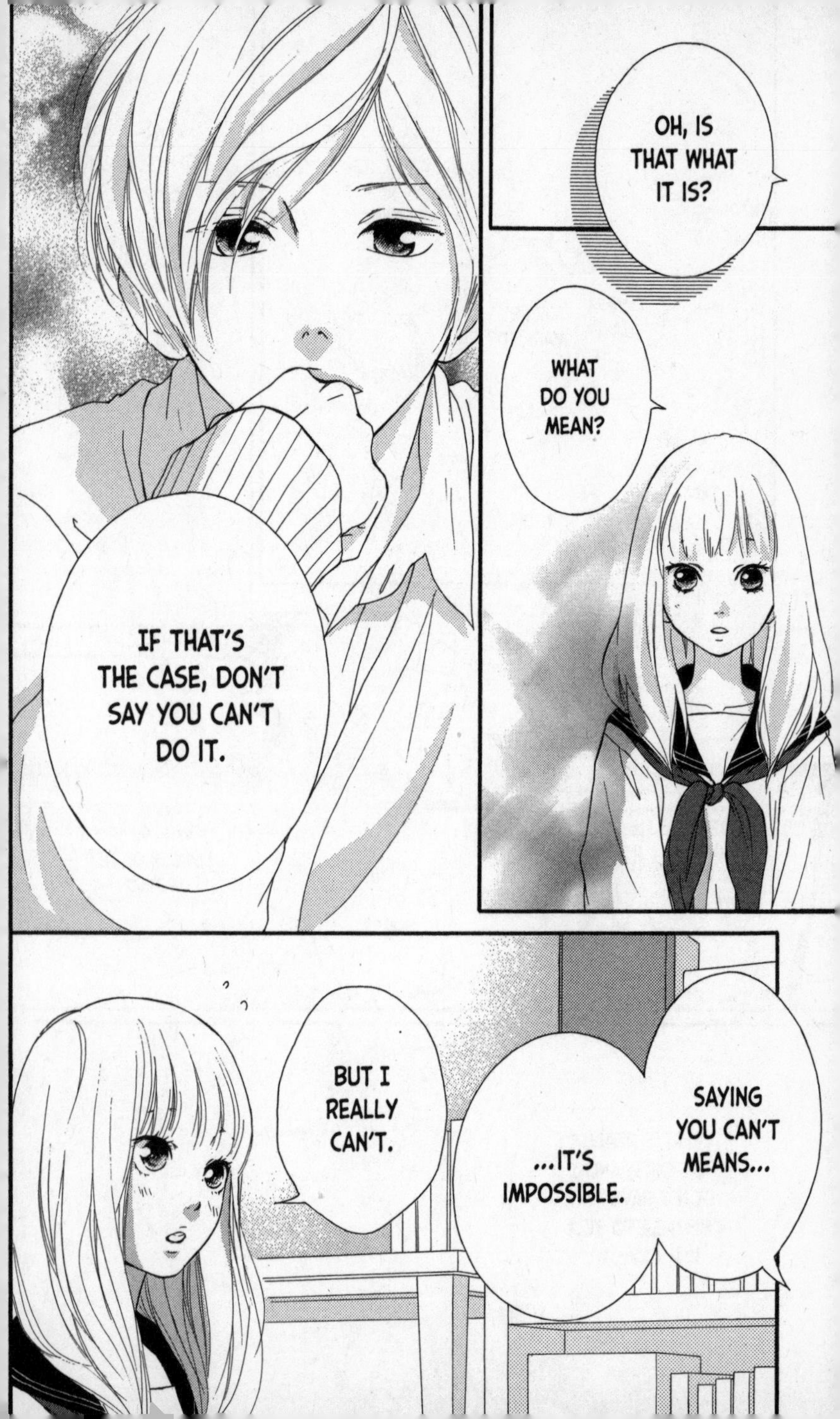
OH, IS THAT WHAT IT IS?
WHAT DO YOU MEAN?
IF THAT'S THE CASE, DON'T SAY YOU CAN'T DO IT.
SAYING YOU CAN'T MEANS...
...IT'S IMPOSSIBLE.
BUT I REALLY CAN'T.

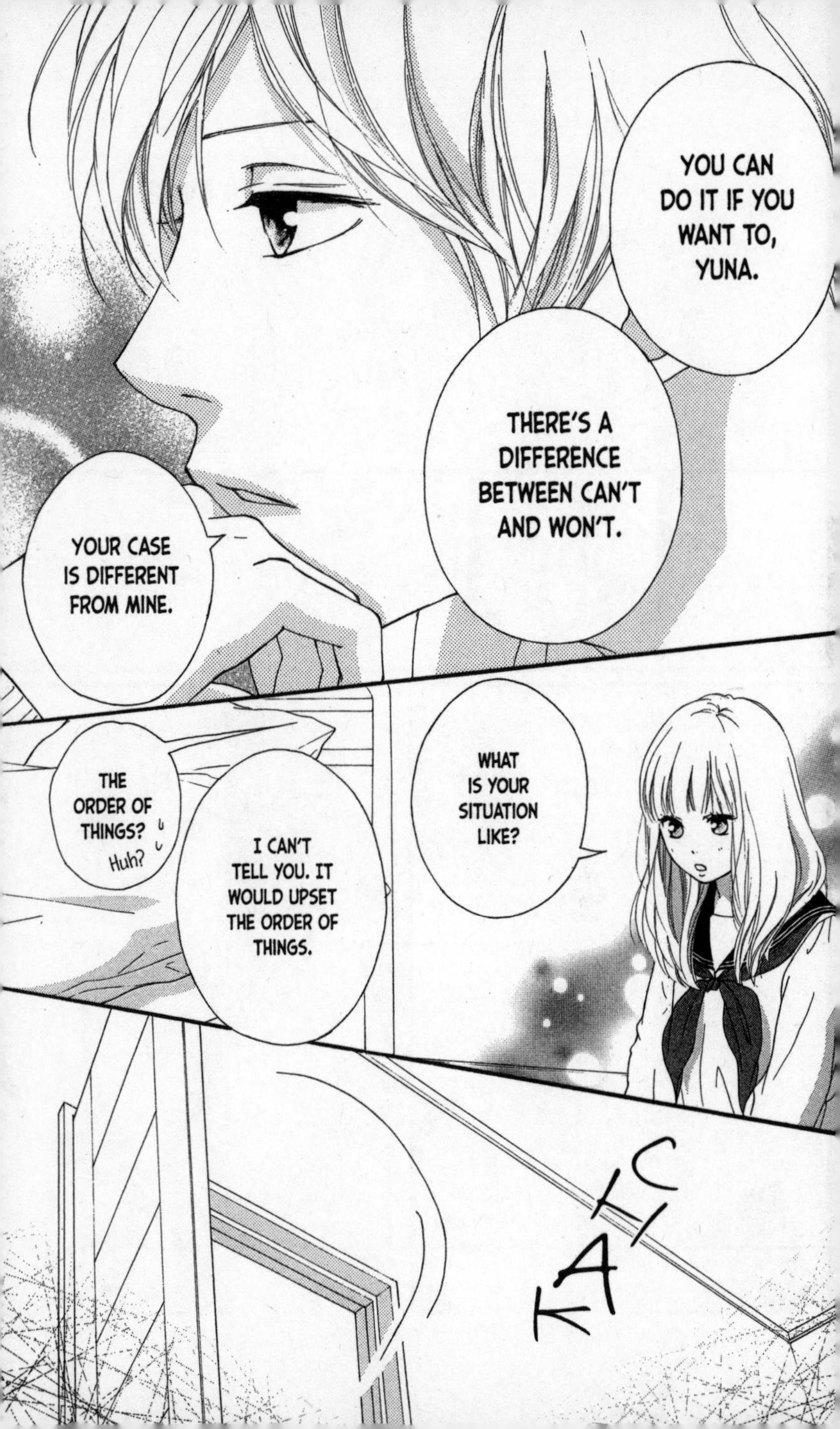
YOU CAN DO IT IF YOU WANT TO, YUNA.
THERE'S A DIFFERENCE BETWEEN CAN'T AND WON'T.
YOUR CASE IS DIFFERENT FROM MINE.
WHAT IS YOUR SITUATION LIKE?
I CAN'T TELL YOU. IT WOULD UPSET THE ORDER OF THINGS.
THE ORDER OF THINGS?
Huh?
KACH

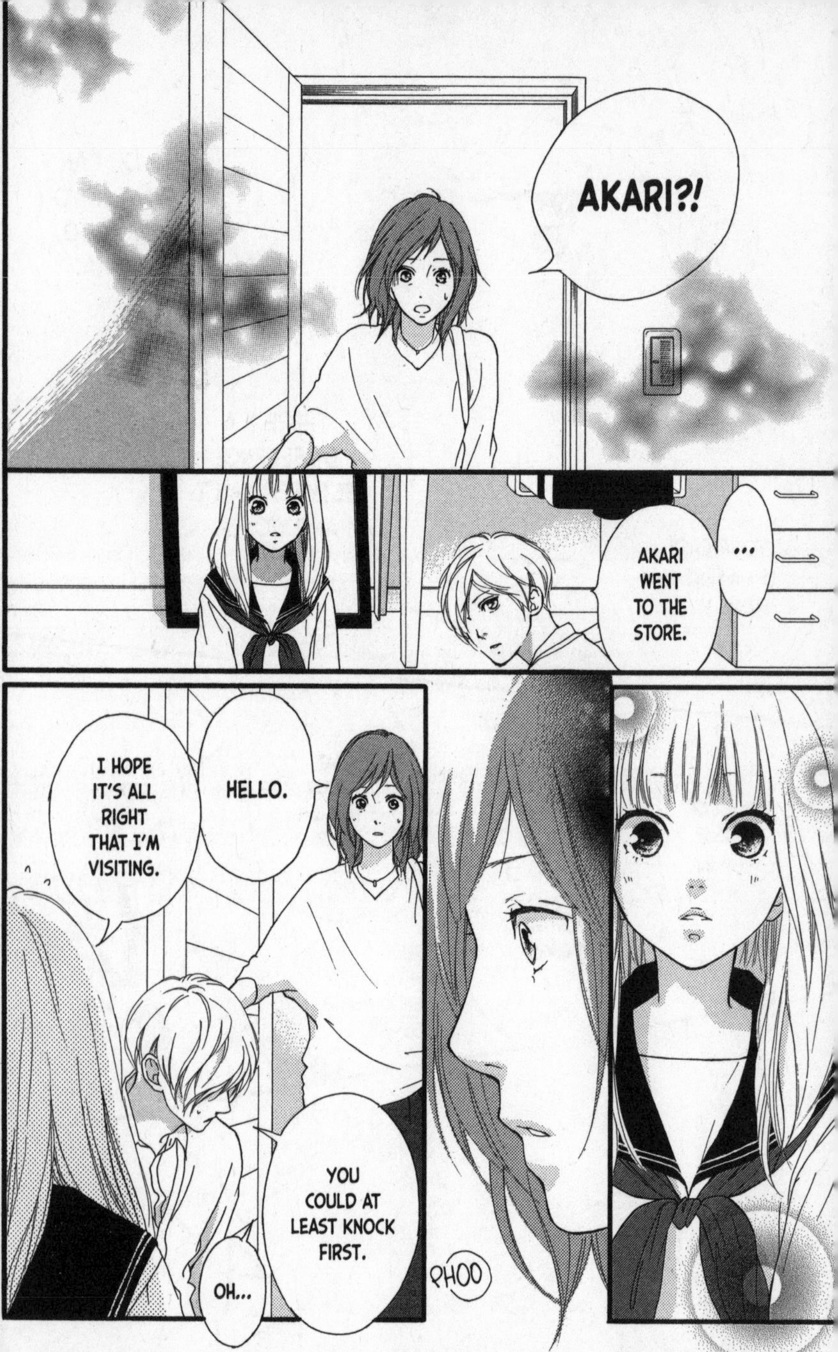
AKARI?!
...
AKARI WENT TO THE STORE.
PHOO
HELLO.
I HOPE IT'S ALL RIGHT THAT I'M VISITING.
YOU COULD AT LEAST KNOCK FIRST.
OH...

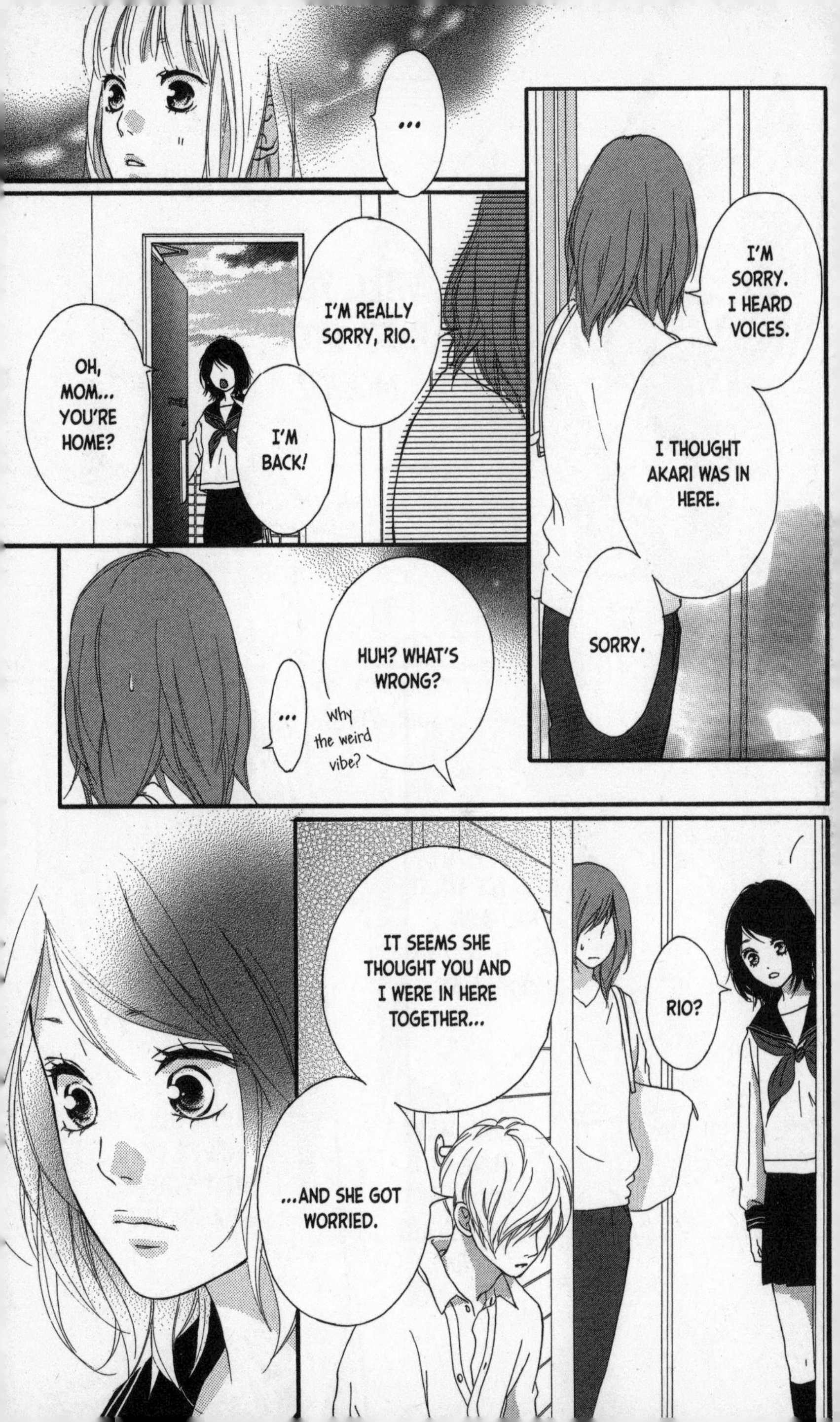
...
I'M SORRY. I HEARD VOICES.
I THOUGHT AKARI WAS IN HERE.
SORRY.
I'M REALLY SORRY, RIO.
I'M BACK!
OH, MOM... YOU'RE HOME?
HUH? WHAT'S WRONG?
Why the weird vibe?
...
RIO?
IT SEEMS SHE THOUGHT YOU AND I WERE IN HERE TOGETHER...
...AND SHE GOT WORRIED.

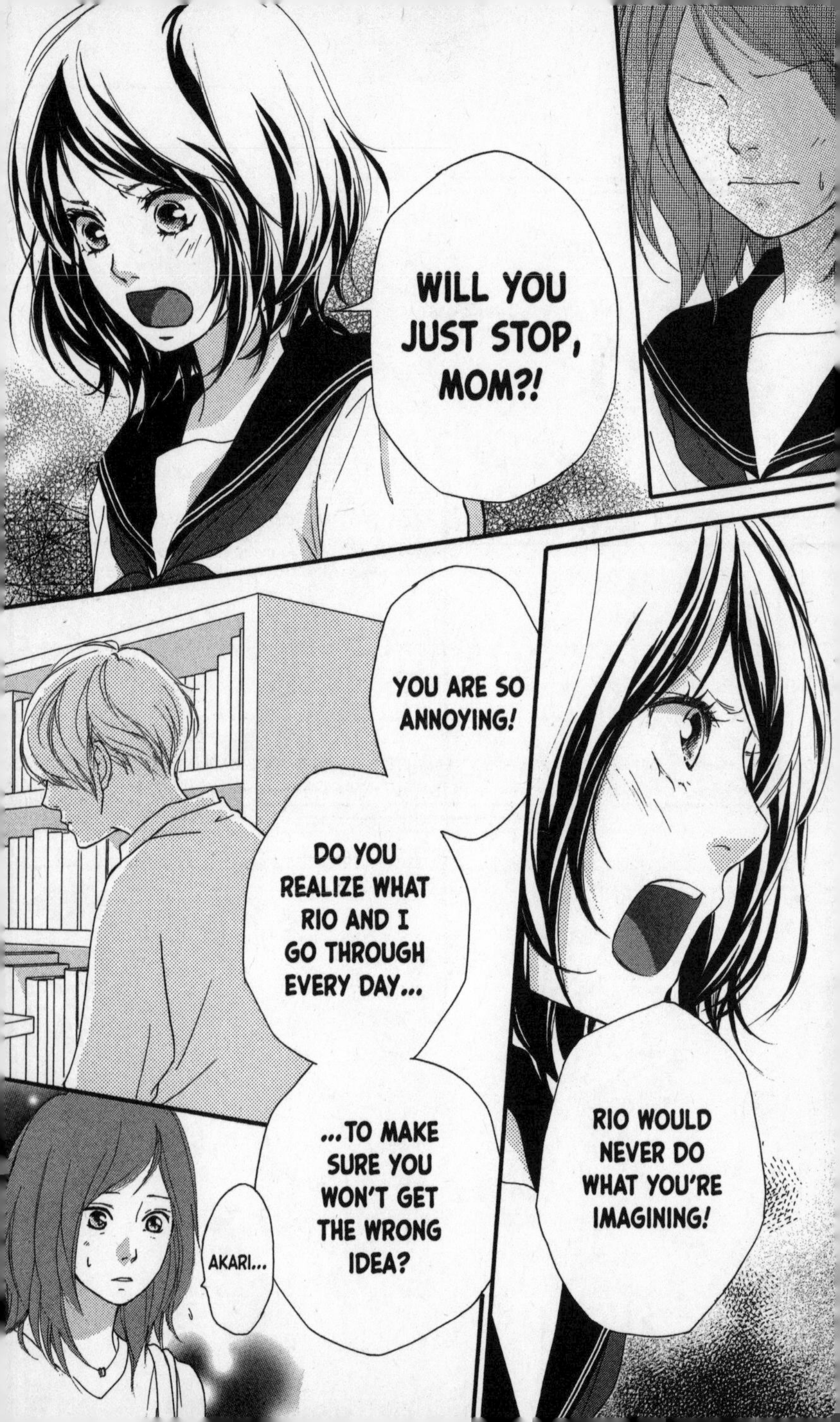
WILL YOU JUST STOP, MOM?!
YOU ARE SO ANNOYING!
DO YOU REALIZE WHAT RIO AND I GO THROUGH EVERY DAY...
...TO MAKE SURE YOU WON'T GET THE WRONG IDEA?
RIO WOULD NEVER DO WHAT YOU'RE IMAGINING!
AKARI...

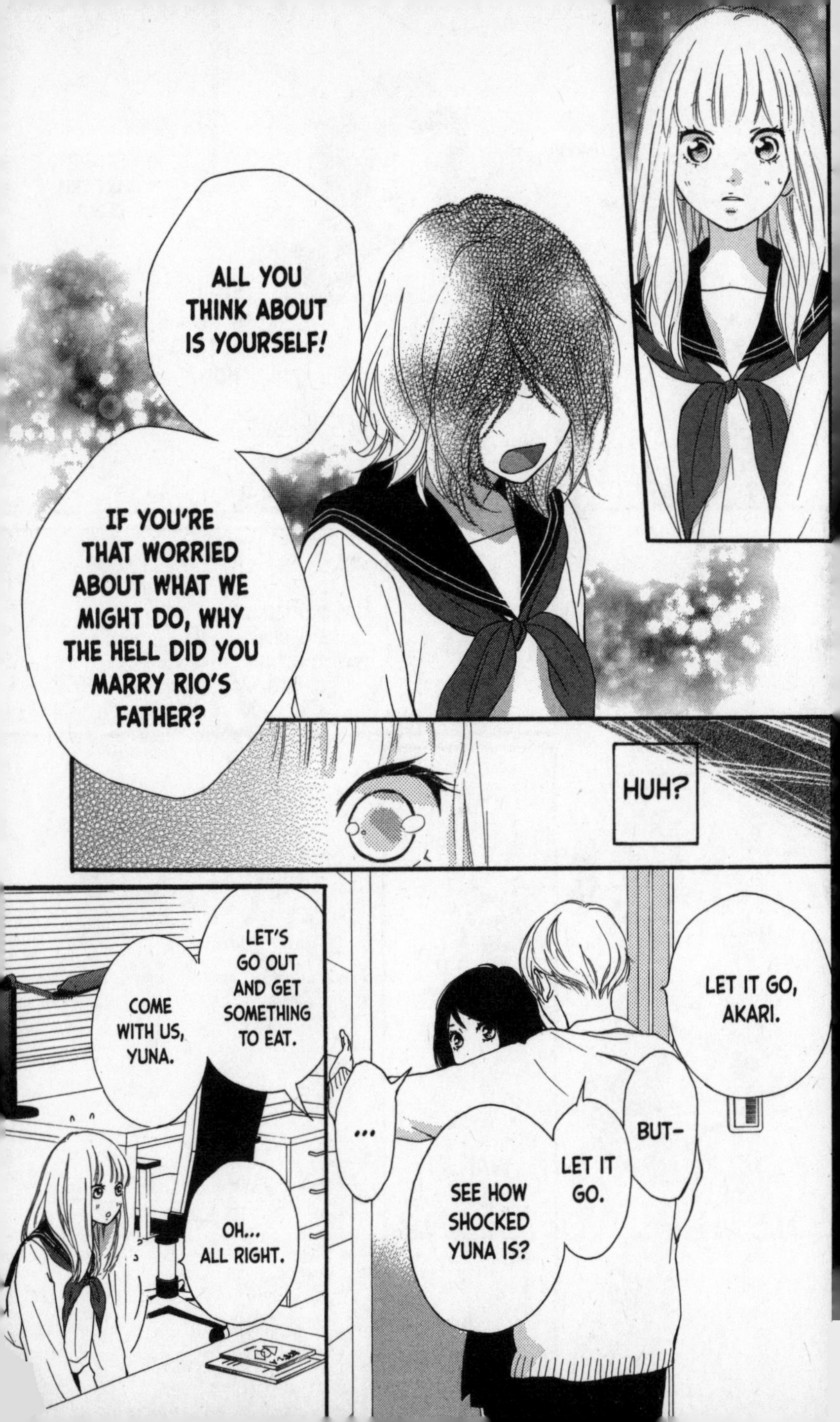
ALL YOU THINK ABOUT IS YOURSELF!
IF YOU'RE THAT WORRIED ABOUT WHAT WE MIGHT DO, WHY THE HELL DID YOU MARRY RIO'S FATHER?
HUH?
LET IT GO, AKARI.
BUT-
LET IT GO.
SEE HOW SHOCKED YUNA IS?
...
LET'S GO OUT AND GET SOMETHING TO EAT.
COME WITH US, YUNA.
OH... ALL RIGHT.

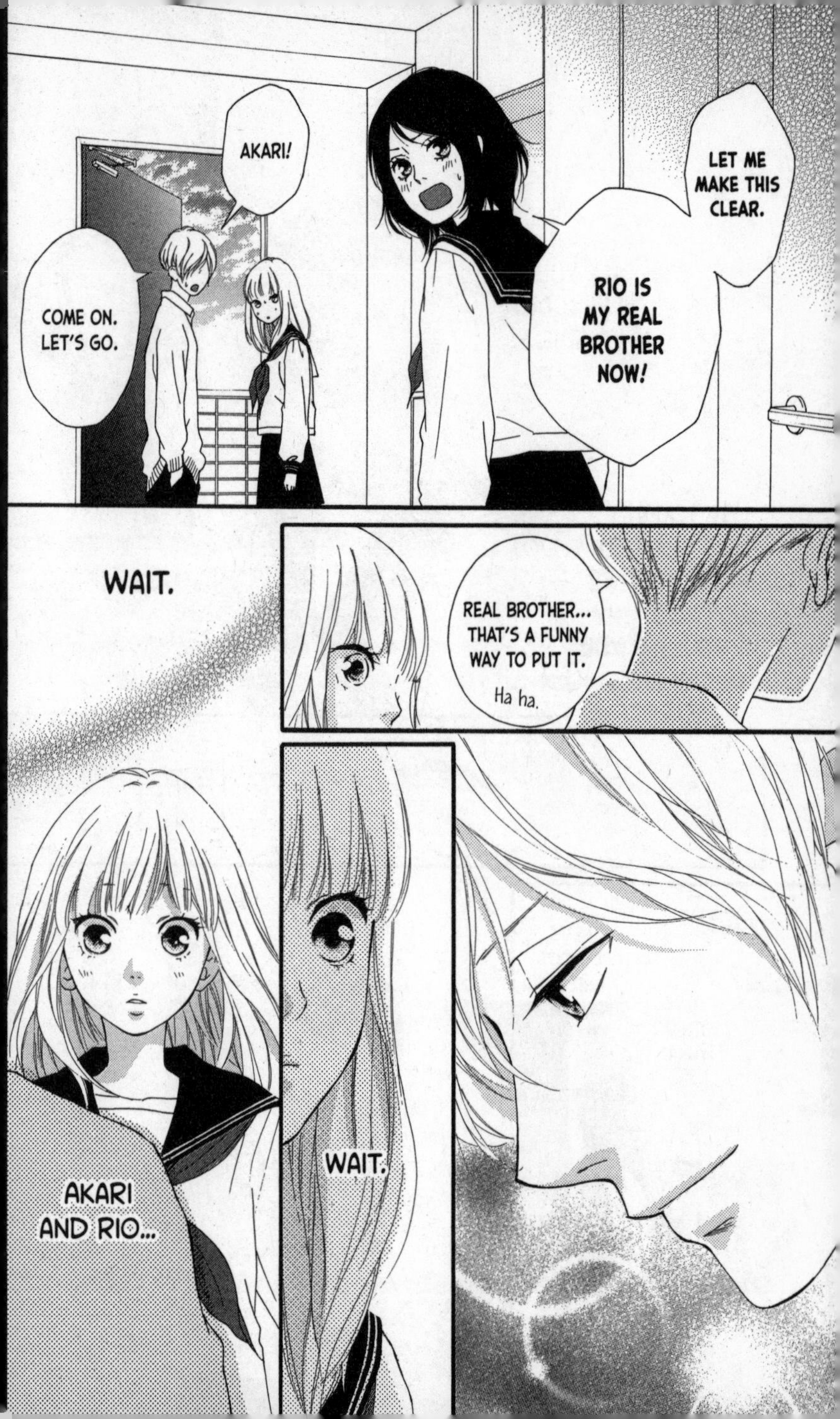
LET ME MAKE THIS CLEAR.
RIO IS MY REAL BROTHER NOW!
AKARI!
COME ON. LET'S GO.
REAL BROTHER... THAT'S A FUNNY WAY TO PUT IT.
Ha ha.
WAIT.
WAIT.
AKARI AND RIO...

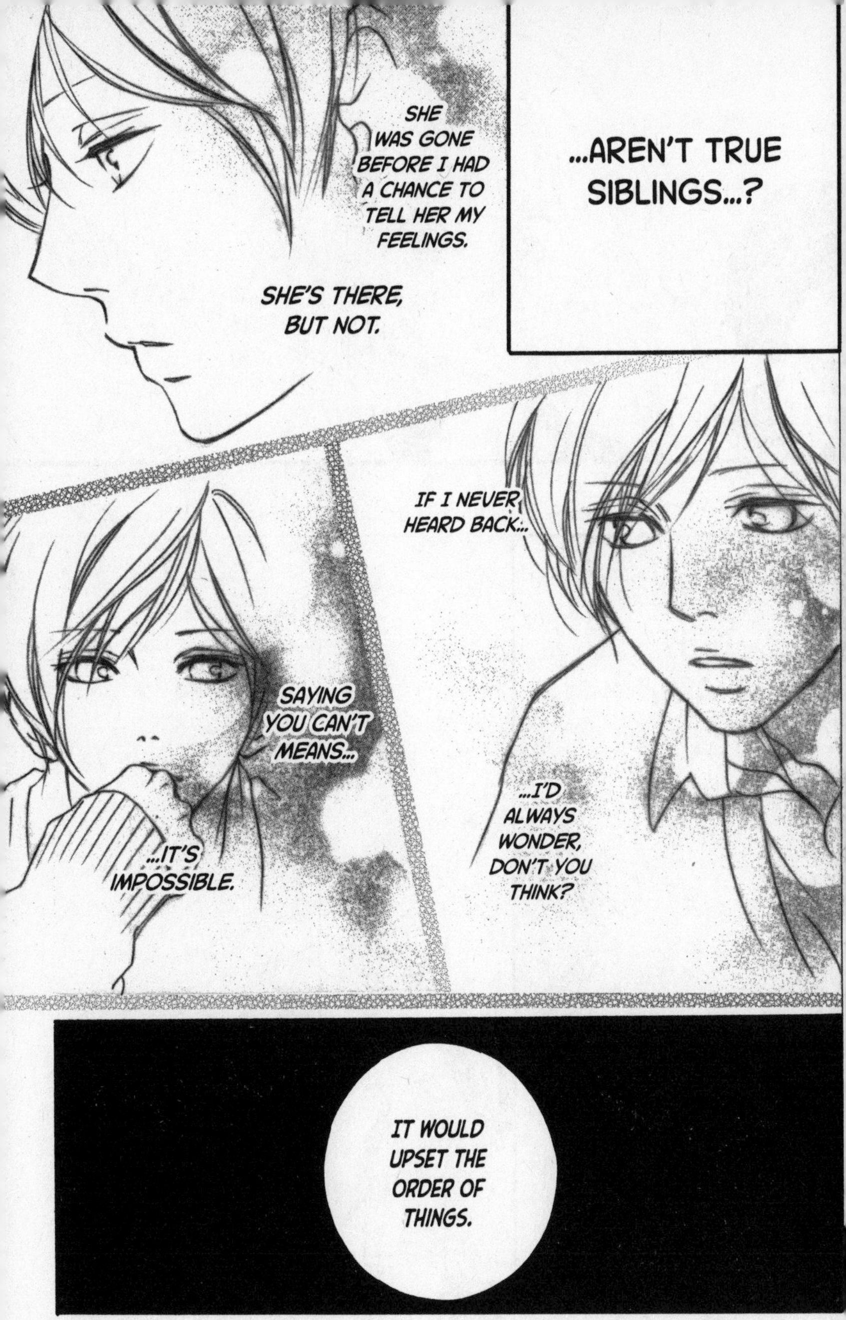
...AREN'T TRUE SIBLINGS...?
SHE WAS GONE BEFORE I HAD A CHANCE TO TELL HER MY FEELINGS.
SHE'S THERE, BUT NOT.
IF I NEVER HEARD BACK...
...I'D ALWAYS WONDER, DON'T YOU THINK?
SAYING YOU CAN'T MEANS...
...IT'S IMPOSSIBLE.
IT WOULD UPSET THE ORDER OF THINGS.

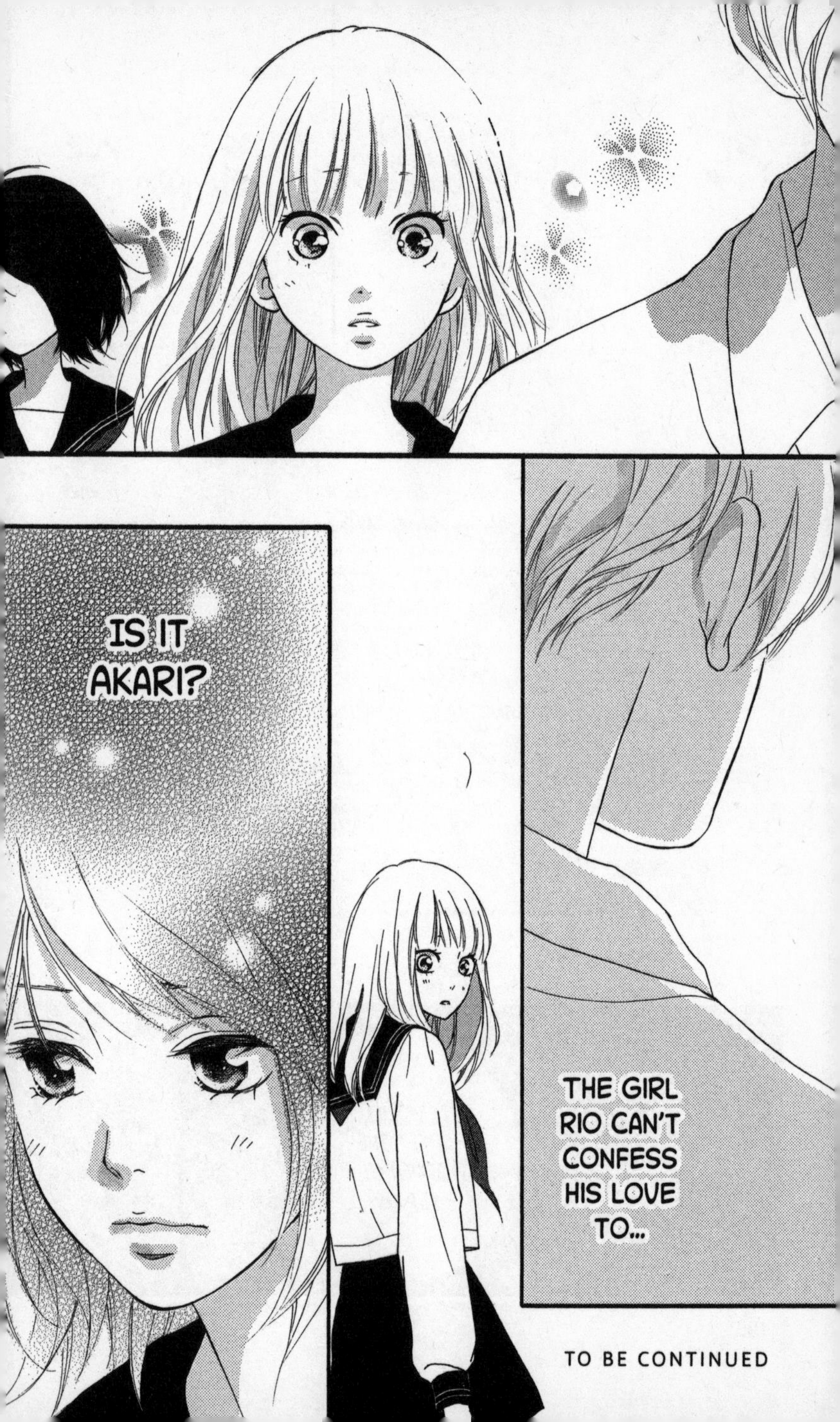
THE GIRL RIO CAN'T CONFESS HIS LOVE TO...
IS IT AKARI?
TO BE CONTINUED

AFTERWORD

Thank you for reading this to the end.

For this series, I have to draw a lot of nautical student uniforms and book bags. I've never had to draw so many of these uniforms, so it feels fresh to me! I find them and the book bags a little difficult to draw. I want to get good at drawing them as quickly as possible. (For your information, they are supposed to be attending a private school.) I wanted their winter uniforms to be black, but that would have involved too many hours of work (by my assistants), so I gave up that idea.

Also, for all you male book-bag carriers who are reading this, I would appreciate any hints or secrets for carrying them in style!

I hope you will continue to read about Yuna, Akari, Rio and Kazuomi in the future!!

Io Sakisaka

This strange blend of excitement and anxiety—particular to the time when a new series starts its run—is something I want to treasure. I hope the excitement just builds from here, and I hope you will love *Love Me, Love Me Not*!

Io Sakisaka

Born on June 8, Io Sakisaka made her debut as a manga creator with *Sakura, Chiru*. Her series *Strobe Edge* and *Ao Haru Ride* are published by VIZ Media's Shojo Beat imprint. *Ao Haru Ride* was adapted into an anime series in 2014, and *Love Me, Love Me Not* will be an animated feature film. In her spare time, Sakisaka likes to paint things and sleep.

Love Me, Love Me Not

Vol. 1
Shojo Beat Edition

STORY AND ART BY
Io Sakisaka

Adaptation/Nancy Thistlethwaite
Translation/JN Productions
Touch-Up Art & Lettering/Sara Linsley
Design/Yukiko Whitley
Editor/Nancy Thistlethwaite

OMOI, OMOWARE, FURI, FURARE © 2015 by Io Sakisaka
All rights reserved.
First published in Japan in 2015 by SHUEISHA Inc., Tokyo.
English translation rights arranged by SHUEISHA Inc.

Printed in the U.S.A.

Published by VIZ Media, LLC
P.O. Box 77010
San Francisco, CA 94107

10 9 8 7 6 5 4 3 2 1
First printing, March 2020

PARENTAL ADVISORY
LOVE ME, LOVE ME NOT is rated T for Teen and
is recommended for ages 13 and up. This story
centers around teenage relationships.

VIZ MEDIA
viz.com

Beat
shojobeat.com

Stop!

You may be reading the wrong way.

In keeping with the original Japanese comic format, this book reads from right to left—so action, sound effects and word balloons are completely reversed to preserve the orientation of the original artwork. Check out the diagram shown here to get the hang of things, and then turn to the other side of the book to get started!

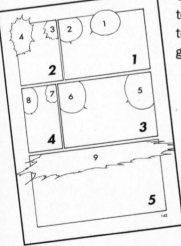